The Possessed and
the Dispossessed

COMPARATIVE STUDIES OF
HEALTH SYSTEMS AND MEDICAL CARE

For a complete list of titles in this series, please contact the
Sales Department
University of California Press
2120 Berkeley Way
Berkeley, CA 94720

For Mimi (ô Dady é!),
so that she may be remembered
as an ancestor;
for my parents,
who have always encouraged my ideas;
and for Paula and Erik, zandriko.

The Possessed and the Dispossessed

Spirits, Identity, and Power in a Madagascar Migrant Town

Lesley A. Sharp

UNIVERSITY OF CALIFORNIA PRESS
Berkeley   *Los Angeles*   *London*

University of California Press
Berkeley and Los Angeles, California

University of California Press
London, England

Copyright © 1993 by The Regents of the University of California

Library of Congress Cataloging-in-Publication Data

First Paperback Printing, 1996

Library of Congress Cataloging-in-Publication Data

Sharp, Lesley Alexandra.
    The possessed and the dispossessed : spirits, identity, and power
in a Madagascar migrant town / Lesley A. Sharp.
        p.   cm.—(Comparative studies of health systems and medical
care ; no. 37)
    Includes bibliographical references and index.
    ISBN 0-520-20708-4 (alk. paper)
    1. Sakalava (Malagasy people)—Rites and ceremonies. 2. Sakalava
(Malagasy people)—Religion. 3. Sakalava (Malagasy people)—Social
conditions. 4. Spirit possession—Madagascar—Ambanja. 5. Ancestor
worship—Madagascar—Ambanja. 6. Ambanja (Madagascar)—Religious
life and customs.   I. Title.   II. Series.
DT469.M277S358 1993
306'.089'993—dc20   92-37296
                                                                            CIP

Printed in the United States of America

The paper used in this publication meets the minimum requirements of American
National Standard for Information Sciences—Permanence of Paper for Printed Library
Materials, ANSI Z39.48-1984. ∞

Contents

Figures

Plates

Textual Notes

In this study I will follow Malagasy systems of spelling, thus:

*The following letters do not exist in Malagasy: c, q, u, w, and x.

*The letter *o* is pronounced like a long *u* or *double-o* in English (thus "tromba" is pronounced "troomba").

*The letter *j* is pronounced like a *z* or *dz* (as in Ambanja).

*The nasal *n* sounds (both velar and palatal) of northern Sakalava (as in rañao and tsiñy) are written as *ñ*, following the preference of local informants (who may also write it as *gn;* see also Baré 1980, 1983; compare, however, Feeley-Harnik 1991). The sound in English which most closely approximates this is the *ng* in "sing."

*In Malagasy there is no difference between singular and plural noun forms. Since the term *tromba*, for example, may refer to one or many spirits, throughout the text I have sought to clarify the number.

Unless otherwise stated, all Malagasy terms are given in the Sakalava dialect. The following abbreviations have been used where it was necessary to specify different dialects or languages: SAK for the Sakalava dialect, HP for high plateaux (Merina), FR for French. All foreign terms used in the text are italicized the first time they appear only. I have sought to limit my use of foreign terms; the most important ones appear in the glossary in Appendix A.

The national currency of Madagascar is the Malagasy franc (*franc malgache* or fmg). During the first six months of 1987 the exchange rate was approximately 750 fmg to U.S. $1. In mid-July there was a devaluation and the franc dropped to approximately 1,300 fmg per U.S. $1.

Acknowledgments

This research would not have been possible without the generous financial support provided by numerous institutions. Two consecutive Foreign Language and Area Studies (FLAS) Fellowships (1984–1986) at the University of California, Berkeley, enabled me to study Malagasy prior to my departure for Madagascar. The following organizations provided funding for fieldwork: the United States Department of Education Fulbright-Hays Doctoral Dissertation Research Abroad Program (Grant number G00864345), the Wenner-Gren Foundation for Anthropological Research, the Sigma Xi Foundation, and the Lowie Fund of the University of California. The Regents and Alice Galloway Memorial Fellowships, also of the University of California, enabled me to devote much of my energies to writing during the first eighteen months that followed my return from the field. Finally, I am grateful to the Academic Grants Committee of Butler University, whose funds allowed me to prepare this manuscript for publication during the summer of 1991; and to Paul Yu for his enthusiastic support of faculty scholarship.

Many people have given of their time throughout the various stages of this project. I owe much to Burton Benedict, Fred Dunn, Nancy Scheper-Hughes, and Michael Watts for their expert guidance throughout the course of the research and beyond. Gillian Feeley-Harnik and Michael Lambek each reviewed a draft of this manuscript with great care, providing invaluable advice on this study of Madagascar as well as helpful suggestions on other related topics. In turn, I have always found their respective research in the Indian Ocean to be informative and inspiring. The following individuals, through conversations and written communication, provided additional comments I have much appreciated: Nancy Abelmann, Elizabeth Colson, Nicole Constable, Steve Foster, Nelson Graburn, Linda Green, Ivan Karp, Jean La Fontaine, and Mary Beth Mills. I also wish to thank those individuals who provided highly skilled technical support. These include Colleen Baker, for the care with which she prepared the maps, and Joe Ader and others at the Butler Computer Center for their time-consuming efforts to reproduce several of the figures. Paula Sharp and Robin Rudell had the kindness and patience to carefully proofread this manuscript at various points, and Marcy Assalone provided superb editorial and other support at the final stage of preparation.

I would like to take this opportunity to thank, as well, a few members of the staff at the University of California Press. These include my acquisitions editor, Stan Holwitz, for his enthusiastic support of this manuscript throughout its various stages; and Michelle Nordon, for her friendliness, patience, and great skill as a project editor. I am fortunate to have had Diane Mark-Walker as a copy editor, for she is truly gifted at her craft. Finally, I wish to thank Diana Feinberg and others for their artwork. Thank you, too, to the countless others at the Press without whose assistance the completion of this project would not have been possible. Any mistakes that remain result from my own carelessness.

I am forever indebted to Hanta and Chris Rideout, who prepared me for the field, and to their kin in Madagascar, who took care of me when I was there. Praise is also due to Marijosée Carlson who patiently tutored me in the Sakalava dialect. Once in the field, any success there was due largely to assistance from the following scholars: Suzy Ramamonjisoa, Fulgence Fanony, Jean-Aimé Rakotoarisoa, Susan Kus, Victor Raharijaona, Hilarion Rakotovololona, Ann-Marie Ralaivola, and Père Robert Jaovelo-Dzao. Innumerable residents of Ambanja and neighboring areas assisted me as well. Space alone prevents me from listing all of their names, but I wish to acknowledge at least the following people: Ampanjakabe Tsimiaro III and his wife and mother, Ambanjakabe Amada and his wife, Dr. A. as well as Mme B. for their warm friendship and hospitality, Members of the Club A., Mme K., Maman'i'H. and Papan'i'H., Mme Z., Mama Rose, Mr. J., and Mr. and Mme E. H.. I am forever indebted to Maman'i'F. for her infinite patience and her expertise as a research assistant, who kept me going and who never lost her interest in this project, and to Mlle. B. A. who led us to many tromba ceremonies. I also owe much to Marie, Mariamo, and a host of other mediums and their spirits, who were my tromba guides. *Misoatra Zana-hary.* Final and special thanks go to Andy Fox: despite crazed *omby*, giant wasps, and unfamiliar smells, he learned to love living—and run-ning—in Ambanja. I wish to thank him, too, for suggesting the title for this book and for his steady support throughout the entire course of this project.

Madagascar

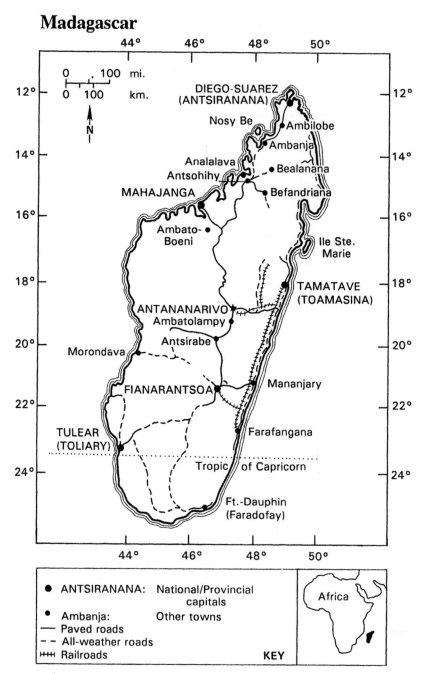

Figure 1.1. Map of Madagascar. Sources: After Bunge (1983: 51); Madagascar-FTM (1986); Société Malgache (1973: 2).

CHAPTER I

Introduction: Possession, Identity, and Power

Theoretical and Methodological Considerations

Women, migration, and power: these are the themes that frame this study of spirit possession and identity in northwest Madagascar. The setting is Ambanja, a booming migrant town in the heart of a prosperous plantation region called the Sambirano Valley. Here identity is shaped by polyculturalism and manipulated through religious experience. Healing rituals, involving possession by ancestral *tromba* spirits, provide an important arena in which to articulate the problems of urban life. In this latter respect this is a study in medical anthropology.

Identity in Ambanja is dynamic and multifaceted, defined in reference to a subjective conceptualization of self, an individual's role as social actor, and cultural—or ethnic—origin. In this migrant town, these three levels of experience are bounded by competing statuses of insider and outsider. Insiders are, specifically, the indigenous Bemazava-Sakalava;[1] outsiders are other Malagasy speakers who have come to this region as wage laborers searching for work. Ethnicity is the most important marker for defining identity and status in Ambanja. Although migrants form the majority of the valley's population, the Sakalava comprise the largest single ethnic group.

These competing statuses define the powerful and the vulnerable, where local ancestors and access to land are pivotal. To some extent, length of stay and material wealth may affect one's position in local arenas of influence, yet indigenous notions of power require that one be symbolically rooted to the land. The Sambirano Valley is the *tanindrazaña* (HP: *tanindrazana*), or "ancestral land" of the Sakalava. The significance of this concept is reflected in indigenous terms that are used to distinguish insiders from outsiders: Sakalava are the *tera-tany* ("the children" or "possessors of the soil") or the original inhabitants of the Valley; while migrants are referred to as *vahiny* ("guests"). These symbolic distinctions also carry significant economic weight, ultimately affecting success or, even, survival. It is Sakalava tera-tany who most often control access to and hold rights over the use of the most important local resource: arable land.

Tromba, as the spirits of dead Sakalava royalty, define the key features of contemporary Sakalava identity.[2] Amid rapid social change, they remain the guardians of local sacred space and they are significant historical actors for collective experience. Possession by the dead is deeply rooted in Sakalava history: among the earliest surviving written accounts is one recorded by Luis Mariano, a Portuguese Jesuit who described this phenomenon when he visted the island in 1616 (Lombard 1988: 23, who in turn cites A. and G. Grandidier, eds. 1903–1920, vol. 2: 251, 255). Spirit possession as an institution subsequently accompanied the rise of royal dynasties and their associated kingdoms in the sixteenth century. Because spirit possession is central to Sakalava culture, descriptions of this form of possession provide a means through which to trace the historical development of the Sakalava as a people, who today are organized into a chain of kingdoms along the west coast of Madagascar (Kent 1968; see also S. Ramamonjisoa 1984). In turn, since tromba spirits are known, historic personalities, spirit possession is an indigenous form of recorded history where Sakalava preserve knowledge of royal genealogies and, ultimately, of who they are more generally. In everyday terms, it is the tromba spirits that define who Sakalava are in contrast to the ever-increasing influx of migrants.

Tromba possession is a mainstay of everyday life in Ambanja. Tromba spirits address the living through mediums, the majority of whom are female. In precolonial times (prior to 1896) there was only a handful of mediums who served as counselors to members of the royal lineages. Within the last fifty years, however, there has been a virtual explosion in the incidence of tromba possession throughout Sakalava territory. Today, tromba spirits proliferate, especially in Ambanja. In this town of approximately 26,000,[3] perhaps 60 percent of all women are possessed, of whom nearly 50 percent are non-Sakalava migrants. Tromba mediums are respected by both commoner Sakalava and non-Sakalava as powerful healers and as advisers on personal affairs. Through the assistance of tromba spirits and their mediums, insiders and outsiders may manipulate their statuses and their personal relationships in this town.

In Ambanja, tromba is perhaps the most significant local instititution for both Sakalava and non-Sakalava, and its importance is reflected in several ways. First, as a key aspect of indigenous religion, it is dynamic, constantly changing in form so as to remain a central defining principle of what it means to be Sakalava. In turn, as an essential Sakalava cultural institution, it also manages or regulates the incorporation of outsiders into the Sakalava community. An important feature of tromba in this polycultural town is that most non-Sakalava may, over time, actively participate in tromba, either as observers, mediums, or mediums' clients. Tromba is the only local institution that enables migrants to permanently transform their identities. Through a complex fictive kinship system, non-Sakalava mediums are symbolically redefined as Sakalava. In this way they become enmeshed in local networks that increase their access to local institutions of power. Since tromba mediumship is primarily a female experience, tromba facilitates the incorporation of migrant women over men, and no comparable institution exists for men.

Tromba possession as ritual has a performative dimension (G. Lewis 1980: 22ff) where the actions, gestures, words, and knowledge communicated during large-scale possession ceremonies and smaller, private healing sessions reveal indigenous conceptions of well-being. For Ambanja's residents, well-being does not hinge simply on one's physical state; it is also mediated by one's status as tera-tany or vahiny. Tromba mediums, as the embodiment of royal ancestral power, assist others in their attempts to cope with the problems they encounter while living in this urban community, one that is dominated by a plantation economy. Thus, embedded in the symbolic order of tromba are critiques of community life and its tensions, the meaning of work, the local political economy, and the dynamics of local power relations over time.

CRITICAL APPROACHES TO THE STUDY OF AFFLICTION

The politics of identity in this town is multifaceted, requiring an integrative theoretical approach. In order to comprehend the many levels of meaning and experience inherent to life in Ambanja, this study will draw from theory in medical anthropology, migration studies, and the study of ritual. A historical dimension is also necessary if we are to comprehend the meaning of power at this particular point in time.

HEALTH AND CRITIQUES OF CAPITALISM

This study is framed by theory generated within the field of critical medical anthropology. In many ways this is highly contested terrain: various authors argue that since the term *critical* is (neo-)Marxist in origin, it is this theoretical stance that should be the primary (or even exclusive) orientation. As a result, there are writers who, assuming the more conservative position, advocate a return to the older label, "political economy of health." Still others strive for a more loosely defined or eclectic approach that draws from interpretative, phenomenological, and epistemological frames of reference.[4] (For more details on this debate see, for example, Baer 1982, 1986; Baer et al. 1986; Doyal 1979; Elling 1981; Frankenberg 1988; Morgan 1987, 1990; Morsy 1979; Navarro 1976a, Scheper-Hughes 1990; Singer 1896.)

This present study is situated primarily within the latter (more eclectic) camp; nevertheless, it seeks to draw from the strengths of each. A key assumption that runs throughout this study from Madagascar is that, first, inequality and power are often significant (or *critical*) factors for understanding health and well-being. This is true not only within highly complex and stratified Western societies, but also in smaller (and, in this case, urban) communities in the Third World, where colonial policies and relations have either introduced new forms of inequality and stratification or exacerbated older ones.

Second, literature written in the genre of the political economy of health assumes the pervasiveness of biomedical (or what I will refer to as clinical) medicine worldwide and focuses on the advantages as well as the disadvantages of biomedicine; nevertheless, this is not the most appropriate focus in Ambanja. Tromba mediums and other indigenous healers are preferred by many local inhabitants over biomedically trained practitioners because they have a clearer understanding of indigenous conceptions of illness and disorder. In terms of daily practice, biomedicine is not hegemonic or heterodox in nature (Baer et al. 1986: 95–98) but instead is perceived as ineffective and is less valued than indigenous forms of healing. Unlike tromba mediums, for example, clinicians do not comprehend or embrace their patients' beliefs about the relationship between the cosmos and the social world. In addition, it is not *medicine* per se that must be the primary focus of the research but, rather, *affliction*, as a broadly defined category of human experience. Thus, in this study from Madagascar, it is not solely disease or sickness that will be investigated, but *individual and collective problems* that are social, economic, and political in nature.

A third assumption is that the human body provides a rich terrain upon which these problems may be played out or expressed. This becomes apparent during healing sessions and other ritual settings. The body may also provide an appropriate medium for transformations in identity, through dress as well as action. This may occur during the pageantry of possession ceremonies, but these in turn may have long-lasting effects on a medium's life and sense of self. Finally, comprehensive critical interpretation requires the investigation of linkages between political-economic, symbolic, and historical elements.

If we begin with critical approaches to affliction, Morgan's (1987: 132) definition of the political economy of health proves useful:

> . . . a macroanalytic, critical, and historical perspective for analyzing disease distribution and health services under a variety of economic systems, with particular emphasis on the effects of stratified social, political, and economic relations within the world economic system.

Morgan advocates that we analyze medicine (and, by extension, medical systems more generally) in reference to competing modes of production; take into account the significance of social class; give greater attention to history, including colonial as well as precolonial periods; and explore capitalism's effect on the declines as well as the improvement of health status (1987: 146).

Although a Marxist orientation offers valuable tools for understanding the effects of capitalism on the local political economy, and on indigenous social relations and healing practices, this definition requires a few adjustments. First, a purely macroanalytic stance (not necessarily something that Morgan herself would advocate) overlooks key aspects of everyday life which are so much a part of anthropological analysis. Thus, for the purpose of this study, the microlevel will be the primary unit of analysis. Following Morsy's approach (1978; 1991: 205ff), the phenomenon of spirit possession will be analyzed against historically based, macrolevel developments.

Second, as Morgan notes, too often the political economy of health relies heavily on world systems and dependency theory, yet such an orientation on its own is outdated. In turn, it is also too restrictive because, as J. Comaroff explains, "the total penetration of the world capitalist system . . . denies determination to forces outside itself" (Comaroff 1985: 154, as cited in Morgan 1987: 141). Specifically, what is at stake here is *local* determination. As the present study will show, the inhabitants of Ambanja are not passive victims of capitalistic forces; rather, ritual forms enable them to *transcend and transform* labor relations, the meaning of work, and future economic development of the region.

MOVING BEYOND CLASS-BASED ANALYSIS:
UNDERSTANDING THE MIGRATION EXPERIENCE IN
NORTHWEST MADAGASCAR

A *class-based analysis* is an essential element in the study of inequality from a Marxist perspective, but this concept, as Strathern (1984: 3ff) has illustrated, does not necessarily translate well cross-culturally. As Comaroff and Comaroff (1991: xi) ask, "how is [consciousness] mediated by such distinctions as class, gender, and ethnicity?" Throughout Madagascar, *ethnicity* is generally a far more important unit of analysis. At times it may correspond with Western conceptions of class; elsewhere it operates independently. For example, on a national scale, the Merina and Betsileo of the central high plateaux have the greatest access to Madagascar's resources, and it is they who form a significant proportion of this nation's elite. This is an issue that is of prime importance to the Sakalava of Ambanja. As case studies throughout this work will illustrate, ethnicity is a much stronger determinant than class for local power relations in this town.

Gender is also a significant category, one that extends beyond the limits of social class or ethnicity. It is especially important to the understanding of the migration process in northwest Madagascar. An assumption running throughout studies of voluntary migration in Africa is that it is predominantly an adult male experience. This process is rooted in colonial policies and subsequent demands of capitalist labor, where indigenous peoples have experienced shifts in the division of labor by gender. Men have become the primary wage earners, while women remain in rural areas, caring for the land, animals, homestead, and offspring. Laborers send remittances home to support kin, and the presence of women in the villages ensures the reproduction of future generations of labor (see, for example, Cohen 1969; Epstein 1958; Mayer 1971; Meillassoux 1982; Murray 1981; Powdermaker 1962; Richards 1951).

Madagascar provides important contrasts. As Little (1973) and

Schuster (1979) have shown, migration can be a liberating experience for women who relocate on their own to towns. In Madagascar, women migrate, often alone. The majority of my female informants in Ambanja were the sole heads of their households, and they were the primary wage earners, often supporting three generations: themselves, their children, and their aging mothers. Women experience the freedom that accompanies migrating alone, but they must also endure the obstacles of migrant status. If migrants are to succeed economically and socially, they must establish networks that will enable them to settle and become integrated into their new community. An important focus of this study is to unravel how women accomplish this. *Age* is yet another dimension: children may also figure prominently in the migration process, although they are relatively invisible in studies on this topic. This problem will be explored in chapter 9.

More generally, capitalism shapes the nature of social relations, and anthropological approaches offer important tools for analyzing the manner in which indigenous forms of social structure respond or are transformed, as well as how capitalist relations are perceived and experienced. Throughout Madagascar a premium is placed on *kinship*, since it is kin-based networks that one may exploit in times of need. In Ambanja, strangers are very vulnerable. They can rely on no one, and so the newly arrived migrant engages in a passionate search for kin or others from the same ancestral land who can help them find work as well as housing, loans, food, child care, and, perhaps, over time, land. Tera-tany status has these advantages, but integration for migrants is very difficult, because Sakalava dislike outsiders. Although marriage is one way in which to become integrated locally, marriage unions in Ambanja are generally short-term and tenuous, making this an unsatisfactory solution.

Kinship and wage labor define opposing categories of social relations in Ambanja. Wage labor is perceived simultaneously as an economic and social relationship, one based on inequality and involving payment in cash for services by an employer to an employee. Wage labor may generate income, which for migrants is essential to survival, but it does not carry with it the permanent and obligatory social ties that characterize kinship. Kinship, on the other hand, is defined by reciprocal relationships that involve the dual exchange of goods and services.

Capitalism and, more generally, colonialism, as social and political forces, have also affected social structure by undermining indigenous power. In the precolonial era, Sakalava defined themselves in relation to their royalty. Throughout the colonial period the French sought to undermine royal authority. As a result, structural rules that defined the relationship between commoner and royalty broke down. This process in turn affected Sakalava principles of commoner kinship. More recently, the opposed categories of insider and outsider have become the most important social categories for daily interactions in Ambanja; these are shaped by national and local ethnic factionalism. Tromba possession is among the few institutions that mediate between the competing statuses of insider and outsider. It also offers its participants a means through which to opt out of wage labor and capitalist relations by embedding them in an alternative social world defined through fictive kinship.

UNDERSTANDING INDIGENOUS NOTIONS OF POWER

If we are to comprehend the nature of inequality in Ambanja, it is necessary to construct a clear definition of power; specifically, we must explore how it is indigenously conceived. Arens and Karp note that anthropological discussions of power rely heavily on Weber's definition (*Macht*) (Weber 1947, as quoted in Arens and Karp 1989: xv). Weber focuses on social actors engaged in rational and "mutually acknowledged" exchanges that are based within established and accepted arenas of authority (ibid. 1989: xiii ff). Arens and Karp argue for the need to break from universalist (and thus ethnocentric) definitions of power to more culturally specific ones, especially in reference to cosmological systems. For the purposes of this study, the greatest limitations of Weber's definition lie in his focus on individual action over collective experience and his preoccupation with formal authority. This study will also explore how power is symbolically expressed.

Arens and Karp suggest that anthropologists consider an alternative definition provided by D. Parkin:

> Power rests [not simply] on the acquisition of land, myth, and material objects but rather that which comes from unequal access to semantic creativity, including the capacity to nominate others as equal or unequal, animate or inanimate, memorable or abject, discussor or discussed. (Parkin, ed. 1982: xlvi)

Even though Parkin's definition focuses on power through discourse, it still offers an appropriate alternative, since it marks a break from a materialist orientation characteristic of Weberians (and neo-Marxists). For the sake of this analysis, I would replace Parkin's term *semantic* with *symbolic*. Furthermore, although *nominate* implies formal political action, the *process of determining status* is essential in Madagascar, specifically in reference to ethnic factions that characterize life at national and local levels.

Arens and Karp also prefer Parkin's definition because "this perspective moves us away from an exclusive emphasis on the exercise of power and provides room for examining the relationship between power and consciousness" (1989: xiv). These authors are especially interested in Weber's distinction between authority and power and stress the importance of exploring the latter: "Power is multicentered and, further, . . . the idea of a center may itself be produced through the ideology of power." As the examples in their volume illustrate, "the source of power resides in the interaction between natural, social, and supernatural realms" (1989: xvi, xvii).

In Ambanja, it is clear that power may be exercised in different arenas: through formal structures (for example, by the French colonial government or the present state of Madagascar), ritual authority (tromba mediumship), and individual action (by Sakalava tera-tany over non-Sakalava vahiny). It also may be manifested through legal action or ritual. Tromba provides an important example for the study of power. It is formal and institutionalized, yet the authority previously invested in living royalty has been transferred almost completely to the spiritual realm. As will become clear below, a consciousness of power relations may be articulated in ritual forms that can have temporary or long-lasting effects.

HISTORICAL CONSIDERATIONS

As Bloch (1986: 157ff) has illustrated in his study of Merina circumcision, rituals may change form over time in response to transformations in power relations on a national scale. In turn, historical and other forms of knowledge, as well as power, may be embedded in ritual, so that ritual may operate as a force of resistance and change against the state or other forces (Apter 1992; see also Fry 1976 and Lan 1985; Sahlins 1985). This pairing of history and power is an important theme underlying tromba possession, since it is not a static religious institution, but one that has responded in unique and creative ways to ever-changing political, economic, and social forces. These transformations are rooted in the manner in which the Sakalava of Ambanja conceive of their recent history, which they divide into three major periods: the precolonial (prior to 1896), the colonial (1896–1960), and postcolonial (1960 to the present). Transformations to the precolonial order is a theme of chapter 3; here I would like to provide a brief summary of recent national developments since they inform contemporary Sakalava perceptions of urban life.

The evolution of the Sambirano into a lucrative plantation economy is rooted in the colonial period. Three policies under the French administration are significant here. First, following conquest, the French removed the Bemazava-Sakalava from the most fertile regions of the valley in order to make room for large-scale plantations. Second, when the Bemazava refused to work as wage laborers, local planters recruited migrant labor from other areas of Madagascar. Third, as part of French *pacification* policies, the colonial government sought to undermine the authority of Bemazava royalty (see chapter 2).

These policies lie behind more recent changes that have occurred within the last three decades. The postcolonial era in turn may be broken down into two major periods. From 1960 to 1972 marks the period of the Malagasy Republic (République Malgache). President Philibert Tsiranana, who served throughout this period, retained many of the colonial structures and continued to employ French advisers and administrators. Also, major industries remained in the hands of private citizens, many of whom were French expatriates. In the final years of his presidency, Tsiranana witnessed the rise of *malagasization*,[5] a nationalist movement that was socialist and anti-French. Originally its advocates demanded that all school curricula be taught in the Malagasy language so as to define and reflect a national—rather than foreign—culture; later they demanded the expulsion of French technical advisers working in the upper echelons of the government. The collapse of the Tsiranana administration was precipitated by a strike of university students in March 1972, followed by a peasant uprising and military coup (the May Revolution) (Covell 1987: 45–46). Tsiranana was expelled, and the country was renamed the Democratic Republic of Madagascar (Repoblika Demokratika Malagasy, République Démocratique de Madagascar).[6]

The Socialist Revolution, which spanned the period from 1971 to 1975, was marked by violence and drastic changes in political orientation under three separate presidents. Following the assassination of Colonel Ratsimandrava, who held office for less than a week in 1975, Didier Ratsiraka was named president (and continues to hold this position today; he was reelected in 1989).* Ratsiraka's early policies included the rejection of institutions based on French models and, subsequently, the withdrawal of much foreign capital. Until 1987, Ratsiraka's administration had been fiercely isolationist and advocated self-sufficiency. The nation's strongest allies have been located in (what was then) Eastern Europe, the People's Republic of China, and North Korea. It was only recently (in mid-1986) that Madagascar chose to strengthen its ties with Western powers. (For more detailed discussions of the recent political history of Madagascar see Althabe 1980; Covell 1987: 29–75; Rabenoro 1986; and Rajoelina 1988.)

Although Madagascar by name is a socialist state, its economy may be defined more clearly as a form of state capitalism, where the ownership of all major industries and land holdings rests with the national government.[7] In the Sambirano, capitalism, and not socialism, shapes the bulk of economic relations. Informants from the Sambirano report that only a few changes in the economic order occurred following the Revolution, the greatest involving land reform policies. In this regard, the holdings of foreign planters were seized by the state, and portions were then resold to local residents, with preference shown for those who could prove that they were tera-tany—that is, whose ancestral land was the Sambirano. Since the Socialist Revolution, state-owned plantations have been referred to as *enterprises* (FR: 'entreprises). The enterprises are among the few profitable export businesses of Madagascar, and several operate fairly independently from the government. Also, state- and privately owned businesses exist side by side in the Sambirano. In the transition to state ownership, workers experienced no major structural changes in their places of employment. Labor unions have been legalized, but they are associated with the national party, AREMA, and so loyalty to the state is mandated by the unions. Some workers report that the most significant change was that their hours were shortened, which in turn shrunk their monthly earnings.

INVESTIGATING POSSESSION: SOCIAL CHANGE, MARGINALITY, AND RELIGIOUS EXPERIENCE

An assumption running throughout anthropological studies of religion is that through the study of belief and ritual we may grasp indigenous

---

* As this book was going to press, national elections were held. On March 27, 1993, Albert Zafy was sworn in as Madagascar's new president.

conceptions of the world; ritual especially provides fertile ground for the expression of social tensions or for coping with sudden change (see, for example, La Barre 1970; Linton 1943; Wallace 1956; and Worsley 1968). Studies set in colonial Africa explore the effects of forced resettlement, migration, and urbanization on the web of social life, and the manner in which religion functions as a means for expressing conflict (Colson 1971; Epstein 1958; Gluckman 1954; Mayer 1971; Mitchell 1956; Powdermaker 1962; Richards 1951; Scudder 1966). Furthermore, it is well documented that the incidence of spirit possession often rises dramatically in times of social disruption and crisis. Colson, for example, found that possession occurred with greater frequency among the Gwembe Tonga (in what is now Zambia) when they were relocated by force after the British colonial administration decided to dam and then flood their valley (1969, 1977). The works of Colson and others remain influential in studies of possession, since this phenomenon continues to be investigated in light of the tensions and uncertainties of everday life. A problem underlying these studies, however, is that indigenous peoples are generally portrayed as powerless victims of change who do not fully comprehend the forces that are responsible for new predicaments in which they find themselves.

RITUAL, SYMBOLIC ACTION, AND POWER

More recent studies of religion have sought to go beyond a functionalist analysis, relying instead on a neo-Marxist framework.[8] These studies are historically situated and set within the complex of unequal relations that characterize colonized societies in the Third World, and they are concerned with economic oppression and exploitation. A primary focus is the dispossessed, the marginal and powerless members of societies who are victims of a world capitalist system. Examples include investigations by such authors as J. Comaroff (1985), Nash (1979), Ong (1987), and Taussig (1980a, 1987), in southern Africa, Bolivia, Malaysia, and Colombia, respectively.

These authors do not reject religious experience as evidence of false consciousness (see Marx 1964: 43–44); instead, religion reveals an indigenous awareness of the inequalities that characterize capitalist economic relations. Although this level of consciousness is not fully articulated in everyday action and discourse, it is, nevertheless, richly interwoven in the symbolic imagery of religious expression. Nash and J. Comaroff both illustrate how religion lends order to the world, symbolically (and temporarily) empowering its participants. Nash describes how Bolivian tin miners attempt to control the hazards of their work through magic and by appeasing Tio, a hungry and greedy devil who lives underground. Comaroff argues that among the Tshidi of southern Africa, the rituals associated with the Church of Zion are evidence of attempts to reorder the world, where military and other symbols of power are incorporated into the regalia and ritual language of the church. Ong shows how spirits that possess young female Malay workers on the shop floor are a manifestation of the exploitative labor relations that characterize the electronics industry. While possessed, these women attack microscopes and other objects that are the instruments of their oppression (see also Lim 1983). Taussig, in turn, describes the disorder and madness that capitalist exploitation imposes on landless laborers in Colombia and the manner in which an indigenous awareness of such chaos is inherent to healing sessions and other ritual spheres.

Thus, as each of these studies illustrates, ritual action may be rich in symbols that reveal a keen awareness of the manner in which capitalist relations define or undermine the local social order. In Ambanja, perceptions of social and economic change are reflected within the context of tromba possession in several ways. First is the theme of historical knowledge, where Sakalava may reflect on and reinterpret who they are in relation to other peoples. In the context of tromba, power and historical knowledge are intrinsically linked, enabling Sakalava tera-tany to manipulate social and economic forces that shape their world. Second, healing rituals, involving tromba spirits, are an important arena for the expression of the meaning of affliction for tera-tany and vahiny.

Third, land, work, and identity are important local themes that are shaped or redefined through the logic of tromba. In the Sambirano, the meanings associated with land are multifaceted, since it is both an economically and symbolically defined category. Madagascar is a nation of peasants: it is estimated that approximately 80 percent of the population acquires some proportion of its subsistence needs from farming (World Bank 1980). Natural disasters—such as droughts and cyclones, coupled with population pressures and deforestation—threaten the viability of a large percentage of the population maintaining rights to arable land (cf. Downs and Reyna, eds. 1988). Severe economic problems also make it difficult for many to find wage labor. Migrants come to the Sambirano hoping to acquire work or land. In this region land is valued as a means of production, since ownership ensures that one may remain economically independent and thus free from capitalist relations that characterize wage labor. But ethnic identity and land are also intertwined, since access to land is defined by the opposing categories of tera-tany and vahiny. Vahiny seek to be rooted symbolically to the local ancestral land because it provides a means to achieve insider status. This is something that may occur through participation in tromba possession. In addition, the importance of this opposition of insiders and outsiders is reflected in the multiple meanings assigned to the word "work" (asa) by Sakalava, migrants, and employees of the French colonial and present governments. The meaning of work may also be redefined through possession.

THE QUESTION OF POSSESSION AND MARGINALITY

The relationship between powerlessness and symbolic expression is central to many studies of spirit possession. This argument is most widely known through the work of I. M. Lewis (1966, 1971, 1986, 1991). Lewis argues that possession gives marginalized people a voice and simultaneously enables them to displace the blame for their actions onto their spirits. This is possible because of the manner in which possession operates: it involves a foreign spirit or entity taking control of a living person, whose spirit, soul, or essence is temporarily displaced. Whatever is said or done during possession is the fault of the spirit, not the person. Lewis notes that it is women who predominate in possession cross-culturally, and so his theory is a corollary to a more general theory in gender studies which assumes the nearly universal subordination of women. A key assumption of this argument is that in any given culture, it is men who dominate formal power structures (Rosaldo and Lamphere, eds. 1974; Ortner 1974; and Reiter 1975).[9]

The question of why possession is so common cross-culturally (Bourguinon 1973) has been a perplexing problem for anthropologists. Numerous authors have sought to break from I. M. Lewis's argument, proposing other lines of inquiry. Dominant themes include exploring possession from psychological or psychiatric angles, either by analyzing the cultural construction of self and personhood (Crapanzano 1973, 1983; Crapanzano and Garrison, eds. 1977; Obeyesekere 1977, 1981), possession as pathology (Krippner 1987), or by challenging the pathological model and, more generally, assumptions about culture-bound syndromes (Bartholomew 1990; Hahn 1985; Karp 1985). Others have proposed a biological model; among the better known is the calcium deficiency hypothesis (Kehoe and Giletti 1981; Raybeck et al. 1989).

Social roles and function provide another focus, including possession's therapeutic role (I. and P. Karp 1979; Prince 1964) and its communicative and performative aspects (Ackerman and Lee 1981; Lambek 1980; Lebra 1982; Leiris 1958; Rouget 1980; V. Turner 1987: 33–71). Others draw on feminist theory (Boddy 1988; 1989) or political-economic approaches (Lim 1983; Morsy 1978, 1991; Ong 1987).[10]

Functionalist arguments about marginality, nevertheless, remain implicit in the majority of writings on possession, since many authors share I. M. Lewis's assumption that possession provides the powerless with a means to symbolically express social, economic, or political oppression. A second assumption that dominates the literature is that possession is a *temporary* experience confined to ritual contexts. In the literature framed by a political-economic approach, for example, possession is viewed as a means to express one's powerlessness relative to established structures, but it has no long-term effects that alter relationships with spouses, employers, and others (see, again, Ong 1987, for example). Psychological studies focus on possession as a means to redefine identity, yet the subjects under study are still assumed to be somehow marginal to the greater society. For example, Crapanzano, in his study of the Hamadsha, presents an interesting case, since it involves men rather than women. He argues that adherents experience shifts in their identity and social roles, yet this institution remains a "peripheral" or "fringe phenomenon" relative to the greater Moroccan society (1973: 7) because they are members of the urban poor who are also psychologically disturbed.

There is, however, a growing body of literature that has begun to challenge the presumed universal association between marginality and the possession experience. Giles argues that women engaged in possession activities in Mombasa are not marginal members of their society, nor is possession, as Lewis advocates, peripheral to orthodox Islam. She advocates that possession by *pepo* (or *sheitani*) spirits is a central aspect of Swahili society, and historical analysis reveals that in the past it was more widespread than it is today. Pepo cults provide their members with close-knit groups that offer social support that extends beyond possession ceremonies into daily life. She also stresses the importance of gender differences for understanding the significance of possession in the community, and that possession cults are among the few places where women and men may interact on equal footing. This is an argument that Boddy (1989) has also taken up in her study of *zar* possession in the Sudan. She stresses that there is insufficient evidence to support the "fantasy" of a dominant male culture that subordinates the culture of women—it is a matter of perspective which is mediated by the gender of the informant (1989: 6) (and, perhaps, the anthropologist).

In Madagascar, several authors have analyzed possession in reference to social and economic change. An assumption running throughout these studies is the *assumed centrality* of possession in the local culture. Althabe (1969: 95–118), for example, illustrates the manner in which tromba possession among Betsimisaraka laborers of eastern Madagascar operates to integrate outsiders into communities located near a large sugarcane plantation. Marriage patterns are exogamous and virilocal; in this context a woman who is a "stranger" may become a spirit medium for the ancestors of her husband's kin. Thus, possession operates as an institution for incorporation, whereby the new wife becomes more closely linked to her affines. In turn she is empowered, since it is through her that the ancestors speak. Fieloux and Lombard (1989), writing from southwest Madagascar, illustrate the usefulness of an analysis that focuses on the local political economy for understanding possession (again, see Morsy 1978, 1991). They describe changes in *bilo* possession which reveal the unease felt by local Masikoro, among whom the introduction of a new cash economy is undermining animal husbandry. Individuals who have grown "rich" and "fat" from their involvement in the cotton industry have lost sight of kin-based social relations, and bilo, as a ritual form, reflects these concerns and transformations.

This study of tromba possession in northwest Madagascar seeks to offer other important counterexamples, where the dominant assumptions about religious experience—and, more specifically, about possession and its participants—are inappropriate. As I will show, tromba possession is not a peripheral domain in the community of Ambanja; rather, it is a *central and defining aspect of Sakalava culture.* Furthermore, tromba possession may be *permanently empowering,* its significance extending beyond the ritual context into everyday life. This case from Madagascar also offers an example of the structural legitimacy of possession, in which kinship is a central operating principle. As a result, tromba carries with it important ramifications for those who occupy competing statuses of insider and outsider. What I will show is that to be active in tromba is a sign that one *is not marginal.*

THE BODY AS A NATURAL SYMBOL

As Mauss reminds us, "The body is the first and most natural tool of man" (1979; quoted in Scheper-Hughes and Lock 1987: 1). Medical anthropology and sociology are rich in accounts that detail how the body serves as a field on which affliction is experienced and expressed (see, for example, Blacking 1977; J. Comaroff 1985; Crapanzano 1973; Martin 1987; Ong 1987; Taussig 1980b; B. Turner 1984, 1987). It is assumed here that spirit possession has a performative aspect and thus, in the context of tromba, the human body is a vehicle for the expression of conflicts through the manipulation of a symbolic order that is shared by members of this community. The aim of this study is to analyze the logic (or, as Taussig [1987] would say, the chaos) of the symbolic meanings that are played out on the body of the medium. Also, tromba possession may be a transformative process that affects different levels of identity.

Scheper-Hughes's and Lock's concept of "the three bodies" is helpful for exploring the symbolic nature of tromba possession, since tromba is significant to individual, social (as well as cultural), and political experiences. As a medium enters and exits trance, she experiences shifts in different levels of identity, shifts that may be temporary or permanent. These include *selfhood, personhood,* and *ethnic identity.* On the first or "individual" level, the first two forms of identity come into play. As these two authors stress, the manner in which the notion of *self* is defined (and therefore experienced) is not universal but culturally specific. In the context of tromba, selfhood is subjectively perceived as shifting in nature as the medium moves in and out of trance. In this sense it operates on a very personal (or psychological) level. Possession also affects notions of *personhood:* in this sense, the medium is perceived as a social being who experiences *structural* shifts in relation to her kin and friends, and these shifts affect her role and status in the community.[11]

On the second level, or in reference to the "social body," indigenous concepts of *ethnic identity* are significant. As a medium for royal spirits, a woman embodies what it means to be Sakalava, and this is evident in her words, attire, and actions. Thus, when possessed, her individual body provides a map of the social body. In addition, an important shift occurs if she is a migrant, because, through tromba possession, her ethnic identity is altered: when she becomes a medium for tromba spirits she is redefined ethnically as Sakalava. Since the concept of ethnic identity is central to this study, unless specified otherwise the term *identity* refers to *ethnicity.*

The third level is the "political body": in this sense possession may be seen as politically charged (see, for example, Lan 1985). The political nature of tromba is defined through ancestral authority, a form of power that is respected locally and legitimated through recent national policies, including malagasization. As a vessel for Sakalava spirits, a medium embodies the Sakalava past: she helps record, shape, and redefine what it means to be Sakalava in the context of social change. She carries the authority of Sakalava ancestral power, and thus it is she who may manipulate relationships between individuals and groups in the Sambirano. This occurs most often during healing ceremonies, where she helps individual clients gain control over events that disrupt their lives. In other instances mediums may dictate the thrust of future economic development in the valley. The economic importance of the Sambirano, at a national level becomes more apparent when it is evaluated against the backdrop of the country as a whole.

THE LOGIC AND METHODS OF INQUIRY

THE SETTING

Madagascar is the fourth largest island in the world (approximately 1,500 kilometers long, with a surface area of 587,000 square miles), yet until recently it has received relatively little attention from scholars outside Madagascar and France. Geographic and political isolation and low productivity contribute to the severity of economic difficulties inherent in life in Madagascar (World Bank 1980; Pryor 1988). In many ways this nation is considered to be a backwater of the Third World. Reasons for this are reflected in recent socioeconomic statistical data for this country. The national population for 1984 was estimated at 9.9 million, with a doubling time of twenty-six years; and the average life expectancies for men and women are 54.2 and 57.8 years, respectively. In addition, the national income has shown a sharp decline over the past twenty years, especially since 1970 (Covell 1987: xiii ff). It is only within the last two years that Madagascar has received much coverage in the popular press (see, for example, *The Economist* 1989; Jolly 1987, 1988; Payer 1989; and Shoumatoff 1988a, 1988b). Although these recent articles focus primarily on environmental depletion through the destruction of precious rain forests, relatively little has been written on the increasing severity of social and economic problems faced by Madagascar's citizens.[12]

Most English-speaking anthropologists are familiar with Madagascar primarily through the works of Bloch (1989) and Kottak (1980), who have written, respectively, on the Merina and Betsileo of the high plateaux. The geographical interests of these two anthropologists reflect a more general trend in the social sciences in Madagascar, where, until recently, the highlands have been a focus for the most intensive research.[13] Another main focus has been village studies of discrete groups of Malagasy speakers. As a result, two main goals of my research have been to provide a much needed study of coastal peoples of Madagascar and to explore the significance of Malagasy identity in a polycultural, urban setting. By focusing on migration, this study seeks to reflect the reality of life as it is experienced by many Malagasy today. Today Malagasy of diverse origins must cope with living together, especially in urban environments, as opposed to the ideal, where peoples of common origins inhabit the same territory.

Migration is very much a part of Madagascar's history and it has shaped ideas about Malagasy identity. Although Madagascar, by virtue of its geographical location, is considered to be an African nation, the Malagasy language is linguistically categorized as Austronesian. Malagasy trace their origins to locations as diverse as Polynesia, the islands of Southeast Asia, East Africa, and the Persian Gulf. The influence of these diverse cultures on what it means to be Malagasy is revealed through social, structural and cultural similarities, including rules of descent, burial practices, styles of dress, cuisine, and physical features. Linguistic analysis also reveals loan words from kiSwahili, Arabic, Malay, French, and English (Southall 1986). Cultural origins are a topic of heated debate among Malagasy intellectuals, who generally prefer to look eastward to Indonesia and Malaysia for their origins. These categories are important for current conceptions of ethnicity.

Another purpose of this study is to analyze the relationship between tromba possession and social change. Spirit possession is among the most common themes found in the literature on Madagascar (see, for example, Althabe 1969: 115ff; Estrade 1977; Fieloux and Lombard 1989; Ottino 1965; Raison-Jourde 1983: 48ff; S. Ramamonjisoa 1984; Rason 1968; Russillon 1908). As my own work progressed in Ambanja, these studies seemed, for the most part, outdated, since they stress the nature of tromba as it should be, set within the royal context. They do not address its dynamic and changing nature over time (for notable exceptions see Althabe [1969], and Fieloux and Lombard [1989], as noted above). Today, tromba possession is common throughout Sakalava territory, but its incidence is unusually high in Ambanja. Tromba is the point at which social, religious, political, and economic forces converge, and so this institution provides a means to explore the dynamic nature of daily life at all levels in this community.

RESEARCH METHODS

The data for this study were collected during a twelve-month period (January 1987 to January 1988), originally for the purposes of dissertation research. Thus, the ethnographic present is 1987. The first two months of research were dedicated to conducting archival work in the Bibliothèque Nationale, the Archives Nationales, and university and seminary libraries located in the national capital of Antananarivo and in the provincial capitals of Toamasina (Tamatave) and Antsiranana (Diégo-Suarez or Diégo).[14]

Anthropological fieldwork was based primarily in Ambanja and the surrounding countryside of the Sambirano. Comparative data were also collected during short-term visits to Diégo in the north and Mahajanga on the west coast, the east coast town of Antalaha, and other locations listed below. The primary methods used for data collection were participant-observation of many facets of daily and ritual life, and personal, often multiple, interviews with a wide variety of informants. These interviews were conducted in Malagasy, primarily in the Sakalava dialect, although some were carried out in other dialects or in French. Two assistants aided me throughout the course of this work. My primary assistant was a young Sakalava woman in her late twenties who was born into a tera-tany family. The second was a high school student who was the child of migrants.[15]

Throughout the course of the year I attended a total of nine large-scale tromba ceremonies, involving as many as twenty mediums at one time. Since many mediums work as healers, I also attended more than twenty private consultations with clients, and I was a regular observer and client in the homes of four mediums. Throughout the course of the year I encountered a total of ninety-eight mediums (of whom four were male). I conducted in-depth interviews with twenty of these (including two men), followed by additional visits and follow-up interviews.

A special quality of tromba possession is that each spirit has a distinct personality, a characteristic it shares, for example, with possession found in Korean (Kendall 1985, 1988), Brazilian (Bastide 1978; S. and R. Leacock 1972; Krippner 1987), Haitian (K. Brown 1991), and west and north African traditions (I. M. Lewis et al., eds. 1991). As a spirit enters a medium's body, it displaces her own spirit, so that she does not remember what came to pass when she was possessed. This gap in knowledge is most clearly illustrated by the following episode. In October I was traveling with a group of five women and a five-year-old girl.

One day the child fell sick with malaria, trembling and delirious from the fever. My adult companions felt powerless to help her because, as one woman explained, "I know nothing [*tsy heko é!*] about how to cure this type of sickness; only my tromba [spirit] knows how [*mahay ny tromba*]." She and the other women assembled and called up her spirit to heal the child. After the session had ended and the medium had left trance, others told her what her spirit had done. (The child eventually recovered.)

Since the knowledge of the spirits is sacred, mediums are reluctant to discuss tromba in detail, fearing that their spirits will become angry and will make them sick. Others who have heard a spirit's words or who are knowledgeable about tromba possession also prefer not to discuss them in any detail. For this reason, I interviewed mediums in and out of trance, collecting life histories from both the living and the dead (cf. Wafer 1991). Mediums' kin, neighbors, friends, and clients were also valuable informants who provided complementary data.

Life histories provided a means through which to explore different areas of mediums' experiences, including possession, migration and work, social ties, education, and health. Several attempts were made to conduct formal household surveys. These were designed to enable me to collect similar data from a broader spectrum of the population. I was forced to abandon this technique since it met with great resistance (and, at times, anger) from my informants and research assistants. Malagasy believe that the government already asks too many questions of private citizens, and I did not wish to alienate potential informants. Instead, much of the information originally requested on the survey was collected during informal discussions on related topics.

Sakalava in Ambanja draw sharp distinctions between what I will refer to as *popular* tromba, or the form that possession takes in town, and *royal* tromba. The latter involves a handful of mediums who are possessed by the greatest royal ancestors, and they live on Nosy Faly, a small island located just off the northwest coast of Madagascar. It is here where the Bemazava-Sakalava tombs are located. These special mediums work solely as advisers to living royalty. Acquiring information on royal tromba was by far the most difficult part of the research, since it was only after eight months in the field that I was able to gain the trust of local royalty. Data on royal tromba were collected through interviews with the Bemazava king, his wife, and advisers and during a visit to Nosy Faly where, under close supervision, I was able to witness a series of royal rituals and briefly interview two royal mediums. I was also invited by the Antakarana king to attend a series of ceremonies in his ancestral village, Ambatoharañana. (The Antakarana are the northern neighbors of the Sakalava; they share many cultural traditions.) Finally, I made several visits to the nearby island of Nosy Be to consult with royalty of the northern Bemihisatra-Sakalava dynasty.

In addition to tromba, there are other forms of possession that occur in Ambanja. Although tromba is primarily an experience of adult women, *njarinintsy* spirits, for example, frequently possess adolescent schoolgirls. These spirits are dangerous and volatile, and they are viewed as a serious illness that must be cured. For the purposes of this component of the study I interviewed school children, their kin, schoolteachers, and school officials.

Clinical medicine, as well as Protestantism, Catholicism, and Islam provide additional insights into local ideas about possession. According to Sakalava logic, possession and madness are believed at times to overlap. The most severe cases may be brought by kin to psychiatrists for treatment (Sharp, in press). More often, however, kin and patients seek assistance from special Protestant groups that have full-time specialists who exorcise spirits through power derived from the Holy Spirit. I made several visits to a bush hospital run by a group of exorcists, and I attended a number of their curing ceremonies in Ambanja. My own residence proved to be a focus for such activities, since I rented a house that belonged to the Lutheran church. The Malagasy pastor who lived there during ten months of my stay was trained as an exorcist. He allowed me, as a member of his household and congregation, to observe him at work and we had many lively discussions on tromba possession. Religions of diverse faiths were also important to this study, since they provide a means for male and female migrants to become socially integrated. I therefore sought out parishioners, pastors, priests, and congregation elders from a variety of faiths, interviewing them on possession and, more generally, on life in Ambanja. Clinical medicine was another important area of exploration, since it provided comparative data that assisted in the evaluation of attitudes toward healing. For this reason I observed the actions of local physicians, nurses, and pharmacists and interviewed them about possession as well as the nature of affliction in the Sambirano.

Since the enterprises are central to the lives of the majority of Ambanja's inhabitants, I interviewed local government officials and enterprise staff and laborers. I also interviewed a wide spectrum of male and female laborers of diverse backgrounds. In so doing, I sought to comprehend the nature of the migrant experience in general terms and to understand variations that might occur as a result of one's ethnic or geographical origin. I made periodic visits to the enterprises, joining the weekly tour with the occupational health doctor in order to watch her and members of her nursing staff work with patients and so that I could interview managers and workers. To grasp the rhythm of the workday and the labor demands associated with agricultural work, I accompanied a woman to work one day and assisted her as she sorted cocoa and coffee.

THE ORGANIZATION OF THE STUDY

This study is divided into three parts, reflecting three different levels of analysis. Part 1, "Historic, Political-Economic, and Social Levels of Experience," provides background information and a framework for exploring the forces that have shaped indigenous notions of identity. Specifically, it focuses on the economic development of the Sambirano and the rise of local polyculturalism over the past century. Chapter 2 is primarily a historical overview of the development of the local political economy of the valley. Chapter 3 describes the nature of factionalism on national and local levels and the relevance of the conflicting statuses of insider and outsider, or tera-tany and vahiny. Chapter 4 provides case studies that illustrate the experiences of migrants in Ambanja and the factors that facilitate or impede their integration into the local tera-tany community.

Tromba is the focus of Part 2, "Spirit Possession in the Sambirano." Within this section, chapter 5 is an overview of tromba and other forms of possession. Chapter 6 focuses on tromba as a locus of power in the Sambirano. Chapter 7 explores the structural principles that are associated with tromba and which enable outsiders to become insiders in Ambanja.

Part 3, "The Conflicts of Town Life," seeks to integrate these two foci—the shifting nature of identity and tromba possession—through discussions on affliction in this polycultural community. Chapter 8 examines the problems that adults face and the role that mediums play as healers of personal and social ills. Chapter 9 explores problems that are specific to children, who form an unusual and especially vulnerable group of migrants. Chapter 10 concludes this study with a discussion of an alternative therapy offered by Protestant exorcists who treat patients troubled by problematic cases of possession.

PART I

Historic, Political-Economic, and Social Levels of Experience

CHAPTER II

The Political Economy
of the Sambirano

The Sambirano Valley is one of the few regions of Madagascar where one finds evidence of prosperity. Malagasy often refer to this region as one of the most fertile and productive areas of the island, providing a sharp contrast to the rest of the nation. The town of Ambanja lies in the heart of this river valley and is the commercial, political (including royal), religious, educational, and entertainment center for the region. Even though national trends exhibit a downward movement of the economy, the Sambirano has become well-known as a region where "there is work" and "money" (*misy asa, misy vola*), so that many people have come here from other regions of the island to "seek their fortunes" (*hidaty harena*). On the whole this nation is plagued by fierce shortages of such essentials as foodstuffs, medicines, and construction materials, but in Ambanja one is struck by the relative beauty of the area and plentitude of goods—though overpriced—that are available. In comparison to other regions of Madagascar, the development that has occurred in Ambanja and the Sambirano Valley is striking. This chapter will explore the factors that account for this over time.

AMBANJA, A PLANTATION COMMUNITY

The greatest economic force existing in the Sambirano Valley is that exerted by the enterprises, the large companies that own much of the land in the valley. Originally these were private plantations, established by foreign planters around the turn of the century. Following the Socialist Revolution of the 1970s, many foreign nationals fled the country, their lands confiscated by the state. By the late 1970s nearly all of these plantations became fully or semi-nationalized, and today they are managed by Malagasy rather than foreign staff. The shift from private holdings to state capitalism has had an effect on land tenure and work relations; it is also important for understanding Malagasy notions of historical experience. For this reason, throughout this study I will use the term *plantation* when referring to these farms during the colonial (1896–1960) and early postcolonial (1960–1972) eras, and *enterprise* when speaking of the period since the Socialist Revolution (1972 to the present).

The plantations (and, more recently, the enterprises) have transformed the geography of the region and shaped, directly and indirectly, the economic, political, social, and cultural orders of the region. Their activities have been characterized by intensive development, the landscape transformed within a few decades into large estates of manioc and sugar cane and, more recently, cocoa, coffee, and perfume plants such as ylang-ylang. During the colonial period, Sakalava living throughout the valley were relocated to make room for plantation lands. Sanctioned by French colonial policies, the activities of the plantations led to the introduction of foreign capital and the proletarianization of local and migrant labor. Colonial efforts to undermine the authority of local royalty also caused the breakdown of local, indigenous power structures and, ultimately, Sakalava cultural identity. As a result of plantation activities, by the 1920s Ambanja had also become a major religious center for the Catholic Church and the district headquarters for the colonial administration. The presence of these forces in the Sambirano has contributed, to a large extent, to the establishment and growth of Ambanja as a major northern urban center.

THE TOWN AND ITS ENVIRONS

Regardless of the direction that one takes out of town, the view is the same: shady, damp forests of cocoa and coffee. Almost all of these lands belong to the enterprises. Occasional breaks in the fields of cocoa and coffee reveal independent villages, a handful of small company worker settlements, and rice fields, fruit trees, or stumpy and gnarled trunks of ylang-ylang. There are also the administrative and production centers of the enterprises. Here one finds warehouses where produce is collected, dried, and sorted by hand in preparation for export and concrete colo-

Plate 1. Main Street, Ambanja. Houses of the more prosperous families line this street, as do the offices and dwellings of the managers of the major enterprises in the Sambirano Valley. The shade trees on either side of the avenue are the same as those found in the fields to protect coffee and cocoa from the tropical sun.

nial-style villas with wide tin roofs and large verandas, which serve as the offices and housing for the management staff. The borders of the enterprises may be drawn where the terrain changes—at the steep ridge of the Tsaratanana mountains to the east; at the semi-arid terrain to the north and south, which is more suitable for wild cashews and for grazing hardy hump-backed zebu cattle; and at the mangrove swamps that flank the seacoast. In contrast to these bordering areas, the land throughout much of the valley is verdant and lush.

The town of Ambanja lies at a major commercial crossroads for the north (see figures 1.1, 2.1; plate 1). One may approach it from the port of Antsahampano (approximately fifteen kilometers to the northwest), from the national capital, Antananarivo, which lies to the south in the central high plateaux, and from Diégo, the provincial capital, which is a day's drive (240 kilometers) to the north. Until a decade ago the only practical way to reach Ambanja from other parts of the island was to fly or travel by boat to the neighboring island of Nosy Be, take a ferry to the small port of Antsahampano on the main island, and then catch ground transport to town.

For a long time this road between the port and the town was by far the best in the area. It was originally constructed for the early plantations and it is still maintained by the enterprises, which use the port to export their produce. The significance of the role played by the enterprises in terms of road maintenance and construction was particularly evident in 1987 when telephone poles and electric wires were installed, stretching from Ambanja all the way to the port on the coast. This ensured that electricity eventually would be available for the inhabitants of the villages along the road. Nevertheless, such progress had its price, since the poles were mounted on the south side of the road, making it necessary to cut down fruit trees in private yards, while the northern side, where there are groves belonging to the enterprises, remained untouched. This road to the port is also used by many people wishing to travel by ferry to the nearby island of Nosy Be, which is both a tourist resort and a site for other large-scale enterprises that grow sugar cane. The ferry provides inexpensive and convenient transportation for passengers wishing to visit their kin or the shops on Nosy Be, while young people may make the journey to enjoy the nightlife of discos and organized parties (bals). Since land on this smaller island is at a premium, zebu cattle, bound for slaughter, are carried from the Sambirano on the boat's lower decks to supply meat for local inhabitants and for the lucrative tourist industry.

Today the conditions of the roads of this region are exceptionally good, since Madagascar is a nation that relies heavily on air and sea travel and invests little in road development and repair. Only in the past few years have these been all-weather roads. For a long time they were little more than footpaths, and until very recently only cars equipped with four-wheel drive were able to traverse them with ease. Within the last decade these roads have been improved considerably, so that now they are graded and large portions are paved. Local Sakalava dislike this new development, fearing that good roads will only make it easier for migrants or vahiny from other parts of an otherwise extremely economically depressed nation to come here to settle.

The south-north road that runs through Ambanja is a major national route, and it is by means of this road that the majority of vahiny arrive in the valley from points south. In the past, the trip from the south was long and difficult: many traveled more than one thousand kilometers by foot in an effort to find work. Today most migrants come to this region by bush taxi (taxi-brusse) by way of the national capital of Antananarivo in the central highlands or from the southern coastal city of Mahajanga. There are also airports in Nosy Be and Diégo with runways equipped for landings by Boeing jets, and Ambanja has a small airport where propeller-driven Twin Otters land twice each week. The northern part of this route is used frequently by those who travel to the provincial capital of Diégo either for business or pleasure. This road is paved as

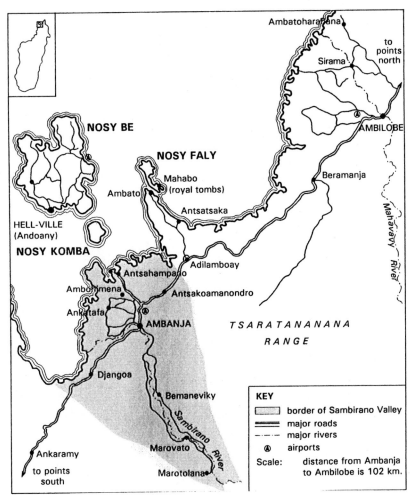

Figure 2.1.   Detail Map of Northwest Madagascar. Source: After Madagascar-FTM (1986).

far as the town of Ambilobe (102 kilometers). This town, like Ambanja, is a county seat, a slightly smaller commercial center, and the residence of the king of the Antakarana who inhabit the neighboring Mahavavy region. Near Ambilobe is another large sugar cane enterprise called Sirama.

Approaching Ambanja from the south, one passes through fields of cocoa and coffee, crosses over the bridge that spans the Sambirano River, and then enters the oldest quarter of town. Here one finds the *bazarbe,* a wide and circular-shaped daily market. Ambanja is a major urban center of the northwest, serving as a county seat for the region,

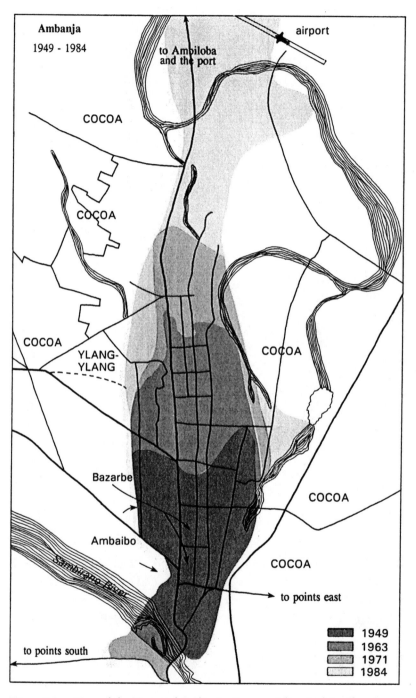

Figure 2.2.   Map of the Town of Ambanja. Source: After Andriamihamina et al. (1987: 6).

and offers many goods, services, and sources of entertainment that are unavailable in other regions of the island. This is immediately evident in the bazarbe. This market is surrounded on all sides by the concrete structures that house the shops and residences for Indian, Arab, Chinese, and Comorean merchants who first came to Ambanja after hearing of the development of the area by foreign planters. Behind the merchants' shops, just to the west and beyond the bazarbe, the top of the Indian mosque can be seen. To the east is the petrol station, a soccer field, and the town cemetery, where a wall separates Christian and Muslim graves. On a Sunday afternoon in the dry season, the music at a *morengy* or boxing match can be heard playing in the distance. On most evenings a crowd will gather before City Hall to gaze at the color television suspended above the front door, while lovers and groups of teenagers stroll by or pause momentarily on their way to a disco or to the cinema. The bazarbe is also one of two stations for the bush taxis, the small Peugeot pickups that serve as the main form of ground transportation in Madagascar. Here in Ambanja they dart madly between the bazarbe and the Tsaramandroso, the site of the Thursday market at the other end of town (see plate 2).

The enterprises are a dominant force in the daily lives of all people living in the Sambirano, whether or not they are employees. The town itself is flanked on the east and west by enterprise lands that, in some places, border streets (see figure 2.2). As a result, urban growth has pushed south along the banks of the river and north following the main road out of town. There is some order to this development, for as neighborhoods expand they continue to form a rough grid of wide, unpaved, and generally very dusty streets. Nevertheless, for the most part, settlement patterns have been sporadic, haphazard, and random. Apart from the old quarter by the bazarbe, it is difficult to categorize any one neighborhood as rich or poor or populated by a majority of any one ethnic group. The structures of the town reflect this diversity. There are a few impressive and imposing two-story villas plopped down among neat two- or four-room houses—made either of corrugated tin or fiber from the traveler's palm (*Ravenala madagascariensis*)—which rest on concrete foundations or on stiltlike wooden legs. Children, chickens, goats, geese, and ducks wander in and out of houses or root about in the grass beneath the shade of mango, banana, coconut, and jackfruit trees.

Since the Sambirano lies in northern Madagascar near the equator (just north of 14°S parallel), it is always hot in Ambanja. There are only two seasons here: the dry season from May to October, and the wet,

Plate 2. Tsaramandroso, the site of the Thursday and smaller daily market. Here the multiethnic makeup of this community is evident, where Sakalava and migrants from other areas of the island come to buy and sell wares as well as to socialize.

hot season from November to April, which is accompanied by the threat of cyclones from December to February. Everyday greetings often include a commentary on the weather: in the dry season, "Ah, the heat, the dust!" (*mafana é! misy poussière!*), or, in the wet season, "Ah, the heat, the mud!" (*mafana é! misy goda!*). Most people prefer to walk along the main street, beneath straight, tall shade trees. These trees were planted earlier in the century, and are the same varieties which are used on enterprise lands to shade cocoa from the heat of the sun (again, see plate 1).[1]

It takes about twenty to thirty minutes to walk, at a leisurely pace (*mitsangantsangana*), from one end of town to the other by way of the main street. Lining this street are small shops that sell colorful fabrics and household necessities; *hotely,* or the small bars and restaurants; the colonial style, wooden homes that belong to select royal families; the impressive and freshly painted structures of the Peasant's Bank and the county seat; a variety of mosques and Protestant churches; and the courthouse, gendarmerie, and prison. All of the enterprises have an office centrally located in Ambanja, since the directors prefer to live in town. These offices are generally placed on the ground level of an imposing villa. Here on the main street there are also offices and agricultural experimental stations of a variety of government ministries, so that as you follow the main street you can see cocoa growing and can smell the pungent blossoms of ylang-ylang.[2]

All along this main street women and young girls sell snacks to passersby, and there is usually a considerable gathering of their stands placed strategically so as to draw clients from the local schools and the municipal hospital. Near the latter is the private occupational health clinic established for the workers and their families and funded by member enterprises and local businesses. Across the street are the grounds of the Catholic Mission school and printery and the tallest building in town, the cathedral. Behind it is the Catholic hospital, which, when completed, will provide the first operating room facilities in the area.[3] Near the other end of town is the Thursday market, (again, see plate 2) where one finds a cluster of oxcarts, yet another bar, the office of Air Madagascar, and many houses of all sizes extending to the town border and beyond. If one visits this second market early in the morning or at dusk, bright red flatbed trucks from the enterprises will have stopped there and men and women—some with small children—will be climbing in or out on their way to or from work.

AN ECONOMIC AND POLITICAL HISTORY
OF THE REGION

PRECOLONIAL HISTORY: THE BEMAZAVA-SAKALAVA[4]

When French military troops arrived in the Sambirano in 1896, this valley was indisputably the territory of the Bemazava, the northernmost dynastic branch of Sakalava speakers, who today form the fifth largest of the eighteen officially recognized ethnic groups of Madagascar (Covell 1987: 12).[5] The Sakalava as a whole are organized as a collection of kingdoms occupying the island's west coast, having been formed as a result of disputes over succession and the subsequent movement north by new founding dynasties.[6] The Bemazava-Sakalava trace their origins to Boina, the royal and sacred capital that lies near Mahajanga on the central part of the western coast. The Bemazava dynasty was established by Andriantompoeniarivo (see figures 2.3, 2.4).[7] According to oral tradition, he left Boina following a dispute over royal succession. Andriantompoeniarivo was accompanied by his followers and by a powerful *moasy* (HP: *ombiasy*) or herbalist named Andriamsara. As they traveled they carried with them royal relics, and among these was a container of sacred water. When the party reached the river valley, however, they discovered that the container had run dry. While trying to decide whether or not to turn back or to use the local river water to replenish their supply, Andriantompoeniarivo is said to have remarked, "it makes no difference, they are each/both water" (*samy ny rano*). Thus the *Sambirano* River was named, and it is here where they chose to settle.[8]

In the nineteenth century, just prior to French conquest, the Bemazava lived in small villages that were scattered throughout the Sambirano. They farmed plots of dry rice and manioc, banana, and other fruits, but the majority of the land of this fertile alluvial plain was used to graze herds of zebu cattle (see Dury 1897). The Bemazava of the Sambirano appear to have been united into a loose confederation under a common ruler (*ampanjakabe*) who was the living successor of the tromba or spirits of the royal ancestral dead. An important royal duty involved the ruler serving as the representative for his or her living subjects in ritual contexts. It was the ruler, with the help of assistants (male assistant: *ngahy;* female assistant: *marovavy* or *ambimañangy*) and tromba mediums (*saha*), who invoked the royal spirits. The ruler also served as a mediator and judge in secular disputes. The Bemazava ruler lived in the coastal village of Ankify, while the island of Nosy Faly served as the sacred ground where royal dead were entombed and where the mediums for the greatest of the royal tromba spirits resided. On Nosy Faly the first Bemazava king, Andriantompoeniarivo, was laid to rest, along with his successors and other members of the royal family (*ampanjaka*). Today both Andriantompoeniarivo and Andriamsara are regarded by the Bemazava as their founding ancestors. They are the most important of the local Bemazava tromba spirits, and their mediums live on the sacred island of Nosy Faly. As will become clear in Part 2, these spirits and their mediums wield much power in the Sambirano.

Prior to 1896, the Bemazava were well aware of the existence of the French, who had been active in the north for approximately sixty years. The queen of another branch of Sakalava—the Bemihisatra of Nosy Be—had previously invited the French to her island. In so doing, she

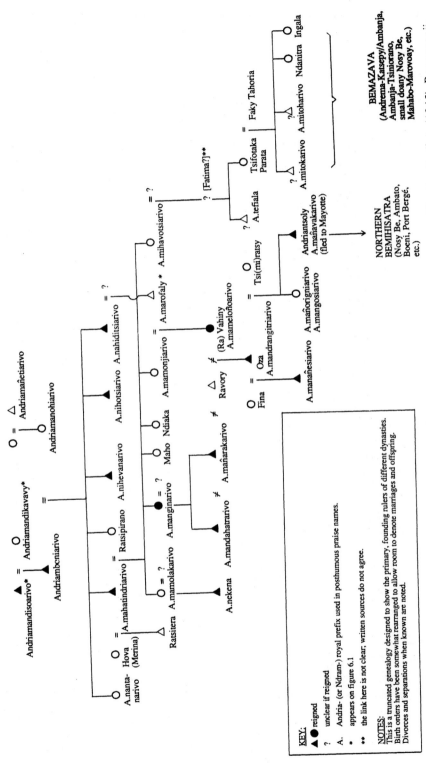

Figure 2.3. Sakalava Dynasties of Madagascar. Sources: De Foort (1907: 130); Feeley-Harnik (1991: 80) after Guillain (1845); Ramamonjisoa (1986: 101).

sought to gain a powerful ally against her enemy, the Merina of the central high plateaux (see Mutibwa 1974 for a discussion of Merina expansion in the eighteenth and nineteenth centuries). She extended this invitation to the French only after she had failed to acquire firearms from the Sultan of Muscat: giving way to his conditions, she and other Bemihisatra royalty agreed to convert to Islam, but the Sultan only sent velvet hats, not arms (Dalmond 1840). In 1840 the French established their first permanent settlement on Nosy Be, and the members of this party included Jesuit missionaries and planters. The latter started sugar cane plantations that still exist today (they are administered from the town of Djamanjary). Although the Sambirano was not far from Nosy Be, contact between Bemazava and Europeans remained fairly limited due to the relative difficulty of traveling to the interior, and to the reputation of the fierceness of Bemazava warriors.

THE ESTABLISHMENT OF FRENCH CONTROL

The end of the nineteenth century marks the beginning of the colonial era in Madagascar. In 1895 Madagascar was declared a protectorate and, in the following year, a colony of France. Under the direction of the military strategist Général J. S. Galliéni, the Merina monarchy was abolished and the queen, Ranovalona III, exiled to Réunion. French troops marched from one end of Madagascar to the other as part of Galliéni's pacification program. Galliéni sent military expeditions to comb the entire island, collecting enormous quantities of data of strategic import, making note of relevant social and cultural institutions, and eventually setting up a network of military posts. From records made by commanding officers, it appears that the Sambirano was visited twice, one battalion moving west from the Tsaratanana ridge to Nosy Be, the other moving up from the ancient northern Sakalava capital of Boina (Boucabeille 1897; Brown 1978: 236ff; Dury 1897; Galliéni 1900, 1908; Raolison 1966; see also David-Bernard 1943). Lieutenant S. V. Dury, who led the battalion from the east, described the Sambirano as follows:

> Dans ces plains [Sambirano and neighboring ones] l'herbe est abondante en toute saisons, ce sont des pâturages magnifiques, qui nourrissent les troupeaux les plus beaux et les plus nombreaux qui existent de la Mahajomba [Mahajanga] au Sambirano. Les boeufs y sont superbes et donnent de 100–150 kilos de viande; on les vends sur place 20 Francs du maximum. . . .

Cette region du Sambirano est donc aussi très riche. Le débouché vers la mer, qui donne dans la large baie de Passandava, est commode et la construction d'une route simplement. (Dury 1897: 443, 445)

It was in 1896 that the first military post, under the command of Captain Verdure, was established in the Sambirano area in the village of Ambato. Ambato lay near the coast en route to the sacred island of Nosy Faly, the location of the Bemazava-Sakalava royal tombs. Within a few years, military men—some with families—had started to farm in the area, and by the turn of the century the Sambirano had become attractive to planters from the neighboring islands of Nosy Be, Réunion, and the Seychelles. In 1903 the French moved the military post to a more advantageous location inland and upstream and situated on a high hill that provided a spectacular view not only of the river but of the entire valley. Placed strategically at a major crossroads, it is around this post that the town of Ambanja eventually grew. From the buildings constructed by the French one may now look down upon the oldest quarter of town which encircles the bazarbe. Throughout the colonial era the post's buildings served as the residence for French colonial officers; since Independence they have been used to house local Malagasy civil authorities.

By the late 1890s, the government of France began to grant land titles to foreign-born planters, titles that were authorized by Galliéni and issued from the national capital of Antananarivo. Within a few years the majority of the land that previously had been used and occupied by Bemazava had been transformed into large private plantations. Much of this land was acquired through purchases of communal grazing lands, transactions the Bemazava misunderstood. Many Bemazava were forced out of the choicest areas of the valley and onto indigenous reserves (FR: réserves indigènes), often pushed up against steep hillsides that were difficult to farm and unsuitable for grazing cattle. This policy of designating territory as indigenous reserves was unique to the northern and western provinces of Antsiranana (in which Ambanja is located), Mahajanga, and only a few areas of the high plateaux. Furthermore, Nosy Be and the Sambirano each had over twenty reserves, while Mahajanga had only two (Service Topographique, Nosy Be, n.d.). This period is also marked by a large exodus of Bemazava to the drier Mahavavy area that lies one hundred kilometers to the north in Antakarana territory. By the 1920s the Sambirano Valley had developed into one of the most prosperous areas of Madagascar. Merchants with origins as diverse as

southern China, southern India, and Yemen came and settled permanently in the town, establishing a large market (the bazarbe) beside the
river and just below the military post.

THE DEVELOPMENT OF THE SAMBIRANO

It is important to realize that the development of Ambanja into a town
and commercial center occurred as a result of, first, French occupation of
the region and, second, the subsequent activities of the early plantations.
Although it is possible that there was a Bemazava village at this location
prior to the arrival of the French, a surveyor's map drawn at the turn
of the century depicts simply a military post with a flagpole to mark it.
As the town has grown, it has developed along a clear axis, sandwiched
between the fields of the large plantation fields of the enterprises that
flank it to the east and west (figure 2.2).

The activities of a number of other foreigners reveal that Ambanja
was growing rapidly into an important cosmopolitan center. The Catholic Holy Ghost Fathers from France were soon active here: in 1921 they
performed their first Catholic marriage, and in 1936 they completed
the construction of the cathedral. By 1927, surveyors were employed
to measure property systematically and lay down landmarks for both
private individuals and the owners of plantations, who thus acquired
official deeds to their lands. An early road map of Madagascar, published in 1938, categorizes Ambanja as a commercial center, complete
with a post office and lodging for weary travelers.

The development of the Sambirano into a plantation area was shaped
primarily by two men, Louis Millot and Guy de la Motte St. Pierre. By
1905, each had acquired land grants from France which together covered nearly all of the Sambirano Valley. In the next few years Millot
and de la Motte St. Pierre also bought out other smaller planters when
their efforts to farm failed.[9] By the 1920s a third plantation had become
active in the Sambirano, one that is now known as the Compagnie
Nosybéenne d'Industries Agricoles (CNIA). This was an extension of
Djamanjary Sugar in Nosy Be.

Both Millot and de la Motte St. Pierre began by planting what was
locally available. Millot chose his fields carefully, and it is said that
he sent soil samples back to Europe for analysis before making large
investments in his lands. He began by planting coconut palms, rice, and
manioc for the production of tapioca. By the the 1930s, he had imported
cocoa plants from the Ivory Coast, and today cocoa remains the domi-

nant crop on Millot lands. In more recent years, this enterprise has also planted some pepper, as well as fields of perfume plants. De la Motte St. Pierre also started with coconuts, but soon switched to sugar. With the arrival of CNIA in the 1920s, sugar remained the dominant crop of the Sambirano until the 1940s.

After World War II, when the price of sugar fell on the world market, it was decided that the sugar companies on Nosy Be, near Ambilobe, and in other regions of Madagascar were sufficient to satisfy the exports needed from Madagascar. As a result, plantations in the Sambirano cut back on sugar production, cocoa production was expanded, and coffee was introduced as a new crop. Eventually cocoa and coffee replaced sugar altogether as the major export crops of this region. Although French planters maintained a monopoly over cocoa production, by the 1950s the government was also encouraging private farmers who had small plots to grow coffee as a cash crop. Tapioca production continued to be a major industry in the Sambirano until the 1970s, when the last factory shut down in response to a diminishing market. Meanwhile, within the last two decades, cashews—which grow wild in the drier areas to the north and west—have joined coffee and cocoa as one of the region's three major export crops. As will become clear, coffee and cashews are important in Bemazava-Sakalava constructions of their local history. The meanings associated with common historical experience are played out through tromba possession, where coffee and cashews figure as prominent symbols (see Part 2).

Following the Socialist Revolution in 1972, all of the large plantations except E. Millot were seminationalized.[10] Millot and the now combined businesses of CNIA/SOMIA (Société Malgache d'Industrie et d'Agriculture) are the largest and most impressive enterprises in the Valley.[11] These have grown out of the original farms of the two men, Millot and de la Motte St. Pierre. The plantation E. Millot had more than seven thousand hectares at its height in the 1940s, although it is now down to two thousand. CNIA/SOMIA, which possesses much of de la Motte St. Pierre's original lands, at one time boasted close to a million hectares.[12] In the Sambirano there are also a number of smaller enterprises, small private farms, and companies (referred to as *concessions*) which buy agricultural produce and prepare them for export.

The labor requirements of the cash crops grown in this region demanded a large and reliable workforce, since each had specific needs for both seasonal and general year-round upkeep and care. The plantations in other regions nearby—such as Djamanjary Sugar of Nosy

Be—recruited prison labor from the south in the early 1920s.[13] In contrast, the Sambirano quickly became well known throughout the island for the availability of wage labor, and so the plantations of the Sambirano did not find it necessary to engage in an aggressive recruitment of workers from other areas of the island.[14] Unlike the Bemazava, who had (and still have) a reputation for being a fixed population, peoples from the high plateaux and the arid south left their homelands and settled in the Sambirano. For example, Betsileo—who are famous in Madagascar for their skills as rice farmers—came and settled on CNIA property as land tenants, developing the area around Antsakoamanondro, just north of Ambanja, into fertile irrigated paddy land. Antandroy, Antaimoro, and other peoples of the economically depressed south and southeast also came to work as manual laborers in the fields.

EFFECTS ON LAND TENURE

Although many of the Bemazava had been alienated from their original territory through relocation, this same policy enabled them to maintain access to arable land throughout the twentieth century. In addition, numerous small villages and private family plots remained scattered throughout the Sambirano, interspersed with plantation lands. A perusal of colonial property records reveals that subsequent transactions of land involving Malagasy were uncommon during the colonial period, so that migrants were unable to acquire land when sales did occur. Instead, priority was given to members of the Bemazava royal family. This was an important trend during the colonial period, whereby the French granted royalty special privileges, assuming that if they could control the Bemazava rulers they could control their subjects. For example, the father of one of my informants was a member of the royal family and was among those royalty (ampanjaka) who were in the direct line of succession; in addition, he was a favorite among a number of French colonial officers. As a result, he was able to purchase several large plots throughout the Sambirano during his lifetime, including one in the 1930s which was nearly fifty hectares in size. Throughout the colonial period, pieces of land of this magnitude generally only went to Bemazava royalty and foreign-born planters.

To some extent, French colonial law favored all local Bemazava, and this enabled commoners as well to maintain control over valuable parcels of land in the valley, albeit smaller in size than those owned by royalty. Among those Bemazava commoners who remained landed, a bilateral rule of inheritance prevailed. Land was generally divided fairly equally among the spouse and male and female offspring when the parent (biological or classificatory) was either too old to farm or had died. For example, two of my informants (one male, the other female) owned two and four hectares of land each, where they grew primarily dry rice. Each had inherited their land from their mothers. The man was an only child whose father had died when he was very young, and previously his mother had inherited land, along with her mother and siblings, when her own father had died. My female informant could trace land inheritance among her kin through six generations. Each time someone died their land was divided fairly equally among their children (sometimes including favorite classificatory offspring) and their surviving spouse. In her kin group land was also acquired in four other ways: as gifts from royalty for performing royal service (*fanompoaña*), as previous residents of indigenous reserves, by periodically purchasing plots of two to three hectares each, or as a result of Napoleonic law, which honors the land rights of squatters who make productive use of land. These methods of land acquisition helped to offset the common trend whereby the size of inherited plots grows smaller with each generation.

Today, tera-tany continue to be favored over vahiny as a result of government reforms following Independence in 1960 and, to a lesser extent, from the sales or confiscation of large private holdings through the nationalization of large private estates that followed the 1972 Socialist Revolution. In the Sambirano, those who own land are truly at an advantage, for even plots rejected by foreign planters give high yields. Land, however, continues to become increasingly scarce, and, as the story below illustrates, it is a source of much contention among kin.

ZALOKY'S HOMESTEAD

Zaloky estimates her age to be about fifty years old, although she looks as though she could be another twenty. She is Sakalava tera-tany, born and raised in an area which, in her childhood, lay on the outskirts of town; within the past twenty years, however, it has become a thriving neighborhood. She lives on a small patch of land (approximately one quarter of a hectare) which she inherited from her widowed mother. In the past she had a garden on an adjacent plot of land but now she is boxed in on all sides by new houses, several of which are concrete. She now farms a small field in her mother's native village, which lies eighteen kilometers from town. Zaloky was married at age sixteen and she had four children. At age thirty-five her husband died; five years later she remarried (by common law) a Tsimihety vahiny named Marcel who would come each year to the Sambirano for the harvest season.

He now works off and on at the enterprises. Because he is old and suffers from a bad back, however, it is difficult for him to find steady work. In 1987 he also worked as a night watchman.

The homestead on which Zaloky and Marcel live is dusty and in disarray; rather than having a neatly swept yard bordered by flowers, like most Sakalava homes, it is littered with metal scrap and old papers that get swept up by the wind and caught in the fence. Marcel sells these items when he can as a way to supplement their income; Zaloky also has two scrawny chickens that she keeps so she can sell the eggs. Their income is meager at best, and nearly every day they beg for food from their neighbors and the Lutheran church that is behind their house.

Her homestead is one that is a source of much conflict: ever since her first husband's death her children have fought to have rights over this land. Since she married Marcel, two of her children (a son and a daughter) have filed a case in court to take it away from her. As Zaloky explains, her children believe that Marcel only married her for her land, and she states flatly that she certainly would rather give it to him than to them! Within the last year a disco has also been built next door, and the proprietor threatens them several times a week, saying he wants them to die so he can expand into their yard. He has already tried to tear down the fence, and so each day Zaloky and Marcel check to make sure it is in its proper place.

Zaloky's problems are extreme: a tale such as this, involving children seeking to evict their mother from her land, is one most Sakalava in Ambanja would listen to in disbelief. Nevertheless, it is instructive, since it reveals the severity of tensions underlying the scarcity of land in the Sambirano. The fact that her second spouse was not tera-tany, but a migrant, brought familial conflicts to the fore. Zaloky's story is one that threads its way invisibly through the following chapters, for she had at one time been a medium for a prestigious tromba spirit, and it was through this work that she met Marcel, who had often consulted her in times of personal crisis. The continuation of her story will appear in chapter 10, for ten years ago she converted to Lutheranism, a choice that (as the next chapter will illustrate) is an unusual one for Sakalava. As tensions with her children, and now her neighbor, have worsened, Zaloky has recently decided to give her land to the church, and the pastor has solicited the national center for funds to pay the surveyor's and lawyer's fees that will enable them to make a formal and legitimate claim.

LOCAL POWER AND REACTIONS TO COLONIALISM

LOCAL AUTHORITY AND POWER

Today the power structure of the town of Ambanja is multifaceted and complex, the town serving as a center for both secular and sacred power.

There are a number of institutions that operate here. First, officially recognized power lies with the state, a structure that originated during the colonial era and which continues today under the independent government of Madagascar. It is composed of a hierarchy of national, provincial, county, town, and neighborhood authorities. There are also other, more informal, power structures at work in Ambanja. The state-owned enterprises wield much control in the Sambirano, since they play an extremely important role economically, one that affects the everyday lives of local people in many ways. Even though directors are state employees, they exercise great freedom in making decisions that affect the local economic and social order of the Sambirano. For example, much of the town's funding for celebrations, transportation, roadwork, and so forth comes from the enterprises, with donations made by the directors themselves. The patron-client relationship between the enterprises and the townspeople is so strong that a common response to an important family or personal problem is to turn to one of the directors for assistance, whose responses can be either rewarding or devastating. Likewise, religious groups—be they Islamic, Protestant, or Catholic—provide support through divine injunction and financial assistance. The Catholic church is by far the wealthiest (as is reflected by the extent of its landholdings in town), and it is also the most influential. The Catholic church also provides access to rare opportunities beyond Ambanja and outside of Madagascar, particularly through education.

Prior to French occupation of Bemazava territory, political power and authority lay almost exclusively with the local royalty, that is, with the ruler and his or her advisers—be they living or dead. As will become clear in Part 2, by far the most important role was played by the tromba spirits and their mediums on Nosy Faly. With the arrival of the French, however, control shifted to colonial administrators and planters. This shift in the power base led to the relocation of the Bemazava ruler from the ancestral village of Ankify to the commercial center, Ambanja. This occurred during the reign of Tsiaraso II (Andriamandefitriarivo), who was the father of the present ruler, Tsiaraso III. Tsiaraso II reigned from 1945 to 1966, and from conversations with informants I assume that the move occurred early in his career (figure 2.4). Furthermore, French policies were designed deliberately to undermine the royal family's power. The most effective effort involved recruiting royal children to be schooled at the local Catholic Mission. These children were trained to be civil servants for the colonial administration, whose loyalties and interests lay with the French and not their own people (cf. Feeley-Harnik 1991b: 137).

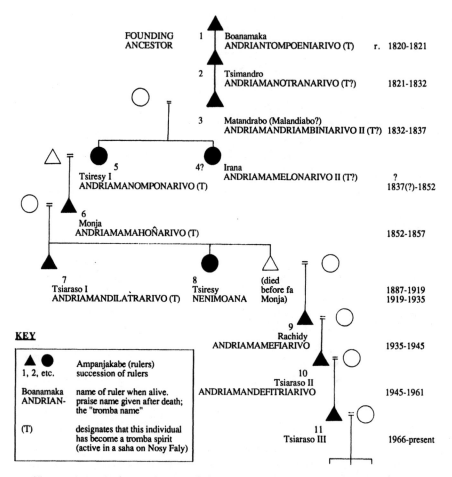

Figure 2.4. Rulers (*Ampanjakabe*) of the Bemazava-Sakalava Dynasty. Sources: Informants accounts; written Bemazava historical records; and De Foort (1907: 130).

Although royal power has diminished considerably (again, cf. Feeley-Harnik, 1991b), the present ruler (ampanjakabe) remains an important figure in the lives of the Bemazava. He is often preferred over the local court as a mediator in private disputes, and as the official living guardian of the local tanindrazaña, he is the first authority one must consult prior to any further development of local land (see chapter 6). Spirit mediums also seek his blessing as well as his guidance in matters involving royal ancestors. The extent to which royalty more generally may become involved in the reassertion of royal power is exemplified in the actions of an Antakarana ruler to the north, who has become heavily involved in the revival and reinvention (Hobsbaum 1983) of royal rituals, which may draw a crowd of thousands of participants.

Local government officials honor the importance of royalty at public (state) occasions. A respect for Malagasy customs (HP/SAK: *fomba-gasy;* also referred to as *fombandrazana/fombandrazaña* or "customs of the ancestors") remains strong in Madagascar. As part of malagasiza-tion, the national government has encouraged and institutionalized the observance of fomba-gasy at public events. Tromba mediums in particu-lar have become very active, since the permission of the spirits must be sought through them, for example, prior to the naming of a local school after a past ruler or at the beginning of each season before boats of a state-owned fishery enter the waters near Nosy Faly (see chapter 6). Nevertheless, one has a sense of cooptation of living royal authority by the state, ironically illustrated by the fact that the present Bemazava ruler is Catholic and works at the county office as a tax collector.

RESISTANCE AND REVOLT IN THE SAMBIRANO

Bemazava reaction to the French occupation and the eventual transfor-mation of the landscape was neither accepting nor passive. As Stoler's work in Sumatra's plantation belt illustrates, what may be presumed to be a peaceful occupation, settlement, and development by colonial forces may in fact be marked by acts of violence by the seemingly power-less against the powerful (Stoler 1985). At first glance, for a number of reasons it does not appear that French activities in the Sambirano were greatly hampered. First, it would have been difficult to present a united front against the French, the Bemazava being relatively few in number and scattered throughout the valley. Second, although Bemazava war-riors were known to be fierce, their access to firearms was limited. Third, they regarded the French as their allies, since they had conquered an old enemy, the Merina.

Nevertheless, acts of violence against the French did occur. An inci-dent cited frequently by the Bemazava involved a private dispute that quickly became a public—and political—one. Shortly after the French military post in Ambato was established, a group of Bemazava men were captured and imprisoned for having killed a Frenchman. The Frenchman had been living in the royal village of Ankify and was mar-ried to a Bemazava woman of royal descent. Jealous of his wife's interac-tions with other men, he had confined her to the house. Since she was royalty (ampanjaka), other Bemazava regarded this as offensive and killed the husband. Captain Verdure had the prisoners beheaded in order to discourage future violence against French citizens. This episode is still remembered with great bitterness by the Bemazava. Much of their anger focuses not only on the French but also on Senegalese soldiers who were brought there by the colonial government to help maintain order. These soldiers are said to have tried to eat the prisoners' bodies until Verdure stepped in to prevent such an outrageous act.[15]

The Sambirano became a politically charged area in 1947, a year that today is commemorated in Madagascar as a time of revolution and early nationalism. The front of resistance was located on the east coast of the island and began in March 1947. Malagasy in other areas of the island subsequently staged their own revolts against the French (see Covell 1987: 26; Rajoelina 1988; Tronchon 1974). Following the lead of revolutionaries elsewhere, inhabitants of the Sambirano behaved disrespectfully to French as they passed in the streets and the workers of some plantations went on strike. By November 1947, a small rebel group had formed in the Sambirano with a camp established in a village southwest of town, where they secretly manufactured knives and guns. Within a few months, however, the leaders were captured and imprisoned, putting an end to a potential uprising.

Resistance may also take more insidious forms, which are culturally more appropriate yet perhaps less effective against foreign invaders (Scott 1985). The *Ramanenjana* or "dancing mania," which occurred in the Merina capital of Antananarivo in 1863, is perhaps the most large-scale resistance movement against foreigners involving religious forces. At this time the streets were crowded with hundreds of people possessed by the dead Queen Ranavalona. The possessed often disturbed and even attacked Europeans, many of whom were Protestant missionaries (see Davidson 1889; Sharp 1985).

Without doubt, during the colonial period Malagasy throughout the island appealed to the ancestors and other spiritual forces for assistance. In the Sambirano, it is certain that Sakalava sought to cause harm to or drive these foreigners from their homeland. They appealed to specialists such as herbalists (moasy), diviners (*mpisikidy*), and tromba spirit mediums, making use of Malagasy medicine, or what Europeans referred to as magic (*fanafody, fanafody-gasy*). According to one informant, at the time of the 1947 revolt in the Sambirano, dead and living forces united against the colonial government; Malagasy who sympathized with the French were victims of "occult forces" (*forces occultes*) including tromba and other spirits, and fanafody. As will become clear in subsequent chapters, the use of fanafody continues to be a powerful way to control events in everyday life. Tromba mediums in particular play a special role in this manipulation of the spiritual realm. In addition, tromba as an institution has been a source of Sakalava pride and identity, as well as a means of Sakalava resistance to foreigners. During this century it has operated as a reminder of things past. It has also provided an idiom through which to critique contemporary experiences.

THE SOCIAL CONSTRUCTION OF WORK

Throughout the twentieth century, by far the most significant form of resistance, in terms of its impact on European attitudes and policies, has been the Sakalava's refusal to work as wage laborers. Although a requirement under the colonial regime was ten days per year of enforced (*corvée*) labor, ownership of land enabled many local Sakalava to avoid having to work full-time for the plantations (for a discussion of similar policies throughout the island see Thompson and Adloff 1965, chap. 23). Furthermore, many Bemazava were able to pay the mandatory head tax through cash-cropping or by selling their cattle. As a result, early in the century the plantations began to hire laborers who came from other areas of the island. To understand the logic behind Sakalava actions, it is necessary to analyze the meaning of work in their society.

Feeley-Harnik, in her discussion of slavery and royal work among the Sakalava in Analalava, states that Sakalava distinguish between two types of work: asa, or work owed to kin, and fanompoaña or "royal work or service that is part of their politico-religious and economic obligation to the monarchy" (Feeley-Harnik 1984: 3). In Ambanja (and elsewhere in Madagascar), *asa* also has other meanings: as a noun, it can mean "task" or "project," and the verb *miasa*, which is often translated "to work," is used more generally to mean "to be occupied" or "active" or "to be working on a task, a project." For example, if a woman is doing the laundry, one says "*miasa izy*" ("she is working"). Beginning in the colonial era, *asa* took on additional meanings, as a result of the penetration of a capitalist economy and its associated labor relations. The French used *asa* to mean wage labor, as well as enforced, mandatory work that involved clearing roads, for example (cf. Feeley-Harnik 1991b, especially p. 349).

French concepts of work ran contrary to Sakalava ones. Since, for Sakalava, work was something that one did out of loyalty to kin and local rulers (Feeley-Harnik 1986, 1991b), requirements imposed by the French government and plantations negated local custom. From a Sakalava point of view (and certainly from a French one as well) fulfilling these work requirements was a sign of loyalty to the colonial administration. Feeley-Harnik (1984), in her discussion of slavery and royal work, argues that this action by the French was deliberately designed to undermine local royal authority and to disrupt the local sociocultural order. (For other discussions of Malagasy conceptions of work see Decary 1956; on the implementation of French colonial policy elsewhere in Africa see Crowder 1964 and Gifford and Weiskel 1974.)

In the Sambirano these efforts were only partially successful. Although royal authority has certainly diminished, many people still look to the local Bemazava king as an adviser and mediator in local disputes. It is also acknowledged that his authority is legitimated by the tromba spirits. Those who today turn to royalty (living or dead) for guidance are not only local Bemazava-Sakalava, but also many others who have become involved in tromba possession and serve as mediums for these spirits. The local government often must rely on the support of the king if it wishes to encourage participation by community members in local activities. On International Workers' Day (May 1), for example, only the blessing of the king ensures that townspeople will help to repair the roads in town—this time as a sign of support for the present socialist state.

Sakalava resistance to work—in the form of wage labor—is often cited today by employers, who speak of them as "lazy" (kamo) or as too independent and proud to be willing to work for others. Sakalava youth express a preference for working in fields owned by kin to wage labor, be it manual or more highly trained supervisory positions. As the chapters in Part 2 will show, tromba possession also provides mediums with a means through which they may resist wage labor, particularly at the enterprises. A sentiment that many Sakalava express is that in such work there is no freedom: the hours are long, the pay is too low, and the fruits of their labor belong to someone else (see plate 3). The refusal to work was and still is a strong form of resistance to capitalist discipline. Such relations involve, first, a readjustment to clock time (Thompson 1967),[16] and, second, the displacement of reciprocal relationships by having services paid for with cash, both of which Sakalava

Plate 3.   Women at work at a local enterprise. Women are hired to sort cocoa, coffee, and cashews. They are paid by the number of bags they can fill in a day.

despise. Throughout this century Sakalava have resisted engaging in such relations with non-Sakalava. In the past, these were foreigners. More recently they are Merina, who now form the majority of managers at the enterprises. This action, however, has its price: after Sakalava refused to work for foreign planters they witnessed the inundation of their territory by a variety of non-Sakalava migrants.

CHAPTER III

National and Local Factions

The Nature of Polyculturalism in Ambanja

As a booming migrant town, Ambanja is a *mélange*, a mixture of peoples of diverse origins, not only from within the boundaries of this large island, but from abroad. This town is a microcosm of factions that operate on a national scale. Of these factions, ethnicity is the primary category, one that overlaps with a variety of other group orientations and allegiances. These are shaped by historically based geographical, economic, and religious differences. Such groupings or identities, when taken in total, reveal the complexity of the tensions operating in Madagascar and, in turn, in Ambanja. An individual's ability to make sense of and become established as a member of one or more groups determines his or her well-being in this community.

The complexity of categories that exist in Ambanja is extreme when compared to other areas where the population is more homogeneous. As a result, in Ambanja and the surrounding Sambirano Valley, defining what it means to be an insider or an outsider is complex. For this reason, the discussion on migration is divided into two chapters. This chapter will address the nature of social and cultural divisions that exist, first on a national scale and then in Ambanja. Chapter 4 provides case studies drawn from migrants' lives and analyzes those factors that facilitate or inhibit their integration into local Sakalava tera-tany society.

Group name	% of population	Group name	% of population
Merina	26.1	Sihanaka	2.4
Betsimisaraka	14.9	Antanosy	2.3
Betsileo	12.0	Mahafaly	1.6
Tsimihety	7.2	Antaifasy	1.2
Sakalava	5.8	Makoa	1.1
Antandroy	5.3	Bezanozano	0.8
Antaisaka	5.0	Antakarana	0.6
Tanala	3.8	Antambahoaka	0.4
Antaimoro	3.4	Others	1.1
Bara	3.3		

Figure 3.1.   Malagasy Ethnic Groups. Sources: Covell (1987: 12), after Nelson et al. (1973), figures from the Institut National de la Statistique in Madagascar, and Thompson (1987). Reproduced by permission of Pinter Publishers Ltd., London. All rights reserved.

NATIONAL FACTIONS: REGIONALISM AND CULTURAL STEREOTYPES

ETHNIC CATEGORIES

The Malagasy

Today in Madagascar there are eighteen[1] (Covell 1987: 12) officially recognized ethnic groups (FR: *ethnie, tribu;* HP: *foko, karazana;* SAK: *karazaña*) which are relevant for census purposes (figure 3.1).

The use of the term *ethnic group* is problematic from an anthropological point of view, since all of these groups are actually subgroups of the general category Malagasy, whose members share common cultural elements such as language and religious beliefs. In other words, the concept of ethnicity is one of perspective and scale. Outside Madagascar, Malagasy are viewed as the dominant ethnic group of the country, and Sakalava, Merina, and other peoples are considered subgroups of this larger category. From a Malagasy point of view, however, Merina, for example, are viewed as the dominant ethnic group, and other non-Malagasy peoples (Arabs, Indo-Pakistanis, Chinese, Comoreans, and Europeans) are grouped separately as "strangers" or "foreigners" (*étrangers*). Since this study is concerned primarily with Malagasy peoples, I will use *ethnic group* as the Malagasy themselves do. These ethnic divisions are significant in everyday discourse, as Malagasy use them to define themselves in relation to each other. Ethnic groups also overlap with

other categories based on geographical, economic, and religious differences.

Ethnic categories have changed over time. As Covell points out, they
are flexible constructs, and although they are in part a reflection of
changes in the political climate of Madagascar, it would be false to
conceive of them solely in these terms:

> This form of identification hardly constitutes a key to Malagasy politics.
> The groups themselves are riddled with internal subdivisions and several are,
> in fact, political constructions created from small groups in the eighteenth
> and nineteenth centuries: the Merina, Sakalava, and Betsimisaraka are the
> most important of these. Others, such as the Betsileo and Bara were first
> grouped together as administrative subdivisions of the nineteenth-century
> Merina empire. (1987: 12)

The French also made use of these categories. They did not begin
systematically to take official censuses, with Malagasy broken down
into different ethnic groups, until 1949, following the 1947 revolt. This
practice was continued by the government of the Malagasy Republic
after Independence (1960) up until the time of the Socialist Revolution
in 1972. For approximately a decade afterward, no census information
was collected (publications in general came to a halt in Madagascar at
this time). In the Sambirano Valley it is only in 1985 that new efforts
were made to gather census data in preparation for national elections
that occurred in early 1989. On these recent censuses, the ethnic categories no longer appear, although logbooks kept of Ambanja's neighborhood residents, for example, still make note of ethnic affiliation. In
everyday discourse these categories are used by Malagasy to label one
another.[2]

Today certain factors unite members of each ethnic group: a shared
dialect of Malagasy; similar religious customs, most notably in regard
to mortuary rituals and a strong regard for local ancestors; observation
of *fady* or taboos; characteristic regional dress; economic activities; and
affiliation with a specific geographical territory (figure 3.2). These categories and their associated characteristics are used by Sakalava as they
define themselves in opposition to others. Ultimately, these differences
define boundaries between insider and outsider. Among some peoples
the boundaries are fluid, while among others they are very rigid.

Non-Malagasy Strangers (Etrangers)

In addition to Malagasy speakers, there are also a number of minority
groups (see Vincent 1974: 377) that consist of non-Malagasy peoples

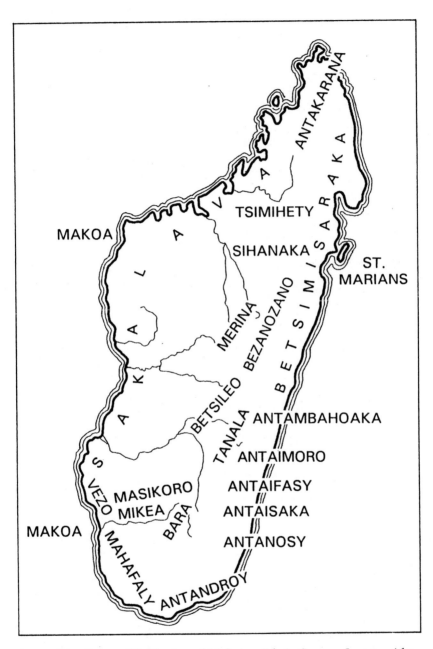

Figure 3.2.   Present Distribution of Malagasy Ethnic Groups. Sources: After
Brown (1978: 16); Kottak (1986, frontispiece); and Société Malgache (1973).

who have settled on the island. The largest of these groups are Arabs, Chinese, Comoreans, Europeans (especially French and some Greek), Indo-Pakistanis, and peoples of mixed heritage from the neighboring islands of Réunion and Mauritius. No recent statistics are available for the size of these populations, and so it is very difficult to estimate their numbers. This is in part due to recent political events. The majority of Europeans fled the island following the Socialist Revolution in 1972. Comoreans and Indo-Pakistanis have also fled periodically, since they have been the targets of violence in the last decade or so. Out of a total estimated population of 9.9 million for the entire island (figure for 1984; Covell 1987: xiii), population estimates for each group of étrangers are: 10,000 each of the Indo-Pakistanis and Chinese; 15,000 to 20,000 Comoreans (Covell 1987; 84–85); and 12,000 French (Bunge 1983: 49; for more details see Covell 1987: 84–85; on the Chinese see also Slawecki 1971 and Tche-Hao 1967).

Malagasy Ethnic Groups: How Difference Is Perceived

A variety of factors delineates boundaries between ethnic groups. To illustrate how these operate, I will briefly discuss two such factors: physical differences and the fady or taboos. Sections that follow provide discussions on other distinguishing characteristics, such as territorial affiliation, economic specialization, and religion.

Highland and coastal peoples (and, in turn, specific ethnic groups) are distinguished from one another by dialect and phenotype, reflecting the diverse historical and cultural origins of the Malagasy. As Bloch explains:

> Madagascar has always been considered an anthropological oddity, due to the fact that although geographically it is close to Africa the language spoken throughout the island clearly belongs to the Austronesian group spoken in Southest Asia; more particularly Malagasy is linked to the languages spoken in western Indonesia. These surprising facts are also reflected in the biological and cultural affinity of the people. Although there is much controversy over the relative importance of the African and Indonesian element in the population, there is general agreement that we find the two merged together throughout the island. In some parts one side of this dual inheritance is more important; in other regions it is the other side that seems to dominate. For example, all commentators agree that among the Merina . . . the Southeast Asian element is particularly strongly marked. (1986: 12)

In addition, style of dress and specific customs serve as markers of difference. Clothing styles vary as one moves from one area of the island to another. In the central and southern highlands, which have a cool, temperate climate, most Merina and Betsileo wear western-style clothes. A style that is considered to be more traditional among these people is the *akanjo,* a knee-length shirt made of plaid flannel which is worn by peasant men throughout the highlands. Merina women (regardless of class) are also easily recognized since they often wear a white shawl (*lamba*) draped over their shoulders for formal occasions. The coastal areas are humid and tropical, and all around the rim of the island men and women wear body wraps made of brightly printed cloth (called a *lambahoany*). Among the Sakalava this consists of the *kitamby* for men, which is a waist wrap worn like a sarong, and for women, a *salova* (*salovaña*), which is wrapped around the waist or chest, and *kisaly,* draped over the shoulders or head. This style of dress is very similar to that worn by Swahili of the East African coast. The far south, which is occupied by such people as the Bara, Mahafaly, and Antandroy, is an arid region. Here men often dress in shorts, a short-sleeved shirt, plastic sandals, and a straw hat, while women wear western-style dresses or lambahoany. Throughout the island different hats as well as hairstyles also serve as markers for ethnicity. For example, the name Sakalava means "[People of] the long valleys,"[3] while the Tsimihety ("Those who do not cut their hair") were so named by the Sakalava after they refused to cut their hair in mourning as an assertion of their independence following the death of a Sakalava ruler (Société Malgache 1973: 46, 47).

Fady (taboos) are another important aspect of Malagasy identity. They are widespread yet specific to particular peoples and regions and have been carefully catalogued in books on Malagasy folklore (see Ruud 1960 and Van Gennep 1904; see also Lambek 1992). Fady work at many different levels: all ethnic groups have their own particular ones and smaller groups, such as villages or kin groups, may observe specific fady. Individuals may have personal fady that are determined at birth by the *vintana* or the Malagasy cosmological zodiac system (see Huntington 1981), or which they have collected over time as a result of sickness or other experiences. Fady may consist of dietary restrictions or clothing requirements, and locations or particular days of the week may have fady associated with them. Complex constellations of fady may surround particular ritual settings or events, such as burials for commoners or royalty. They are also a key aspect of tromba possession.

Among the Sakalava, the following are important examples. Pork is fady for many, requiring that they avoid contact with pigs and their products. Nosy Faly ("Taboo Island," *faly* being an older form of the word *fady*), is Sakalava sacred space that requires respectful behavior from all visitors. One can not enter the village of the royal tombs (*ma-habolzomba*) on a Tuesday, Thursday, or Saturday, and so visitors who arrive on these days camp out on the beach, waiting for a more auspicious time. In the tomb village (Mahabo) one must go barefoot, and women are prohibited from wearing a kisaly on their heads. Dogs are prohibited and must be killed if they enter. Tortoises, on the other hand, are sacred, and it is fady to harm them. Because of these and other fady associated with the village, visitors must carefully monitor their actions so as not to incur the wrath of the local royal ancestors. Non-Sakalava visitors to Nosy Faly must also conform to local, Sakalava fady. Thus, on this sacred island and elsewhere, when one is among strangers, fady serve as markers of difference. They also operate to control the actions of outsiders. Visitors are expected to respect local fady or risk harming themselves or others. For this reason, Malagasy, when they travel, generally inquire about local fady, and they are usually listed in tourist guidebooks (see, for example, Société Malgache 1973).

GEOGRAPHICAL TERRITORY AND ETHNICITY

The Highlands versus the Coast

Among Malagasy, distinctions are made in reference to geographical areas and their corresponding ethnic groups, which in turn are relevant to the development of political power in Madagascar. There are, first, the peoples of the high plateaux. The most important group here is the Merina. The Betsileo, who live to the south of the Merina, occupy an ambiguous position in the minds of other Malagasy, since they are of the plateaux but are non-Merina people. I know of no general term in common usage that is applied collectively to Merina and Betsileo. Instead, more specific ethnic labels are used. Contrasted to these two highland groups are the *côtiers* ("peoples of the coast"), a term coined during the colonial era by the French to label all other Malagasy groups, many of whom Covell (1987: 13) points out live nowhere near the coast. The term *côtiers* is used most frequently by highland peoples and carries somewhat derogatory connotations.

These two general geographical categories have evolved out of politically defined divisions as a result of Merina expansion and subsequent French occupation of the island. During the eighteenth and nineteenth centuries, the Merina conquered much of the island and established a powerful kingdom. By the early 1900s Merina royalty in Antananarivo established an alliance with the British against the French, but this alliance ended when the French conquered the island. Throughout the twentieth century the distinction between Merina and all other peoples has remained significant. With Independence, President Tsiranana (who himself was from the coast) and his party members "tried to mobilize support by portraying themselves as defenders against 'Merina domination'" (Covell 1987: 13). Today, this tension persists. As Covell states, "The conflict cannot be reduced either to ethnic or class competition, but has elements of both" (1987: 13; she in turn cites Tronchon 1975).

Relations between members of these two major geographical groups are characterized by mistrust and racist attitudes. African versus Austronesian origins are a subject of important debate in Madagascar. Merina and Betsileo claim to be the most "Polynesian" of the Malagasy (see Bloch 1971: 1–5) and look disdainfully on coastal peoples, whom they often refer to as being "more African." These comments are made most often in reference to skin color and hair texture. For example, the term *Makoa* (which often appears on censuses as an ethnic category, see figures 3.1, 3.2, 3.3) is used as a descriptive (and somewhat derogatory) term for people who have dark skin and kinky hair. Makoa were originally brought to Madagascar as slaves from an area in the interior of Africa that is now part of Mozambique (see Lombard 1988: 88 and Smith 1963 on the "Makua," especially pp. 257 and 273). Highlanders in general view côtiers as backward and uneducated. Coastal peoples, in turn, express resentment of Merina who were once favored by the French and who form the majority of the population in the capital city. Merina continue to dominate the national political arena and maintain access to the best education, health care, and other services and facilities, and they fill many of the country's civil service jobs. (For a discussion of these trends after Independence, especially in reference to education, see LaPierre 1966.) Ideas shared by members of each of these groups toward one another also include notions of uncleanliness; concepts of physical beauty, especially in regard to skin color ("white/black": HP: *fotsy/mainty*; SAK: *fotsy/joby*); and a reluctance to intermarry (cf. Bloch 1971: 1–5, 198–201; J. Ramamonjisoa 1984).

The Tanindrazana or Ancestral Land

The most important concept used to define personal and group identity is that of the ancestral land (HP: tanindrazana; SAK: tanindrazaña). This may not necessarily be the locality where one lives or even grew up; it is where one's ancestors are located and, ultimately, where one will be entombed. For all Malagasy, identity is intrinsically linked to the ancestral land. Although it is considered rude to ask what one's ethnicity is, asking the question "where is your ancestral land" (HP: "*aiza ny tanindrazanao?*") will generally provide the same information (see Bloch 1968 and 1971, especially chapter 4).

Even when Malagasy migrate to other parts of Madagascar, the notion of the ancestral land continues to tie them to a particular locale. It is not simply the geographical space, but the ancestors themselves that serve as the locus of identity and that define an individual's point of origin. As a result, as one moves about the island, one continues to have a strong sense of ethnic identity that is geographically defined. As Keenan states of the Vakinankaratra (a group that is culturally considered to be Merina), "The worst fear of a villager is to travel far from the tanindrazana and fall sick and, perhaps, die alone" (Keenan 1974). The same may be said for the majority of Malagasy, regardless of origin.[4] Migrants and their children, who are born far from their ancestral land, may continue to invest money in a family tomb that is hundreds of miles away, so that they can be placed there when they are dead.

ECONOMIC SPECIALIZATION

Another system of ranking and categorization is based on forms of economic specialization that, in turn, correspond to ethnic and geographical categories. In a country where, for the majority of peoples, the staple is rice (see Linton 1927), highland peoples pride themselves on their talents as paddy rice farmers. The abilities of Betsileo farmers are a source of great national pride: their paddies are located in the valleys and tiered on the steep hillsides of the temperate regions of the southern plateaux. Coastal peoples of the east, west, and north practice swidden agriculture, where rice is, once again, a major crop (see Le Bourdiec et al. 1969: map no. 51).

The peoples of the arid south (for example the Antandroy, Bara, and Mahafaly) are pastoralists who raise cattle and goats. Although some grow rice, manioc is an important staple. Among many Malagasy—coastal and highland alike—pastoralists are regarded as being "simple," "primitive," and "African," and are said to speak dialects that are unintelligible by the vast majority of Malagasy. Pastoralists are feared by others who say that they are thieves (*mpangalatra*). This comment is made in reference to (and is a result of a misunderstanding of) the *dahalo*, or cattle raiders, since among these groups cattle raiding is an important social institution for young men. Antandroy and other pastoralists are taller than many Malagasy and the men often carry long staffs with large blades mounted on one end. As a result, other Malagasy are wary of them.

Conditions are severe in the south, made worse by a drought that has extended throughout the past decade. This has forced a large proportion of men to spend their lives as migrants, working in different parts of the island and sending remittances home (usually by registered mail) to their spouses and other kin, where much of the cash is invested in animals.[5] These migrants are drawn to the major urban centers of other regions where they are hired as night watchmen and as cowherds. They are preferred by employers because they are willing to brave the elements and sleep outdoors, even during the cold, wet winters so characteristic of the highlands (for detailed discussions of southern pastoralists see Decary 1933; Faublée 1954; Frère 1958; Huntington 1973).

RELIGIOUS AFFILIATION

Religions of foreign origin—Islam, Catholicism, and Protestantism—provide another means for distinguishing Malagasy from one another. They define divisions that are both ethnic and geographical. Estimates for religious affliation for the entire island in 1982 are as follows: 57 percent adhere to traditional (or what I will refer to as "indigenous") beliefs (fomba-gasy) and 40 percent are Christian, with equal representation of Roman Catholics and Protestants (Bunge 1983: 62). I assume that the remaining 3 percent is mostly Muslim, but also includes Indian Hindus.

Islam is strongest in the north and west. In contrast to other Malagasy, many Sakalava and Antakarana are faithful to Islam, their conversion having occurred in response to their efforts to find allies against Europeans in the eighteenth and nineteenth centuries. In addition, Arabs, the majority of Comoreans, and many Indo-Pakistanis are Muslim (see Delval 1967, 1987; Dez 1967; Gueunier and Fanony 1980; Vérin 1967).

Christianity has played an important role in shaping factions in modern Madagascar (Gow 1979; Mutibwa 1974; Southall 1979). Attempts were made by Portuguese and French Catholics to Christianize coastal peoples in the fifteenth and sixteenth centuries (Brown 1978: 30ff; Bunge 1983: 14), but these missionaries were killed by indigenous peoples shortly after they arrived. The first successful missionaries were Protestants from the London Missionary Society (LMS), who were wel-

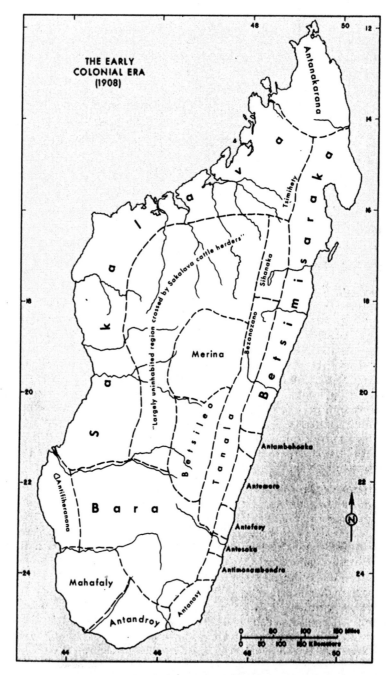

Figure 3.3 A and B. Distribution (and Migration) of Malagasy during the Twentieth Century. Source: Originally published in the Department of the Army Publication DA Pam 550-154, Area Handbook for *Indian Ocean: Five Island Countries*. Frederica M. Bunge, ed., 1983.

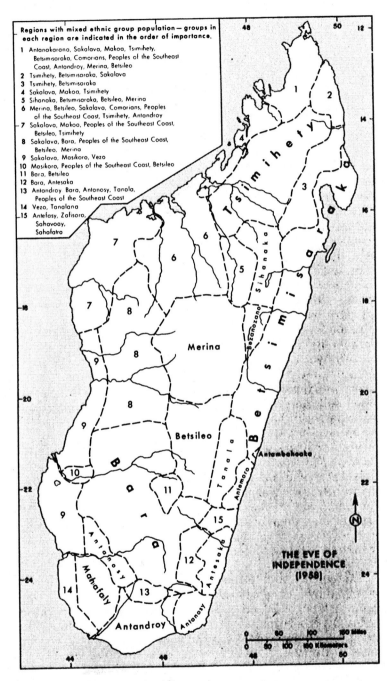

Regions with mixed ethnic group population — groups in each region are indicated in the order of importance.

1 Antanakarana, Sakalava, Makoa, Tsimihety, Betsimisaraka, Comorians, Peoples of the Southeast Coast, Antandroy, Merina, Betsileo
2 Tsimihety, Betsimisaraka, Sakalava
3 Tsimihety, Betsimisaraka
4 Sakalava, Makoa, Tsimihety
5 Sihanaka, Betsimisaraka, Betsileo, Merina
6 Merina, Betsileo, Sakalava, Comorians, Peoples of the Southeast Coast, Tsimihety, Antandroy
7 Sakalava, Makoa, Peoples of the Southeast Coast, Betsileo, Tsimihety
8 Sakalava, Bara, Peoples of the Southeast Coast, Betsileo, Merina
9 Sakalava, Masikoro, Vezo
10 Masikoro, Peoples of the Southeast Coast, Betsileo
11 Bara, Betsileo
12 Bara, Antesaka
13 Antandroy Bara, Antanosy, Tanala, Peoples of the Southeast Coast
14 Vezo, Tanalana
15 Antefasy, Zafisoro, Sahavooy, Sahafatra

THE EVE OF INDEPENDENCE (1958)

Figure 3.3 A and B.   *(continued)*

comed into the Merina kingdom in 1818 by royalty who sought to have the British join them as allies against the French. Other sects soon followed and rivalries developed as they sought to stake out territory and win converts. While Protestants won the favor of Merina royalty (*andriana*) and elites (*hova*), Catholics worked outside the capital. Among the highland Merina they were most successful with the slave population (*andevo*). They also worked among the Betsileo and throughout the coastal areas of the island. In 1863, Protestants were expelled from the island by the Merina Queen Ranavalona I, but they were eventually allowed to return in the 1880s following her death (Brown 1978: 152ff; Gow 1979; Mutibwa 1974).

Rivalries between different sects have been fierce up to the present. According to Covell, the number of Christians has declined since Independence (1987: 95; she in turn quotes Raison 1970). As she states, "The Christian Churches of Madagascar claim an estimated four million 'adherents'; a term that obviously covers a wide range of commitment. Both Catholic and Protestant churches have their largest number of adherents in central Madagascar, and one of the common physical features of the plateaux villages is the presence of two spired churches, usually confronting each other from the opposite ends of the village" (1987: 95).

Today, certain faiths are associated with specific ethnic groups. The Catholic Church is strongest in the southern plateaux among the Betsileo and in coastal areas. Protestantism is split between those churches that have a tradition of strong political ties with the Merina in Antananarivo and others in the south; the latter rely on regional missionary activities (for example, American and Scandinavian Lutherans have been active in southern Madagascar since 1866). In recent years, attempts have been made to forge new unions, alleviating the competition between Protestants. The FJKM church (Fiongonana Jesosy Kristiany Malagasy or the Malagasy Church of Jesus Christ) was formed in 1970 and draws adherents from such Protestant groups as the original LMS, Quaker, and French Protestant Mission churches (Covell 1987: 95). Subsequent ecumenical agreements among Protestant sects have led to their working in what was predominantly viewed as each other's territories. (For more detailed discussions on the Catholics see Chandon-Moët 1957; Decary 1966; Hübsch 1987; Judic 1987; L'Hermite 1968. On Protestants see Belrose-Huyghues 1979; Birkeli 1957; Gontard 1971; Gow 1979; London Missionary Society 1881–1900; Vérin et al. 1970.)

The majority of Malagasy remain faithful to indigenous religion or fomba-gasy, in which ancestors are central. In a sense, fomba-gasy touches the lives of all Malagasy, regardless of faith, since all Malagasy express an interest in their origins and a concern for their respective ancestors. The contrasts and contradictions between fomba-gasy and other religions have served as a means to divide peoples throughout the recent history of the island. This is certainly true for the inhabitants of Ambanja.

SOCIAL AND CULTURAL DIVISIONS IN AMBANJA

Malagasy are, historically, migratory peoples, first in terms of the original settlements of the island and, more recently, in terms of subsequent movements within the boundaries of this island (see Deschamps 1959). The movements of peoples have increased dramatically throughout this century (figure 3.3). Individuals and entire groups have moved for a variety of reasons: to find new grazing lands in response to population pressures (the most important case being that of the Tsimihety, see Molet 1959 and Wilson 1971); accompanying the expansion of Sakalava and Merina kingdoms (see Brown 1978; see also assorted essays in Kent, ed. 1979 and Kottak et al., eds. 1986); and in order to flee from more powerful enemies, as was true with the Tanala (Linton 1933: 24ff). Throughout the latter part of this century, Malagasy have also migrated in search of wage labor, and the Sambirano is an important destination.

THE SOCIAL CATEGORIES OF AMBANJA

As a result of the in-migration of non-Sakalava to Ambanja, the classification of its inhabitants is extremely complex. The most important distinction is between insiders and outsiders, or tera-tany and vahiny. When loosely defined, *tera-tany* may refer to anyone who owns land, but in the strictest sense, this term refers to the indigenous Bemazava, who form the largest single group represented in the area.[6] *Vahiny* is used to refer to other migrant Malagasy. Much tension exists between members of these two social categories. In addition to Malagasy-speakers, French, Comoreans, Chinese, Indians, Arab-Yemenis, and Greeks have also been drawn to the Sambirano. As mentioned above, these peoples are "foreigners" (étrangers; Western Europeans are also called *vazaha*), and this label applies even if they were born in Madagascar.

1950	2,000
1960	4,000
1975	11,334
1986	27,288

Figure 3.4.   Population Figures for the Town of Ambanja, 1950–1986. Source: Madagascar (1950–1971, 1986).

According to the 1986 census, foreigners collectively numbered 493, or 0.5 percent of the total population of the Sambirano Valley.

Contrary to customs of ethnic endogamy observed in other regions of Madagascar, in Ambanja intermarriage is common, not only between different groups of Malagasy-speakers, but also between Malagasy and peoples of foreign origins. *Métisization*—that is, intermarriage between members of diverse groups and their subsequent offspring—involving all groups is extremely high. Special labels are used when speaking of the offspring of these unions, and they reflect that an individual's parentage is a mixture of Malagasy and foreign heritage. For example, a child of a Sakalava mother and an Arab father is called "Arab-métis(se)." Ambanja has developed into a polycultural community, marked by the sharing and overlapping of cultural and social norms of diverse peoples. As a result of this blurring of ethnic boundaries, what it means to be tera-tany or, more specifically, Sakalava, has become increasingly problematic, so the terms *insider* and *outsider* require constant redefinition.

Malagasy Ethnic Groups and Their Points of Origin

Ambanja, as a migrant town, may be viewed in certain ways as a microcosm of Madagascar as a whole, since all groups—regardless of whether they are defined by ethnic, geographical, or religious categories—are represented. According to the 1986 census, the town had a population of 26,288 (25,945 nationals and 343 foreigners)[7] (Madagascar, Service du Planification, 1986). Over the latter half of this century the population of the town has doubled every ten years, whereas the average national growth rate in Madagascar is 3.1 percent per annum (Covell 1987: xiii), the national doubling time being approximately twenty to twenty-five years. This population increase in the Sambirano has occurred as a result of the immigration of non-Sakalava. The rate of immigration has increased dramatically since 1975, following the Socialist

ETHNIC GROUP	1950*	1960*	1962-1963**	1965**	1969**	1986
Sakalava	15,886	17,672	19,550	26,383	32,976	--
Adults:	5,047M; 5,420F	4,967M; 5,958F	4,007M; 5,396F	5,864M; 6,828F	9,204M; 8,515F	
Makoa	7,730	5,605	5,542	5,697	5,589	--
Adults:	2,119M; 2,493F	1,680M; 1,901F	1,070M; 1,049F	1,381M; 5,697F	1,287M; 1,376F	
Tsimihety	7,709	6,496	6,661	5,683	6,326	--
Adults:	2,189M; 2,588F	1,729M; 2,528F	1,294M; 1,329F	1,254M; 1,685F	1,327M; 1,626F	
Antaimoro		2,805	1,829	1,875	2,367	2,113 --
Adults:	1,024M; 737F	617M; 536F	381M; 330F	615M; 488F	594M; 525F	
Antandroy		1,767	1,881	1,968	1,992	1,858 --
Adults:	802M; 432F	801M; 523F	628M; 387F	674M; 404F	606M; 395F	
Betsileo	1,464	1,414	1,473	1,618	1,454	--
Adults:	465M; 514F	501M; 427F	436M; 306F	473M; 345F	364M; 320F	
Merina	593	570	565	645	808	--
Adults:	150M; 154F	162M; 150F	142M; 565F	173M; 168F	105M; 255F	

TOTAL POPULATION:

	1950*	1960*	1962-1963**	1965**	1969**	1986
Malagasy only:	42,946	39,669	42,216	50,337	57,784	93,298
with foreigners: (étrangers)	43,280	41,602	43,777	51,909	61,026	93,791

KEY

The cutoff point used for determining adult status changed in 1962:
*   1950-1960: adults are those individuals over 14 years of age;
**   1962 - early 1970s: adults are those over 21 years of age.
By the 1980s, adults were those individuals over 18 years of age.

Census material is available for the following years (collected during the preceding year):
1950, 1959, 1960, 1961, 1965, 1968, 1979. Thus, figures for the years up to 1960 were collected by the colonial administration; subsequent censuses were conducted under the direction of the government of Madagascar. The figures change dramatically at this time: for example, as noted above, the cutoff point for adult status changed from 14 years to 21 years. It is for this reason that I provide figures for the years 1961 and 1962-1963.

Source: Madagascar (1950-1971, 1986).

Figure 3.5.   Population Statistics for Major Ethnic Groups of Ambanja District (Sambirano   Valley),   1950–1971,   1986   (totals).   Source: Madagascar (1950–1971, 1986).

Revolution and the subsequent expansion of state-run agricultural enterprises (Andriamihamina et al. 1987: 25). Estimates for the population of the *town* of Ambanja since 1950 reveal this doubling of the population (Andriamihamina et al. 1987: 21) (figure 3.4).

Statistics on the ethnic breakdown of the population of the *district* of Ambanja (the entire Sambirano Valley) are scanty, since they were collected regularly only from 1950 to 1971. Further problems arise since changes were made in the size of the district over time, as well as in the procedures used to collect census information. It is also unclear whether or not these figures include temporary residents of the valley. Since 1985 the timing of the census has been designed to avoid the coffee season (June and July), when there are many temporary laborers in town. The figures are now collected by local representatives for each neighborhood, drawn from registration books where they keep a log of all residents living there during the course of that year. Despite these disadvantages, I have reproduced these figures since they provide a rough picture of the ethnic composition of the Sambirano Valley (see figure 3.5).

These figures show that, first, the Sakalava remain the largest single group, comprising 37 to 54 percent of the population. Second, all officially recognized categories are well represented in each census, reflecting the presence of large numbers of non-Sakalava. The most significant groups, in terms of number (listed in descending order) are as follows:

1. *Makoa* are the descendants of African slaves; Makoa was an official ethnic category as late as the 1970s. Makoa are now considered to be indigenous to Sakalava territory in western Madagascar and are sometimes subsumed under the category designated for Sakalava. From the point of view of local Bemazava, they occupy an ambiguous category vis-à-vis tera-tany status: although they are perceived as a distinct group, they have special rights and privileges in reference to this status because they served the Sakalava in the past.

2. *Tsimehety* are pastoralists who originally came from the south and who have since migrated northward throughout this century. Today they occupy the territory to the south of the Sambirano; many also live along the northeast coast in an area referred to as the "Vanilla Triangle."

3. *Antaimoro* are from the southeast, near Farafangana.

4. *Antandroy* are pastoral peoples from the far south.[8]

5. *Betsileo* and *Merina* are the two major groups that occupy the high plateaux.

Dating the arrival of these different migrant groups to the Sambirano is difficult. By consulting the records of land titles held by one of the first plantation owners, de la Motte St. Pierre, it is clear that by 1907 he had worker villages situated on his lands (Title 140, Le Gabés) and by 1908 the Sakalava were living on indigenous reserves (Title 130 B.P.) (Service Topographique). Planters on Nosy Be used slave labor until slavery was abolished by the French parliament in 1896. After that they relied on land tenants and corvée labor. Attempts were made throughout Madagascar to recruit foreign laborers from China, Yemen, and the

Comoro Islands, but these efforts were relatively unsuccessful (see Brown 1978: 249–250; Stratton 1964: 95–96; and Thompson and Adloff 1965: 442ff). The first Antandroy laborers were brought to Nosy Be in 1922 by Djamanjary Sugar (established 1918). These workers were recruited from the prison in Tulear and brought to Nosy Be by boat. Many of these Antandroy settled permanently in the north. It is possible that a few planters in the Sambirano continued this recruitment practice until migrants began to arrive on their own.

Betsileo are also among the early migrants to the Sambirano; evidence of their work can be seen on the road to Diégo, just north of Ambanja, where there are large rice paddies. As one Betsileo informant explained:

> My parents decided to come north in the 1920s to search for work, and they came directly to the Sambirano, having heard that there were colonists here who needed laborers. My father came to work in the sugar cane and manioc fields, and he became a land tenant of one of the plantation owners. Under a system called *miasa-talata* [lit. "to work on Tuesday"; the French called these workers *talatiers*, cf. Feeley-Harnik 1984: 11] he was given land to farm where he grew rice; in exchange he worked every Tuesday for the landowner. When French and other large landowners left Madagascar in the 1970s, my father bought the land, so that now he owns approximately 110 hectares.

Today my informant's father farms his land successfully with the assistance of a tractor and the labor of his wife and fifteen descendants, including children and grandchildren. Clearly, by the second decade of this century, the Sambirano was well-known throughout Madagascar as a place where one could find work, and it attracted people from all areas of the island.

In the 1959 census, Jonoro Houlder, the Chef du District, devoted special attention to a discussion of immigration and emigration of peoples to and from the Sambirano. He noted that a number of non-Sakalava were well established in the area, contracted by European planters to work as manual laborers. These included the Tsimehety (from Analalava, Antsohihy, and Bealanana), and peoples from the south and southeast (Antandroy, Antanosy, Bara, Antaimoro, Antaisaka). Others from the east coast (Betsimisaraka) and high plateaux (Betsileo and Merina) had also arrived in the area and had put down roots:

> Le district d'Ambanja est un district plutôt d'immigration et d'emmigration. Il forme une plaque tournante où transitent obligatoirement tous ceux qui, venant d'Analalava, d'Antsohihy ou de Bealanana par voie de terre, se dirigent vers Ambilobe et Diégo-Suarez. . . . Dans cette région particulièrement

favorisée par une terre riche, la colonisation européene a introduit des trav-
ailleurs salairiés ordinaires du Sud, engagés par contrat, et qui forment l'ess-
entiel de sa main-d'oeuvre: Antaimoro, Antaisaka, Antandroy, Antanosy,
Bara. . . . Profitant de la décadence et de l'apathie des Sakalava qui peuple-
rent initialement ce pays, d'outres éléments allongènes plus laborieux, se sont
infiltrés et y ont fait solidement souche: Betsileo, Tsimehety, Hova [Merina],
Betsimisaraka, etc. (Madagascar 1950–1971, report from 1959: 2)

Houlder then went on to discuss the presence of non-Malagasy, including Comoreans and Indians, and their activities as local merchants.

Similar comments are made about the immigration of Malagasy in
the report from 1965, where the author spoke again of the importance
of contract workers, especially Antandroy and Antaimoro; he also commented on Tsimehety migration, which had continued to grow. He
stressed that most Tsimehety came from Bealalana (which is about 350
kilometers south of Ambanja) and that Tsimehety villages had been
established in the Sambirano (Madagascar 1950–1971, report from
1965: 2).

A recurring theme in subsequent reports is the reluctance of Sakalava
to emigrate to other areas of Madagascar. Such a statement is made by
Houlder, above, and is reiterated by the author of the 1968 report: "les
elements aborigènes sont ordinairement sedentaires et quittent diffi-
cilement le village natal" (Madagascar 1950–1971, report from 1968:
1). The authors of these reports comment on Sakalava resistance to
work as wage laborers (cf. Feeley-Harnik 1984: 6, 1991b, especially p.
191ff and chapter 5).[9] As discussed in the previous chapter, today these
are themes which are voiced by Sakalava about themselves as well as
by frustrated employers. The complexities that have arisen as a result
of this constant immigration of non-Sakalava will be discussed below
in this chapter, as well as in the chapter that follows.

Local Territory and the Ancestral Land

As described above, the tanindrazana or ancestral land is central to
Malagasy notions of identity, both personal and collective. In the strictest sense, the region of the Sambirano is the exclusive ancestral land of
the Bemazava-Sakalava. Since Malagasy identity is tied to the ancestors
and, thus, to the land, all other peoples, regardless of how long they
have lived here, are outsiders by virtue of this rule.

Sakalava maintain tombs that are located throughout the valley,
often in small remote villages that may be a long drive or walk from

where they reside.[10] In some cases these tombs are fairly new. When the French relocated Sakalava, they obliterated all traces of old cemeteries, so that the Sakalava had to create new tombs for their dead (cf. Colson 1971 for similarities with British colonial policy).

Some migrants have established their own tombs or cemeteries on land they or older kin have bought. This is especially true for the Antandroy, who bury their dead locally, since for them the costs for transporting a body as far as one thousand kilometers to their ancestral land in the south is prohibitively high. In the town of Ambanja there is also a cemetery where Christians and Muslims are buried, and it is used by both Sakalava and non-Sakalava. Migrants who choose to be buried locally may not be accepted as full-fledged tera-tany by Sakalava. Nevertheless, by Malagasy rules of affiliation, such a choice is an indicator that one's sentimental ties to the region are strong, since where one is buried carries the sense that one is from—or belongs—there.

ETHNICITY AND ECONOMIC SPECIALIZATION

In Ambanja, different economic activities are associated with different ethnic groups. In reference to the four largest migrant groups represented in the Sambirano (see above), the following generalizations can be made.

Tsimihety have an established history as labor migrants throughout this century (Deschamps 1959). Many come to the Sambirano as temporary migrants during coffee harvest season in June and July. Others have settled permanently in the Sambirano.

Others from the *south and southeast,* such as the Antaimoro and Antandroy, were among the earliest migrants to the region. Today they form the bulk of manual laborers at the enterprises and at businesses in town. Antandroy men also work as night watchmen (see Frère 1958: 117–140 for information about the Antandroy).

It is the Betsileo and Merina who hold university degrees and who fill the majority of civil service and other government sponsored positions. As state employees, they are schoolteachers, the managers and engineers of the enterprises, the president of the local bank, the doctors at the town's hospital and worker's clinic, and the directional staff of government agricultural and communication agencies. There are also a number of rural peoples from the high plateaux who have set up small businesses or who work as "traveling merchants" (*mpivarotra mandeha*). The best known of these are the Vakinankaratra, a group occupying a southern region of Merina territory around the town of Ambato-lampy (which lies to the south of Antananarivo). Many of these traveling merchants have established Ambanja as their home base, and they travel periodically to the national capital where they buy goods, return to Ambanja, and sell them in the local market at a significant markup.

RELIGION

Ambanja is the religious center for the Sambirano and adjoining regions. Reflecting national trends, Muslims, Catholics, and Protestants are divided along ethnic lines. Estimates of religious affiliation in the Sambirano are 4–6 percent Muslim, 6 percent Catholic, up to 6 percent Protestant, and approximately 80 percent fomba-gasy (Jaovelo-Dzao 1983, 1987, and personal communication). The faiths of foreign origin which boast Sakalava membership are Islam and Catholicism. Protestants, on the other hand, usually are non-Sakalava from the high plateaux and the south.

Islam

As mentioned in chapter 2, in the nineteenth century, the Bemihisatra-Sakalava royalty of Nosy Be converted to Islam. Pierre Dalmond, a Catholic priest who arrived in Nosy Be in 1840, reported in his journal that when he was first received by Tsimiaro I, the king of the Antakarana, the ruler was dressed as a Muslim, wearing a white robe and a hat of red velour (Dalmond 1840). A photo taken perhaps half a century later of "Tisaraso [Tsiaraso I] (1871–1919), souverain des Sakalava Bemazava" (see Raison-Jourde, ed. 1983, between pages 128 and 129) shows the ruler clothed in similar fashion. It is this same style of dress that mediums wear today when they are possessed by the greatest of the Bemazava, Bemihisatra, and Antakarana tromba spirits.

Today, among the Bemazava, the majority of Muslims are royalty. Most are "sympathetic Muslims" (SAK: *muselmans/silamo sympatiques*) who do not go to mosque regularly and only observe the fast of Ramadan (SAK: *Ramzan*). A Sakalava expression that reflects their lax attitude is *tsopa tsy haramo*, which literally means "[drinking] tsopa [a small bottle of very strong alcohol] does not violate the Koran" (Jaovelo-Dzao, personal communication; compare the kiSwahili expression *chupa tsi haramu*, J. Bergman and M. Porter, personal communication).

There are five mosques in Ambanja, each identified according to the ethnic makeup of the majority of its members. These are the Comorean (the majority of members are originally from Anjouan); Comorean and métis (Comoreans and Malagasy of mixed origins); Arab-métis (offspring of mixed marriages between Arabs and Sakalava); the Indian mosque; and a splinter group that I will refer to as "Modern Islam" (see chapter 10), whose members are primarily Sakalava, Antakarana, and some Comorean. These labels aside, membership in all mosques (except that of the Indians) is fairly heterogeneous, reflecting the town's high rate of intermarriage between peoples of diverse backgrounds. The number of regular members (that is, those who attend Friday prayer) of each mosque varies between fifty to one hundred, with perhaps half as many attending daily prayer. The largest is the Comorean mosque.

The Catholic Church

When the northern Sakalava failed to acquire firearms from the Sultan of Muscat, they turned to the French for assistance against the Merina. Captain Passot led the French military into Nosy Be in 1840, and he brought with him Catholic missionaries. Among these was the Jesuit priest Dalmond, who had already been active on the small islands off the east coast of Madagascar (see Dalmond, n.d.). Nosy Be became an important northern post for Catholic activities, while additional evangelical work was conducted on Nosy Faly, Nosy Mitsiosioko, and in the Sambirano Valley. In the early part of this century, however, Ambanja replaced Nosy Be as an important colonial and commercial center. By 1921 the Catholics were active in Ambanja, having followed the military there, and in 1936 they built a cathedral, which continues to be one of the largest buildings in town. The Catholic church has by far the largest congregation in Ambanja, the cathedral seating approximately two thousand (it is packed during Easter). Catholic adherents include Sakalava as well as well as Tsimihety, Antandroy, Antaimoro, and some Betsileo and Merina.

Catholicism is far more popular than Protestantism among the Sakalava, and the style of Catholic evangelizing has much to do with this. Although Sakalava royalty have remained Muslim, Sakalava commoners were encouraged to attend the mission school, and those who did so often converted to Catholicism. The present king, Ampanjakabe Tsiaraso III, is an anomaly: tera-tany insist he is Muslim, but he himself professes to be Catholic, since he converted to the latter faith when, as a child he attended the mission school. The Catholic church has been successful in winning Sakalava converts because it is especially sensitive to Sakalava culture. In recent years this approach has been formalized under a policy known as *enculturation* which evolved following Vatican II. Enculturation encourages the tolerance of local beliefs and customs and emphasizes syncretism over orthodoxy. This policy plays an important role in shaping Catholic practice in Madagascar, as in many other parts of Africa (cf. Aubert 1987).

Although Ambanja's Catholic clergy includes nuns and priests from France, Italy, and Germany, the majority are Malagasy, who are primarily Sakalava. The leaders of the church in Ambanja and nearby towns are all locally born Sakalava, while Europeans occupy the backstage in terms of policy matters. In addition, whereas the Protestant Bible is written in official Malagasy (and thus is based on the Merina dialect), the Catholic Bible used in Ambanja has been translated into Sakalava. Catholic services are also performed in the local dialect. They are lively and innovative and incorporate elements that characterize local town life. For example, the church hosts discos as fundraisers and has an electric guitarist who accompanies the singing of hymns at Sunday services. Rumor also has it that a number of priests have taken mistresses and have had children by them, and that several of the nuns delight in dancing with their students at the church discos.

The Catholic church has made attempts to incorporate local customs into the services. It is also tolerant of fomba-gasy, including tromba possession. In contrast, the Protestant groups regard fomba-gasy as sinful and the work of Satan (the full ramifications of this stance will be discussed in chapter 10). Furthermore, while Protestants complain about the Sakalava's lack of respect toward such social institutions as marriage, the Catholics perform several marriage ceremonies each year (this rarely occurs at the Protestant churches).

Protestantism

Thus, Sakalava, if they "pray" (*mivavaka*), are Muslim or Catholic; they are rarely Protestant. Sakalava and their Antakarana neighbors have resisted Protestantism since they associate it with their enemies of the past century, the Merina, among whom Protestants have been active since the nineteenth century. Today it is rare to find Protestant Sakalava in the Sambirano. The only northern people who historically have been associated with Protestantism are the Tsimihety.

Ambanja is, nevertheless, home to a wide variety of Protestant churches. The oldest of these is the FJKM, which has been active in the area since the 1930s. Other groups include Lutherans, Adventists, Anglicans and a handful of Pentecostal groups that split from the FJKM more than a decade ago. The FJKM is the largest Protestant church in town, with approximately 250 to 300 people who regularly attend Sunday services. The Anglicans, Adventists, and Lutherans all have small churches that can hold up to about two hundred people, but on a regular basis there are only, perhaps, ten to thirty in attendance. Each of these churches is relatively new, having been established within the last ten to twenty years, following an ecumenical agreement among different sects to allow one another to expand into each other's territories. In contrast to the Sakalava, the majority of migrants are Protestants. The Lutherans, for example, who are associated with southern Madagascar, established a church in Ambanja in 1975. This congregation is composed primarily of peoples from the south and high plateaux, although they hope to gain converts among the Sakalava. More generally, the parishoners of all Protestant churches are Betsileo, Merina, Tsimehety, and Antandroy and Antaimoro. In Ambanja, Protestantism is an institution that embodies that which is *not* Sakalava.

Fomba-gasy, or Malagasy Religion

As the figures for religious affiliation show, fomba-gasy remains the dominant religion in Madagascar; in Ambanja, the percentage (80 percent) is much higher than the national average (59 percent), because Sakalava of Ambanja have been reluctant to convert to faiths of foreign origin. Jaovelo-Dzao attributes their resistance to Christianity to the power and influence of the Bemazava royalty.[11] Since royalty had already converted to Islam prior to the arrival of Catholic priests, they dissuaded commoners from converting to this new religion. Following the dictum of royalty, Sakalava often state that it is fady for them to embrace other faiths (*fady mivavaka*, lit. "praying is taboo"). It is also easier for a Muslim to marry a Sakalava than it is for a Christian to do so, since Sakalava marriage and other institutions have incorporated elements derived from Islam (Jaovelo-Dzao 1983; personal communication).

Sakalava hostility toward non-Sakalava has played a role in their resistance to conversion. For the Sakalava, the fomba-gasy define what it means to be Sakalava, and so to give up tromba and other local practices would, from a Sakalava point of view, require denouncing one's ethnic identity. Sakalava express their reluctance to attend Protestant services by saying that many of the pastors, and other officiants, are from the highlands. Several Lutheran evangelists spoke to me of the Sakalava with bitterness; since they themselves are Merina, it is impossible to gain converts. During the course of my fieldwork two young Sakalava men joined the church, and the pastor and evangelists hoped that at least one would choose to be trained as a pastor and return to Ambanja to evangelize among his own people. Catholicism and Islam reveal a tolerance for fomba-gasy, but Protestants are strongly opposed to these traditions. Tromba possession, which is central to Sakalava religion, provides an appropriate example. Protestants say they are *fady tromba* ("[have a] tromba taboo") and so only those mediums who choose to opt out of possession by having their spirits exorcized by the Protestants convert (this will be discussed in chapter 10).

Studies of Zionist churches in Africa provide examples of how faiths of foreign origin may answer questions that arise as a consequence of massive social change (Comaroff 1985; Jules-Rosette 1975; see also Colson 1970). Yet in Ambanja, a town so rife with conflicts, the general population shows little or no inclination to convert to Christianity or Islam. Instead, what has occurred is a virtual explosion in the incidence of tromba possession, involving Sakalava and vahiny.

THE EFFECTS OF POLYCULTURALISM

Although there are no statistics available for the valley's present ethnic composition, it seems clear that Sakalava remain the single largest group represented. Sakalava own the majority of small, privately owned plots of land which are scattered throughout the Sambirano. Many are peasants who raise both subsistence (especially rice) and cash crops (especially coffee and cocoa). Those who live in town usually own the land they live on, supporting themselves by running small family-owned groceries on the premises. Others sell produce, charcoal, and other essential items in front of their homes. Townspeople may also own land in the countryside. It is the Sakalava who, more generally, dominate formal power structures. Since they comprise the largest voting block, Sakalava dominate elected positions in the city and county governments. The only other group that has managed to have a few members elected are the Tsimihety. Sakalava royalty—both living and dead—also wield power in the Sambirano. Because Sakalava exercise the greatest influence of any ethnic group in the Sambirano, it is important to understand how they perceive the social world of Ambanja.

SAKALAVA PERSPECTIVES

Sakalava characterize other Malagasy groups as being closer to or farther from themselves. These conceptualizations in turn reflect notions

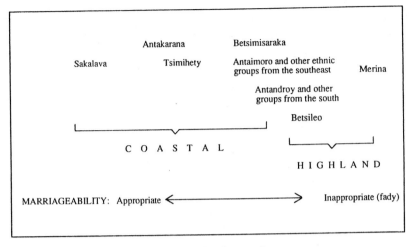

Figure 3.6.   Sakalava Conceptions of Other Malagasy.

of similarity and compatibility on the one hand and dissimilarity and distrust on the other (figure 3.6).

These categories have profound implications for patterns of informal association. They may affect more formal decisions as well, as in choosing an appropriate spouse or electing an official to the local government. On one end are groups thought to be the most similar to the Sakalava: these are their neighbors the Antakarana and Tsimihety. Makoa occupy a slightly more ambiguous position since they are the descendants of slaves who served local Sakalava in the past. The other extreme includes pastoralists from the south, like the Antandroy and the Merina of the high plateaux. Sakalava, like many other non-southern peoples, rank themselves above pastoralists, regarding themselves as more sophisticated. Like other coastal peoples, they express resentment and distrust of the Merina (whom Sakalava refer to derogatorily as *borzany*). There is a body of fady which places Merina in an extreme position outside the realm of association for Sakalava. Some Sakalava tromba are said to be *fady Merina* ("[having a] Merina taboo"), so that Merina may not attend tromba ceremonies, nor may they approach Sakalava tombs or other sacred locations. Many Sakalava extend this fady to everyday interactions as well and deny Merina access to their homes. More generally, there are fady and other customs that set various groups outside the Sakalava realm. Among the most common is the ingestion of pork, for the majority of Sakalava have a pork taboo (SAK: *fady komankory*).

What I wish to stress here is that it is difficult to pass as Sakalava: dialect, name, dress, and physical appearance give away a person's ethnic background.[12] Overlapping and confusion generally only occur among peoples from the same general regions of Madagascar. For example, *Antandroy* is a label often applied to Mahafaly and Bara. Also, a number of my informants were Merina but in public they claimed to be Betsileo to facilitate interactions with Sakalava. In general, peoples such as the Merina, Sakalava, and Antandroy have distinct physical characteristics that make it easy for the trained observer to distinguish one from the other. Malagasy are accustomed to thinking in this way about each other. Maps of Madagascar, for example, often include photos of people who are considered to be archetypal of their given ethnic group (see for example Société Malgache 1973; map opposite p. 40).

The logic of the Sakalava framework of similar and dissimilar peoples is based on several general principles. The first involves a sense of shared cultural features and historical origins. For example, in the past, Sakalava and Antakarana were members of one group. As a result of a dispute over royal succession, the Antakarana split off and moved north, so that now Sakalava and Antakarana are members of related yet separate descent groups. These descent groups of the northern Sakalava and Antakarana are called the *Zafin'i'mena* and *Zafin'i'fotsy*, or "Grandchildren of Gold" and "Silver," respectively. Relations today between the two are cordial. The mother of the present king of the Antakarana, for example, is of the Bemazava-Sakalava royal lineage. Sakalava and Antakarana share many fady and honor many of the same ancestors. Ceremonies are similar and at times indistinguishable: tromba ceremonies may include the same spirits, and at royal occasions for either one may see a dance called the *rebiky* performed (see Feeley-Harnik 1988).

The second principle is one of proximity. The Sakalava's closest neighbors are the Tsimihety (to the east and south) and Antakarana (to the north). This places all other peoples geographically at a distance from them. As one moves farther away to the east (towards the Betsimisaraka) and to the south (into the high plateaux and farther south and southeast), social distance increases. With the Merina, however, historical factors take precedence, for they are still seen as enemies while the Betsileo, who live farther to the south, are tolerated to a greater extent.

DEFINING TERA-TANY AND VAHINY

The increased immigration of non-Sakalava to the Sambirano Valley creates a dilemma for the Sakalava. Since they would rather not work for the enterprises, they are faced with the constant influx of unwanted strangers who are willing to do so. Sakalava express anxiety about migrants, and this anxiety has increased since the recent improvement of the north-south highway, which connects Ambanja with Mahajanga and, ultimately, Antananarivo. In 1987, it was being turned into an all-weather road, and the Sakalava feared it would bring still more people, leading to an increase in crime rates and other problems characteristic of other urban centers in Madagascar.

The lack of social cohesiveness among members of different groups is graphically illustrated in the haphazard layout of the town. Malagasy exhibit a preference for socializing with individuals who share similar regional or ethnic origins. Nevertheless, in Ambanja, like peoples are rarely clustered together in neighborhoods. Instead, each area of town presents a wild array of people of diverse origins and class backgrounds. The effects that accompany the ever-increasing influx of migrants have become a major concern in the town. A recent study conducted by the Urban and Housing Service of the Ministry of Public Works (Andriamihamina et al. 1987: 7–9) echoed these concerns, particularly the potential dangers associated with water shortages and insufficient sewer facilities. They stressed the need for more careful city planning if these problems were to be avoided. An area of special concern was the neighborhood of Ambaibo, near the bazarbe, where houses are now crammed against the banks of the Sambirano River (see figure 2.2).

Since Sakalava are the dominant group of the Sambirano, it is they who determine who is tera-tany or vahiny (insider versus outsider). The factors that define these social categories should be clear by now. Yet the dynamic between Malagasy kinship and ethnic identity often blurs these categories. In Madagascar, offspring are said to share the ethnic identity of their biological father. In Ambanja, individuals born into families that have lived in the region for generations, who own land, and who identify culturally with Sakalava generally consider themselves to be tera-tany. Nevertheless, others may insist that they are, and always will be, vahiny because they ultimately share the identity and thus origin of their father (or father's father, and so on).

The concept of ancestral land and the way in which it is interpreted in Ambanja is central to these definitions. Tera-tany and vahiny have conflicting views on how burial choices define one's identity and proper place in the Sambirano. As described above, the place where one will be buried is of central concern for Malagasy, as it is tied to concepts of kinship identity and home. The kin of Malagasy who die far from home will go to extreme lengths to make sure that the body will make its way back to the family tomb. In Ambanja there are families that, even after living in the town for a number of generations, are still tied to tombs elsewhere. They are, however, a minority. Migrants who settle permanently in Ambanja generally choose to be buried in this region. Nevertheless, although migrants may think of Ambanja as home, psychological alienation may persist because of Sakalava notions that define what it means to be tera-tany or vahiny. In other words, even for those who choose to buried in the Sambirano and who consider it their (new) ancestral land, Sakalava may still consider them to be vahiny.[13] As will be illustrated in the following chapter, it is very difficult to shake the migrant or outsider status, regardless of how long an individual or cluster of kin has been in the area and regardless of their burial choices.

CHAPTER IV

Tera-Tany and Vahiny

Insiders and Outsiders

The complexity of factionalism makes migrant status a perplexing one in Ambanja. Clearly there are advantages to being an insider: one has first rights to the land, a greater access to and an understanding of local power structures (be they formal or informal), an understanding of Sakalava culture, and, most important, social acceptance among Sakalava. Since the essential characteristic of insider status is Sakalava ethnicity, the boundary is a fairly rigid one. Migrants face the contradictions between how they perceive their own identities, based on their sentimental ties, and how others perceive and label them.

For newly arrived migrants, having contacts in the community is essential if they are to succeed in finding lodging and employment. They must establish new networks, seeking out kin and, sometimes, friends, who come from the same region of the county and who can help ease their transition into town life. While tromba enables migrant women to be symbolically transformed into Sakalava, there are other institutions that facilitate the partial integration of migrants more generally, offering avenues that are open to both men and women. Some migrants join ethnic associations, which help to maintain ethnic distinctions, or they choose to be buried locally, instead of in their original ancestral land. Others attempt to become integrated into the Sakalava community by marrying tera-tany, or by changing their behavior, dress, and dialect. But even though these actions bring a migrant closer to Sakalava in everyday interactions, from a Sakalava point of view they do not transform the individual's ethnic identity. The purpose of this chapter is to explore the nature of migrants' experiences with these issues in mind. The first section illustrates this through case studies drawn from informants' life histories. The second is an analysis of the important social institutions that facilitate or inhibit the incorporation of outsiders into the community of Ambanja.

MIGRANT STORIES

The examples that appear below have been selected in order to illustrate the relevance of the factors mentioned in the previous chapter: ethnicity and associated characteristics such as fady or taboos, religious affiliation, areas of economic specialization, and so forth. They also reveal why migrants come to Ambanja and how they cope with life in this town. The examples presented here are for the most part success stories; the chapters in Part 3 will focus on the more extreme problems that migrants face in Ambanja.

In such a diverse community, distinctions must be made between different categories of migrants. In his study in northern Nigeria, Cohen draws on distinctions made by urban Hausa, who divide migrants into "settlers" (Dan Kasa) and "strangers" (Baki). Length of stay is significant, but it alone is insufficient to determine settler status. Instead, these two categories are defined primarily by social roles, particularly through participation in political, religious (in this case Islam), and economic arenas. More specific criteria include rights to housing within the Hausa quarter, occupation, residence patterns of wives and children, and primary relationships, including one's relationship with the local chief (1969: 32ff and 222, nn. 9 and 10).

Cohen's (or the Hausa's) categories prove helpful in sorting out the dynamics of the social world of Ambanja. Cohen's use of the term *stranger* is, however, problematic, since the equivalent of this term in Madagascar (étranger) is only applied to non-Malagasy. Thus, for the purposes of this study, I will divide the vahiny of Ambanja into two major categories: *short-term* or *temporary migrants;* and *long-term* or *permanent migrants,* whom I will also refer to as *settlers.* As with the Hausa, length of stay is, in part, a determining factor of status. In addition, as was illustrated in the preceding chapter, participation in particular types of economic, religious, and political activities are important aspects of identity. There are certain differences, however, between these two communities. Although social roles are important in Ambanja, temporary migrant and settler statuses have additional dimensions. First, whereas in Cohen's study all migrants share a similar cultural background (they are all Hausa), in Ambanja one finds a multitude of groups, in which ethnicity is of primary importance. Thus, for members of certain groups, the desire to become a settler is already, in many cases, predetermined by point of origin. Tsimihety, for example, are more likely to settle permanently than are Antandroy. Second, Sakalava attitudes toward migrants differ according to their ethnic origin. Sakalava feel most comfortable with Antakarana, but they avoid contact with Merina. As will be made clear below, adherence to particular fady is often a clear marker of difference. A third key factor is what I will refer to as migrants' *sentimental* ties to life in this town. As Wilson (1971) has illustrated, the idea of "sentimental structure" is important for Tsimihety pastoralists, who, often with each generation, move away from the place where they were born. They must, therefore, eventually choose their burial location, and this is determined by, essentially, their emotional ties to a particular place or to certain kin. As will be clear throughout this study, this idea of sentiment is a crucial one for migrants in Ambanja, evident in their daily activities, personal ties, marriage patterns, burial plans, and participation in tromba or other religious and cultural institutions.

Thus, in Ambanja, temporary migrants are those who have come to the Sambirano searching for work and who only intend to stay long enough to make their fortunes. Although some may live in Ambanja for more than a decade, they do not consider it to be their home. For these people the ancestral land lies at their point of origin, often where they were raised, and their strongest sentimental ties are with kin who remain there. Temporary migrants try to send remittances home regularly, money that is used to help support kin and is invested locally in land and animals. Temporary migrants also attempt to visit their ancestral land as often as possible (generally once a year) and they intend to return there to live permanently and retire. Although they may take lovers in Ambanja, they often have spouses and children back home. Temporary migrants also show a stronger tendency to socialize with people of similar origins; since they do not intend to stay in Ambanja, they are not particularly interested in becoming incorporated into the Sakalava community. Examples of temporary migrants, whose stories are detailed below, include the men of the handcart (*posy-posy*) team and Mme Razafy.

Permanent migrants or settlers, on the other hand, are those individuals who come to Ambanja and stay. For some, this was their original intention (as with Botabe's father, see below). Others were temporary migrants whose sentimental ties to the region changed over time as a result of economic or other forms of success. In time, they have chosen to settle permanently in Ambanja. Of those who were settlers from the start, the majority come to Ambanja alone, and they may permanently sever ties with their kin in their original ancestral land. Another common pattern among settlers is to marry locally, often with Sakalava tera-tany rather than with other vahiny. Over time, their manner of speaking and style of dress also reflect their adoption of Sakalava customs. There are still others who come to the Sambirano, either accompanied by their spouses or who have their spouses (often with children) join them there later. Some of these people still feel tied to the original ancestral land and may prefer to be buried there. Their children, however, will generally choose to be buried locally in the Sambirano, considering it to be their new ancestral home.

Children of migrant parents (temporary or permament) characteristically have strong sentimental ties to the Sambirano, especially if they have never visited kin living in their parents' original ancestral land. One day a Betsileo friend of mine, for example, looked at her four-year-old with a puzzled expression when he used an unfamiliar Sakalava term that he had learned from his playmates. She later said, laughing, "ah-ah, he is a child of the Sambirano!" playfully using the Sakalava expression for this (SAK: *tsaiky [ny] Sambirano*, HP: *zanaka [ny] Sambirano*). Ultimately, what determines where children's sentiments will lie once they are adults depends somewhat upon their parents' patterns of association and, to a greater extent, upon their own experiences, especially in reference to the peers with whom they associate.

Finally, the notion of what it means to be a vahiny varies. From a Sakalava point of view, all people regardless of their length of stay in or their sentimental ties to the Sambirano—are vahiny if they are not Sakalava by birth. They are forever, as the word *vahiny* implies, "guests" to the region. This occurs regardless of most attempts they might make to become assimilated. In general, the only exceptions to this rule are post-partum practices (which will be described later in this chapter) and, as will become clear in Part 2, tromba possession, both of which affects primarily women. From the perspectives of different categories of migrants, however, the appropriateness of the term *vahiny* varies. Temporary migrants generally consider themselves to be vahiny, since they have no intention of staying in the Sambirano. As the story of L. Botabe below illustrates, settlers may face a dilemma that arises from conflicting perspectives on their status: while they may consider themselves to be tera-tany, Sakalava continue to label them as vahiny.

ANTANDROY MIGRANTS: THE STORY OF GUARDIAN

Guardian is approximately twenty-six years old and is an Antandroy man from the south. He prefers not to use his real name but instead asks that people use a term of address which is a reference to his line of work: night watchman. His employer, a lawyer in town, does not even know what his real name is.[1] When I first met Guardian he had been living and working in the Sambirano for six years; the lawyer had been his employer for the last eight months.

When I asked Guardian why he had come to Ambanja, his reply was a typical one: "hitady harena"—"to seek [my] fortune"—in the Sambirano, where it is known that there is money (misy vola). As he explained, "It took me several months to make it here, traveling much of the way on foot. . . . it was a long trip. . . . my village is near Tulear [in the south and more than one thousand kilometers away]. In Tulear it is very beautiful, but there is no rain and no food.[2] I stopped and worked for a while in Antananarivo to earn the bush taxi fare to the north, but life was so difficult there—it was too cold, and there were thieves everwhere! One night when I was sleeping in a doorway someone stole the sandals off my feet!"

"...When I first arrived in Ambanja I sought out my brother [FaBrSo]; he worked at a local enterprise and he helped me get a job as a laborer. . . . There I cut branches from cocoa trees and cleared the underbrush. I also worked at the loading station, piling sacks of prepared cocoa on transports bound for the nearby port. . . . Eventually I saved enough money to buy several head of zebu cattle from people living in the countryside. These I fattened up and then sold to buyers in Nosy Be, where there is no local beef. Sometimes I also sold milk and beef to neighbors." (He then imitated the sound of a conch shell being blown, which I sometimes hear in my neighborhood at dawn to notify people that there is fresh beef for sale.) "After three years I was able to make a trip home; there I bought several goats which my father now tends for me. . . . I also brought my wife back to Ambanja with me."

Guardian and his wife have since had a son, who is now two years old. Although well settled, he plans only to stay as long as necessary to make his fortune, so he can then return to his ancestral land and live there when he is an old man. He now has a herd of ten zebu in Ambanja and many goats at home.

Guardian's story is typical for pastoralists from the far south, whose kin, for several generations, have come to the Sambirano to work as temporary migrants and who later return home.

THE TRAVELING MERCHANTS FROM THE HIGH PLATEAUX

Population pressures, land shortages, or natural disasters (especially from floods and cyclones) have led many from the high plateaux to migrate to the Sambirano. The people best represented in Ambanja are the Vakinankaratra, who culturally are identified by other Malagasy as Merina. They come from the region of Ambatolampy, which lies to the south of Antananarivo (for a detailed study see Keenan 1974). Many of these people are traveling merchants (mpivarotra mandeha): they buy goods in the great Zoma market, which is held on Friday in Antananarivo. (Zoma is said to be among the largest markets in the world; it is here that people come from all areas of the island to sell goods.) The traveling merchants take their newly purchased goods and go to other, less central areas to sell them, generally at significant markups. A pastor I knew in Ambanja started to do this in order to supplement the meager income from his church. After an initial loan of 100,000 fmg (approximately U.S. $75 at the time) from a kinsman of his wife, he made one trip by bush taxi to Antananarivo, bought goods there, and then returned to Ambanja to sell what he had purchased, making a profit of approximately 100 percent. After this he would send money in installments to his mother, who would buy additional goods for him and then ship them by mail to Ambanja. Within a period of only four months, he managed to raise his standard of living considerably, buying luxury food items and new furniture, changes that greatly upset his parishioners, who criticized him behind his back for being a man who "loved money" (HP: *tia vola izy*).

Many of the traveling merchants live clustered together in the heart of the old section of town, next to the bazarbe, where the majority of them sell goods on a daily basis. It is here one can always find hats, sewing and electronic supplies, watches, ready-made clothing, and cooking utensils. One kingroup I knew had started out as traveling merchants and later set up a small factory making aluminum pots, pans, and spoons by melting down scrap aluminum (figure 4.1).

ROLAND'S COOKWARE FACTORY

Roland first came to Ambanja in 1981 as a traveling merchant, selling aluminum cookware to people throughout the Sambirano. When he arrived here he had no kin (*havana*) but made friends locally among Betsileo, Merina, and Vakinankaratra from his region. He has been married since 1979 to

Nadine, who came to Ambanja to join him with three of their four children in 1987. Their oldest child lives with Nadine's mother's sister so that she can go to school in Ambatolampy.

Today Roland runs a thriving business in Ambanja with the help of eight adult kin. When I first visited their settlement, I was awestruck by the size of the operation. This group rents two buildings made of corrugated tin which rest on concrete foundations. The first has two rooms (one bedroom and one workroom) which they rent for 6,000 fmg per month. The second has three bedrooms, costing 5,000 fmg per month. Although the rents they pay are high by Ambanja standards, the group turns a good profit. They buy their aluminum by the kilo from a nearby village that specializes in collecting salvage metals. On average they make about thirty pots and three hundred spoons a day, although the rate at which they sell them varies greatly according to the season. The leanest months are December through February, when they sell perhaps thirty pots a week. The peak time is the coffee season in June and July, when people have more money. At this time they make as many as fifty pots a day (pots cost 1,500 to 6,000 fmg, spoons go for 300 fmg). Roland pays each worker 40,000 fmg per month, which is more than the salary paid to a junior high school teacher (who has a high school education) or a full-time manual laborer at one of the enterprises.[3] Recently they have also built a pig shed, so that they can eat pork. (Highland peoples love to eat pork but cannot buy it in the Sambirano because pigs are fady for Sakalava and Muslims. As a result, Betsileo and Merina must go elsewhere to buy it; many make a point of buying pork sausages when they are in Diégo.) Their pig shed is a source of tension because many of their neighbors are Sakalava and Muslim. Their landlord, who is Sakalava, has permitted them to build the shed there.

I asked Roland how he had started his factory. "In 1985 I went back to Ambatolampy and persuaded several of my [male cognatic and agnatic] kin to join me here in Ambanja. I wanted them to come with me to help set up a shop for making aluminum cookware. . . . .You see, at the time, there was no one producing these items locally. The merchants who sold these goods were buying them elsewhere and then charging a lot of money for them. . . . Eventually François and Clarence joined me [in 1985]: They were followed by Georges and Louis Sr. [1986], and Louis Jr., Paul, and Narda, along with Nadine and three of our children [1987]."

Although a number of these men are married, Nadine remains the only adult female of the group; all other married men have left their wives back in Ambatolampy. Since the majority are men, and a number of them are single, I asked if they go out with local women and, if so, what type (HP: foko/karazana). To this Clarence replied, "We usually go out with women from Antananarivo." When I asked why not Sakalava, he said, "Oh, they do not speak the same dialect as we do" and then added, with a smile, "and they don't eat pork" (fady kisoa; SAK: fady komankory).

Roland and his kin today run one of the most profitable small businesses in Ambanja. They may stay a decade or more, yet their actions

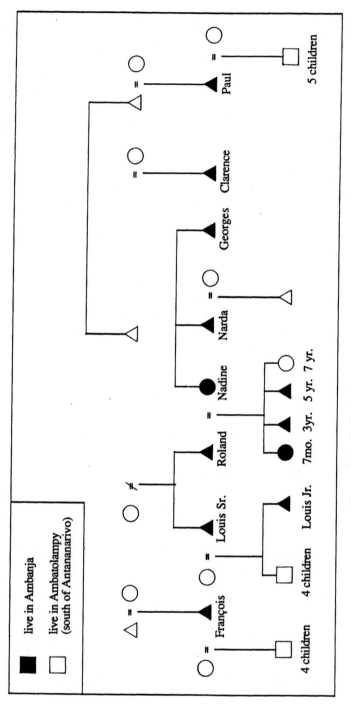

Figure 4.1. Roland and His Kin: The Cookware Factory.

reveal a decision to remain distinct from Sakalava. Although their clientele are of all backgrounds and they live in a Sakalava neighborhood, their closest social ties are with other highland people. Nearly all members of this group pray, for example, at a local Protestant church where the majority of parishoners are Merina and Betsileo. Since they are Merina, it is difficult, if not impossible, for them to become integrated into the local Sakalava community. Their choice to raise pigs in town is an obvious transgression of local Sakalava fady, one that asserts their separateness. Their marriage (and dating) patterns also reveal that they are ethnically isolated from other groups.

THE ANTAISAKA HANDCART TEAM

As stated before, in Madagascar, ethnicity is often paired with economic specialization, providing stereotypes for different groups. The Antaimoro, Antaisaka, and others from the southeast, for example, are well-known for their strength. Many of them work as pullers of handcarts called posy-posy (FR: *pousse-pousse*, lit. "push-push" or rickshaw). These handcarts have a seat that holds two people, shaded by an awning that unfolds over the seat when needed. This is an inexpensive form of transportation used in all major coastal cities, and the majority of pullers are from the southeast coast.

> Ambanja has a team of five men who started a handcart business here a year ago. They range from twenty to twenty-six years in age and are originally from a village near Farafangana. Doda and Aimé had first worked in Diégo for fifteen months, going there by bush taxi directly from their ancestral land. There they worked for a man who owned several handcarts and who hired them as pullers and provided them with a place to sleep. Aimé had heard from customers that there were no posy-posy in the Sambirano, and so he came here to investigate. He returned to Diégo and arranged to have his own cart built, and then encouraged Doda to join him as a coworker in Ambanja (figure 4.2).
>
> Within a few months, these two men had set up a business in Ambanja and were then joined by Franz, Tiana, and Piso ("The Cat"), who are from their home village in the southeast. The five men share the small cramped space of a two room house made from traveler's palm. Here there is barely enough room for the five men to lie down at night. Each man has his own handcart, and although they do not take passengers(the town is too small for pedestrians to want to hire them) they do a lucrative business by carrying goods from one part of town to another. The largest share of activity involves delivering bottled drinks to local bars and groceries. They make anywhere from 2,500 to 10,000 fmg each day. Together they pay 1,500 fmg per month in rent for their house, which they found out about through a Tsimihety friend who works at one of the beverage distributors in town.

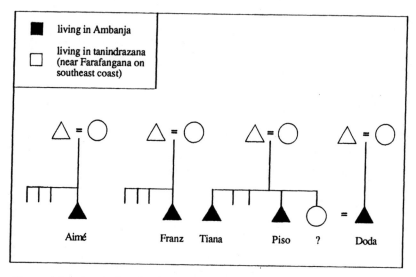

Figure 4.2.   Antaisaka Handcart (*Posy-Posy*) Team.

All of these men intend to settle in their ancestral land after working in the Sambirano for several more years. Both Piso and Tiana have managed to go home since settling in Ambanja (Piso has done so once, Tiana twice). Only Doda is married. These men say they often seek out girlfriends (*sipa*) in town, but find this to be difficult, their experiences echoing those of the Vakinankaratra men. As Franz put it, "we prefer the Sakalava women, but they don't like us! Really! They don't like men who pull handcarts, they would be ashamed to be seen with men like us." Piso then added, "I love to eat pork, and so no Sakalava woman will have me." They all hope to get married, but prefer to settle with women back home, finding them to be more serious about their commitments to marriage.

These men are not unusual for many young temporary migrants. They have come to the Sambirano to make a living and earn savings and then return home, where their sentimental ties lie. Although they may attempt to socialize with local Sakalava—especially in reference to sexual liaisons with young women—they remain outsiders and look forward to later establishing more long-lasting relationships back home with women of the same ethnic background.

THE BOTABES

Laurence Botabe is fifty years old and is the patriarch of one of the largest corporate kin groups in Ambanja. Twenty-three kin members live in one compound, and another nineteen live close by in other parts of Ambanja or the Sambirano (figure 4.3). Laurence has been married twice (his first wife

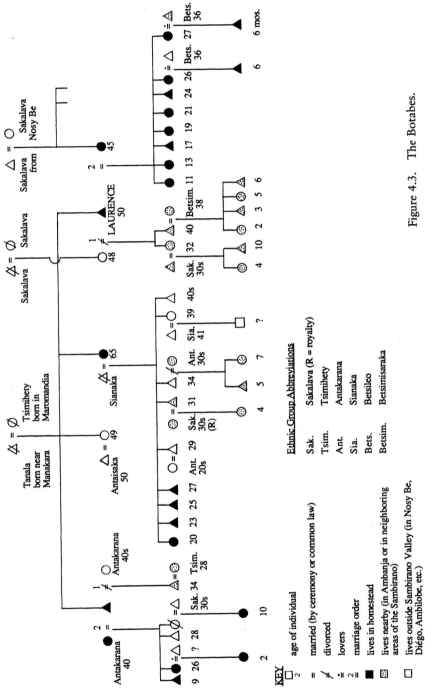

Figure 4.3. The Botabes.

KEY

□ 2	age of individual
=	married (by ceremony or common law)
≠	divorced
∴	lovers
2 2	marriage order
■	lives in homestead
▦	lives nearby (in Ambanja or in neighboring areas of the Sambirano)
□	lives outside Sambirano Valley (in Nosy Be, Diégo, Ambilobe, etc.)

Ethnic Group Abbreviations

Sak.	Sakalava (R = royalty)		
Tsim.	Tsimihety		
Ant.	Antakarana		
Sia.	Sianaka		
Bets.	Betsileo		
Betsim.	Betsimisaraka		

died ten years ago), both times to Sakalava women. He and his siblings conjointly own land in town which includes five houses where they live with their respective wives, children, and grandchildren. The land they own was originally purchased by their father, a Tanala man from the southeast who came to the Sambirano more than half a century ago to work for what were then sugarcane plantations. Their father married a local Tsimihety woman who had come to Ambanja with kin from Maromandia (ninety-six kilometers south of Ambanja). When their father died, Laurence and his siblings decided to occupy the homestead together rather than split up the land, and it is Laurence and his brother who manage it now. Originally there were three houses, but they have since built a fourth structure that serves as a kitchen and dining room. Together they also purchased a two-room building across the street where their widowed sister now lives. Several of the teenage boys sleep in the room next door.

All older kin group members living in the compound work for wages, unless they are students. Laurence holds the salaries of his children in a safe place (and thus maintains control over how they spend their cash). The economic activities of the household's members are diverse and generally quite profitable. This kin group also owns collectively several hectares of land in the countryside, where they grow enough rice to feed the entire homestead for eight months out of the year. The Botabes live simply yet comfortably, and they have enough capital to enable them to send the majority of children to the private Catholic school in town(they are Catholic and all children have been baptized). Laurence, who is in his late fifties, recently retired as a truck driver for a local enterprise. He now helps his wife run several businesses out of their home. Both travel into the countryside to purchase goods that they sell out of their compound, Laurence buying supplies for building houses of ravinala palm, and his wife charcoal from nearby foresters. One daughter is a seamstress and another is a typist for a local lawyer. One son, in addition to being a high school student, works for the local radio station during his vacations, playing songs that are popular in the discos and at morengy boxing matches.

The Botabes are well-rooted in the community, especially in terms of their ties to those active in the local political machinery. Laurence knows many powerful people at the enterprises through the job he has held for much of his life. Having married Sakalava women, Laurence also has ties to the Bemazava royalty, since his second wife's sister married a member of the royal family. His brother, who was recently elected as the neighborhood president, is responsible for taking census information and serving as a local mediator for disputes.

Unlike Guardian, Roland and his kin, and the members of the handcart team, Laurence considers himself to be tera-tany, since he was born and raised in the Sambirano, owns land, and has married Sakalava women. Nevertheless, townspeople (especially Sakalava) insist that the Botabes are vahiny, because the older male members of this kin group are considered to be Tanala by birth, and this affects subsequent off-spring as well. (Many townspeople are also under the mistaken impression that he is Antaimoro because his father was from the southeast.) This categorization as vahiny becomes blurred, however, as one moves down through the generations. Laurence's children, having been raised by Sakalava mothers, consider themselves to be Sakalava and are so regarded by many other Sakalava, rather than being Tanala like their father. For example, the son who works for the radio station is becoming famous throughout the Sambirano. He is an object of great local pride since he prefers to play salegy music with lyrics that refer to local events and items that are typically Sakalava. Postpartum practices, which will be discussed below, also help to endow the offspring of unions between Sakalava and non-Sakalava with Sakalava qualities.

MME RAZAFY, MERINA SCHOOLTEACHER

Mme Razafy is twenty-eight. She was born of Merina parents and was raised in Morondava on the southwest coast. After completing high school she went to Antananarivo to study at the university, where she received her degree in education. It is here where she met her husband, who is Merina and from Antananarivo.

In Madagascar, schoolteachers are government employees and must apply to the state for job placement. Jobs are very scarce, and so when she and her husband received assignments in towns that were more than three hundred kilometers apart, they felt compelled to accept them, living separately and visiting each other only during school vacations (this was in 1982). She described the experience as follows: "The second year was especially difficult. I became pregnant and had a child. It was then that I decided to take a leave of absence for a year and join my husband . . . and I worked at home as a seamstress to earn more money."

"Three years ago we finally managed to acquire jobs together in Ambanja where I was originally stationed. . . . Once we were both working again I tried to hire a maid to help me, but I had little success. . . . I went through a series of local women, none of whom worked out: several did not show up for work, one left town suddenly with a lover bound for Nosy Be. . . . Another made me so angry! She pinched the baby all the time. . . . Then my [mother's sister], who lives in Antananarivo, eventually sent me a maid . . . This was a young Merina woman named Fanja [age twenty-one]. . . . Fanja has been living with us for two years now ." I later asked Fanja how she felt about living in Ambanja, to which she replied, "tamana, tamana be aho! [I am very content here]." When I asked why, she replied, "At home there are too many people, all of them hungry. Here in Ambanja there is work and food, and I have enough money to buy some nice clothes, too."

In contrast to Fanja, Mme Razafy and her husband hope to be able to leave Ambanja in the next few years. "It is difficult to teach in the school

here, because the students are hostile toward us because we are Merina.[4]. . .
The students are not very motivated, either; they are more concerned with
matters of love and money, not schoolwork. . . . We would like to resettle
in Antananarivo, but it is very difficult to find a teaching post there." Mme
Razafy, unlike Fanja, is not content: "I am homesick [ngaoma] for my mother
and sisters because they live far away in Antananarivo."

"TE HO MODY": I WANT TO GO HOME

There are two concepts that are especially important for migrants when
they are expressing their sentimental ties: these are tamana (contentment) and ngaoma (homesickness); among people who express the latter, they also use the expression *te ho mody* (the desire to return/go
home). It is through these constructs that inhabitants of Ambanja articulate their experiences in this town. They are used deliberately either as
statements of one's personal feelings, or as questions put to others. As
a foreigner, I was asked almost daily whether I was tamana or ngoama.

Because of the availability of work and the quality of the soil in the
Sambirano, physical survival is rarely a problem. It is often said that in
this region of Madagascar no one is really poor and rarely do people
go hungry. Although I have seen sick and emaciated individuals—especially children of migrants with large families—this is a rare sight.
Ambanja and other northern towns are distinct in this way from much
of the rest of Madagascar, where many people are starving and where
the streets are full of beggars, especially children and women. Antananarivo has a large population of people living on the street who have
lost their houses, crops, or cattle to droughts and cyclones. These are
the *katramy* (from the French *quatre-murs*, called this because they are
people who are without "four walls"). In Ambanja, this term is not
known. Throughout 1987 there were only three people who begged on
a regular basis, two of whom were considered to be mad by townspeople. My point here is that it is not simply economic problems that make
life difficult for Ambanja's migrants, but social and cultural ones, all of
which are tied to the tensions and factionalism that operate locally and
on a daily basis. Ngaoma (homesickness) and tamana (contentment) are
sentiments that help differentiate between the experiences of temporary
migrants and settlers.

Tamana is a term that is used by those who feel they belong in Ambanja. These in general are the tera-tany and permanent migrants or
settlers. For example, people who would use these terms are Laurence
Botabe and his kin and Mme Razafy's maid, Fanja, who has no desire
to return home. For vahiny, however, tamana is not devoid of tension,

for in order for a migrant to feel tamana in the new place of residence, it means that he or she has left behind (and forgotten) other kin who remain in the original ancestral land. To neglect kin, ancestors, and ancestral land is a trying experience for any Malagasy. It is rare that a migrant feels no uneasiness about this. One must wait for the offspring who, born locally, are zanaka Sambirano, or "children of the Sambirano," before sentimental ties to the original ancestral land are weakened or altogether broken. Temporary migrants are more likely to say they are ngaoma. It is they who feel they do not belong and who stay in the Sambirano Valley for economic—and not sentimental—reasons. Examples include Mme Razafy and the Antaisaka handcart team.

There are also other individuals who fall somewhere in between these two extremes. Examples include Guardian, especially after he was joined by his wife and after he had accumulated enough capital to invest in several heads of cattle, and Roland, who has been joined by kin and who runs a successful business in Ambanja. Neither, however, intends to settle permanently. On a daily basis they say they are content (as Guardian says with a Sakalava inflection: "Oh, the cattle are so big and fat here!" [bodabe ny omby an-Ambanja é!]), yet they still miss things and people more familiar to them and they look forward to the day they can return to their respective ancestral lands. Both Guardian and Roland have married women from their own regions and tend to associate with peoples of similar ethnic backgrounds.

Another expression that distinguishes the content from the malcontent is tsy malala fomba (lit. "don't know how to do the customs"). This expression implies that an individual has coarse manners and was ill-raised. It is generally only used to describe children when they commit faux pas; when applied to adults it is an extremely rude thing to say. In the context of interactions between vahiny and tera-tany, it takes on a special character, and it is used by people of one background to describe the customs of others. Sakalava sometimes use it when they joke about vahiny ways of doing things. More often, it is used by migrants (especially those from the high plateaux) when they reflect on Sakalava customs. In reflecting back to the categories of temporary migrants and settlers, it is more common to hear this expression voiced by temporary migrants to express their disgust for Sakalava customs. Settlers are less critical of Sakalava, since typically they choose to be assimilated as or at least be accepted by Sakalava.

The question of where the ancestral land lies for migrants is a complicated one. Even settlers sometimes (especially among those of the first generation) prefer to be buried in the area where they were born, and they or their kin will spend enormous amounts of money so that the body of a deceased member may be transported to a family tomb located in the original ancestral land. For example, the parents of the Betsileo described earlier came to the Sambirano more than fifty years ago, yet they plan to be placed in a tomb in the southern plateau region near Fianarantsoa. Their son, however, is married to a local woman who is Indian métisse. Since it is fady for a non-Betsileo to be placed in his parents' tomb, he plans to be entombed locally: in this way his body can lie with his wife's. He has already built a tomb in the Sambirano for this purpose. Among the temporary migrants, only Antandroy as a group exhibit a pattern of being buried locally, because, as they explain, the cost for transporting a body more than one thousand kilometers to the southern end of this island is prohibitively high.

PATTERNS OF ASSOCIATION AND MEANS FOR INCORPORATION

The above case studies reveal how migrants who have recently arrived in Ambanja seek the assistance of kin and, sometimes, friends from their ancestral lands. There are also a number of institutions that help them to meet each other and to become involved with settlers and tera-tany. As the African literature illustrates, voluntary organizations and other forms of association are important for helping migrants to become integrated (and to be successful) in urban communties (see Cohen 1969; Epstein 1958; Hellmann 1948; Hopkins 1972; Little 1957, 1962; Mayer 1971; Meillassoux 1968; Powdermaker 1962). In Ambanja such institutions exist and they may be formal or informal. Some enable migrants to maintain ties with people of similar ethnic backgrounds, and others facilitate their assimilation into the local Sakalava community. Although tromba possession primarily enables women to become active in local Sakalava power structures, there are other local institutions that are more readily available to men and women of a variety of ethnic backgrounds. These include churches, mutual aid societies, political organizations, and sports. The following examples briefly illustrate the most common experiences.[5]

PRESERVING ETHNIC DISTINCTIONS: MUTUAL AID ASSOCIATIONS

At one extreme are ethnically based, mutual aid societies that are designed to help individual members in times of need. Because of the composition of their membership, they also help to maintain ethnic factionalism in the town, or, as one Betsileo friend put it, "they only promote regionalism and racism, problems which are already too much a part of life in Madagascar." A number of such organizations exist in Ambanja, and most of these are registered with the city government. These include an association for people of the Mahavavy (an area to the north of Ambanja, near Ambilobe, which is inhabited by Sakalava and Antakarana); another for the Sakalava of the Sambirano; one for migrants from Vohemar and other nearby towns on the northeast coast (inhabited by Antakarana and Betsimisaraka); a neighborhood association where the majority of the inhabitants of that section of town are Antandroy; and three Tsimihety associations. During my stay in 1987, a Betsileo association was also being formed. There are certainly other, nonregistered groups. The members of these associations come from a wide variety of economic and educational backgrounds. Each pays dues regularly which are used by the association to assist members when they are sick or, should they die, to help transport their bodies back to their ancestral land.

POLYCULTURAL GROUPS

The middle ground is occupied by an assortment of formal groups and organizations as well as informal associations that tend to be polycultural in their makeup. These include groups that are based on ties developed at the workplace, local churches and mosques, different subgroups of the national party which exist for youth, workers, and specific neighborhoods, and, among men especially, soccer and other athletic teams. Studies from the colonial period throughout Africa reveal that such organizations may operate not only as social clubs but as forces for political organizing (see, for example, Epstein 1958 and Powdermaker 1962). In Ambanja, church organizations provide potentially powerful lobbying groups for local social causes, such as water, sewage and garbage control. The Alliance Française is not only a popular gathering place in the evenings for the local educated elite, but it also exerts pressure from time to time on educational policies in local schools. Athletic clubs are rallying groups for men during their off hours. One form of athletic activity which has become highly suspect in Madagascar is kung fu and other forms of martial arts, since the government fears their potential military strength.

Because of the great tension between tera-tany and vahiny, it is extremely difficult for outsiders to become insiders and, in turn, to become involved in Sakalava power structures. Polycultural groups provide a few ways in which migrants may gain access to politically powerful positions. This is difficult, however, and possibilities differ for men and women. Men, for example, try to become involved in local politics and seek to be elected to the town or county government, but so far only Tsimihety have managed to do this. Civil service appointments, which are made through Antananarivo, present another possibility, and in this context many vahiny (especially Betsileo and Merina) have been appointed to work in the Sambirano as teachers, agricultural extension agents, and directors of the local enterprises. The managers of the enterprises occupy very powerful positions, especially in relation to the national and local economy. Since they tend to be wealthy they are also able to buy favors and manipulate the outcome of decisions in the local court. Nevertheless, they are very unpopular because of their ethnic backgrounds. As a result, recently the staff in the central offices in Antananarivo have attempted to replace them with others whose backgrounds are more acceptable to Sakalava. For example, one director, who has become very popular in the area, is a métis whose background includes French, Sakalava, and Betsileo heritage. He has married a local Sakalava woman and their children were born and raised in the Sambirano. In addition, they live in the heart of town, rather than on company grounds fifteen kilometers away, as is the case for several other local directors. Because he maintains a favorable reputation among vahiny and tera-tany alike, each morning people confronted with financial or other problems line up outside his door. Other vahiny who fail to acquire such positions of power may have access to these individuals through their membership in polycultural associations.

CHANGES TO SAKALAVA SOCIAL STRUCTURE

To understand how Sakalava identity is defined and how their authority is asserted, it is important to outline briefly recent structural shifts that have occurred. The most important distinction that must be made is that between commoner and royalty. Sakalava royal descent is based on truncated patrilineages that are traced primarily through past rulers. These lineages are still preserved and recorded with care by living royalty. Nevertheless, the undermining of royal authority by the French has led to a shift in focus among commoners from living to dead rulers.[6]

Today the names and deeds of dead rulers are preserved and celebrated primarily within the context of tromba lineages (see Part 2).

Prior to French conquest, Sakalava commoners defined and organized themselves in reference to their royalty. Commoners were grouped into small village-based clans (firazaña).[7] These political entities were organized hierarchically in reference to specific duties or work that each was expected to perform periodically for royalty (fanompoaña; asam-panja-kaña) (see the discussion on work in chapter 2). Clan membership was defined in reference to shared territory, ancestors, and tombs. In addition, there were the Sambarivo, royal slaves of diverse (often non-Malagasy) origins. Although they occupied the lowest rank, the Sambarivo were considered to be closest to royalty, since they were (and still are) responsible for tending to living royalty and the royal tombs. Sambarivo, however, as slaves, had no ancestors (see Feeley-Harnik 1991b). To quote Feeley-Harnik, "'clans' seem to be seen as having a lineage-like cohesiveness that is not born[e] out by actual relations on the ground . . . firazaña [are] very much a product of local political relations" (Feeley-Harnik, written personal communication). In addition, Baré, in his study of the Bemihisatra-Sakalava of Nosy Be, also stresses that clan membership was sentimentally determined by the "cycle de développement" (1980: 193):[8] clan identity often hinged on where one had spent much of his or her life. In general these clans appear to have been bilaterally conceived and exogamous (although endogamous unions did occur following the performance of specific rituals that lifted marriage bans or fady). Since clans were ranked, marriages between particular clans were deemed to be the most appropriate unions.

In addition to clans, a second form of affiliation was the kindred (tariky), which was composed of matrikin and patrikin. Residence usually determined how one conceived of one's tariky. Different clans showed different biases toward patrikin vs. matrikin, with sentimental ties affected by residence patterns determined by the political order. Virilocality was the norm, but Sambarivo women, for example, could not leave their native villages. Similarly, members of high status groups tended to be uxorilocal. Often choice of residence after marriage was determined by the advantages and disadvantages perceived by cognates and their offspring. Baré cites an example of a man whose father settled uxorilocally, and so Baré's informant was therefore raised among his mother's kin. As an adult he had rights in his father's village, but he preferred to remain where he had been raised. In order to be accepted as a full member of his mother's kin group, he had undergone a series of ceremonies. As he told Baré: "je ne suis pas en bonne position ici (*tsy tamana*)" (Baré 1980: 92; note that this is the same expression used by migrants in Ambanja to mean they are "not content").

The third organizing principle was the distinction made between the "children of men" (*zanakan'lahy*) and the "children of women" (*zanakan'vavy*), which distinguished paternal and maternal kin. In conjunction with this was the concept of uterine kin, or "children of the same belly" (*kibo araiky*) who shared their mother's ancestors. These principles set restrictions on marriages between the children of sisters and excluded foster or adopted children from full participation in their adopting clan's royal work.

In the Sambirano, clan membership is no longer a significant organizing principle. Clans have virtually vanished, save for the Sambarivo, who still live separately in special villages in the Sambirano Valley and on Nosy Faly, where they guard the royal tombs. Today few Sakalava are aware of these categories and, if they are, rarely do they know from what group their own ancestors came. Although two young adult informants stated with pride that their grandmothers had been "servants to the royalty" (*mpiasam-panjakaña*), they did not know what their duties had been. A major change that has occurred is the use of broader terms to define identity. Whereas two or three generations ago clan names served as markers for personal identity, today people of the Sambirano resort to using broader categories to define themselves as tera-tany, stating that they are Bemazava or, more generally, Sakalava. This practice stands out in contrast to the Sakalava of the Analalava region, for example, where so broad a term as "Sakalava" is rarely used by the indigenous people to label themselves (Feeley-Harnik, personal communication). Today it is the category of kindred or tariky that is important. As mentioned above, the kinship system of commoners is bilateral.

Sakalava kinship terminology is fairly complex (figure 4.4). Kin terms vary according to the sex and sometimes with the relative age of the speaker. Labels for siblings are as follows: for a male ego, brother is *rahalahy*, sister is *anabavy;* for female ego, brother is *anadahy*, and sister is *rahavavy*. The term used to address older siblings (male or female ego) is *zoky* and for younger siblings it is *zandry*. Structurally, parallel and cross-cousins are regarded as being the equivalent of siblings. The siblings of ego's parents are differentiated from one another, again according to the sex of ego. Thus, for either a male or female ego, on the father's side: *baba* (father), *bababe* ("big father," or father's older brother), *babakely* ("little father," or father's younger brother), and *angovavy* (FaSi). On the mother's side: *nindry/Mama* (mother), *nindrihely/mamahely* ("little mother," mother's younger sister), *nindrihely/mamabe* ("big mother," mother's older sister), and *zama* (MoBr). Spouse's siblings are *rañao*, and in turn their spouses are structurally regarded as siblings. In the past, there was a joking relationship between agnates of opposite sex (for female ego: *rokilahy*, for male ego: *rokivavy*). A special term, *asidy*, is used instead of *zanaka* for the children of ego's opposite sex sibling.

As figures 4.4 and 4.5 show, changes have occurred in kinship terminology and they are significant for several reasons. First, they reflect the effects of Sakalava contact with French and other peoples. Various indigenous terms (and, thus, structural concepts) have been replaced with French ones. Sakalava now use the terms *mama(n)*, *papa*, and *tonton*. Sakalava younger than thirty or so are unfamiliar with the terms that designate joking relationships with agnates (*rokilahy* and *rokivavy*). Also the term *asidy*, for sibling's children, is used less frequently. Finally, Sakalava kin terms (and the shifts that have occurred in the movement from village to town) are important in the context of tromba possession (this will be discussed in chapter 7). To illustrate these changes, figure 4.4 provides the older ("village") kinship terms, while the second set in figure 4.5 corresponds to those used in town.

These structural changes—where clan membership and older (village) kinship terms have been forgotten—illustrate an important shift in how Sakalava conceive of their collective identity. Whereas in the past clan membership served to distinguish different groups of Sakalava from each other, today other categories operate to distinguish Sakalava from non-Sakalava. The broadest of these are tera-tany and vahiny. The use of Sakalava kin terms also serves as a marker for Sakalava identity or affiliation: terms such as angovavy and zama are distinctly Sakalava. Ironically, so are maman, papa, and tonton, since Sakalava are unusual among Malagasy speakers in reference to the number of French terms they have incorporated into their vocabularies (Dalmond, n.d.).[9] When vahiny use French-derived Sakalava kinship terms they do so to signal their affiliation with the tera-tany, since kinship terms vary somewhat as one moves from one region of Madagascar to another. Sakalava kinship terms are also very important in the context of tromba, where they are operational in establishing links of fictive kinship among the living and between the living and the dead (chapter 7).

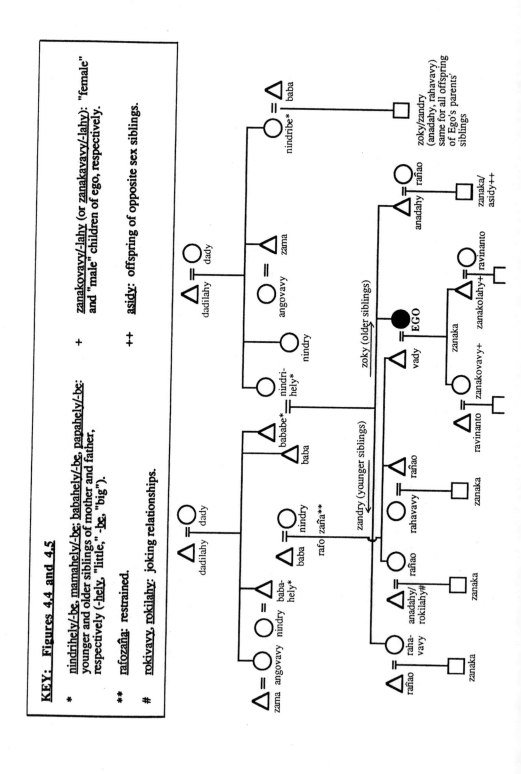

KEY: Figures 4.4 and 4.5

nindrihely/-be, mamahely/-be, babahely/-be, papahely/-be: younger and older siblings of mother and father, respectively (-hely, "little", -be, "big").

zanakovavy/-lahy (or **zanakavavy/-lahy**): "female" and "male" children of ego, respectively.

* **nindrihely/-be, mamahely/-be**

+ **asidy:** offspring of opposite sex siblings.

** **rafozaña:** restrained.

++

\# **rokivavy, rokilahy:** joking relationships.

zoky/zandry (anadahy, rahavavy) same for all offspring of Ego's parents' siblings

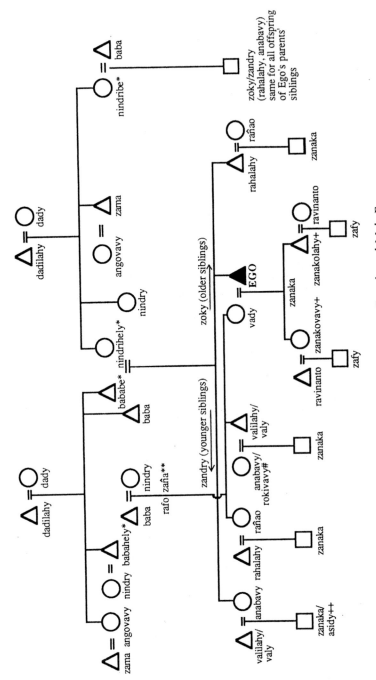

Figure 4.4. Village Kinship Terms: Female and Male Egos.

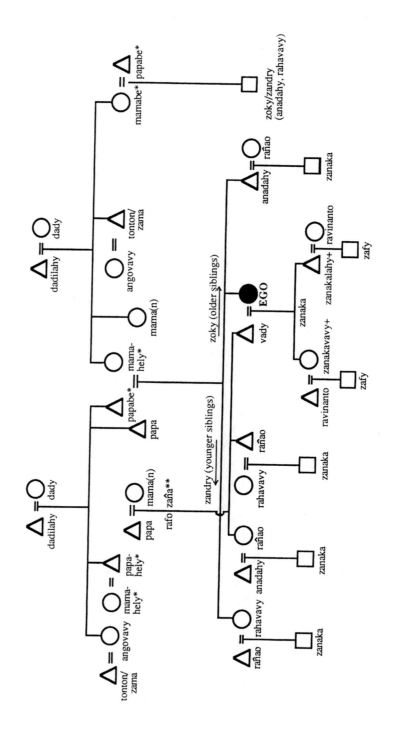

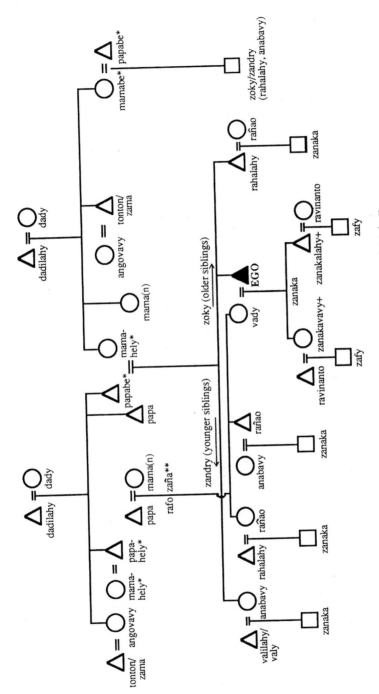

Figure 4.5. Town Kinship Terms: Female and Male Egos.

MARRIAGE ACROSS ETHNIC LINES

At first glance marriage would seem to offer vahiny an easy means for their integration and acceptance by tera-tany, but Sakalava ideas about paternity (which will be described in more detail below) and ethnicity make this difficult. Sakalava attitudes towards non-Sakalava vary, and so it is much easier for Antakarana and Tsimihety to form unions with Sakalava than it is for groups from the south or high plateaux (it is almost impossible for Merina). The experiences of the men of Roland's factory and those of the Antaisaka handcart team provide examples of this.

Nevertheless, the rate of ethnic exogamy is high in Ambanja when compared to other regions of Madagascar. Unions between Sakalava and non-Sakalava have led to a greater blurring of ethnic boundaries, so that defining what it means to be Sakalava is becoming increasingly problematic. As a result, tracing lines of descent and reckoning ethnic affiliation in such unions, local informants now resort to rules that are legal or what I will refer to as *bureaucratic* in nature. Today, by national, semilegal ways of reckoning, the father's ethnic identity determines the "official" ethnic label to be used for offspring. This breaks down with each subsequent generation. The case of the Botabes provides an example of this: Laurence is considered to be a vahiny even though he was born and raised in the Sambirano, owns land, and has consecutively been married to two Sakalava women. Officially his children are Tanala like him and his father. By less formal rules, however, his children are generally accepted as tera-tany (they are referred to as being Sakalava), since they have grown up among Sakalava and they were raised by Sakalava mothers. Culturally (and physically) they dress, act, and speak like Sakalava, and so their status as tera-tany is rarely questioned. In other words, it is the children—or, in the case of the Botabes, the grand-children—of migrants who may be considered to be tera-tany. Thus, marriage unions between Sakalava and non-Sakalava do not affect the ethnic identities of spouses but, rather, only potentially those of their offspring.

Some settler families have developed creative measures for determining an individual's kin group in cases where relatives are of different ethnic backgrounds. Again, the Botabes provide an apt example. In this kin group, all female children are given a surname derived from the names of their mother's female kin, and male children carry a different surname that they share with a male member on their father's side. This is a creative embellishment on a bureaucratically defined assumption, since many Malagasy people do not have surnames. As a result of this system of naming, female children tend to be sentimentally tied to their mother's Sakalava kin, but male children are closer to their father's Tanala kin. This system also determines patterns of inheritance among the Botabes, so that female offspring inherit from tera-tany, and male from vahiny.

Sakalava marriage as an institution has also been affected by the changes that have occurred in response to colonial presence. These changes in turn further complicate the manner in which the affiliation of offspring is determined in any generation. In precolonial and early colonial times, Sakalava households were defined by monogamous or polygynous unions, their offspring, and extended kin. A marriage ceremony (fehim-badiaña, Baré 1980: 212) was performed to legitimate the union, but now this ceremony is rarely undertaken. Laurence Botabe, for example, performed such a ceremony with his first wife, but not with his second. Among his children, only one daughter has done so. Her other married siblings went either to City Hall or the Catholic church to confirm their unions. In the urban setting in particular, indigenous marriage ceremonies have been uncommon for the past two generations. Although marriages that are sanctioned either by institutionalized religion (Catholic, Islamic, Protestant) or by City Hall do occur, they are infrequent. Unions are extremely fragile. By the time they have reached their forties, most adults in Ambanja have been involved in a series of unions, each of which has lasted only a few years.

Linguistic analysis reveals that this abandonment of marriage ceremonies has become institutionalized. The term vady is used in Ambanja (and neighboring areas of northern Madagascar) to refer to an individual's primary partner, be they a spouse (through a union confirmed through a ceremony) or a lover (common-law spouse).[10] When Bemazava-Sakalava of Ambanja are compared to Malagasy in other parts of Madagascar, what is striking is that elsewhere the term vady is usually used only to refer to unions confirmed through a ceremony. Baré also notes this, saying the term has become more popular among the young generations of the Bemihisatra of Nosy Be, but he stresses that "adultery" or relationships outside of marriage (vamba) were common in earlier generations as well. Bemazava informants report that unions of their grandparents' and older generations lasted much longer: although several unions may have occurred in a lifetime, the turnover was much less frequent. Interviews with elders on their marriage histories confirm this. Feeley-Harnik (1991b: 200ff) also describes how, for the Bemihisatra of the Analalava region, the search for a compatible partner (vady; *namana*: "friend") is an important yet difficult quest; the same is true in Ambanja. As will become clear in chapter 8, tromba mediums specialize in helping clients solve problems associated with romance and marriage.

Today, many children of the Sambirano are the offspring of such tenuous unions. Some remain with their mothers, although the majority are raised by their mothers' kin (typically by their maternal grandmother) while their mother lives and works elsewhere, sending remittances back to her mother. In cases where the father of the children is absent (and, perhaps, his identity not known by others), children are considered to be culturally the same as their mother and structurally they are considered members of their mother's kin group. Thus children of a Sakalava mother and an absent non-Sakalava father will be considered to be tera-tany. There is also a postpartum practice that is distinctly Sakalava, one that helps to incorporate non-Sakalava women and their offspring into the Sakalava community.

POST-PARTUM PRACTICES AS A FORM OF RITUAL INCORPORATION

Determining the ethnic affiliation of a child who is born of a mixed union between a Sakalava and a non-Sakalava parent can be problematic. By the bureaucratic rule of reckoning, as mentioned above, the child is Sakalava only if his or her father is. In the past, the identity of the mother often was important for determining clan affiliation among the Sakalava. Also, uterine siblings or "the children of women" (zanakan' vavy) had special privileges in traditonal Sakalava society that were not extended to adopted children. These categories still operate in ritual contexts, where zanakan' vavy and zanakan' lahy ("children of men") must both be present and participate if a cermony is to be performed properly. Although clan affilation is no longer important, uterine ties are operative. For example, today the responsibility for raising children of temporary mixed unions usually falls with the mother's kin, as mentioned above. Also, postpartum practices that are distinctly Sakalava help to determine the ethnic identity of offspring of mixed unions. Through such practices non-Sakalava women who bear children by Sakalava men may temporarily and symbolically become Sakalava.

All Malagasy but northern Sakalava are said to be "hot" or *mifana*

(SAK; HP: *mafana*) in reference to their postpartum practices.[11] During a specified period (typically six weeks or forty days), a woman with a newborn child is expected to take special precautions to keep herself and her infant warm, so that she will heal quickly and so that her infant will grow strong and remain healthy. Following labor, the umbilical cord and afterbirth are put in a warm place to ensure the protection of the child. The mother must also bathe several times a day with hot water and eat heated food. Some Malagasy place hot coals under the mother's bed to keep her warm (see Hart et al. 1965 for descriptions of similar practices of "mother roasting" in southeast Asia). Among northern Sakalava, postpartum practices are very much the same as that of other Malagasy, with one important difference: they alone are *ranginalo*, observing a postpartum categorization that is "cold" rather than "hot."[12] Following ranginalo involves placing the umbilical cord in a cool place, often inside the house, and burying the placenta in a cool, shaded spot in the courtyard. The mother is expected to bathe in cool water several times a day and eat only cold or cooled food.

Marriage among peoples of similar ethnic backgrounds presents no problems as to which practice should be followed, since both parents share the same tradition. When Malagasy marry non-Malagasy, the mother must decide between doing what her own mother did and what is common among her non-Malagasy affines. In choosing one practice over the other, the mother is making a statement about where her sentiments lie, as well as about the identity of her child. I met several Chinese women married to Malagasy men who each chose to follow their husband's mother's orders. Malagasy women married to non-Malagasy men, however, tended to do whatever their mothers had done. In other words, women in mixed marriages that produced métis offspring generally follow the Malagasy custom deemed appropriate by their Malagasy kin. Most informants agree that Chinese, Comoreans, and Arabs are hot. As for Europeans, no one seemed sure, although since most Europeans prefer warm bath water to cold, they tend to be categorized as hot as well. No problems arise between most Malagasy and non-Malagasy, since the practice is basically the same.

It is in marriages between northern Sakalava and other groups where the decision regarding postpartum practices is complex. Sakalava insist that raginalo or "cold" is stronger (*mahery*) than "hot," and so in cases where one parent (mother or father) is cold, it outweighs hot. If the mother does not practice ranginalo, she runs the risk of having great harm befall her child. In general, for Sakalava, coldness (*manintsy*) is associated with health. Coolness promotes healing: this is why water and kaolin (a type of clay; SAK: *tany malandy* or "white earth," HP: *tany fotsy*), which are attributed with cool properties, are used by tromba mediums to heal patients. A Sakalava word for "sick" is *mamay*, which also means "hot." Heat (*mafana*) is associated with danger and death, principles that are the opposite to those of other Malagasy groups.[13] For the Sakalava, for example, June and July are said to have "cool" qualities, and it is during these months that royal work is performed at the tombs on Nosy Faly. When a royal person has recently died, it is said to be a "hot" time, and so no one may enter the tombs.

In interviews with thirty women of assorted backgrounds who had borne children from mixed unions, all but two said they had chosen to practice cold over hot. In both cases these women insisted that they felt more comfortable in doing what their mothers had done. One was living with her mother at the time, and they both thought it riskier to try to follow a practice with which neither one was familiar. The other woman was Sakalava and married to a man of Arab and Comorean heritage (hot). At first she practiced hot, but she fell ill. She was then instructed by her husband's mother to switch to cold, after which her health improved. As one informant put it, "If you have to make a choice, go with cold, because it is the stronger of the two." The diagrams provided in figure 4.6 illustrate how this system works.

Structurally, the choice to observe the cold over the hot practice has a number of effects. From the point of view of the male Sakalava parent, it is straightforward. Having the child's mother follow the cold practice provides him with a means to assert his paternity, since it symbolically illustrates that the child is endowed with Sakalava qualities. (The child is already recognized as such by the bureaucratic rule that stipulates that a child shares the ethnicity of its biological father.) Since the mother must use the cold system, her offspring—as well as all future generations of children—will always be considered to be cold. If the mother is Sakalava and the father is not, however, the effect is different. It serves to label the child as being partly Sakalava and endows it and its progeny with coldness, a Sakalava trait. As a result, here it works to assert the *maternal* tie to the child, regardless of the bureaucratic rule. In this way it also *distinguishes* the child from its father, since the child will be cold like its mother while the father is hot. In cases where the father has left or his identity is unknown by others, the decision made by the mother following labor will serve to identify the child as hot or cold (and ultimately as Sakalava or something else). The offspring of a woman who

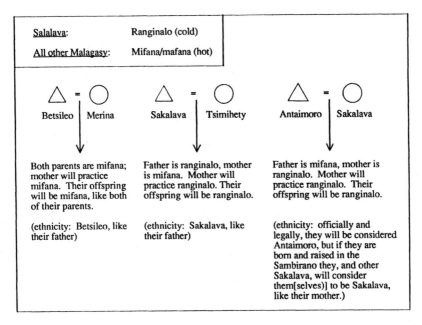

Figure 4.6.   Postpartum Practices and Ethnicity.

has performed ranginalo (cold) are viewed as having Sakalava characteristics and they, in turn, will consider themselves to be cold when they
are adults and have their own children.

Ranginalo, as a Sakalava postpartum practice, affects mothers in
ways that it does not affect fathers. In unions between Sakalava men
and non-Sakalava women, this cold system serves to incorporate women
into the community of Sakalava. Each time that a non-Sakalava woman
has a child by a Sakalava man, she must perform ranginalo. In so doing,
she participates in a Sakalava institution and generally does so in the
company and under the direct supervision of those who know how to
do it properly: other Sakalava women. Since men are not involved in
postpartum practices, it does not operate in this way for them. Instead,
it serves to exclude or distinguish non-Sakalava men from their Sakalava
spouses (and children). In essence, maternal ties to the child take precedence or they override paternity.[14]

To summarize, although the first generation of male settlers will never
be considered to be Sakalava, non-Sakalava women become incorporated as insiders following the births of any children whose fathers are
Sakalava. All offspring of mixed unions—regardless of whether it is
the mother or father who is Sakalava—will be endowed with a quality

that is distinctly Sakalava. In this way, through ranginalo, offspring are retained as Sakalava, so that Sakalava-ness is not altogether lost through the effects of polyculturalism.

As this chapter has shown, significant elements of Sakalava social structure have changed dramatically within this century, but some continue to work to define what it means to be Sakalava. In the past, various categories distinguished Sakalava royalty from commoner, and, in turn, different clans of commoners from one another. Today broader categories work to distinguish Sakalava as a whole from all other groups: Sakalava conceptions of their own ethnicity, on the one hand, coupled with migrants' participation in forms of economic specialization and voluntary organizations on the other, foster the continuation of ethnic isolation. These factors maintain the distance between adult tera-tany and vahiny. Even though marriage fails as a means for vahiny to become integrated as tera-tany, kinship is, nevertheless, the organizing principle that allows for the integration of outsiders. Postpartum practices, for example, operate in such a way as to temporarily incorporate non-Sakalava women and to permanently incorporate their offspring. As will become clear in Part 2, these same structural principles are key to understanding the significance of tromba for tera-tany and vahiny.

PART II

Spirit Possession in the Sambirano

CHAPTER V

The World of the Spirits

Tromba possession is the quintessence of Sakalava religious experience. Throughout Madagascar, ancestors and other spirits are an important aspect of everyday life, yet no form of possession is more widespread than tromba (see Estrade 1985). For the Sakalava, the spirit world is inhabited by royal and common ancestors, lost souls, nature spirits, and malicious, evil spirits. Tromba, as the spirits of dead Sakalava royalty, are the most significant and influential in terms of daily interactions that occur between the living and the dead. As Huntington has observed, the "royal ancestors belong, in one sense, to everyone" and are regarded as "the 'national ancestors' " of the Sakalava (Huntington and Metcalf 1979: 95).

Tromba as an institution provides keys for understanding Sakalava notions of the world, offering explanations and solutions for misfortune. It is also an important part of any major celebration. Tromba spirits affect the lives of both Sakalava royalty and commoner, and they are active in public and private spheres. These spirits appear in such diverse contexts as royal events, healing rituals, after the birth of a child, and during domestic disputes. Furthermore, a tromba ceremony may be viewed as an encapsulation of Sakalava experience in time and space. Tromba spirits enable Sakalava to record and interpret historical experience. They also offer ways to understand how Sakalava perceive the local geography of their ancestral land and the nature of their responses to economic development. For these reasons, one can not fully understand what it means to be Sakalava without understanding tromba.

In the past, tromba possession was a purely Sakalava institution, tying the living to the dead, and commoner to royalty. Although tromba in Ambanja continues to be a marker of Sakalava identity and tera-tany status, it has undergone radical transformations during this century. Accompanying the increased immigration of non-Sakalava to this region, there has been an explosion in the incidence of possession within the last thirty years, involving the incorporation of new tromba and other spirits and the participation of peoples of diverse ethnic backgrounds. When Malagasy speak of Ambanja, they often remark that there is a lot (*misy tromba maro*) or, perhaps, too much tromba (*laotra ny tromba!*). Today the incidence of possession in Ambanja is high when compared to other regions of Madagascar as well as neighboring areas of Sakalava territory.

Discussions of the causes of spirit possession are best argued when rooted in the internal logic of the culture in which they are found (cf. Boddy 1988: 12, who in turn cites Crapanzano 1977a: 11). The interpretation becomes flawed and misleading if it draws exclusively from Western conceptualizations of the body and mind as distinct categories, a notion that only distorts indigenous notions of possession (see also Scheper-Hughes and Lock 1987). The purpose of this chapter is to give the reader a general impression of what possession looks like and to provide an overview of the Sakalava spiritual world.

THE DYNAMICS OF TROMBA IN DAILY LIFE

Tromba are perhaps the most well-known—and best documented—of the spirits of Madagascar. The term *tromba* is sometimes used in Madagascar in a general sense to refer to any form of possession. In the strictest sense of the term, tromba are the spirits of dead Sakalava royalty (ampanjaka) whose lineages are based throughout western Madagascar.[1] The recent proliferation of spirits in Ambanja is rendering this definition of tromba increasingly problematic. Today, tromba continues to play an important part in preserving records of these royal genealogies, providing a shorthand account of the succession of royalty (most often rulers). In recent years it has also become a more flexible category so that it now includes a wide assortment of other spirits. They, like their mediums, are in a sense "strangers" to these lineages, since not all are important rulers from the past.

TROMBA IN ROYAL CONTEXTS

In the Sambirano one finds many types of tromba and other spirits. From a precolonial point of view, the key figures of the Bemazava spirit world are those that only appear in mediums on the island of Nosy Faly, in the village that guards the royal tombs (zomba, mahabo). These are the oldest and most powerful of the Bemazava ancestors, and they are often referred to as the *tromba maventibe*, or the "greatest tromba." Each of these spirits possesses only one medium, who is referred to as a saha ("valley" or "canal"). Saha live full-time at Nosy Faly (there were four living there in 1987), and their sole purpose is to serve the living royalty. Periodically, members of the royal family come to pay tribute to or consult their ancestors (cf. Baré 1980, especially chap. 6). Since it is forbidden for rulers to approach the royal tombs when they are alive, their personal counselors regularly visit the island to seek advice on issues that affect the well-being of Bemazava royalty and, more generally, tera-tany who inhabit the kingdom.[2]

Two assumptions are central to Sakalava tromba: that all spirits were royalty when they were alive, and that any member of the royal lineage may become a tromba spirit after death (this usually takes about twenty years). When a great royal tromba possesses a medium, it takes her to the tombs: in other words, she will travel to and arrive at the tombs in trance. The royal guardians (ngahy), who reside at the tombs, will test the tromba spirit to make sure it is the ancestor it claims to be. I have heard two accounts from living royalty who have been summoned to the tombs to help administer and witness an examination of a tromba. In both cases the spirit passed, since it was able to pick out personal possessions from a pile of paraphernalia presented to it by the ngahy, and it described the appearance and location of an item that was in a private area of a witness's house.

The recent proliferation of lesser spirits outside of Nosy Faly make it necessary to distinguish between different types of tromba spirits. Kent (1968) and other authors (cf. Lombard 1973 and Baré 1980) use the term *dady* to refer to the royal cult of ancestors and *tromba* to refer to other Sakalava possessing spirits. Perhaps these definitions were true in the past in Ambanja, and they are used elsewhere in Madagascar (see Lombard [1988] on the southern Sakalava of Menabe). In Ambanja, however, the medium serves as the point of reference and the means for distinguishing between these spirits. Royalty and commoner alike draw distinctions between the great tromba of Nosy Faly and other spirits who appear in town by saying that only a medium who has passed an exam (and who usually then takes up residence at the royal tombs) may be referred to as a *saha*. When speaking of other mediums one simply says that she "has a tromba" (*misy tromba*, lit. "there is a tromba"). Today the term *dady*, which means "grandparent," is a generational term used to refer to the tromba spirits of the greatest age and stature. The founding ancestor of the Bemazava, Andriantompoeni-arivo, for example, is affectionately referred to as *dadilahy* ("grand-father") by living royalty. This spirit's saha, in turn, is referred to as *dadibe* (meaning "big-" or "great-grandmother"). This is because a me-dium is structurally defined as the spouse of her spirit (see chapter 7).

Unfortunately, it is cumbersome to refer to the medium's status in order to distinguish between these two types of possession. For this reason I will use the spirit's audience (and its function) as the point of reference when comparing these two forms. Thus *royal* tromba are the most important of the Bemazava ancestral spirits that appear only at Nosy Faly, and *popular* tromba are those that possess mediums in town. Since the town of Ambanja is the focus of this study, the reader should assume that I am speaking of the *popular* spiritual realm unless spirits are referred to specifically as "royal tromba."

THE POPULARIZATION OF TROMBA

The term "popularization," as I am using it here, has several meanings. First, it refers to the shift in emphasis from royal tombs to the commu-nity of commoners. As in the past, royal spirits are central to the lives of royalty. Yet today Sakalava of common descent possess little under-standing of the old order. Only elders have any knowledge of the roles and duties their own grandparents had in relation to living and dead royalty. For most Sakalava in contemporary Ambanja, the royal tromba and their saha seem distant and only occasionally touch their lives, since they are far away on the smaller island. Instead, it is the popular tromba spirits of Ambanja which are important for commoners. The respect that commoners express for royalty is manifested in ceremonies that occur in town, involving spirits of much smaller stature than those that can be found at the royal tombs. Second, accompanying this shift from the tombs to town is the dramatic increase in the incidence of tromba possession over the last few decades. Older informants living in Am-banja report that in the 1940s and 1950s there was only a handful of mediums operating in town, possessed by the stately spirits of old royalty. These mediums assisted commoners, primarily as healers. Today tromba possession is widespread; my data collected throughout 1987 reveal that roughly 50 percent of all women are possessed. Today, tromba possession touches the lives of nearly all of this town's inhabitants, since almost everyone either knows a medium personally, has consulted a tromba spirit, or has friends or kin who have done so. A third characteristic of popularization is that it involves widespread participation of non-Sakalava female migrants in what was previously an almost exclusively Sakalava domain (the ramifications of this proliferation—generally speaking and in reference to migrants—will be discussed in greater detail in subsequent chapters, especially chapter 7).

Fourth, popularization marks an increase in the number and types of spirits that are now identified as tromba spirits. Although the majority of these new popular tromba spirits are Sakalava, tera-tany often say that Tsimihety and other groups are responsible for bringing them from the south to Ambanja. In addition, recent trends reflect the incorporation of obscure royalty and, potentially, non-royalty into the world of tromba. Many of the spirits that now appear in Ambanja are not members of the Bemazava lineage but are distant kin, coming primarily from the region near Mahajanga. The vast majority of these spirits are obscure members of the Zafin'i'mena royal lineages. Although these spirits usually can be located in the royal genealogies, they are considered to be royalty of low status, for many of them died young without having ruled or accomplished much in their lifetimes. Finally, these new tromba spirits also reflect the nature of contemporary town life in Ambanja. Whereas the stories of the greatest royal tromba are well-known and cherished, few mediums in Ambanja know the details of the lives of popular spirits. The spirits active in town are not the staid and powerful royalty of the past, instead, they are cowboys, boxers, soccer players, and prostitutes. Their life stories often echo the experiences of people who live in the urban environment of Ambanja. They have been in automobile accidents, they like to drink and dance, they frequent boxing (morengy) matches, and several have died at the hands of their lovers or rivals.

The popularization of tromba is now beginning to reveal a shift away from royal status through the incorporation of a few non-royal spirits. The most important of these are spirits who are not direct descendants of royalty, but who are affines who appear to have achieved royal status over time and through association with other tromba spirits. Others are commoners who have retained their lower status after death. For example, a number of informants hoped that friends or kin who had died in a recent ferryboat accident would one day become tromba so that they could talk to them, and there is already a young woman in Ambanja who is possessed by her twin sister who died in this accident. I also know of a spirit whose dog, named Markos, has become a tromba, and these two accompany each other at ceremonies.

Another recent trend involves the incorporation of Christian personalities into the tromba world. In Diégo, the Virgin Mary (Masina Marie) occasionally appears in mediums. In 1988 John the Baptist (St. Jean) arrived in a medium in the middle of a Catholic service. This spirit stood and began to evangelize in the style of a Protestant pastor, infuriating the officiating priest. From a Sakalava point of view, these spirits are confounding, as they defy all rules of tromba. As one of my assistants wrote recently, "I do not consider St. Jean to be a tromba; he is really just some type of *njarinintsy*" (an evil spirit; see below). These examples are important, since they reveal that tromba is not a static institution but is dynamic and evolving.

THE ORGANIZING PRINCIPLES OF TROMBA

There are several organizing principles inherent to tromba possession which are significant in both royal and popular contexts. First, tromba spirits (like all northern Sakalava royalty) are divided into two major descent groups: the Zafin'i'mena ("Grandchildren of Gold") and Zafin'i'fotsy ("Grandchildren of Silver"). (These are abbreviated versions of *Zafinbolamena* and *Zafinbolafotsy* [see Lombard 1988]). Gold (*vola mena*, or "red money") and silver (*vola fotsy*, or "white money") are symbols of Sakalava royalty, and these metals are represented by the colors red and white during tromba ceremonies and other rituals. Thus, Zafin'i'mena tromba spirits dress in red and Zafin'i'fotsy dress in white.

Each descent group can be further broken down into a collection of lineages. Each of these corresponds to a different Sakalava dynasty that has its own royal tomb. Tromba genealogies serve as truncated versions of these lineages. Within each lineage, tromba spirits can be divided into three generational groups: the oldest are the Grandparents (dadilahy; grandmothers: dady), of whom the *tromba maventibe* ("very big" or "biggest tromba") are the most powerful (and the ones that are generally only found at the royal tombs). Beneath the Grandparents are the "Children" (zanaka) and "Grandchildren" (zafy).

Since each spirit is tied to a specific royal tomb, it is also important to locate it within the context of Sakalava sacred geography. In this context, the tanindrazaña or ancestral land provides a way to refer to types of tromba spirits. Among the Zafin'i'mena, for example, there are *baka atsimo* (lit. "coming from the south") who are from the region of Mahajanga.[3] Similarly, there is a category of Zafin'i'fotsy tromba which is referred to as the *baka andrano* (lit. "coming from the water"). These are the spirits of Sakalava royalty who, in the eighteenth century, chose to commit suicide by drowning to escape serving under their Merina conquerors (cf. Feeley-Harnik 1988: 73). It is the baka atsimo and baka andrano who appear most frequently at the ceremonies in town.

Finally, since tromba were at one time living persons, their deeds and personal histories are also important, and these are often reflected in their names. It is fady to utter the given names of Sakalava royalty after they have died. As noted earlier, after death, a royal person is given a new praise name (*fitahina*). If he or she becomes a tromba spirit, this is the name the spirit will adopt. For example, the former Bemazava ruler was Tsiaraso II; his tromba name is Andriamandefitriarivo, which means literally, "the ruler who is tolerant of many." Today, many Sakalava only observe this name taboo in a loose sense. During interviews with informants I found that many would shyly refer to the most recent rulers by their living names when they would trace the royal lineages, and use the tromba names when referring to the same persons specifically in reference to spirit genealogies. Because tromba names are long, many of the better known spirits have nicknames: thus Ndramiverinarivo ("the king to whom many return"), a very well-known tromba spirit, is often referred to as either "Ndramivery" or "Zaman'i'Bao" ("Bao's Uncle").

These genealogical, generational, and geographical categories comprise the essential operational principles of tromba possession. Their importance is evident in several contexts. If one wishes to invoke a spirit, one must cite its genealogy in descending order, calling first upon the ancestors on high, the *Zanahary*. The tromba spirit must then be located within its general descent group—the Zafin'i'mena or Zafin'i'fotsy—by calling on the more important tromba spirits of this lineage, the Grandparents. One then descends through the tromba's specific lineage, and only then does one address the spirit. The spirit should be able to identify itself when it arrives, stating its genealogy (cf. Ottino 1965) by naming its classificatory Grandparent(s) and Parent(s). It should also be able to tell the story of its death. Finally, during a ceremony the order in which spirits arrive and depart reflects these descent groups and the hierarchy of the three generations. In essence, a tromba ceremony is a dramatization of the genealogical system.

THE POSSESSION EXPERIENCE

Tromba possession permeates much of everyday life in Ambanja. Large-scale ceremonies that involve a gathering of mediums (and their spirits), kin and neighbors, musicians, and clients occur frequently in this town. This is especially true during the dry months from May through September,[4] because at this time it is easiest to travel. Children are out of school on vacation, and since it overlaps with the coffee season, many adults have the cash needed to host ceremonies. Throughout the course of the year in 1987 I attended a total of nine ceremonies and knew of two dozen more; a third of all of these ceremonies occurred within earshot of my house.

Tromba ceremonies are lively dramas where the spirits of dead royalty come to life and interact with the living (cf. Firth 1967 and Lambek 1988a on possession as performance; see also V. Turner 1987, especially pp. 33–71). This they do by possessing mediums, the majority of whom are female. Tromba spirits may be aggressive and, at times, physically threatening, playful, or flirtatious. Their characteristics vary according to their age and unique personality. Tromba, unlike other Sakalava spirits (as well as many others found cross-culturally), have elaborate histories and highly developed personalities, and each spirit has its own style of dress, behavior, and body of fady, making it easy for the trained observer to identify the spirit once the medium has entered trance. Because of these attributes, when tromba spirits possess their mediums, one often forgets that they are not actual living persons. Since the majority of mediums are female, while spirits tend to be male, the most striking aspect of tromba possession is that one watches a female medium transform into a male spirit.

The issue of gender is integral to understanding the nature of tromba possession in Ambanja. Spirits may possess men, but this is unusual: where 96 percent (94 out of 98) of the tromba mediums I encountered were women. The reasons given for this by the living (and by the spirits as well) is that women are more susceptible to possession because they are "weak" (*malemy*) and it is difficult for them to resist the advances of spirits, in contrast to men who are "strong" (*hery*). In addition, since most spirits are male, they are attracted to women. Marriage provides the idiom for expressing the relationship between male spirits and female mediums, who are said to be each others' spouses (vady). As will be described in further detail in chapter 7, tromba mediumship correlates with adult female status, marked by marriage and first pregnancy (which may or may not be carried to full term; see figure 7.1 and Appendix A).

Although the majority of participants at tromba ceremonies are female, tromba possession is not exclusively a female domain. The majority of mediums and observers at ceremonies are teenage girls and adult women, while the musicians and spirit interpreters (*rangahy*) are men. This division of duties along gender lines replicates what occurs at the royal tombs, where the saha for the most powerful royal tromba are female, and male tomb guardians (ngahy) who serve as the spirits' interpreters when living royalty wish to consult them. (The significance of gender and the role of the rangahy will be discussed in more detail in chapter 7.)

Should a person show signs of tromba possession, she must accept it, for if she resists the spirit, it may cause her great physical harm. Most often possession is precipitated by an onslaught of chronic symptoms, including headaches, dizziness, persistent stomach pains, or a sore neck, back, or limbs. Typically, the victim has consulted a wide array of healers, including staff at the local hospital and indigenous healers, including tromba mediums, herbalist-healers (moasy), and diviners (mpisikidy). Eventually it is suggested to her that perhaps it is a tromba that is making her ill, the spirit being angry because she is resisting possession. The victim is then instructed to visit an established tromba medium in order to have the diagnosis confirmed. If it is indeed a tromba, she is expected to undergo an elaborate series of ceremonies in order to permanently install the spirit within her.

Once established, a tromba spirit remains active in the medium throughout her lifetime, and although it may become dormant once the medium has reached old age, the spirit departs only after she is dead. The spirit does not constantly reside within her. Instead, the spirit lives in the royal tomb, which it leaves temporarily in order to possess a medium; she in turn serves as a temporary "house" (*trano*) for the spirit whenever she goes into trance. When the spirit enters the medium's body (or head, since it is often said "to sit" [*mipetraka*] here), her own spirit departs and remains absent throughout possession. After the possession experience has ended she does not remember what came to pass, so that a third party is required to serve as a witness or interpreter (rangahy) for her.[5]

One medium may have several tromba spirits, and often the older the medium the greater her spirit repertoire, since she collects increasingly powerful (and older) spirits as she herself ages. A medium can only be possessed by one spirit at a given point in time. Although the greatest royal tromba have only one saha each, the majority of tromba spirits are active in many mediums, and each can only be present in one medium at a time. In the past, when a medium became old or died, one of her daughters would usually inherit her spirits. (Lambek 1988b provides an excellent description from Mayotte of how children inherit their parents' spirits.) Over the course of my fieldwork I knew of only one medium who had inherited her mother's spirits. Instead I found that in Ambanja tromba possession often affects clusters of women who are friends or who are structurally related through kinship. Often these women are possessed by the same spirits. Special bonds defined through fictive kinship are established between mediums who share the same spirits or whose spirits are members of the same genealogies. Tromba possession affects a medium's life in many other ways: in addition to being an important part of her personal experience, tromba spirits often become integral members of her household. As a vessel for them she may also become a respected healer in the community.

Tromba ceremonies are entertaining and suspenseful events. Spirits love music, and it is the lively sound of an accordion or stringed valiha[6] which generally alerts passersby to the fact that a ceremony is taking place inside someone's home. The tunes of these instruments are complemented by faray, wooden rattles made of bamboo which are shaken and thumped on the floor to produce sophisticated poly-rhythms. These ceremonies are held for specific purposes: for a woman who is thought to have a new spirit; for the established spirits of a medium in order to introduce them to a new family member (such as a new child); or to show them a new house where the medium (and thus, the spirits, too) have moved. For these ceremonies the sponsor must spend much money for food, drinks, and payments for other mediums, their spirits, and for hired musicians (an accordionist or valiha player). These are often large-scale social events, sometimes attended by as many as twenty mediums (and their spirits), as well as kin, neighbors, and other friends. Tromba ceremonies generally begin in the daytime and run throughout the night and into the next day. The time when a tromba ceremony is held is chosen with care so as to fall within auspicious, complementary phases of the solar day and the lunar calendar.

ANGELINE'S TROMBA CEREMONY

Angeline is twenty and was born of Sakalava parents who live in a village thirty kilometers from Ambanja. She has been married to Jean (age twenty-nine) for two years. They met four years ago at the junior high school where she was a student and he was teaching French as part of his national service (required before continuing on to university). Jean is also from Ambanja and is the son of a Sakalava mother and Tsimehety father. His parents live in town, but are divorced. When Angeline and Jean informed their parents that they wished to marry, Angeline's parents said she had to wait until she had finished her studies at junior high school; a year later Jean left for eighteen months to attend university in another province. During this time Angeline became very sick, possessed temporarily by an evil njarinintsy spirit, but she was eventually cured. She later finished her studies but had to repeat the final year. She did not pass the exam that would have enabled her to continue on to high school. Jean later decided to discontinue his studies at the university, and he returned to Ambanja to marry Angeline. He now works as a shift supervisor at a local enterprise. Since their marriage Jean and Angeline have lived in a small, neat two-room house made of traveler's palm which was built on land that belongs to Jean's maternal grandmother.[7]

Eight months after they were married, Angeline became ill again: she was weak, lost her appetite, and suffered from chronic stomachaches, dizziness, and periodic headaches. During this time she also became pregnant, but miscarried in the middle of her third month. Jean's mother came and cared for her, cooking meals for Angeline and Jean. Being a tromba medium herself, she suspected that perhaps Angeline's suffering was caused by a tromba spirit. It was not simply the chronic symptoms that led her to think that this might be true. She also suspected that, perhaps, it had been a tromba spirit that had given Angeline a njarinintsy because she was resisting possession. Jean's mother finally decided to approach Angeline in private to see if she could learn more.

When she asked Angeline about her past experiences with possession, Angeline told her mother-in-law in a low voice that she had, in fact, been diagnosed as having a tromba. At first, when she had attacks of njarinintsy, friends and kin had told her parents that she needed to go to a tromba medium or other healer to have the spirit driven from her. Her parents are devout Catholics and did not believe in njarinintsy. When the doctor at the local hospital failed to cure her, however, they became very distressed and finally decided to do as others had suggested. A tromba medium was eventually able to drive out the njarinintsy, but suspected that Angeline also suffered from tromba possession. The medium said Angeline appeared to be possessed by a young baka atsimo tromba of the Zafin'i'mena descent group. Angeline's parents had never arranged for the appropriate ceremonies, refusing on religious grounds to let their daughter become a tromba medium. They also feared that Jean would no longer wish to marry their daughter if he knew that she had a tromba spirit.

Angeline and her mother-in-law decided to approach Jean and explain the circumstances to him. He agreed to host a tromba ceremony (romba ny tromba). This ceremony is called mampiboaka ny tromba ("to make the tromba come out"), since it is at this time that the spirit makes its debut. When I later asked Jean what his reaction was when he heard the news he said, "I was surprised, but not upset—you see, I grew up with tromba, since my mother has several spirits. Although tromba spirits can be demanding, they are there to help the members of their households." The greatest problem was finding the money to pay for the ceremony: it cost 95,000 fmg, the bulk of which Jean saved, with additional assistance from his mother and his maternal grandmother (Angeline did not work). The ceremony was postponed on three different occasions because royalty from different lineages had died throughout the course of that year, thus, "the doors [to the royal tombs] were closed" (nifody ny varavaraña), making it taboo to hold tromba ceremonies for several months. The tomb door was finally "opened" (nibiaña ny varavaraña) in September, and the ceremony was scheduled to begin around 9:00 A.M. on a Saturday, when the phase of the moon was nearly full. Jean's mother and maternal grandmother helped with the arrangements, and although Angeline's mother did not attend, her mother's sister, with whom Angeline had lived while a student in Ambanja, was an observer at the ceremony. Jean was also an important observer throughout the ceremony, since he would be introduced to his wife's spirits. An implicit understanding was that he was there to begin to learn the role of rangahy or medium's assistant.

By 9:15 A.M. two men arrive, one bearing an accordion. These musicians have been hired to play music that will entice the spirits to come.

They will take turns playing and will split the 5,000 fmg Jean will pay them. Five mediums have also been invited to attend; Jean will pay between 750 and 2,000 fmg for each spirit that has been invited to officiate at the ceremony, the amount being determined by the spirit's stature (see figure 5.1). The first of the mediums to arrive at the house is Dady Soa, a woman in her early sixties. She is possessed by a powerful spirit named Ndramarofaly, and it is this spirit that will officiate at the ceremony. Dady Soa is accompanied by a man named Anton, who will serve as the rangahy or interpreter for her spirit. He, like Dady Soa, will be paid 2,000 fmg. No one knows Dady Soa personally, but she has been recommended to Jean's mother by several friends as an accomplished medium. Within half an hour four other mediums arrive. These include two women in their forties: one named Mona, who is a cousin of Jean's mother, and Alice, Mona's friend. The other two are Marie and Jeanette, who were Angeline's schoolmates and who are now her neighbors. All five mediums carry small baskets that hold the costumes for their respective spirits.

The mediums sit down in the house and face the eastern wall. This direction is associated with the ancestors and the location of the royal tombs.[8] Dady Soa occupies the northeast corner. Anton, her rangahy, is seated slightly behind her and to her left, and the other mediums are to her right. In front of the mediums is a short-legged table that Jean's mother has set up to serve as an altar for the spirits. On this she has placed items needed to summon the spirits: an incense burner in which a piece of resin now burns, issuing a sweet aroma into the air; a plate holding water and crumbled kaolin (tany malandy); a small cup with more kaolin that has been crumbled and mixed with water to make a paste; several bottles that are painted with designs of white kaolin and which hold a mixture of burnt honey and water (SAK: barisa generally refers to the container; the contents is tô mainty/joby; HP: toaka mainty);[9] and an assortment of goods that will be given to the spirits to "eat" (mihinana) or consume. These include a small vial of honey, a small bottle of local rum, three one-liter bottles of beer and two others of soda pop, and two packets of cigarettes. Other similar supplies rest on the floor in a basket, waiting to be added to the table when needed. The mediums have already bathed before coming to the house, but Jean's mother has placed a pitcher of water beneath the table for periodic hand washing and drinking during the cermony.

The house soon fills with other people. The two musicians sit to one side, while Angeline, Jean, and Jean's mother approach the front and sit next to the rangahy along the north wall. Friends and neighbors have also begun to assemble in the room. The majority are teenage girls and adult women, several of whom hold babies on their laps. Out of respect for the ancestors all present are barefoot, have their heads uncovered, and wear lambahoany, a body wrap that is an essential element of Sakalava dress. A dozen children crowd in the doorway and crane their necks inside the windows to watch the ceremony just inside.

When all are seated, the rangahy and mediums consult with Jean's mother to review the reasons for why the ceremony has been arranged. Dady Soa, Mona, and Alice untie their knots of hair so that their long plaits hang down to their shoulders. This is a gesture they make in deference to the royal spirits that will soon arrive. They then assume a cross-legged position and, while facing east, they hold their palms up in deference to the ancestors; several members of the audience do this as well. The rangahy says the invocation (*sadrana*), asking the ancestors for their assistance. He first addresses the Zanahary, or Gods on High, and then those spirits who have been requested to attend this ceremony. As he does this, Jean's mother hands him two 100-fmg coins made of nickel, which serve as an offering of "silver" (vola fotsy) for the spirits. The rangahy places these in the plate that is filled with water and kaolin. A musican then begins to play a lively tune on the accordion.

The atmosphere in the room is not calm, nor are the members of the audience austere. This is a time for excitement and rejoicing, for if the spirits are pleased, Angeline's spirit will make its debut in her. When the musicians begin to play, one woman begins to sing and three others soon join her, while two additional women each pick up a rattle (faray) and beat out the rhythms of the tune. The time between the prayer and the arrival of any spirit is always one of great anticipation, for no one is ever sure how long the wait will be or if the spirit will come at all.

The first medium to go into trance is Dady Soa, and this she does with ease. She trembles slightly and then, abruptly, she stands. She is now possessed and has become the male spirit NDRAMAROFALY.[10] Jean's mother jumps up to help this spirit, who draws his clothes from Dady Soa's basket and begins to dress. As Jean's mother holds up a cloth between Ndramarofaly and the spectators, the spirit drops Dady Soa's waist wrap and puts on an old peasant-style white shirt and two tattered and faded pieces of red cloth, one of which he wraps around his waist, draping the other over his shoulders. He then sits down and washes his hands. Then the rangahy hands him a wooden baton (*map-*

ingo) that is tipped with silver. Jean and his mother speak to the spirit with the assistance of the rangahy, who repeats what each party says. In this way the spirit learns why he has been summoned. Throughout this Angeline is silent. The spirit takes the plate of water and blesses Angeline by pouring a bit onto her head, and then pours some more into his palm, which he wipes on her face.

Tromba spirits are arranged hierarchically in relation to one another, according to their positions in the royal genealogies. The order in which they arrive at Angeline's ceremony reflects these positions: the Grandparents (dady; dadilahy), who are the oldest and most powerful spirits arrive first, followed in turn by younger generations, the Children (zanaka) and Grandchildren (zafy). Thus, Ndramarofaly, who is the most powerful spirit to attend this ceremony, must arrive before other mediums can enter trance. Now Mona and Alice begin to draw on their bodies with kaolin paste. These markings designate which spirits will arrive in them. Alice also ties a white cloth around her chest. Within a few minutes both of these mediums show signs of possession. First their bodies shake violently, then Mona begins to shake only her head, and then she falls on her belly, with her hands behind her back. Alice, meanwhile, begins to hiss, holding one trembling arm outstretched before her. She, too, falls on the ground, and then they each draw a white cloth over their bodies and heads. Two other young women come to their aid, helping them to rise and dress and shielding them with draped cloths. They emerge as two brothers, RAOVOAY ("Crocodile Man") and RALEVA, who are both young affines of Ndramarofaly. These are the spirits of royalty who served under the colonial administration and their clothes reflect a European flair: in addition to a small baton and a red-print lambahoany waist wrap, each wears a white, four-pocketed shirt and a fedora.

Upon arriving these spirits must greet their elder, and so they approach Ndramarofaly and put their heads on his lap. He then blesses them by placing his hand on their heads. While Grandparents like Ndramarofaly remain calm and somewhat detached throughout tromba ceremonies, younger spirits interact with the living. Typically, a Child or Grandchild will light up a cigarette and then greet members of the audience with a special tromba handshake; this is just what Raovoay and Raleva do.

Again, the spirits confer. All wait and watch Angeline, who now sits calmly behind the spirits. She has recently untied her long, braided tresses and they now hang down onto her shoulders and back. She sits cross-legged and has a lambahoany draped over her shoulders. The music continues, people chat, and children come in and out of the room. Still, nothing happens.

An hour later one of the two youngest mediums, Marie, starts to go into trance. Grunting, she violently spins her head from side to side, so that her tresses fly. A young woman runs to grab her: first she smears white kaolin along Marie's jawbone, and then she wraps a towel firmly under her chin and up over her head. All know by now that this is the spirit of MAMPIARY, the cowherd and the son of Raleva, who is trying to make his entrance. When this spirit died he broke his jaw, and so when he arrives the medium's head must be supported so that she will not be injured in a similar way. The young woman holds Marie, who is kneeling and whose body begins to jerk while her head moves up and down. Meanwhile Jeanette has drawn lines of white kaolin on the backs of her fingers, hands, and up her arms, and she now begins to box the air. When members of the audience realize she is aiming for one wall, they laugh and nervously jump away, while Jean's mother quickly smears kaolin on the wall. Just as she withdraws, Jeanette strikes the wall with her fists and falls—she is possessed by the boxer, BE ONDRY ("Big Fist"), who is the brother-in-law of Mampiary (see plate 4). Marie and Jeanette, possessed by their respective spirits, each stand and dress. Their clothes are similiar to those of Raovoay and Raleva: they, too, wear lambahoany, although Marie's is green and Jeanette's is orange, and they wear boater or panama hats. Once dressed, they greet the other spirits and then turn to the audience and playfully shake each person's hand. Mampiary also jingles a collection of bottle caps that he has in one of his pockets. Although in appearance these two Grandchildren resemble the Children who are their elders, they are playful and reckless in their actions. These two spirits speak in high voices, and throughout the ceremony they will drink, smoke, and dance with members of the audience. When clowning Grandchildren are present, it is the dead who are the life of the party.

These five spirits will play important roles during Angeline's ceremony, having been summoned because her spirit is believed to be a member of their lineage (again, see figure 5.1). These spirits appear frequently in Ambanja, each possessing mediums of ages that correspond to those present at Angeline's ceremony. Throughout this ceremony other spirits will arrive and depart in these and other mediums,

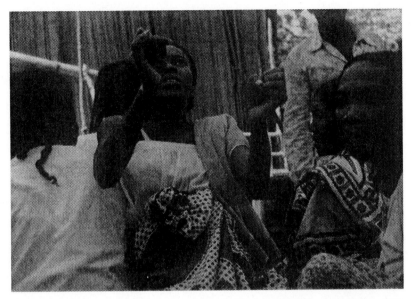

Plate 4.   Medium entering trance. The medium is making two fists, which indicates she is about to be possessed by one of the boxer spirits, Djao Kondry or Be Ondry.

so that any medium may undergo a series of transformations, changing personae as different spirits arrive and depart in her body. Since tromba spirits are powerful healers, passersby may also drop in and request their services. Most of these clients are adults who bring small children by for treatment. Periodically there are breaks in the ceremony; at these times the musicians pause to rest or to eat with members of Angeline's household. Anyone else who is present will be invited to join them. Sometimes mediums leave trance so that they can eat, but more often they refrain, remaining possessed throughout the ceremony.

Once these five spirits have assembled, all attention is again focused on Angeline in anticipation of her spirit's arrival. Occasionally she shows signs of possession, shaking and moaning, but she only collapses, exhausted, on the floor. These moments are tense and exciting. The musicians, anticipating the spirit's arrival, play faster, and the beat of the rattles grows harder and louder. Women also begin to ululate or sing loudly, hoping to excite the spirit and encourage it to arrive. Each time, too, the younger spirits run quickly to Angeline's aid, holding her up, consoling her, and asking her spirit to be kind to her and arrive

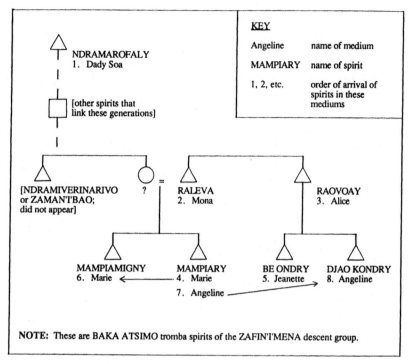

Figure 5.1. Spirits and Mediums Present at Angeline's Ceremony.

smoothly and quickly. This continues throughout the afternoon and into the night, but still her spirit does not arrive. When she shows signs of fatigue following fits of partial possession, the spirits have her drink from the plate of water, or they wipe her face and arms with kaolin paste: both have healing properties because they are cool (manintsy) and because they are sacred, being associated with the spirits. The spirits and a number of observers begin to suspect that Angeline may be possessed by Mampiary since, at one point, when Marie was temporarily possessed by another spirit, Angeline waved her head up and down when showing signs of possession. Mampiary is instructed by Ndramarofaly to leave Marie, who then becomes possessed by another spirit, MAMPIAMIŃY ("Limpness"), Mampiary's brother. His style of dress is slightly different: he wears a purple cloth that is similar to Ndramarofaly's and a shirt and hat like that of the Children. Also, unlike Mampiary, he is quiet, sitting limply on the ground at the front of the room. By this time Angeline is exhausted and she retires for an hour to the bedroom next door.

Around dawn Angeline's spirit finally arrives. This is the moment of the day that is, in J. Mack's words, "the most auspicious time in the Malagasy calendar" (1989). Since the spirit is making its debut in Angeline, it is important that it be identified, stating its name and position in one of many genealogies. In this way its relationship to other spirits and to Angeline can be determined. Possessed, Angeline is brought to the front of the room to consult with Ndramarofaly and the other tromba. After much discussion, her spirit finally utters its name: it is, indeed, MAMPIARY. A series of additional conferences are then held, involving Ndramarofaly, the rangahy, and members of Angeline's household.

The arrival of the long-awaited spirit is the climax of the ceremony. The neophyte may remain possessed for less than an hour, her spirit quickly departing, or her spirit may stay and enjoy the celebration, clowning with other spirits and members of the audience. In Angeline's case, it leaves quickly, but soon she shows signs of being possessed by yet another spirit. She assumes a boxing position, and at this time others prepare her in the same way as was done for Jeanette. Angeline suddenly hits the wall with her fists, collapses, and then sits up. The spirits and her kin confer and determine that Angeline is possessed by a second spirit, DJAO KONDRY ("The Guy Who Boxes"), the brother of Be Ondry.

After this second spirit departs from Angeline, the ceremony is nearly completed. The spirits that remain must depart in an order that mirrors their arrival, the youngest leaving first, the most powerful departing last. Angeline's ceremony lasts for another hour because Be Ondry refuses to leave until Jean has bought him yet another bottle of beer. Since it is early in the morning, Jean has to wait for a nearby store to open before he can send a child to purchase a bottle for the spirit. Be Ondry guzzles this down, and then he is cajoled into leaving by the other, more powerful spirits. He finally agrees to leave so that other spirits may follow. Each spirit leaves in a style similar to the way it arrived. As the younger and more active spirits depart, unpossessed members of the audience run to catch each medium, massaging her arms and back with quick slaps and jerks in order to relieve her somewhat of the pain and stiffness she will feel afterward. All mediums are in a daze when they reenter their own bodies and they ask for a summary of what happened, since they do not recall what came to pass. Although they are tired, they do not feel the effects of any alcohol they consumed.

This ceremony will be followed by another equally expensive ceremony called *manondro ny lamba* ("to give the clothes"), when the spirits will be presented with their appropriate attire and they will be given items they like to eat. For Mampiary and Djao Kondry these goods are beer and cigarettes. They also will be properly introduced to Jean, since he is a member of Angeline's household, and they will be paraded seven times around the courtyard of the house. Anytime that a major change occurs in Angeline's life—if she bears a child, or if she moves to another residence, for example—she must hold a ceremony to officially inform her spirits of this. Since these ceremonies are expensive, mediums are often forced to postpone them for a year or more until they can assemble the necessary capital or gain the assistance of kin to help pay for the ceremony. Postponement is dangerous, however, and causes the medium much anxiety, since her spirit may become angry with her and decide to harm her or others close to her. Throughout her life she may accumulate several other spirits, and generally the stature and power of these new spirits increase as she herself ages. If she wishes, she may participate in similar ceremonies held for other neophytes.

In addition to the large-scale ceremonies such as the one described above, many established mediums work alone at home, holding private sessions, by appointment, with clients. These ceremonies are more austere than the larger, public ceremonies, and they are always held in a quiet and dark room. They are attended by the client, the medium and her assistant or rangahy (who is usually her husband, although it may be a woman who is a friend or a relative), and, perhaps, an assortment of other observers such as friends or kin of the medium or client. In addition to prearranged ceremonies, tromba spirits occasionally arrive suddenly and unannounced. This almost always occurs when the spirit has been angered, either by the medium or by someone who is close to her.

OTHER MEMBERS OF THE SPIRIT WORLD

The spirit world of Ambanja is complex and varied. Tromba are by far the most important spirits. It is they who appear most frequently in mediums and who are most significant in terms of daily interactions between the living and the dead. As the spirits of Sakalava royalty, structurally they are also of prime importance. Although tromba dominate the spirit world, they can not be understood fully unless explored in relation to other spirits.

In Ambanja, spirits are categorized in a number of different ways

ORIGIN	POSSESSING SPIRITS + Involves Mediumship good, beneficial (tsara)	POSSESSING SPIRITS - Possession Sickness evil, dangerous (raty/ratsy)	NON-POSSESSING SPIRITS
Human:	tromba (royal ancestral spirits)		razaña (ancestors of commoners) lolo (ghosts of unidentified dead)
Nature:	tsiñy kalanoro		
Origin Unknown:		njarinintsy (tromba hely; tromba raty/ratsy) masoantoko shay-tuan bilo (from southern Madagascar)	

Figure 5.2.   Spirits of Ambanja.

(see figure 5.2). They may be grouped according to their origins and by human or nonhuman qualities. In addition to the tromba, who are royal, historical figures, there are also the ancestors of commoners (*razaña*), ghosts of the lost dead (*lolo*), nature spirits (*tsiñy* and *kalanoro*), and a variety of lesser, amorphous, evil spirits (njarinintsy, *masoantoko, shay-tuan,* bilo). Although all spirits are potentially dangerous, spirits generally are grouped by Sakalava as being either good (*tsara*) or bad (*raty, ratsy*).

Mediumship also provides a means by which to group spirits. Just as tromba spirits require mediums, so do the nature spirits tsiñy and kalanoro. All spirits are potentially dangerous, especially when angered, but spirits that work through professional mediums are regarded as being, in general, benevolent. In Sakalava cosmology, the Zanahary, or Gods on High, are distant and vaguely conceived creator spirits or dieties to whom the living do not give much thought. Ancestral spirits especially serve as intermediaries between the living and the Zanahary. (In Malagasy Christian theology, the Zanahary have been replaced by the Christian God, *Andriamanitra,* or "the King of Heaven"; sometimes Catholic mediums will address this God instead when they invoke tromba spirits.) Although nature spirits that require mediums are feared, they, like tromba, are respected as authority figures and as specialists in times of crisis. They are also revered as knowledgeable healers.

Finally, positions and meanings assigned to spirits within the Malagasy cosmos are further manipulated, restructured, and redefined through the doctrines of Christianity and Islam. In these contexts, *all* spirits are considered to be evil and are referred to as devils or jinn (*devoly, jiny*). Values collide in the realm defined by the spirit world, as devotees of Christianity and Islam (as well as urban intellegentsia and foreigners) struggle to make sense of the pervasiveness of Malagasy customs (fomba-gasy) in light of their own beliefs based on alternative moral and ideological systems (this will be elaborated in chapter 10).

OTHER SPIRITS OF HUMAN ORIGIN: RAZAÑA AND LOLO

Like royalty, Sakalava commoners have their own personal ancestors (SAK: razaña; HP: *razana;* the latter term is used throughout Madagascar for ancestors), but, in contrast to tromba spirits, razaña do not possess mediums (cf. Rason 1968).[11] Instead, they communicate with the living either through dreams or through a third party, such as a tromba medium, whose spirit, in turn, serves as an intermediary and interpreter.[12] These spirits interact with the living when they are angry or troubled and must be appeased when necessary. An angry razaña may also be identified by a healer as the cause for an individual's sickness or misfortune. They sometimes disturb the living because their bodies have been lost or forgotten. For example, an ancestral spirit may be angry because it has long been dead and its burying place forgotten, or because it was never placed in the family tomb. Reasons for this may vary. Perhaps the person died while traveling, or the body was never recovered, or the body was intentionally neglected, left to rot somewhere in the woods because of a major trespass committed in life.[13] The healer, most often a tromba medium, will then instruct living kin how to placate the troubled spirit, explaining where to find the remains, or what other actions the ancestor wishes its kin to take. Personal ancestors are also honored annually on the Day of the Dead (*Fety ny Maty*), since many Sakalava in Ambanja are Catholic.[14]

Lolo (pronounced "lu-lu") is a term used throughout Madagascar for ghosts. These are, in essence, orphaned spirits with no structural ties to anyone. They are similar to razaña, the difference being one of perspective. Razaña are one's own lost ancestors; lolo, on the other hand, may be seen as the lost ancestors of strangers: they bear no structural affinity to those whom they disturb.[15] Lolo are the ghosts of people who have died in tragic or violent ways, whose bodies were never recovered and placed in a tomb. Lolo haunt the scenes of past accidents, such as regions of the sea where people have drowned or under bridges where there have been automobile accidents. These are jealous and vicious spirits that cause their victims to die in ways similar to their own deaths. For example, the sea near the east coast town of Toamasina is very rough, and it is said that many lolo dwell there. Similarly, people crossing the channel between Nosy Be and the main island often fear that the ghosts of those who drowned in boating accidents will cause them to meet similar fate.

The theme of lost bodies is a common one in Madagascar. As Bloch (1971) has shown, it is in the tomb that Malagasy invest the greatest amount of money and sentiment, for it is the tomb that defines where home is, tying the individual to past, present, and future kin. A lost body is very frightening, and Malagasy tell elaborate tales of trying to recover and transport the body of a loved one who has died far from home, either in a remote part of Madagascar or abroad. During the course of my interviews with an old Sakalava man he told me I should move out of my house because there were lolo living there, since it was built, along with the neighboring Lutheran church, on top of an old Sakalava cemetery. One of my assistants and I later challenged him on the truth of this story (topographical records revealed that a cemetery had in fact existed near the church, but not on its grounds). He later retracted his statement and agreed that it was unnecessary for me to move. I believe that his statement had much to do with my needing to clarify for him my relationship with the Lutheran church, which was not particularly popular with the Sakalava.

NATURE SPIRITS THAT REQUIRE MEDIUMS:
TSIÑY AND KALANORO

In addition to tromba, there are two categories of nature spirits that also possess mediums. These are the tsiñy and kalanoro. A tsiñy is a nature spirit associated with a specific location where it is said to live, such as a sacred tamarind tree (*madiro*) or a rock. Tsiñy, when they possess their mediums, wear clothes that are similar in appearance to Zafin'i'fotsy tromba. In addition to being periodically possessed by their spirits, tsiñy mediums also serve as the exclusive guardians or caretakers of the spirits and their habitats, so that a tsiñy medium is said "to have a tsiñy" (*misy tsiñy*, lit., "there is a tsiñy"). This issue of guardianship is important. Since a tsiñy's dwelling is sacred, people may wish to leave offerings for the spirit without actually consulting with it directly. In order to do this, however, one must acquire permission from the spirit's guardian. The location of a tsiñy is easy to recognize, since it generally has a fence built around it for protection, and pieces of white cloth, left as offerings, will be draped on a pole or, if it is a tree, a branch. Unlike tromba, tsiñy possession is not widespread in Ambanja. Tsiñy locales and mediums are few and are located in small villages throughout the countryside.

Kalanoro are by far the most mysterious, frightening, and bizarre (*hafahafa*) of the Malagasy spirits, having a quality that Kane (1988) aptly describes as "surreal" in speaking of the *duende* spirits of Panama. Kalanoro are found throughout Madagascar, and in other regions of the island they go by such names as *kotoky* and *vazimba*.[16] Kalanoro are rarely seen, because they live deep in the forest. They are short and some informants say they have long fingernails and red eyes. Their hair is long and possesses magical qualities. I know of one moasy (herbalist), for example, who derived his power from a small packet of magical substances which included kalanoro hair. The most striking aspect of kalanoro is that their feet point backward, so that if one wishes to track a kalanoro, it is important to remember to follow the footprints in the direction they appear to be coming from, rather than where they seem to be going. Kalanoro eat raw food and may leave evidence of a meal—such as the cracked shells of a crayfish on a rock in the middle of a river.

As is true of tsiñy, kalanoro mediums are said to have or keep these spirits and act as their guardians. Unlike tromba and tsiñy possession ceremonies, however, the client is not permitted to view a kalanoro when it possesses a medium. Instead, during the consultation, the medium sits behind a white curtain in a darkened room. There are only a few kalanoro mediums working in the Sambirano Valley, and they, like those with tsiñy, live out in the bush. Although I was never able to consult a kalanoro, I was told by informants who had done so that when the kalanoro arrives it can be heard walking and banging on the ceiling and walls of the house and that its speech is quick, choppy, and high pitched, so that it is difficult to understand. It is taboo to have a dog present during a kalanoro seance, because dogs can see them. Malagasy are generally wary of kalanoro because of their strange qualities. The few informants I knew who had consulted kalanoro did so either out of curiosity or as a last resort after the efforts of numerous tromba mediums and other healers had failed.

Although tsiñy and kalanoro are similar to tromba spirits in that they operate through mediums and work as healers, they differ in a number of ways. First, kalanoro and tsiñy are associated with nature, and so many of their clients seek their assistance because of a trespass they have committed against such a spirit by violating a sacred locale. Second, the mediums for these nature spirits serve as their guardians and, thus, each spirit is only associated with one person, whereas a tromba spirit may possess many mediums. Third, they are much rarer. Over the course of a year, I met only three tsiñy mediums, and I was never able to locate a kalanoro. Because of this, their services are usually more expensive than those of tromba mediums, which accounts in part for why they are a last resort for clients. Fourth, although the majority of tromba spirits possess women, kalanoro guardians are men and women. Tsiñy possession, on the other hand, appears to be more common among men: of the three tsiñy mediums I encountered during one year, only two of these were male. Finally, whereas tromba possession occurs in the context of large-scale ceremonies, tsiñy and kalanoro work in the privacy of the guardian's home.

EVIL SPIRITS

Njarinintsy, Masoantoko, Shay-tuan

All spirits that operate through mediums—tromba, tsiñy, and kalanoro—become permanent fixtures in their mediums' lives. There are also evil (raty, ratsy) possessing spirits—njarinintsy, masoantoko, and shay-tuan—which are harmful and are often regarded as a special form of *possession sickness*. These spirits are said to be recent arrivals to the Sambirano region.

Of these malevolent spirits, njarinintsy are the best known and claim the greatest number of victims. For this reason njarinintsy will be the focus of subsequent discussions of possession by evil spirits (see especially chapter 9). Njarinintsy possession is a relatively new phenomenon in Ambanja, occuring only within the last fifteen years. Most informants say that they first heard of njarinintsy in the 1970s, and Sakalava argue that it was brought by Tsimihety migrants. Cases of njarinintsy are reported from other areas of the north as early as the 1960s and informants describe these as clowning spirits. In more recent years, however, njarinintsy have become increasingly violent. Njarinintsy possession is viewed as a grave illness with symptoms that include shaking and chills (this is reflected in the spirit's name, which is derived from *manintsy,* which means "coldness");[17] uncontrollable screaming and crying; loss of memory; and mental confusion. As with tromba possession, the majority of njarinintsy victims are female. They experience temporary fits of possession or madness when they wander the streets aimlessly and may even, in extreme cases, attack people. If an individual is in a possessed state she does not recognize anyone, nor will she remember what happened once the fit has ended.

Sakalava often speak of njarinintsy in reference to tromba. Njarinintsy may be viewed as structurally akin to tromba, for it is sometimes said that they are the "children of tromba" (*tsaiky ny tromba, zanaka ny tromba*). They are also referred to as *tromba hely* ("little tromba") or *tromba raty/ratsy* ("bad tromba"). Informants insist, however, that njarinitsy are not a type of tromba for, unlike tromba, njarinintsy are malicious and extremely dangerous, and must not be allowed to inhabit the living. In many ways these spirits are defined in opposition to tromba—they are everything that tromba are not.[18]

Masoantoko and shay-tuan are very similar to njarinintsy, and so I will describe them only briefly. A masoantoko (lit. "group of eyes" [?] from *maso,* "eye," and *antoko,* "group"[?]) disturbs its victim while she sleeps, giving her terrible nightmares. Informants opinions on shay-tuan differ, particularly in reference to their origin. Some informants say they are Chinese spirits, referring to the local spelling of the name, but others say they are Muslim. More likely they were brought to Madagascar by slaves or Swahili traders from East Africa (compare with the Arabic term *shetwan,* for "devil"; *setoan* in Feeley-Harnik, 1991b: 95; also sheitani spirits of East Africa, see Giles 1987; Gray 1969; Koritschoner 1936). According to one informant, shay-tuan smell bad (*maimbo*). Odors can be important in distinguishing different categories of spirits from one another. Tromba, for example, can be enticed into arriving in a medium by burning sweet smelling resin or other types of incense. Shay-tuan (and lolo, see above), however, can be driven from a room by burning the same type of incense or a piece of cloth. For this reason adults often burn one of these substances in a room before children enter it to sleep at night.

Bilo

A final form of possession sickness found in Ambanja is bilo. Bilo does not occur with great frequency in Ambanja, being an affliction primarily of peoples who have come from the south, such as the Betsileo and Antandroy. The symptoms associated with bilo are much like njarinintsy in that its victims may become violent and temporarily crazed. Some bilo spirits are animals, such as snakes, and they cause their victims to crawl on their bellies while they are possessed.[19]

RESPONSES TO POSSESSION SICKNESS

The responses to possession involving evil spirits—njarinintsy, masoantoko, shay-tuan, and bilo—reflect the gravity of the situation and the necessity for collective action. In Malagasy communities, individual illness is a time when kin and close friends congregate to care for, watch over, and socialize with the afflicted. This is especially evident in cases involving spirit possession. Tromba, tsiñy, and kalanoro require that the individual go through a series of ceremonies to instate the spirit permanently within her; in contrast, an evil spirit must be driven from its victim. If it is not, she may become increasingly ill and may even go mad or die. When an evil spirit strikes, the assembled group provides not only a united front against the spirit, but also helps to give the victim strength to resist possession. The presence of kin ensures that the afflicted will be taken to a healer. Furthermore, she has witnesses to the entire process. This is, I believe, essential: regardless of the type of possession, the possessed is never aware of what happens when she is in trance, and so part of the healing process involves the recounting of events to the victim (see Lambek 1980 for a similar discussion from Mayotte).

Possession sickness involving evil spirits most often affects adolescent girls between the ages of thirteen and seventeen, and many tromba mediums and other healers specialize in exorcising these spirits. Malicious spirits generally do not possess their victims through a will of their own but have been sent by an adversary, who has used magical substances or bad medicine (*fanafody raty/ratsy*) to harm someone. The victims of evil spirits are those who have come into contact with fanafody that was meant for them or, in some cases, through accidental contact with fanafody that was meant for someone else. As the case of Angeline shows, they may precede tromba possession, the evil spirit having been sent by a tromba to harm a woman who is resisting mediumship. In these cases, once the evil spirit is exorcised, the tromba then makes its debut.

Although njarinintsy possession is a grave illness, if a cure has been successful, long afterward kin and friends will tell lively, comical stories of the problems encountered in trying to restrain the possessed and keep her calm during transportation in an oxcart or taxi and, finally, what came to pass with the healer. Njarinintsy are, in general, uncooperative and demanding spirits. The role of the healer is to strike a bargain with the spirit, making arrangements to give gifts to it or later to leave certain goods in strategic locations—by a sacred tree, for example—so that the spirit will be content and will leave the victim. This process is not always successful. It may take several visits to a number of different healers before the spirit agrees to leave. The process is further complicated by the fact that njarinintsy do not always appear alone, for they are said to prefer working in groups of seven. Thus, even if one spirit is driven away, there may be others that remain inside the victim. Once the spirit or spirits have departed, the individual is cured. A failure to cure is a grave matter, for the person will continue to have fits, and it is said that she may be driven mad or even die from the harm caused by the presence of the spirit. If indigenous healers fail to coax an evil spirit from its victim, her kin might then go to a Protestant or Muslim exorcist.

Most Christians and Muslims in Ambanja state that they are opposed to possession. According to Christian doctrine, all spirits are considered to be devils (devoly). Although the Catholic church in Ambanja is fairly tolerant of possession activities, Protestant churches in Ambanja (and in other regions of Madagascar as well) are actively involved in exorcism activities. The FJKM, Lutheran, and a number of other churches have a long tradition of specialists called *fifohazana* (HP, from the verb *mifoha*, meaning "to wake" or "to arise") or *mpiandry* ("shepherds") who exorcise tromba and other spirits through the power they derive from the Holy Spirit. Under Islam, all spirits are similarly regarded as being jinn (SAK: jiny), and, like the Protestant churches, a number of Muslim sects in Ambanja also have specialists who are able to exorcise them. Tolerance of possession varies from one Muslim sect to another, and attitudes toward possession often depend on how troubled the victim is. Rarely do kin seek help from Protestant exorcists and only in extreme cases. (This alternative form of therapy will be explored in chapter 10.)

Thus, tromba and other forms of possession now form a vital part of daily life in Ambanja. The social, demographic, economic, and political forces outlined in Part 1 have led to the popularization of tromba. As the chapters that follow will show, tromba provides Sakalava with a means to reflect upon their shared experiences and to document, re-shape, and constantly redefine relationships with peoples of diverse origins. In turn, since tromba possession continues to be viewed as a Sakalava institution, it enables tera-tany to regulate the participation (and thus incorporation) of outsiders. For vahiny, it provides them, too, with a powerful vehicle to express their own experiences within the context of migration, and with a means of integration into the local community. In these ways, possession in Ambanja is an important aspect of both collective and individual identity.

CHAPTER VI

Sacred Knowledge and Local Power

Tromba and the Sambirano Economy

In the Sambirano, power, authority, and independence hinge on access to and control over land. At first glance it may appear as though it is outsiders (first, French and, more recently, highland Malagasy) who exert the greatest control in the valley, since throughout this century they have been the managers of the plantations and now the enterprises. In this region, much local power lies, however, with those most familar with and integrated into its institutions: these are the Sakalava tera-tany. Managers rarely occupy their positions for more than a few years and so their influence is limited. Sakalava maintain long-term control over important social, economic, and political arenas since they outnumber other groups; occupy the majority of elected positions; own the greatest number of private landholdings; and define the thrust of local culture. The final factor is significant because shifts in national policy in the early 1970s have underscored the necessity of showing respect for local custom, and so today outsiders find they must maintain a delicate balance with the Sakalava tera-tany if they are to accomplish their goals.

This chapter will explore the manner in which Sakalava collectively view and interpret local power and, in turn, how they maintain their influence in the valley. As will become clear, the power of tera-tany hinges on their ability to resist capitalist relations and to undermine or manipulate the future development of the region by the state. In order to fully comprehend this process, it must be explored from a multitude of angles. First, social cohesiveness is an essential element: among the

Sakalava this is defined through the ancestors, the concept of a shared historical past, and the occupation of a common territory, their tanindrazaña (cf. Keyes 1981). For the Sakalava, like other Malagasy, these domains of time and space are sacred. Since these contexts are defined by the actions of royal ancestors, tromba spirits are an essential element of local custom and identity.

Second, as the studies of such authors as Comaroff (1985), Nash (1979), and Taussig (1980a, 1987) show, ritual may be rich in symbolism that reveals an indigenous awareness of the disruptive and alienating nature of development. The symbolism associated with tromba serves to record, reorder, and critique collective experiences that occur under drastic economic development. In essence, tromba possession rituals operate as a form of ethnohistory, providing an arena in which to retell and reflect upon relations with non-Sakalava.

Third, and perhaps most significant, tromba possession goes beyond critique: it also empowers the Sakalava of the Sambirano. Apter (1992) has argued that, in the context of Yoruba religion, ritual knowledge and power may be intrinsically linked and may ultimately challenge the political order on a national level (cf. Lan 1985). Tromba spirits (through their mediums), embody sanctioned ritual authority, occupying pivotal positions that affect power relations in the Sambirano and the subsequent development of the landscape of the tanindrazaña. Such authority affects not only individual experience but also directs collective reponses to the state. Through popular tromba, individual mediums may manipulate their actions in the context of labor relations, while the saha of Nosy Faly control the actions of outsiders and monitor economic changes that disrupt the order of the local sacred geography as a whole.

TROMBA AS ETHNOHISTORY

The preservation of historical knowledge is an important task among the Sakalava, and often this takes the form of written histories (*tantara*) where stories of royal succession and deeds are preserved (see, for example, Feeley-Harnik 1991b: 22). An essential element of written as well as oral Sakalava history involves recording royal—and thus tromba—genealogies. There are several authorities to whom this duty of preserving such knowledge is allocated. Many communities (in Sakalava territory and other areas of Madagascar as well) have an elder (usually male) who is designated as the official local historian.[1] In Am-

banja this position is held by a man in his seventies who is a counselor
to the king; often when I sought information on the history of the
Sambirano Valley I was referred to him. The role of historical authority
has also become bureaucratized. School-teachers are respected as historical authorities because of the knowledge they acquire through their
studies. Because of the nature of their work, they are regarded as very
articulate. In Ambanja there is a second elderly man (he is in his sixties)
who is a self-appointed historian. He was raised in the Sambirano,
served in the colonial administration, and later worked as a school ad-
ministrator in Diégo. He is often referred to as a "living encyclopedia"
(*Monsieur l'encyclopédie vivante*) by his friends and by professors at
the provincial university, and occasionally he is invited to give presenta-
tions at conferences at the Académie Malgache in Antananarivo. Although these two men will speak freely of the French conquest, the
development of the Sambirano, and the influx of non-Sakalava into the
town, the details on more sacred subjects are the prerogative of royalty,
special royal advisers or counselors, the tomb guardians, and the tromba
spirits themselves.

Royalty, their advisers, and the tomb guardians may be knowledgeable, yet they often defer to the tromba, for it is these spirits who are
regarded as the true authorities and as the guardians of sacred knowledge. Only tromba spirits will speak in detail of the deeds of past rulers
or on matters related to spirit possession over time. Part of the logic
here is that they, after all, can provide firsthand knowledge, since they
were eyewitnesses to these events. This knowledge is regarded as sacred
(*masina*) and should not be treated lightly or spoken of freely. Since
one gains access to the tromba through the mediums, it is women who
have the greatest access to, and who thus, in essence, serve, as the gatekeepers to this sacred knowledge. Furthermore, since it is women who
predominate at tromba ceremonies, it is they who are able to recall the
names of royalty and recite their genealogies with the greatest accuracy.

DEAD MEN DO TELL TALES: POSSESSION AS
COLLECTIVE MEMORY

Historical knowledge is conveyed in direct and indirect ways. When a
spirit arrives, it is expected to be able to identify itself by name; recite
part of its geneaology (the name of its father and grandfather, for example); locate itself geographically by stating the location of its tomb; and

tell the story of its death. This is especially important when a spirit makes its debut, but it occurs in other contexts as well. For example, one may ask questions of or interview a spirit in detail regarding its past or that of other tromba spirits. This is done not only by inquisitive anthropologists, but also by Sakalava, who may seek to locate another spirit in the genealogy or to test to see if it is a real or a "fake spirit" (tromba mavandy).

Historical knowledge is embedded in the operational principles of tromba (see the previous chapter). As should be clear from Angeline's ceremony, tromba ceremonies are a form of pageantry, where history is dramatized and displayed through the dress, mannerisms, dialects, and actions of the tromba. Sakalava history is both embedded and embodied in tromba, conveyed not only through the words and behavior of the spirits, but also on the body of the medium. While she is possessed, the medium's body carries evidence of the spirit's history. The color and style of the clothes she wears indicate the spirit's point of origin and its place in the genealogical hierarchy (see plates 5 and 6). She may also put marks on her body that reflect the injuries the spirit sustained at the time of death: white kaolin on her cheeks to indicate the broken jaw of Mampiary or skeletal marks on her hands which are the sign of the boxers Be Ondry and Djao Kondry.

As one watches a tromba ceremony, it becomes evident that generations of royalty are collapsed into three generational categories of spirits—Grandparents, Children, and Grandchildren.[2] These correspond to three major epochs of Sakalava history: precolonial (prior to 1896), colonial (1896–1960), and postcolonial (1960 to the present) (see figure 6.1). This is reflected in their dress, personal stories, and their behavior. The Grandparents are the oldest of the spirits, both in terms of their age when they died and historical depth of time. Their clothing also reflects that they are of an older era. Typically spirits of Ndramarofaly's stature wear clothes that are reminiscent of the styles of a century ago: red waist and shoulder wraps called lamba mena (or "red cloths")[3] and a white, simply-cut (peasant style) pullover shirt. The predominance of the colors red or white is generally an indication that the spirit belongs to the Zafin'i'mena ("Grandchildren of red [metal, i.e., gold]") or Zafin'i'fotsy ("Grandchildren of white [metal, or silver]") royal lineages. In one hand they hold a long wooden staff tipped with silver (mapingo), which is an emblem of royal authority and power (see also the description in Feeley-Harnik 1991b: 92). Their clothes may be very old. No

Plate 5.   A Grandchild spirit. The medium's dress and the marks on her chin signify that she is possessed by the spirit Mampiary, who broke his jaw falling from an ox cart. The marks left on her arms and hands are remnants of an earlier possession by the boxer spirit Djao Kondry.

one may destroy the clothes of a tromba and no one, save a special class of royal attendants (the Sambarivo), may wear them as everyday dress. When a medium dies, her family is expected to take her tromba clothes to the living ruler, who will then take care of them or redistribute them to mediums who have the same spirits. A medium who has inherited her mother's spirits will also inherit the spirit's clothes. In the context

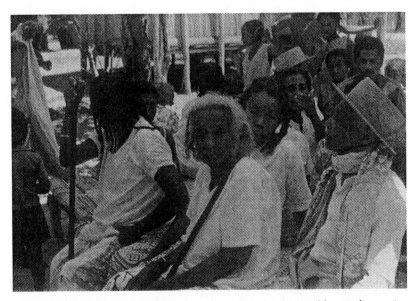

Plate 6. Tromba ceremony (*romba ny tromba*) involving older mediums (including one who is male). These mediums are possessed by older and staid Grandparents. They sit on a raised, open-air platform that can be found in villages throughout the Sambirano. In contrast, mediums in the town of Ambanja prefer to hold ceremonies inside private homes.

of royal tromba possession, saha wear the clothes that rulers wore during their lifetimes. These are kept by the tomb guardians when they are not being used.

As one moves to the next generational group of spirits, to Children such as Raleva and Raovoay, the style of dress changes to one reminiscent of the colonial era. Many Sakalava royalty received an education and were trained by the French to be civil servants in the colonial administration. In Ambanja, many of these spirits continue to wear the sacred color red, but instead of donning the traditional red cloth (lamba mena), they prefer a factory printed waist cloth (lambahoany) that bears a red design printed on a white background. Today the lambahoany is considered to be the traditional dress of the Sakalava, although the living may not wear a red one since this color is reserved for tromba. Instead of wearing the old peasant cut shirt of the Grandparents, this generation of spirits prefers the *quatre-poche,* a white, four-pocketed short-sleeved shirt. In addition, the shoulder cloth has been replaced with a terrycloth towel.[4] Other paraphernalia include a fedora or boater hat (the black band of the latter being decorated with stars, moons, and

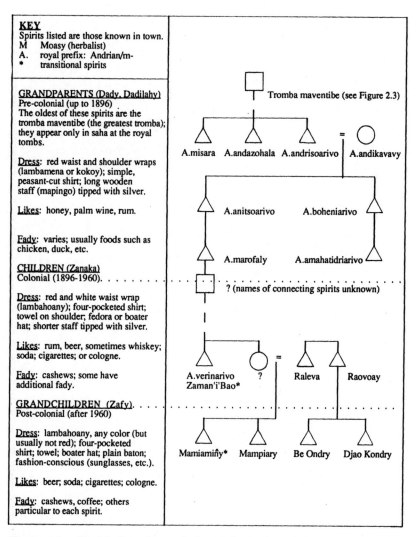

KEY
Spirits listed are those known in town.
M   Moasy (herbalist)
A.   royal prefix: Andrian/m-
*   transitional spirits

GRANDPARENTS (Dady, Dadilahy)
Pre-colonial (up to 1896)
The oldest of these spirits are the
tromba maventibe (the greatest tromba);
they appear only in saha at the royal
tombs.

Dress: red waist and shoulder wraps
(lambamena or kokoy); simple,
peasant-cut shirt; long wooden
staff (mapingo) tipped with silver.

Likes: honey, palm wine, rum.

Fady: varies; usually foods such as
chicken, duck, etc.

CHILDREN (Zanaka)
Colonial (1896-1960). . . . .

Dress: red and white waist wrap
(lambahoany); four-pocketed shirt;
towel on shoulder; fedora or boater
hat; shorter staff tipped with silver.

Likes: rum, beer, sometimes whiskey;
soda; cigarettes; or cologne.

Fady: cashews; some have
additional fady.

GRANDCHILDREN (Zafy). . . . .
Post-colonial (after 1960)

Dress: lambahoany, any color (but
usually not red); four-pocketed
shirt; towel; boater hat; plain baton;
fashion-conscious (sunglasses, etc.).

Likes: beer; soda; cigarettes; cologne.

Fady: cashews, coffee; others
particular to each spirit.

Tromba maventibe (see Figure 2.3)

A.misara A.andazohala A.andrisoarivo A.andikavavy

A.anitsoarivo   A.boheniarivo

A.marofaly   A.amahatidriarivo

? (names of connecting spirits unknown)

A.verinarivo ? Raleva Raovoay
Zaman'i'Bao*

Mamiamiñy* Mampiary Be Ondry Djao Kondry

Figure 6.1. Partial Genealogy of the *Zafin'i'mena, Baka Atsimo* Tromba
Spirits.

other tromba symbols reminiscent of Islamic influence), and in their
hands they often carry a silver-tipped staff, but generally it is shorter
than that of the Grandparents.

Finally, Grandchildren, such as Mampiary and the boxers Djao
Kondry and Be Ondry, exhibit a style similar to that of the parents,
except that they have abandoned the royal color of red. Their waist

wraps are generally blue, green, or purple on white. Their accoutrements are similar to those of the colonial spirits in that they hold a small, plain baton and wear Panama hats. Their style of dress has more flair, however, and when they possess mediums in town they are by far the most fashion conscious of the spirits. Their clothes may be color coordinated, so that a blue lambahoany will be accompanied by a blue shirt and towel, and some even sport sunglasses.

Since tromba were at one time living (and supposedly well-known) persons, each spirit also has a personal story. These are lively, dramatic tales that record the more important events of the Sakalava past. As Estrade (1977: 217) states, these stories operate as a form of *mémoire collective* (cf. Rosaldo 1980). The stories of tromba are often very detailed and reflect the nature of life during the period in which the tromba spirits were alive and ruled. These stories may be part of their their individual or categorical names as well. As stated earlier, Sakalava royalty change their names at the time of death, so that the name they used when alive can no longer be uttered. The new praise name or "tromba name" often reflects great deeds they performed during their lifetimes. Other spirits take names that reflect the manner or circumstances under which they died. Thus, since many of the Grandparents reigned or were well-known royalty, their names provide a shorthand for their deeds.

The life stories of the Children and the Grandchildren are not as well known, since these spirits never ruled. The stories of their deaths are usually more developed, and reflect the nature of the lives of those born in the present century. The stories of the Grandchildren are by far the most involved and spectacular and reflect the experiences of town life in the Sambirano. Behavior also marks the status and the associated historical period, for while Grandparents are staid and aloof, like old rulers, Children and Grandchildren are more accessible to the living and more understanding of their daily affairs, since they have had similar experiences themselves.

What follows are descriptions of a number of popular Zafin'i'mena spirits that appeared at Angeline's ceremony and which correspond with the chart in figure 6.1. Nearly all are baka atsimo spirits who are entombed to the south near Mahajanga. I have also included a description of a few Zafin'i'fotsy spirits, since they appear frequently at ceremonies in Ambanja. These versions of spirits' stories are drawn from descriptions provided by informants living in the Sambirano. They do not necessarily correspond with versions from other regions of Madagascar and so for contrast I have occasionally included information from Estrade, who has carefully catalogued Sakalava tromba spirits elsewhere in Madagascar.

Grandparents

Ndramarofaly (full name: *Andriamarofalinarivo*;[5] in Ambanja, this name is translated to mean "the King who is always happy" [*faly*, happy]). Most mediums in Ambanja are unfamiliar with this spirit's story but state that they believe he died by hanging. This spirit is considered to be one of the most important of the Grandparents, and he often officiates at cermonies in Ambanja. (Spirits listed above this point in the Zafin'i'mena genealogy appear only rarely in mediums in town.) Like an old king, he is very quiet and calm when he is present. An important fady for this spirit is the guinea hen. He likes to consume honey (a food that is given as an offering to ancestors throughout Madagascar), palm wine (*trembo*), and rum. (According to Estrade [1977: 207] his name means "the King who has many taboos," *faly* being an older version of *fady*, as with Nosy *Faly*. Estrade reports that this name is ironic, referring to Ndramarofaly having defied the fady imposed by a sorceror. While lost in a forest, he went mad and hanged himself from a cashew tree; as his body putrified, it was surrounded by guinea hens. Another fady is a perfume called *sakona*, which is made from the cashew.)

Ndramandenta (full name: *Andriamandentarivo*, "the King who slit the throats of many"). He is a spirit that many find frightening because when he arrives he is usually very angry. Still, as a Grandparent, he is a powerful healer, and so clients occasionally ask for his advice. This spirit died by having his throat slit, and so when he arrives he coughs up blood, making mediums reluctant to call him up. Ndramandenta likes to drink palm wine and he eats honey. (According to Estrade [1977: 212] he was a mighty warrior who was stoned to death. Estrade also reports that this spirit likes to consume blood.)

Kotofanjava, Kotomena, and Kotovazaha are representative of the baka andrano ("coming from the water") spirits of the Zafin'i'fotsy descent group. These spirits are from Analalava, which lies to the south of Ambanja near the mouth of the Loza River. They and an assortment of other spirits of the same generation chose to commit suicide by drowning rather than become the subjects of their Merina conquerors in the late eighteenth and early nineteenth centuries (cf. Feeley-Harnik 1988: 73). (Estrade [1977: 211], in his description of these spirits, stresses the severity of this action, saying drowning is an unusual form of suicide for Malagasy.) It is fady for Merina to approach these spirits. Since Zafin'i'fotsy spirits usually appear at ceremonies in Ambanja, people of Merina descent may not participate. Other fady include shark and an assortment of other fish that feasted on their corpses; chicken is also fady for some. (Estrade [1977: 211] only lists firearms as their taboo.) These spirits like rum.

Zaman'i'Bao ("Bao's Uncle") or Ndramiverinarivo (full name: *Andria-*

miverinarivo, "the King to whom many return") was among the first of the popular spirits to possess mediums in any great number in the Sambirano. Zaman'i'Bao's story is colorful and reflects the changes and experiences associated with colonial rule. Several informants say that Zaman'i'Bao died as a young man when he was enrolled as a student in the Merina city of Antananarivo. Two versions of his death were told frequently by informants: that he choked on a mixture of alcohol and cashews, or that his drink had been poisoned by a Merina rival. One informant, however, told a slightly different version: "Zaman'i'Bao was the *chef de canton* in an area near Mahajanga. There was an old woman who hated him because he was a Christian, and so she decided to poison his drink, *toaka mahabibo* [which is made from cashews]. When he drank the poison, it made him cough and spit up a lot of blood." When this spirit arrives in a medium he coughs uncontrollably; to signify possession (and to protect herself from harm) a medium marks her chest with kaolin before going into trance. As the latter informant said, "It is dangerous for a medium to be possessed by this spirit very often; if so, she will die young." Unlike other Grandparents, an important fady is cashews. Zaman'i'Bao likes rum, as well as drinks of foreign origin, such as beer and imported whiskey.

(Estrade [1977: 219] provides a more detailed account of the circumstances of his death: Zaman'i'Bao was enrolled in the Ecole le Myre de Villers in Antananarivo, and he died either as a result of Merina witchcraft or after he drank from a glass that was infected with *bacille de Koch.* [This seems unlikely, however, since this is the bacterium that causes conjunctivitis, and it is not fatal.] He went home drunk and got in bed with his wife, who pushed him away. He then took a double dose of an alcoholic drink called *betsa-betsa* and died. His wife mourned terribly because she believed that she was responsible. She went to the royal tomb of Betioka [Ambato-Boeni], crying and saying that she was to blame for her husband's death. But Zaman'i'Bao then rose from his tomb to comfort her. Today he consoles Sakalava women.)

Children

Raleva is perhaps one of the most "popular" of the spirits active in Ambanja today—he is well known to all mediums and inevitably appears at any tromba ceremony. Few of the mediums I interviewed were familiar with the details of his life, although several said that he served in the colonial administration, having been schooled as a child by the French. In his dress and actions he mimics a colonial officer.

One medium for this spirit told his story as follows: "Raleva worked for Zaman'i'Bao as his secretary, and he was married to Zaman'i'Bao's sister. . . . The two men were inseparable: they worked together and inhabited the same house. When Raleva heard that Zaman'i'Bao had been killed, he was so distraught that he committed suicide. This he did by climbing up in a tree, and then he jumped, landing on his head. As he fell, he hit some branches and broke his forearm and neck. This is why a medium puts kaolin [tany malandy] on her arm and neck before she summons the spirit." This medium then added: "It is true that Raleva was not royalty by birth, but shortly after the deaths of these two men, a young girl in Mahajanga became possessed by Zaman'i'Bao, and through her the spirit said, 'Raleva is to be respected just as I am . . . because we were close in life and thus it should be so with our tromba [spirits].' " The medium asserted that Raleva had died only within the last decade or so and that his niece, who was about seventy years old and who lived in Mahajanga, had toured the north several years ago, visiting mediums and testing them while in trance to make sure they were in fact possessed by Raleva. (This is the only example I have of tests being administered for popular tromba.) The most important fady for Raleva is cashews, although individual mediums sometimes list others that the spirit has designated for them throughout their lives. Although Tuesday is a taboo day for all baka atsimo spirits (in reference to activities that occur back at the tomb), Thursday is also taboo for Raleva, since he died on this day. He likes to smoke cigarettes, and although he will drink rum and palm wine, he prefers drinks of foreign origin, especially beer and whiskey; sometimes he will also drink soda pop. He enjoys wearing French cologne.

Raovoay ("Crocodile Man"). As with Raleva, mediums are unfamiliar with the details of Raovoay's life, and they know only a bit about the circumstances of his death. Raovoay was eaten by a crocodile (*voay*) while trying to cross a river, and for this reason a medium's motions imitate this animal when this spirit arrives and departs. Raovoay's fady and preferences are the same as Raleva's.

Grandchildren

Today, *Mampiary* is usually the first spirit that young women of the Sambirano acquire. Mampiary was a cowherd or "cowboy" (*koboy*) who died in an automobile accident when he was young. This happened when he was intoxicated and driving across a bridge in an oxcart filled with coffee. A car (which some say was gray, the color of most bush taxis in Madagascar) ran into him. When he fell from the cart, he broke his jaw and died. These circumstances account for his fady, which are oxcarts, coffee, and gray automobiles. Just as for his "Fathers" Raleva and Raovoay, cashews are fady. In addition, as mentioned in the description of Angeline's ceremony, one must take special care to make sure the medium does not injure her jaw when the Mampiary arrives. He likes beer, soda pop, and cigarettes.

Djao Kondry and *Be Ondry* were both young men who loved to box at morengy matches. Morengy occur frequently throughout the dry months (May to August), and this is a popular sport among young Sakalava and Tsimihety men. These matches usually take place on Sunday afternoons and attract contenders as well as young women who wish to watch. It is a time of romance, when sweethearts meet and court each other and when rivals fight one another. The boxing is carefully supervised so that opponents pull back from one another following each successful contact; the match ends after one opponent has successfully touched the other three times. The one who wins then seeks a new challenger from the circle of spectators, and whoever is willing to accept the challenge steps into the ring. Although most matches last no longer than a minute, after the official morengy is over rivals stay and fight each other in less structured settings. It is at these times that boxers may be seriously injured. Both Djao Kondry and Be Ondry died at morengy matches, killed by rivals. Their preferences and fady are the same as Mampiary's. A medium for either of these spirits is also forbidden from making a fist when she is out of trance. A few mediums say that they can not eat other foods, such as certain types of hot peppers.

Mampiamiñy This spirit's name means "to make limp" or "limpness," and when he possesses a medium he sits quietly and slumped over. He is not nearly as well known (or as active) in Ambanja as his brother or the two boxer spirits. He, like them, worked for the colonial administration, but the story of his death is not clear. One medium said she thought that maybe he died with Mampiary, riding in the same ox cart. His dress is not as stylish at that of the other Grandchildren. Instead, Mampiamiñy, as with an assortment of other Zafin'i'mena spirits, wears a purple waist wrap (*so-boya*) like that used by the Grandfathers, along with a white, four-pocketed shirt and fedora hat. Like Zaman'i'Bao, he appears to be a transitional spirit, since, in addition to coffee and cashews, his taboos include a kind of duck (*drakidraky*), milk, and french bread.[6]

As cross-cultural studies of possession reveal, spirit possession provides a powerful idiom for preserving collective and historically based memory. This is illustrated, for example, in Brown's (1991) study of a Haitian vodou priestess living in Brooklyn, New York. Embedded in the the dress, tastes, and tales of vodou spirits are generations of knowledge shared by displaced peoples. These include the experiences not only of those who choose to migrate from Haiti to the United States, but also of slaves taken involuntarily to the Caribbean from Africa. Giles has also argued that possession among kiSwahili speakers of the East African coast reflects indigenous notions of peoples of diverse origins whom they have encountered over time. Spirits incorporated into Swahili possession cults include Somali, Arab, Maasai, and even Malagasy and "hard-drinking European Catholic priests" (1987: 249).

Similiar themes are embedded in Sakalava possession. At present, tromba stories comprise a special genre that reflects different epochs of Sakalava history. Through these stories and associated dress and behavior Sakalava both learn about their past and interpret it. The tromba stories recorded above, for example, reflect local perceptions of historical experience that are specific to the Bemazava, since they do not necessarily correspond with those collected elsewhere by Estrade and others. For the Bemazava-Sakalava, Grandparents are powerful and influential rulers from the Sakalava past. Their greatest concerns are with the ancestors and with an old order that existed prior to French conquest. Informants are generally reluctant to tell the stories of these powerful tromba spirits, fearing their wrath, and it is their behavior that is the most important marker of their status: they are staid and serious, and they generally do not speak directly with the living, but through an interpreter. When these tromba spirits arrive, they speak of major events and relationships with other non-Sakalava. These include disputes over royal succession and subsequent relocation; battles with the Merina in the eighteenth and nineteenth centuries; the arrival of the French in the 1890s; and the 1947 uprising. Each time these spirits arrive, they (and their mediums) reconstruct the past and critique collective precolonial and early colonial experience.

SPIRITS FOR COMMON FOLK: ZAMAN'I'BAO, RALEVA, MAMPIARY, DJAO KONDRY, AND BE ONDRY

As one moves to the more recent generations there is a sudden shift in emphasis in both the genealogical system and in the behavior of the spirits. The first of these is Zaman'i'Bao, who occupies a pivotal position. Zaman'i'Bao is the first of the popular spirits, one who, by the middle of the present century, became well known among commoners as a powerful healer. Like the Grandparents, this spirit is associated with the precolonial era (as is evident in the way he dresses) and he has a royal name, Ndramverinarivo. He is more closely associated with the Children, however, since he does not appear in the saha of Nosy Faly but in mediums in town. Whereas the stories of Grandparents focus on the deeds these royalty performed in life, that of Zaman'i'Bao and other Children and Grandchildren focus on the nature of their deaths.

It is the spirits who follow Zaman'i'Bao whose actions and concerns parallel those of townspeople of the recent past and of today. The first of these are Zaman'i'Bao's brothers-in-law, Raleva and Raovoay. It is very difficult to date the arrival of these popular tromba spirits, but it seems that these Children appeared in Ambanja in the late 1950s or early 1960s. Shortly after Independence in 1960 they were followed by Mampiary the cowherd (who is the child of Raleva), and the boxers Be Ondry and Djao Kondry (two brothers and the children of Raovoay). These three spirits are considered by Sakalava to be royalty (ampanjaka), although Raleva and Raovoay and his sons are affines to the royal family. In essence, they are honorary royalty.

What becomes clear is that the most recent shifts in forms of spirit possession, involving the Grandchildren, closely parallel the experiences of the town's youth. As mentioned earlier, older—and especially royal—Sakalava are skeptical of these spirits, describing them as fakes (tromba mavandy), stating that they are not royal ancestral dead at all but only njarinintsy, or arguing that they are not Sakalava but were brought by Tsimihety migrants (see Deschamps 1959 for information on the migrations of the Tsimihety up to this time). Nevertheless, this category of spirits defines the most widespread of the popular forms of tromba possession in the Sambirano. In essence, the older spirits no longer fulfill the needs or expectations of the younger people of the town, who make up the majority of the population.[7] Older forms of tromba harken back to a time that is not part of the collective memory of the young. Even though Grandfather and Children spirits continue to oversee tromba ceremonies, and it is from them that spiritual power and knowledge are derived, nevertheless, the active participants at these gatherings and at healing consultations are most often the Grand-children.

Grandchildren spirits are young, reckless playboys who have died as a consequence of their behavior. When they interact with the living at ceremonies, their actions are similar to those who enjoy the town's nightlife. Sometimes spirits such as Mampiary even wander into discos and bars and demand something to drink or attempt to dance with women there, behaving as young men sometimes do when they are drunk. Although they are royalty (ampanjaka), their experiences parallel those of contemporary folk living in an urban world, where there are fast automobiles, cash crops, and rowdy boxing matches. It is these spirits that proliferate in Ambanja, and mediums report that they receive the greatest amount of requests from clients to consult with them: since these spirits grew up in the late colonial and postcolonial eras, they have a firsthand understanding of their clients' problems. Issues such as love and romance, work, and physical injury are important domains for them, these problems being typical of life in town and the surrounding plantation economy (see chapter 8).

Thus tromba provides an encapsulation of Sakalava perceptions of their collective experience. It is a form of ethnohistory, where the dress, actions, and stories of each generation of spirits reflect the nature of life in three epochs of time—precolonial, colonial, and postcolonial. In more recent years, tromba possession has involved the participation of increasing numbers of non-Sakalava. Tera-tany and vahiny both are now involved in the construction of local history, especially through the Grandchildren, who are most active in mediums today.

TROMBA, WAGE LABOR, AND ECONOMIC INDEPENDENCE

This historical order associated with tromba does not simply provide a means to record or reflect on past experience. It is also a major force that affects daily individual and collective action of both tera-tany and vahiny. The taboos associated with each spirit may influence the economic activities of individual mediums. On a grander scale, the royal tromba of Nosy Faly today monitor any additional economic developments that affect the local ancestral land.

TROMBA AND THEIR FADY

Just as dress serves as a marker of precolonial, colonial, and postcolonial epochs, the various fady associated with spirits reflect changes in the local economy which accompanied the introduction of foreign produce. These fady record these changes. They may also affect the daily activities of their mediums. In the Sambirano and neighboring areas, as one moves down through the Zafin'i'mena genealogies, it is plantation cash crops that slowly have been incorporated into the system of fady. This process reflects changes in the economy of the Sambirano over time and attempts by local Sakalava to resist and control the effects of these economic changes on their collective and individual lives.

The fady associated with the Grandparent spirits are the least restrictive. Many of these spirits impose none on their mediums, save for limitations associated with certain days of the week when the medium may not go into trance. (These taboo days affect all spirits and correspond to activities that take place on a regular basis at the tombs.) These spirits usually prefer to be fed certain items that existed prior to the French conquest: honey, palm wine, and, sometimes, rum. Honey and rum are regarded as appropriate foods for ancestors throughout Madagascar.[8]

It is among the Children that one begins to see the acceleration of preferences and aversions for foreign goods. Bloch (1971: 8–9; 32ff) has noted that the Merina often express a certain ambivalence toward foreign goods and customs, which they contrast to things Malagasy (thus there are *fomba vazaha*, or foreign customs, and fomba-gasy, or Malagasy ones). Similar distinctions are made in Ambanja: there are *Malagasy* chickens and ducks that are distinguished from *foreign* breeds, for example. In the case of produce and animals, often the latter category connotes better quality, yet the ambiguity remains (Bloch mentions this as well).

In the context of tromba, a distinction is also made between foreign imported goods and cash crops that are of foreign origin. Although Children and Grandchildren enjoy (and demand) foreign cigarettes, rum, beer, soda pop, and sometimes even whiskey (which is very expensive), certain cash crops are taboo. For the Children an important fady is cashews (*mahabibo*) and for the Grandchildren, cashews and coffee (*kafé*). In the context of tromba there exists both a recording of the introduction of foreign goods and a subtle critique of them.

WORKING IN THE SAMBIRANO

In order to understand the significance of these fady, it is necessary to return our attention to the economy of the Sambirano. In the warehouses of the major enterprises, women are employed to sort and clean three main crops: cashews, coffee, and cocoa. Of these cash crops, two are major fady for the majority of tromba spirits active in Ambanja. Although cashews grew wild throughout the west coast prior to the colonial era, it was during the period of French occupation that cashews became a major cash crop. This is especially true around the area of Mahajanga, which is often referred to as the "capital of tromba" by the northern Sakalava, since it is near there where many of the Zafin'i'mena spirits are entombed. Mahajanga is also referred to affectionately as "Mahabibo," for it is a city of cashews. Similarly, indigenous coffee grew in Madagascar, but it was in the 1940s when new domestic strains were introduced and when much of the countryside was transformed into coffee plantations where the crop was grown for export.[9]

It is not coincidental that residents of Ambanja are referred to as the "possessors of the soil" or tera-tany. Although in part this is a general reference to the Sambirano being the ancestral land of the Bemazava-Sakalava, it is also the Bemazava who are identified as those who originally used the land prior to the arrival of the French, other foreign nationals, and Malagasy migrants. Today, in the Sambirano, it is the enterprises that occupy much of their territory. Private plots are scarce and highly valued, for several reasons. Here, the soil is very fertile and farming is profitable. Also, personal economic freedom is associated with land ownership. If one has even a small plot of land on which to grow rice and other subsistence crops, one may not have to work as a wage laborer. This is the most important distinction made between tera-tany and vahiny, since many of the former own land, while the latter are landless proletarians who hope one day to acquire arable plots.

In the Sambirano the enterprises are the largest employers of unskilled labor. There are significant benefits associated with this work. Salaries at several enterprises are relatively high: in mid-1987 a full-time laborer could earn 30,000 fmg per month. Although this is barely enough to feed a small family, laborers who are single can live fairly comfortably on this salary. Enterprises provide women who have no other employa-ble skills with a ready means for economic independence. Two of my informants, for example, who were having marital troubles, were able to move out of their husbands' houses and rent one of their own with money they saved from their salaries. In addition, health care is free or available on a sliding scale for laborers and members of their house-holds. Still, cash and health care are not as highly valued as economic independence.

Throughout this century, Malagasy have resisted wage and contract (corvée) labor. As Feeley-Harnik notes, by World War II Madagascar had more labor laws than any other French colony. French colonial officers "noted that Malagasy had 'a veritable fear' of labor contracts. By signing them, they felt 'a little like prisoners' " (1984: 8; she in turn is quoting Thompson and Adloff 1965: 449). Among the Sakalava, wage labor means losing control over one's time and becoming entwined in unequal social relations. According to the Sakalava "morality of ex-change" (Parry and Bloch 1989) the reciprocal exchange of goods and services is coveted, but payments made in cash are generally not desired and are often refused.[10]

Most laborers hope eventually to find other employment, since enter-prise work is difficult and time consuming. Many newly arrived migrants begin by working at an enterprise and then, as soon as they have accu-mulated enough capital, they start a small business of their own. Antan-droy, for example, travel south to Befandriana and Antsohihy where they buy rice and then resell it in Ambanja, while others go north to purchase cattle. These they then take back through Ambanja and then on the ferry to Nosy Be, where sugar cane plantations monopolize lands that could otherwise be used for grazing. Here the cattle are slaughtered for sale in the market, where much meat is needed to satisfy the demands of the local tourist trade (see the case of Guardian in chapter 4).

Although most enterprises have one worker village on their grounds, the majority of laborers' homes are in town or are scattered throughout the rural areas of the Sambirano. Laborers begin their workday around 6:00 A.M., when they catch a transport (usually a large flatbed lorry or dump truck) for the hour-long ride to the company warehouses. Women (who may be accompanied by children) sit in shaded areas and sort and bag produce (again, see plate 3), while men load these bags and other heavy items onto trucks bound for the port. Men, women, and sometimes children work in the fields, cutting branches, clearing underbrush, and harvesting produce. While most women's salaries are determined by the number of bags they fill (these are weighed at the end of each day), men are paid slightly more and receive a flat salary. Since the enterprises are far from most laborers' homes, the majority carry their lunches in small baskets. A typical meal consists of leftover rice with, perhaps, a little broth sprinkled over it. Laborers are allowed thirty minutes to an hour for lunch, but women often prefer to eat quickly or skip lunch altogether so they can bag more than the minimum quota or finish early and rest at the end of the day. The workday is scheduled to end around 3:00 P.M., but delays occur frequently, since trucks may be needed for other purposes. As a result, laborers may not reach their homes until 5:00 or 6:00 P.M., if not later.

One of the greatest complaints expressed by laborers concerns the time requirements of their work. Since they usually work six days a week, they feel they live only to work, sleep, and work again (*miasa, matory, miasa koa koa*). Each day they return home late and exhausted, unable to perform other necessary tasks. They have no time to visit with kin and neighbors or keep house. For this reason women and single men usually rise as early as 3:00 or 4:00 A.M. to clean their homes and shop before catching the transport to work. They are unable to attend the Thursday market, where one finds the greatest selection of items and the lowest prices and where townspeople can look forward to visiting friends and kin who live in the rural areas. Sunday is their day off, but on this day hardly anything is available in the two markets in town. Enterprise work is especially hard on single women with children, since they must also rely on kin for help with childcare. If a woman has no kin living nearby, she must bring her children to work with her. Children who are sick usually accompany their mothers to work so that they can be cared for there. The degree to which this is tolerated varies from one enterprise to another; in some cases a woman may risk losing her job if she pays too much attention to her children.

As discussed in chapter 2, land in the Sambirano is associated with economic freedom. This feeling is especially strong among the Sakalava. As one Sakalava engineer said, "I have planted coffee on my father's land so that in another five years, when the plants are mature, I can quit this horrible job and control my own life, my time." As the story of Botabe's homestead (chapter 4) illustrates, both tera-tany and vahiny are freed from such constraints of capitalist labor by nonenterprise work and through the acquisition of land on which to grow rice and house kin. Laborers and supervisors alike often speak of a desire to purchase a bit of land one day so that they will not have to rely on the enterprises for their livelihood. The preoccupation with land is reflected in the activities of the local county court, where approximately 70 percent of all cases involve land disputes. Although employers refer to the Sakalava as lazy (kamo) because of their reluctance to work as laborers, the Sakalava regard their resistance to wage labor as their strength. It is partially a result of colonial policies that many Sakalava have been able to avoid working for the enterprises. Sakalava were alienated of the richest farmland, and those who remained in the valley and lived on indigenous reserves continued to farm and graze animals. Other non-Sakalava worked as laborers. Following the Socialist Revolution, land reform laws have favored tera-tany. Sakalava have also maintained land rights without purchasing their plots since, by law, whoever puts the land to good use is the rightful owner.

TROMBA AS A CRITIQUE OF CAPITALIST PRODUCTION AND RELATIONS

Feeley-Harnik, in a discussion of Sakalava royal work, argues that Sakalava taboos served to exempt individuals from labor requirements imposed by the French during the colonial era (1984: 11). In the Sambirano, the fady associated with tromba operate in a similar fashion. Tromba possession enables a medium—who may be Sakalava or non-Sakalava—to manipulate her economic relations to her advantage.

Spirits like Raleva and Raovoay, as well as Mampiary and his classificatory brothers Be Ondry and Djao Kondry, are extremely active in mediums in the Sambirano, which means that many mediums have coffee or cashew taboos. Because of this, a medium with one of these spirits must avoid these agricultural products. If she does not, her spirit may become angry and make her very sick. Mediums often shift their economic activities as a result of new restrictions imposed on them by their tromba spirits. I encountered several mediums who had these fady and had continued to work at the enterprises, but they had to make sure to sort only cocoa and avoid coffee and cashews. Generally this is not a problem if one works at an enterprise where, on a daily basis, a choice is possible. Coworkers, foremen, and employers are often aware of and respectful of tromba fady. As the case of Berthine, below, shows, a more common scenario is that a woman quits her job when she learns that she is possessed by a spirit with a coffee or cashew taboo.

BERTHINE'S PAST EXPERIENCES AS AN ENTERPRISE LABORER

Berthine is about forty years old. She has been single for ten years, ever since her husband left for Diégo with his mistress. She lives with three of her four children (the other child lives with her sister). Her oldest child is now twenty, and he works as a laborer at one of the enterprises to support the household. Berthine is severely crippled as a result of an automobile accident fifteen years ago; she can move only if carried or if she drags herself on the ground. As a result, she is not much of a housekeeper. Her house is in shambles and leans to one side, and both the interior and the surrounding yard are dusty and messy, atypical for homes in this town. Berthine was born of Betsileo parents near Fianarantsoa, but they moved often when she was a child, since her father was a gendarme. They came to Ambanja in 1951 and she has stayed here ever since. Both of her parents are dead.

Like her son, Berthine once worked for one of the enterprises. As she explained, "Eleven years ago my husband persuaded me to get a job to help support the household; this was just one year after our youngest child was born. But I had no skills, and so I went to a neighbor, who worked at one of the enterprises, and I asked her to help me find a job. . . . I was hired to sort and bag produce with women and other girls who were about my age. . . . Oh, the work there was very hard! You sit and work from early morning into the late afternoon. . . . I sorted coffee and cashews, and I worked there for about six months. . . . It was around this time that I started to feel sick: I was dizzy, and I had terrible headaches that would not go away. Eventually I went to a medium, who told me I had a tromba . . . when the tromba arrived we knew it was Mampiary [for whom cashews and coffee are taboo]. . . . My husband was furious, but he and my sister helped me instate the tromba. . . . We held a small ceremony with three mediums six months later." I asked her if this has affected her life in any way since and she said, laughing, "It causes no problems, except that we must never bring coffee into the house!"

Berthine's story is typical: pressures at home (and, specifically, from her husband) forced her out into the labor market. She, like many other mediums I encountered, reports that subsequently she had been forced to quit her job at the enterprises because of the sudden arrival of a spirit whose fady prohibit its medium from coming into contact with cash crops. When mediums quit their jobs they then turn to other means of support. This includes selling goods such as charcoal, vegetables, or palm fiber (for house construction) from their yards; finding work at a business in town; or seeking financial support from kin or a lover. Even though these activities are generally not as lucrative as enterprise work, they enable a woman to remain economically independent, stay close to home, and control how she spends her waking hours. Reminiscent of spirits in Malay factories (see Ong 1987), tromba provides a medium with a means by which to articulate her sentiments regarding wage labor in symbolic ways and through the words (and fady) of her spirits. But whereas in Ong's example outbursts of group possession provide only temporary relief from the drudgery of the shop floor, tromba possession has long-term effects that permanently liberate the medium from the demands of wage labor.

The requirements of tromba fady are not rigid, but can be altered or manipulated by mediums when necessary. In the case of Angeline (chapter 5), for example, problems arose after it became clear that she was possessed by Mampiary and Djao Kondry. Her example illustrates the flexibility of these taboos, revealing that distinctions can be made between wage labor and favors to kin. From a Sakalava point of view, it is not the *cash crops alone* which present problems but the *nature of labor relations* that endow these items with harmful properties.

ANGELINE'S PROBLEMS WITH COFFEE

After it was clear that Angeline was possessed by two tromba spirits that had coffee taboos (Mampiary and Djao Kondry), her in-laws were faced with a significant problem. Although Angeline had never worked as a wage laborer, her affines expected her to work in their fields, since Jean's mother had looked after Angeline when she was first married and, later, whenever Angeline had been sick. Jean's mother grows coffee in her fields; since Angeline's spirits forbade her from coming into contact with this crop, she could no longer help with the care of the fields and with the harvest each year. Angeline's labor is valuable to her kin, and so she and Jean's mother finally decided to ask Angeline's spirits for a dispensation. They did this by holding a private ceremony in Angeline's house. Jean's mother called up each spirit in turn and asked if it would be possible to exempt Angeline from this taboo.

As members of her household, her spirits wished only the best for Angeline and her kin, and so each spirit gave Angeline permission to work in her mother-in-law's fields, but they forbade her from ever working at the enterprises. As Jean put it later, Angeline may handle raw coffee berries, but *processed coffee is strictly taboo* (informant's emphasis).

These taboos are a creative *local* response to an awareness of exploitation associated with capitalist relations, as revealed by data from other regions of Madagascar. For example, Feeley-Harnik reports that coffee and cashew taboos may perhaps be spreading south to the Analalava region. In the 1970s these fady were not associated with tromba there, yet by 1989 informants told her a story of a medium of Mampiary who died after falling asleep against a bag of coffee. Although this is not a plantation region, coffee has become a more popular drink in recent years and is associated with European customs (fomba vazaha) (written personal communication, 1991). The flexibility associated with possession in Madagascar allowed Angeline and her kin to redefine the relevance of her spirits to work activities (cf. Fieloux and Lombard 1989). Her spirit's coffee fady saved her from wage labor relations and simultaneously allowed her to assist her in-laws through principles defined by kin-based reciprocity.

TROMBA AND COLLECTIVE POWER IN THE SAMBIRANO

In the precolonial era, tromba was central to social and political control in Sakalava society (Ottino 1965). Today this role remains evident in the actions of the royal tromba spirits of Nosy Faly. In the past, their advice could affect the lives of all subjects, although today it is generally limited to the private matters of royalty. In this aspect tromba spirits have become marginalized because of the displacement of power from royalty to the state. Within the last fifteen years, however, the power of royal tromba has been extended in new ways, so that these spirits affect the activities of both tera-tany and vahiny. As a result of recent developments in government policies, tromba spirits have entered the arena of economic development of the Sambirano.

MALAGASIZATION AND ECONOMIC DEVELOPMENT

Throughout the colonial period, spirit possession and other rituals associated with honoring Sakalava royalty were suspect and were often suppressed by local French authorities. The level of surveillance increased dramatically following the 1947 revolt, which began on the east coast and quickly spread throughout the island. In response, tromba mediums in the Sambirano essentially went underground, holding tromba ceremonies in private and hidden places.[11] As Feeley-Harnik reports, the Analalava region shared similar experiences: the French required that the Bemihisatra-Sakalava acquire their permission for all forms of royal rituals. As a result, secret tromba meetings were held. In some cases, however, French officials appear to have looked the other way, as long as such ceremonies did not interfere with the power of French authority. Since women were not perceived as a political threat by the French, "that contributed to the indecision of French officials and thus their inconsistent and ultimately inconsequential efforts at suppression"; therefore tromba possession appears to have spread, rather than declined in this area (1991a: 112, n. 27).

In contrast to the colonial period and the first fifteen years following Independence, malagasization marks a new, dramatic shift at the state level, beginning in the 1970s. Malagasization has been incorporated into the national policies of President Ratsiraka's administration, mandating the rejection of many French-derived practices (fomba-vazaha) and the promotion of Malagasy customs (fomba-gasy). Its effects are widespread. They include a shift from French to Malagasy as the language for teaching in the schools (see chapter 9) and the nationalization of privately owned plantations. By government edict, respect must also be shown for local customs (fomba-gasy, fombandrazana).

The attitudes that accompany malagasization vary radically from that of colonial officials and those who served in the early post-Independence years. Bemazava attribute outbreaks of njarinintsy possession in local schools (which began in the 1970s) to the earlier actions of the French, since they built these and other buildings with total disregard for Sakalava tombs and other sacred locales. The construction of these buildings disrupted and displaced spirits, who have subsequently become angry and have caused harm to the living. The more recent emphasis on malagasization is reflected in the increase in tromba. Mediums in Ambanja report that around 1972, following the Revolution, tromba possession became a sanctioned activity, so that it was no longer necessary to be discrete about holding ceremonies. Ceremonies started to occur with greater frequency and spirits began to appear in public settings such as bars and in the street.

Royal tromba has also been affected by malagasization. The tromba spirits of Nosy Faly are respected as the guardians of sacred space by both tera-tany and vahiny. Since the mid-1970s, the role of the royal tromba has become increasingly important in the Sambirano. Whenever the local terrain is disrupted or changed, respect must be shown for local customs and for the geography—and thus the spiritual order—of the local ancestral land. In the Sambirano, deferring to the tromba spirits of Nosy Faly has become an aspect of local protocol. A new coffee factory, for example, bears evidence of a *joro*, a ceremony that is held to honor the ancestors and give thanks for their blessing and assistance. Cow skulls are mounted on the fence surrounding the factory, a sign that zebu were sacrificed, and in the courtyard there is a plaque at the foot of the flagpole which commemorates the date of the joro. Today this sight is a common one throughout Madagascar. Two examples illustrate recent participation of royal spirits in the Sambirano's economic order in post-Revolutionary times.

THE FISHERY IN NOSY BE

Seafood is an important export commodity for northern Madagascar, and in the early 1970s a fishery was built on the island of Nosy Be to harvest and process local sea products. In 1973 it started to fish near Nosy Be for giant prawns (*makamba*). The allocation of fishing rights became an important issue since the richest waters surround Nosy Faly. Fishery management consisted of French nationals, Merina, and Betsileo. They knew that if their fishing boats were seen near the island it would cause an uproar among the Sakalava. For this reason they decided to hire someone who was Sakalava who could help them approach the Bemazava royalty and gain access to the waters. The man they hired is a member of the northern Bemihisatra royal family (which is based in Nosy Be) and is knowledgeable in both financial and royal affairs.

Gaining initial and continued access to the waters involved complicated negotiations and private conferences with both living and dead royalty. This emissary first approached the Bemazava king and his advisers, who eventually gave him permission to visit Nosy Faly. There, in the village of the royal tombs, he had to confer with the tomb guardians who, in turn, helped him gain access to the saha and thus the tromba spirits themselves.

The standing agreement reached between the fishery and the royal tromba spirits requires that at the opening of each season the emissary visit Nosy Faly and acquire permission to fish in the local waters during that season. If the fishing season is a successful one, the fishery must then host a joro and rebiky (a royal dance) in honor of the royal ancestors. This contract is similar to that made by any client who consults with a tromba spirit in town: one makes a request (for medicine, to be cured, and so forth) and then promises to return to thank and repay the tromba spirit with goods or money if the tromba's actions were effective. The first ceremonies were held in 1975, and every year since they have done the same. Each time the fishery hosts a joro or rebiky, both living and dead royalty preside.

THE NEW HIGH SCHOOL

The population of Ambanja has been increasing steadily and so in the early 1980s the town decided to build a high school. Up to this time, it was necessary for all students in the county to go to Diégo to continue their studies beyond junior high. The naming of the new school became a major political issue in Ambanja, where tensions between insiders and outsiders surfaced. Two factions emerged: Sakalava (especially royalty) wanted to name the school after Tsiaraso I, a former Bemazava ruler. Non-Sakalava preferred to use the name of a Sakalava national hero who was instrumental in the 1947 uprising against the French. When the vote was taken at a public meeting, Sakalava royalty made sure that it was well attended by their supporters so that they carried the vote.

After the decision was made, the present king, Tsiaraso III, went to Nosy Faly[12] and requested permission of the tromba of Tsiaraso I (Andriamandilatrarivo) to use his name. Naming the school after Tsiaraso I is significant because, as stated earlier, the name that a royal person has in life may not be uttered after his or her death. To put the name Andriamandilatrarivo on the front of the school, however, would be an even greater breach of tradition, since it is a sacred name. Tsiaraso I served as an appropriate compromise, because today there are many people who disregard royal rules regarding name taboos.

Today the school is an imposing structure on the edge of town, occupying lands acquired from one of the enterprises. It is a source of civic pride: in 1987, the Independence Day celebrations on June 26 (the most important holiday in Madagascar) were held on its grounds. A lengthy parade, which included nearly everyone in town—schoolchildren, workers, different elements of the national party, and local clubs—filed past a grandstand of local dignitaries who watched from the shade of the school's veranda. The school opened its doors to students in the fall

of 1987. Its name and the manner in which it was constructed under-
score that it is a focus of collective identity among Sakalava.

BEMAZAVA SPIRITUAL AUTHORITY AND ECONOMIC DEVELOPMENT

As Comaroff has asserted in her work *Body of Power, Spirit of Resistance* (1985), it is a mistake to view traditionalism as an archaic response
to change or as an oblique form of protest. In Madagascar, shifts in
national policy in the early 1970s have stressed the importance of showing respect for local customs. As a result, the authority of the Bemazava
tromba has been revitalized, and these spirits have entered the arena
of economic development. Whenever the local terrain is disrupted or
changed, respect must be shown for local customs, the geography, and
the spiritual order of the Bemazava kingdom.

The authority invested in tromba spirits is very similar to that of
spirits among the Shona during the struggle for independence in Zimbabwe, as described by Lan in *Guns and Rain* (1985). In this context,
spirit mediumship was not an oblique form of control, but a vital force
during a time of great change. As in the Bemazava example, Shona
spirit mediums serve as vessels for royal ancestral spirits, who are the
guardians of local, sacred ground. Spilled blood can pollute the land
and harm its inhabitants, and thus Shona mediums imposed restrictions
on and served as advisers and ritual specialists for ZANU (Zimbabwe
African National Union) guerillas, teaching them about the terrain and
monitoring their access to the land and its people. Following Mugabe's
victory, Shona mediums were recognized as heros of the revolution. I
do not maintain that tromba mediums are revolutionary leaders; nevertheless, Lan's example is useful, since it underscores the potential power
of traditionalism as an agent of control in social change, rather than
simply viewing it as a vestigial and archaic cultural form (this will be
explored in chapter 9).

The purpose of malagasization has been to assert Malagasy customs
over those of foreign origin, but in the Bemazava kingdom it has led to
the assertion of local custom over all others. Following malagasization,
the government has become self-conscious about how its actions may
affect Malagasy people as a national body. In the Sambirano, the French
built their structures with total disregard for sacred locales, placing
buildings on top of tombs and moving villagers to other areas. Bemazava
hold the French responsible for outbreaks of possession by evil spirits

which have occurred within the past decade: they argue that displaced ancestral spirits are angry and so they now harm the living. If the present government of Madagascar were to disregard the sacredness of Bemazava land, its actions would parallel those of the former French colonial government.

This example from Madagascar illustrates the dynamic of traditionalism in a contemporary African state. On the one hand, it is an important aspect of nationalist policies. On the other, it provides particular groups with a means to assert their authority over that of the dominant political body (see also Apter 1992). In the northwest, Sakalava tromba spirits (and their mediums) impede development, since negotiations take time, money, and a lot of patience. Ong (1987), in her study of possession in Malaysian factories, illustrates that possession may slow capitalist production or bring it to a temporary halt. The actions of the tromba, however, are more influential than the spirits (and the possessed) in Ong's example. They are sanctioned by the state and they are accepted by Malagasy, who, throughout the island, embrace a belief in and a respect for ancestors. Malagasization assures that Bemazava may exercise authority over Merina and other migrants; ultimately, it elevates local authority over that of the state. As the terms *tera-tany* ("children of the soil/land") and *tompontany* ("masters/owners of the soil/land") imply, it is the tromba of the Sambirano who are, essentially, the true landlords of sacred space who manage and control the means of production in the context of state capitalism. Since managers of state businesses rarely occupy their positions for more than a few years, the extent of their influence is limited. Today, these outsiders must maintain a delicate balance with the tromba spirits if they are to proceed smoothly in their pursuit for profit in Bemazava territory.

CHAPTER VII

Spirit Mediumship and Social Identity

Since tromba is a vital aspect of Sakalava culture, participation in tromba possession confirms tera-tany status. Strictly speaking, tera-tany and Sakalava are synonymous, yet the recent participation of migrants in tromba possession necessitates a looser definition. For those who have only recently arrived in Ambanja, tromba is an exclusive and unfamiliar institution but, over time, virtually any outsider may participate. The manner and rate in which they become involved in tromba is determined by their social networks, length of stay, economic constraints, compatibility with Sakalava, and desire to be integrated into the tera-tany community. Tromba creates a sense of belonging, a social cohesiveness that is unmatched by other local institutions. Sakalava structural principles that are associated with tromba possession favor women over men. As this chapter will show, participation in tromba may alter a woman's life in profound ways. First, as a medium, she may experience shifts in her identity. This process is facilitated by a special form of fictive kinship which has especially profound ramifications for non-Sakalava. In turn, a shift in her social relations occurs, affecting those who know her in the privacy of her home as well as the public sphere, where she strengthens her personal networks with other mediums and, if she works as a healer, with clients. In essence, tromba enables a medium to redefine her social status and gain access to local power structures.

SELFHOOD AND PERSONHOOD IN THE CONTEXT OF POSSESSION

Tromba possession affects identity on multiple levels. As a medium moves in and out of trance, she experiences shifts in her identity on three different levels: the first is what Mauss (1987: 2) referred to as the idea of *moi* or "self," that is, her private (and psychological) sense of who she is as an individual operating in the world. The second is her "person" (*personne;* again, see Mauss 1987: 2ff), or what I will refer to as her *social persona:* how she is perceived by others within her social milieu.[1] For example, as a medium a woman elevates her social status when she becomes a healer. She also shifts from being a commoner to a royal personality. The third shift is one that is experienced by mediums who are migrants. They experience a shift in their *ethnic identity*, that is, their *cultural persona*. A complex fictive kinship system associated with tromba enables a medium to make these shifts in her social and cultural personae.

SHIFTING SELVES

A medium, because she is a vessel or "house" (trano) for spirits, has multiple selves: her personal (unpossessed) self and each of her spirit's selves. Thus, a medium with two spirits has, essentially, three selves. Gender is also an important elements of selfhood. As a medium she is female; when possessed, she is usually male. The boundaries between these different states of selfhood are clearly demarcated for the observer as a woman goes in and out of trance, yet these multiple selves blend into one another and carry over into her daily (unpossessed) life.

As the last chapter illustrated, spirit possession provides fertile ground on which to record and interpret collective experience. In turn a dynamic may also develop between *collective and personal histories*. As Brown deftly illustrates in her study *Mama Lola* (1991), in the context of Haitian vodou there are multiple layers of history recorded, shaped by Haitian history, generations of mediums within a given kindred, and the personalities of the spirits that possess them. As we learn through the unraveling of the personal and family history of her key informant, Alourdes, different spirits (who are African and Haitian, male and female, and so forth) are, for example, more appropriate for particular time periods, settings, and temperaments of mediums. In this way, not only is possession subjectively experienced, but history, as well, is interpreted from a subjective point of view by a medium, through her spirits. This process in turn has a profound effect on the medium's sense of selfhood.

This overlapping of histories is also central to tromba possession. A tromba medium, as well as others around her, perceives herself as a composite or a gestalt of interlocking and overlapping selves. This is evident in the way that tromba mediums and their spirits recounted their personal histories during my interviews with them. I found that the events in mediums' personal lives were often reflected in their versions of their spirit's personal histories. At times, tromba stories provided a more appropriate arena for articulating a medium's personal problems. For example, in interviews with a medium named Mariamo, I had great difficulty in collecting any details on her life. After numerous attempts one afternoon proved futile, I asked her to call up her spirits so that I might interview them. Two appeared: the first was a prostitute spirit named Mbotimahasaky, whom I quickly learned had had serious conflicts with her father, brother, and lover, and she had killed her first and only baby as a result of neglect. The second spirit was a soccer player named Djaomarengy. After these two spirits had departed, her assistant (rangahy) and I retold the spirits' stories to Mariamo, who then explained that she herself had worked as a prostitute for sixteen years in Mahajanga. Previous to this event she had sometimes alluded to her inability to have children, but it was only during (and then after) these interviews with the spirit Mbotimahasaky that Mariamo was able to articulate the great sadness she felt about her barrenness. As I later learned, the antics of the spirit Djaomarengy usually paralleled events in the life of Mariamo's lover, who was an avid soccer player. As this story illustrates, there is a richness in narrative form here that may allow for a deeper level of introspection than is generally possible in daily social discourse among Malagasy. In essence, mediums may in fact experience a deeper or more integrated sense of self than do non-mediums (cf. Obeyesekere 1981).[2]

THE SOCIAL PERSONA, OR MEDIUMSHIP AND PERSONHOOD

For Mariamo, this overlapping of selves is one that carries over into her everyday life, and which affects her *social persona* (person) or how she is viewed by others in her social world. Mariamo perceives herself as being composed of all of these personalities, and others do as well:

she is both male and female, royal and commoner. This is especially true since she works as a healer. Even in her unpossessed state she experiences this shift, because she is respected and feared by others who are aware of her association with ancestral spirits. Possession also affects how a medium is defined structurally in relation to others. As will be made clear below, her personal relationships with kin and friends are temporarily altered as she shifts in and out of trance yet, by virtue of her being a medium, they are permanently altered as well.

Gender, Age, and Possession

Historically, the majority of mediums for tromba spirits have been adult women. At Nosy Faly, for example, saha are usually women in their forties or older, while men play complementary roles as interpreters for the spirits. In general, a Sakalava ritual cannot be performed if the two are not present and represented.[3] This is evident, for example, during activities that take place at the royal tombs on Nosy Faly. There are both male and female tomb guardians (male: ngahy; female: marovavy or ambimanañy), each with their specified duties. When living royalty come to pay tribute to their ancestors, both male and female guardians must participate in order for the spirits to be invoked. Similarly, when the greatest of the royal tromba spirits are consulted, both the female saha and the male ngahy must participate.

Thus, in the precolonial context, possession in Sakalava culture was not evidence of marginal status (cf. Giles 1987 on possession on the East African coast). Instead, it was a central institution associated with adult female status. Similarly, in Ambanja today, tromba possession continues to be almost exclusively a female experience. Tromba spirits may possess men, but this is unusual. Only four (of a total of ninety-eight) of the mediums I encountered throughout the course of my field-work were male. In addition, different categories and generations of spirits are associated with different ages and statuses. Possession sickness, involving njarinintsy and other malicious spirits, occurs most often during adolescence, their crises coinciding with troubled or failed love affairs and pregnancy outside of marriage (see chapter 9). Tromba mediumship, however, is associated with culturally sanctioned adult female status: out of eighteen female tromba mediums I interviewed in detail, nearly all had been married (by ceremony or common law) at least once before the onset of tromba, and thirteen had had at least one pregnancy that may or may not have been carried to full term at the time of having a tromba spirit instated (see figure 7.1 and Appendix A).[4] Marriage itself is the idiom that is used to describe tromba possession: a medium and her spirit are defined as each other's spouse (vady). As will be explained below, this concept of marriage has significant implications for household dynamics. It also provides a framework for a medium to expand her social networks.

The age of onset for tromba possession is typically between eighteen and thirty years, although I did encounter two cases involving girls under fourteen years of age.[5] In addition, different categories of tromba spirits make their debuts at different stages in a medium's career, so that mediums accumulate more powerful spirits over time. Grandchildren spirits frequently arrive in women who are seventeen to twenty-two, Children arrive most often in women twenty to thirty-two, and Grandparents are almost exclusively seen for the first time in mediums who are thirty-two to forty years of age (again, see figure 7.1).

Boddy's (1988, 1989) work on zar possession among women in northern Sudan provides clues for understanding gender as a factor in possession experience. She argues that zar is related to concepts of female identity and selfhood and that possession occurs in response to women's attempts to cope with circumcision and the overwhelming demands associated with adult status: in the Sudan, female "selfhood is . . . culturally overdetermined" (1988: 16). Even when women have been properly socialized and circumcised, they may still fail to be fertile. As Boddy explains, "When a woman's fertility mandate is impaired—for whatever reason—her self-image, social position, and ultimately general health are threatened"; it is zar spirits that are "held responsible for procreative mishap" (1989: 186, 188). Within this context it is married and childless women who are most likely to become possessed by zar spirits.

Tromba in Ambanja is likewise associated with female status, but in this case it serves as a confirmation that female status has been achieved. As a woman takes on the role of tromba medium, her identity is transformed in terms of the way it is perceived subjectively and collectively. While in a state of trance, her personality and behavior change in ways that are only limited by the boundaries of her spirit repertoire. Her spirit(s) also impose(s) a new order on her daily life through the complicated categories of taboos that are part of each spirit's identity and history. Furthermore, as a powerful and respected healer, a medium imposes order on the lives of others: her family, her friends, and her clients are all within her sphere of influence. If she is possessed by a very powerful spirit, then she may affect the actions of living royalty

PREG/ MEDIUM	AGE	RESIDENCE STATUS				ADULT STATUS		SPIRIT REPERTOIRE				SCH
		VAHINY										
		T-T	ST	SET	CSET	MAR	OFSP	PS	GChld	Child	GPar	
FEMALE MEDIUMS												
1. BASELY	19				X	0	0		1?			ps
2. ANGELINE	20	X				1	1 p	1	2			jhs
3. BERTHINE	20				X ms	1	0		1?			jhs
4. LEAH	20	X				1s	1 p	2	2			jhs
5. ALICE	28				X ms	2	3		2	3		hs
6. MARIE	28				X	1s	1	2	2	2		jhs
7. BEATRICE	30	X				2s	4	1	1?			jhs
8. FLEURETTE	32				X ms	1	2		1	1		hs
9. PERLINE	33	X				2	0 i		1	1		hs
10. MONA	34	X				1	0		3?			jhs
11. MARIAMO	34		X	ms		2	0 i	1	3	1		ps
12. MARIVOLA	36		X			1	4			3	1	hs
13. GERTRUDE	37				X	1s	4		2			jhs
14. ELODIE	39	X				2s	6		1	1		jhs
15. ELISABETH	42	X				2s	2			3	2	ps
16. ZALOKY	50	X				2	4			1		ps
SAHA												
17. DADIBE	39	X				1s	2			3	1	ps
18. MBOTISOA	50	X				1w	3			3?	1	ps
MALE MEDIUMS												
19. ROMAIN	30			X?ms		1s	1	1				jhs
20. GABY	38	X				1s	0			2		ps

Figure 7.1. Table of Mediums. Note: See Appendix A for more details and for descriptions of women who have experienced only possession sickness.

as well. Finally, she joins a special collective of mediums who share the same spirits or who have other spirits from the same genealogies. As will be described below, these women, as spouses to their respective spirits, are redefined in relation to one another as sisters, mothers, and co-wives. Power is inherent to the tromba world, and social integration is also an essential characteristic.

THE CULTURAL PERSONA: CHANGING ETHNIC IDENTITY

Since it is ancestors that are pivotal in defining Sakalava (and, more generally, Malagasy) identity, it is exclusively through tromba that out-

GENERALIZATIONS:

RESIDENCE STATUS	No. (n=20)	%
Tera-tany:	11	55%
Vahiny:		
Short-term migrants:	0	0%
Settlers:	3 (1-2 sm)	15%
Children of Settlers:	6 (3 sm)	30%

CATEGORY of SPIRIT	MOST COMMON AGE OF ONSET AMONG FEMALE MEDIUMS/ (Number of Mediums)
Grandchildren:	17-22 yrs. (6/8total)*
Children:	20-32 yrs. (9/12 total)*
Grandparents:	32-40 yrs. (3/4 total)*

* These figures reflect only those mediums who had spirits fully instated and for whom the spirits' names are known. Figure reflects age when first spirit for this category was acquired.

KEY:

RESIDENCE STATUS
T-T:	Tera-tany
ST:	Short-term migrant
SET:	Settler
CSET:	Child of settler(s)
ms:	Mother is Sakalava

ADULT STATUS
MAR:	Total number of marriages
s, w:	separated, widowed NOTE: if married more than once, these were serial marriages (separated with first spouse)

PREG/OFSP:	Total number of pregnancies/offspring; unless otherwise noted, the number given refers to children born:
p:	Specifies number of pregnancies that were not carried to full term.
i:	Infertile

SPIRIT REPERTOIRE
PS:	Number of cases of possession sickness
GChild:	Number of Grandchildren spirits (instated)
Child:	Number of Children spirits (instated)
GPar:	Number of Grandparents spirits (instated)
?	Number or status unknown

SCH:	Schooling; completed some or all of the following:
ps:	primary school
jhs:	junior high school
hs:	high school

Figure 7.1. *(continued)*

siders may be structurally recognized as Sakalava. Through this process they also gain access to local ancestral power. The significance of tromba in the context of migration is evident in the types of people who experience possession. In the past, tromba possession was exclusively a Sakalava experience; in recent years, non-Sakalava mediums have become involved. They are either settlers or the children of settlers. For these reasons it is not surprising that half of the mediums interviewed during 1987 were themselves migrants, participating in what is viewed as a Sakalava institution. The involvement of migrants in tromba possession has occurred through an unusual set of kinship principles that are activated by the spirits. The reasons for this have much to do with local notions of social identity and status and Sakalava conceptions of gender and adulthood.

Migrants as Mediums

Although tromba possession is regarded as a Sakalava institution in Ambanja, the recent proliferation of possession in this town has occurred in part as a result of the active participation of vahiny. As noted earlier, Bemazava royalty especially bemoan the popularity of new and less important Grandchildren spirits, saying that Tsimihety migrants are to blame for bringing them to Ambanja. Nearly all tromba spirits continue to be members of Sakalava royal lineages, either by birth or honorary incorporation (as with Raleva, Raovoay, and their offspring), but tromba mediums are peoples of diverse origins. They include, for example, many Tsimihety, as well as Antakarana, Betsileo, Antaimoro, and métisse. Only Merina are denied the possibility of ever participating, regardless of their personal networks. This is because Merina are taboo to many spirits (they are "fady Merina"). As a result, members of the most powerful ethnic group on a national scale remain among the most peripheral locally in Ambanja. They can never fully participate in tromba, and they are never welcome as members of the Sakalava tera-tany community.

Although I estimate that approximately half of mediums participating in tromba today are of migrant status, they are not short-term (temporary) migrants but settlers or the children of settlers (see figure 7.1 and Appendix A). Drawing again from the sample of twenty mediums (male and female) whom I interviewed in detail, eleven were tera-tany (born locally of a Sakalava mother and father) and nine were vahiny. These vahiny can be broken down into two subgroups: three were settlers (two of whom had Sakalava mothers), and six were the children or grandchildren of migrants (three of whom had Sakalava mothers). All nine were born in the Sambirano. I encountered no short-term (temporary) migrants who had become tromba mediums.

Possession as a means for social integration in Madagascar has been described elsewhere by other authors. Althabe (1969), in his study of possession among the Betsimisaraka of the east coast, has argued that in an area where exogamous virilocal settlement was the rule, possession served as a means to incorporate women into local lineages. Mediumship guaranteed a woman's participation in her husband's ancestral lineage, providing her with a way to be involved in local decisions that affected her and her affines. In Ambanja, this incorporating nature of possession has taken one further step. Through tromba, outsiders are incorporated into local Sakalava culture and society. Unlike Althabe's example, they are not simply affines who are, in a sense, strangers, but more distant non-Sakalava migrants and neighbors. The reason why tromba is so successful in integrating non-kin migrant women is that it operates on kinship-based principles.

TURNING OUTSIDERS INTO INSIDERS: MEDIUMS' SOCIAL NETWORKS AND PERSONAL RELATIONSHIPS

Tromba ceremonies are major social events that involve a large group of people and may span several days. As is often true cross-culturally, mediums who participate at these ceremonies are generally part of a network of women who, on a regular basis, attend the same ceremonies. Similarly, zar ceremonies in the Sudan may be a daily social event where women gather to gossip and drink coffee (Kenyon 1991: chap. 6). Giles, writing from the perspective of Mombasa, Kenya, states that possession activities provide cult members with a "close-knit group or 'family' for support in a heterogeneous and complex social setting, especially in urban areas" (1987: 248). In Ambanja, tromba networks are composed of women who might be kin, neighbors, or coworkers or who were friends at school when they were young. Socializing among these women extends beyond the spatial and temporal confines of the ceremony. It is in the ceremonial context, however, that these ties are underscored and strengthened.

Active participation in large tromba ceremonies helps to create special bonds between mediums. One network of women I followed throughout 1987 will serve as an example. It was composed of six women: one Antakarana, two Sakalava, two Tsimihety, and one Antaimoro. Five of these six women were mediums. All six participated regularly in ceremonies sponsored by royalty living in town (for example, to celebrate the birth of a child, a child's first hair cutting, or the circumcision of a son). Four of these women had known each other since childhood, having gone to school together. Two had befriended the remaining two (the Antakarana and one of the Tsimihety women) while they were working at a tapioca factory, which is now defunct. (Today they all work in town.)

During the past decade, these six women have helped each other find housing so that now they all live in the same neighborhood, an area where rents are cheap and where several royal households are located. As dwellings have become vacant, they have alerted each other that a new house is for rent, and now they are clustered as two sets of next-door neighbors, four on one side of the street facing the other two. These women visit each other daily, sitting on the porch or in the yard of one of their houses, chatting, braiding each other's hair, or preparing food for their evening meals. Two of the six women are single, and all six assist one another in times of need: they watch each other's children; take turns going to the market; and they keep an eye on each other's possessions should one of them leave town. The Antakarana woman's sister had left a son under her care. Near the end of my fieldwork the boy died of diphtheria, and her five friends came to mourn his death and accompany her to the cemetery as if they were kin.

To understand the significance of these ties, one must analyze the structural implications of tromba. It is not simply friendship that binds these six women. In Ambanja, being friends (*drakô,* an intimate term used between women; or *kamarady,* from French *camarade*) is not enough to bind individuals. Among Malagasy, friends do favors for one another, but only kin (SAK: havañana; HP: havana) are obligated to help each other in times of need. As Keenan says of the Vakinankaratra of the high plateaux, "The ties that bind descendants are thought to be the strongest of any interpersonal relationship" (1974: 61). In small villages, neighbors are usually kin (see Bloch 1971), but in Ambanja one generally has no kinship ties to those who live nearby. Among these six women it is participation in tromba ceremonies which cements these ties.

Involvement in tromba in Ambanja is simultaneously evidence of an individual's integration into the local community and a means to achieve this end. In this community, it is not simply affines who are incorporated but, more importantly, people of diverse ethnic (and thus ancestral and geographical) origins. In order to instate a spirit in a medium, a woman must have either kin or close friends who can help pay for and sponsor the ceremony. She, or others she knows, must also have contacts within a network of mediums who will agree to participate in and run the ceremony for her. Migrants who have been in town for only a short period of time have not had time to develop such networks; those who plan to return home soon are not interested in developing them. Tromba serves as a mechanism that regulates the pace of integration. The personal qualities and sown status of the migrant determine whether she may become a medium. Whereas Angeline's cermony (chapter 5) provides an example of successful possession, the case of Basely illustrates that if networks are weak, a tromba spirit cannot be instated in a potential medium.

BASELY AND THE ANGRY, UNREQUITED SPIRIT

Basely is nineteen and was born of Tsimihety parents. She moved to Ambanja with her parents and her older brother when she was ten. Basely shares a house in Ambanja with her father, but she spends much of her time there alone. Her mother died when she was twelve, and her brother died a few years ago. Her father, who is both an alcoholic and unemployed, is rarely home, preferring to live instead with a string of lovers in town who support and feed him (and eventually throw him out). Basely reports that her father is cruel to her—he often beats her when he is home, and he never provides her with food to eat or money with which to support herself.

Four months ago Perline hired Basely as a part-time house servant. Perline is thirty-three, Sakalava, and married. She was born in the Sambirano and she owns the land on which she and other members of her household live. Although she has no children of her own, she cares for her present husband's two children by a former marriage. Perline's day is very busy: she runs a small grocery store with the help of her husband, and she is an accomplished tromba medium with a large clientele. For two years her younger sister lived with them and helped Perline with household chores, but six months ago her sister went to live in Ambilobe with a lover. Perline found it difficult to see to her housework while running two businesses. Since one of her sisters was, at one time, married to Basely's brother (who is now dead), Perline decided to hire Basely to wash dishes, carry water, and do the laundry.

Perline pays Basely a minimal salary and feeds her two meals a day. When Basely is in the yard, just out of earshot, Perline often speaks to me of Basely. As she said on one occasion: "I feel so sorry for Basely . . . she is a little crazy (adaladala)—she is not quite right in the head. . . . This is because Basely has had a tromba for almost a year and a half now, but she has no one—no friends or living relatives—who will help her raise the money for the spirit so it can be established within her. . . . Her tromba makes her feel weak and dizzy because it is angry with her. . . . Oh, it is terrible—back at her house she lives like a dog,[6] eating scraps when she can find them!" Before Perline had decided to pay part of Basely's salary in the form of meals, Basely used to come by between work hours and beg for food to eat. Now Perline feels she is helping Basely while saving herself some money in the bargain. Perline is worried that if a ceremony is not held soon, Basely will suffer even more than she does already.

Basely's situation illustrates the necessity of having a supportive network of either kin or a strong social network of friends (something that most tera-tany, settlers, and the children of migrants have). Basely has neither. Since Perline does not consider Basely to be close kin, she is unwilling to help pay for Basely's ceremony.

TROMBA AS FICTIVE KINSHIP: SPIRITUAL
POLYANDRY AND POLYGYNY

Perhaps a generation ago, the bonds between these women might have been legitimized by a form of fictive kinship called *fatidra* or "blood brother/sisterhood" (Tegnaeus 1952), yet it appears that this practice no longer operates in Ambanja. I met several Malagasy in Ambanja who had heard of fatidra but I was unable to find anyone, male or female, who had a blood brother or sister.[7] Through tromba spirits, women establish bonds through a complicated fictive kinship system, characterized by inverted and shifting perspectives. Kinship serves as an idiom for defining relationships that a medium has with the spirits and other mediums, and those that exist between her kin and her spirits.

The most important defining principle is marriage. Lambek, in his analysis of possession in the Mayotte, compares *trumba* initiation ceremonies to weddings since, structurally, the two are quite similar (1981: 141). He also draws a comparison between a spirit and a groom (1981: 143). In Ambanja this relationship is a reality, for a medium's spirit *is* her "spouse" (vady) (figure 7.2). An important structural component of tromba is symbolic polyandry (cf. Karp 1987 on polyandry and spirit possession in Kenya). If a tromba medium is possessed by numerous male spirits, all of these spirits are her husbands. If she has a living husband, when she is not possessed, he, too, is her spouse. When she is possessed, she *becomes* the tromba, and this spirit and the living husband regard each other as "friends" (kamarady) or as "brothers" (*miralahy*).[8] The ranking of spouses is also important. If a female medium has more than one spirit, these are ranked according to their relative location in the spirit's genealogical hierarchy. All spirits, in turn, are regarded as being superior in rank to the living husband. Thus, when a female medium is possessed, she becomes the dominant male in her household, and she may appeal to her tromba spirit for assistance in ways that a living spouse should help her. When I asked Mbotisoa, who is widowed and who is a saha at Nosy Faly, if she ever thought of remarrying, she replied, "I have no need for a [living] husband! My tromba [spouse] takes very good care of me." Mbotisoa is simultaneously a widow, a woman married to a spirit husband, and the embodiment of that spirit husband. She had freed herself from what she perceives to be the constraints of marriage.[9]

Other relationships defined by marriage are also at work here. Polygyny was often practiced by Sakalava royalty in the past, since having several wives was a sign of power and prestige. Since one spirit may

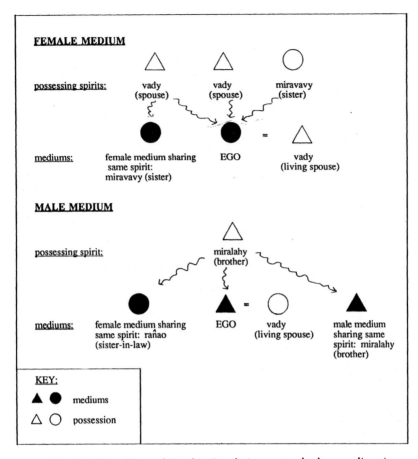

Figure 7.2. Mediumship and Kinship Bonds (terms used when medium is out of trance).

possess many mediums, structurally all of these mediums are co-wives. When they are together at a tromba ceremony they will sometimes refer to each other as "sisters" (miravavy). If a woman has a female tromba spirit, it, too, is regarded as her "sister." Men, too, can be mediums, yet they are only possessed by male spirits who are defined as their "brothers" (singular: rahalahy; plural: miralahy) (figure 7.2).

GOING IN AND OUT OF TRANCE: MALE VERSUS
FEMALE IDENTITIES AND THEIR ASSOCIATED
KINSHIP TIES

This concept of having shifting male and female selves is also structurally embedded in the complex kinship system that is associated with tromba possession. Accompanying tromba marriage are other principles that affect not only the medium but her living kin as well, and these principles follow general rules of Sakalava kinship, where terms of address change according to the sex of the speaker. In order to examine the relationships of a female medium, the two parts of figure 4.4 (chapter 4) are needed. First, it must be noted that while in everyday practice Sakalava utilize "town" kin terms that are influenced by french vocabulary, in the context of tromba one relies on older, "village" terminology. This is done out of respect for the ways of the past (*taloha*), since tromba spirits are ancestors. Also, charts for female and male egos are relevant. The terms for the female ego operate when a female medium is not possessed and is addressing her own living kin and the kin of her spirit (spouse). The chart for the male ego becomes relevant when the medium is possessed by a a male spirit. At this time, she is a male spirit who uses this set of terms when he speaks of or to his "wife" (the medium's displaced self) and his own spiritual kin. This restructuring of relationships between the living and the dead is also relevant to all of the medium's living kin. I have heard one medium (when out of trance) address another woman as "older sister" (zoky) (figure 4.4, female ego), and then, as soon as she enters trance, refer to her as "sister-in-law" (rañao) since, as a tromba spirit, he (the tromba, that is) is married to the medium who is that woman's sister (figure 4.4, male ego).[10]

Since spirits have genealogies of their own, mediums are also integrated into a spiritual kinship order. If a medium is possessed at a ceremony, then it is likely that she is surrounded by tromba spirits who are related to her own possessing spirit. When she is possessed, she becomes that spirit, and so she addresses all other related spirits by their proper kinship terms—they are the spirit's "children," "parents," "grandchildren," "nephews," "brothers," and so forth (see again figure 4.4, male ego). Mediums for different spirits are related to one another as affines, so that if one woman is a medium for Raleva, for example, and another for Be Ondry, they address each other as "father" (baba) and "son" (zazakely, zanaka, zanakalahy). Finally, if a medium is not possessed and is in the presence of spirits who are related to her own, she will address these spirits as relatives of her tromba "husband" (figure 4.4, female ego). As should be clear by now, the terms of address shift constantly, depending on whether the medium (and others around her) are in or out of trance.

As a result, unrelated women become kin to one another through a kinship system that involves constantly shifting perspectives. As the above examples illustrate, women involved in tromba are quite comfortable with this notion of shifting selves. Since the majority of mediums are female, it is women who experience the richness of this experience, which ultimately can deepen her social networks in this community. As a migrant, a female medium becomes established as a member of the tera-tany. This occurs in a number of ways. She becomes Sakalava, since through possession she is transformed into a Sakalava ruler or member of the royal lineage. She embodies the Sakalava past and becomes active in the construction of Sakalava notions of their historical experiences. Ultimately, her actions may be significant within the context of local power. In addition, through fictive kinship, she is incorporated into a network of established mediums who are not only her friends, but who are defined, for example, as her "sisters," "co-wives," and "mothers," bonds that carry with them the obligations of kinship. Through tromba possession a medium joins an "old girls" network that enables her to strengthen and extend her local social ties. Finally, as a healer, she may become a central figure in the community, assisting both tera-tany and vahiny in times of personal crisis. Since tromba is simultaneously the epitome of Sakalava experience, yet one that is associated primarily with female status, it is far more difficult for vahiny men to become integrated as insiders than it is for women.

TROMBA IN THE HOME

Tromba possession also affects a medium's relationships in her household. Among the most significant are those with her husband and children. If the medium and her living spouse have children, then they are also regarded as being the "children" (either direct or classificatory) of the spirit. As one tromba spirit said of his medium's family, "her husband is my brother, and so his children are my children." The children, in turn, address the spirit as "father" (papa, baba, or sometimes dada). When Perline (see above), for example, speaks to her children of her youngest spirit, Raleva, she says, "and, so, how is your father's friend?" (kamarady, or zalahy, the latter being an intimate term of address used between men, similar to drakô, which is used by women). When she and all other members of her household speak of her most powerful spirit, they refer to him as "Grandfather" (Dadabe or Dadilahy).

Spirits become integral members of their mediums' households, as the following case illustrates.

ALICE AND HER MERINA HUSBAND: TROMBA AND MARRIAGE

Alice is a medium who is twenty-eight years old. Although she is the child of a Betsileo (settler) father, she considers herself to be tera-tany and Sakalava, since she was born and raised in the Sambirano by a Sakalava mother. She is possessed by five spirits (claiming that three of these arrived when she was six years old) and she works full-time as a medium. Alice met her present (second, by common law) husband, Gaby, four years ago. For the past three years they have lived together in a house she owns.

Both report that they are happy in their marriage. This was not always so, however. Alice had assumed that both of Gaby's parents were Betsileo, but soon after they started to live together she learned that although his mother was Betsileo, Gaby's father was Merina. This caused serious problems for Alice, since it was taboo for at least one of her spirits (Kotofanjava) to be near anyone of Merina descent. As Alice said: "After I learned this, I had many restless nights and I would wake up very tired in the morning. I thought that my tromba was responsible for this, but I was too afraid to consult the spirit to ask what to do. . . . Then, one night, in the middle of dinner, I collapsed. . . . I don't remember what happened, but Gaby later told me that Kotofanjava suddenly arrived, without warning. . . . Gaby said I dropped my spoon and fell over. Then I stood up, and he realized I was possessed."

Gaby later added: "The spirit sat up abruptly and started to yell at me, saying that as a Merina living in the house, I was making it dirty. I was so scared! You know, Kotofanjava does not like filth [tsy tiany maloto]. He wanted to know why Alice had allowed me, a Merina, to enter her house and live there with her. The spirit was very angry, saying I shouldn't have assumed I was welcome here. . . . I asked what I should do. . . . I said I cared about Alice and I was happy living with her as her husband. . . . The spirit said he would like to think about it, and that I must make a request to speak to him a second time. Alice fell to the ground again and then she sat up and she asked me what had happened. It was then that I told her the story that I've just told you."

They decided that the best thing to do was to call up the spirit later that month, when the moon was in an auspicious phase. This they did one morning and the spirit stated its terms: Gaby must host a ceremony in order to formally introduce himself to each of Alice's spirits, and at this time he was to pay a fine of 2,000 fmg to each. This would serve as recompense for his transgression. Gaby agreed to the terms. Although it took more than eighteen months for him to assemble the necessary funds, he did eventually host a ceremony at which time each of the five spirits arrived, greeted him, and, after being paid the fines, gave him their blessing.

Gaby has since become involved in helping Alice with her work as a medium. In addition to working at a restaurant in town, during his days off he also serves as her rangahy. Alice's spirits know him well and trust him; they often commend him for his skilled work as interpreter. He now brings new clients to Alice, since customers at the restaurant sometimes ask him if he knows of a competent tromba medium in town. When Alice is tired following possession, Gaby cooks their evening meals and washes the dishes afterward. On some days he also goes to the market for her if she needs to get ready to receive clients in the morning.

Tromba spirits are expected to watch over and take care of a medium and her kin. If the medium is married, ideally her spirit and living spouse regard each other as friends or brothers. As the story of Alice and Gaby illustrates, a husband may become familiar with tromba possession through his wife's activities as a medium. Also, he may become integrated into the local community through her, since, as a medium, she has a network of friends and clients whom she knows through her possession activities. If the couple has children, a woman's spirit is regarded as a second father who helps raise them along with the living husband.[11] In this household, tromba strengthened the bond between spouses.

MEDIUMS AND THEIR RANGAHY

Although men are not very active in tromba as mediums, they often serve as the rangahy or assistant to one, especially if the medium is his spouse. This relationship illustrates another form of the complementarity of male and female that is so common in Sakalava ritual. Gaby is now indispensable as Alice's rangahy. The story of Angeline in chapter 5 illustrates how a new husband may begin to learn this role through example, watching another skilled rangahy perform the associated duties as spirits are instated in his spouse.

If a medium works as a healer, it is essential that she have a rangahy, an assistant who helps her as she goes in and out of trance and who can interpret the wishes of the spirit for her clients. Also, since a medium does not remember what came to pass while she is in trance, the rangahy serves as her witness, recounting the events for her (cf. Lambek 1981: xiiff, 70ff; 1988a). Generally the rangahy is not a medium, but is someone who is, nevertheless, very familiar with possession. He or she may be someone who attends ceremonies on a fairly regular basis, for example. The rangahy must also be someone the medium can trust, since it is the rangahy who prevents the medium from hurting herself while she is in trance and who tells her what happens during interactions with clients.

It is also the rangahy who serves as the go-between for the medium and her clients, helping to make appointments. If a medium wishes to work full-time as a healer, she needs help to ensure that her household duties are done (cleaning, cooking, fetching water, going to market, and so forth). It is the rangahy who often performs these duties for her. Since this requires much work on the part of the rangahy, the rangahy is most often the spouse, other kin (for example, a sister-in-law), or a close friend. These are individuals who are tied to the medium in reciprocal relationships that carry with them the obligation to assist one another.

The case of Marie presents an unusual example, since her rangahy, Monique, was a schoolmate and a former client. This case illustrates the closeness of the bond that develops between a medium and her rangahy when the rangahy is not already her kin.

MONIQUE AND HER MEDIUM FRIEND, MARIE

Monique is Marie's closest friend. These two women seem inseparable, for I rarely see one without the other. Monique and Marie met when they were schoolmates in junior high school.

Monique is Tsimihety and came to the Sambirano with her parents when she was seven (she is now twenty-one). She had been an excellent student when she attended grammar school in the village where she lived. Six years ago (when she was thirteen), her schoolteacher convinced her parents to let her continue on to junior high school in Ambanja. Since she had no kin in town, the schoolteacher accompanied her parents there and helped them find lodging for Monique. They found a small, two-room house made of traveler's palm. This Monique shared with three other schoolgirls. Her mother tried to visit her at least once each month, coming to town for the Thursday market and bringing Monique rice and other food to eat. Although Monique did well her first two years, in her third year, when she had just turned fifteen, she started to go out with a man from Diégo who delivered the mail each week to Ambanja. She began to fail in her studies. Things got worse when, near the end of the school term, she became pregnant and her lover abandoned her for an older woman who worked at the post office. She failed her studies and was told she would have to repeat the year.

When Monique went back to her parent's village over the school break, she became very ill, possessed by a njarinintsy spirit. In the middle of the night she would wake up and cry, then run out into the street and wander aimlessly for hours. Her mother, father, and older sister cared for her and took her to four different tromba mediums, but none were able to cure her. She continued to be troubled by fits of possession, when she would scream and cry. Her parents were very worried but they were also angry with Monique because she had become involved in the town nightlife, and this had caused her to do poorly in school (and become pregnant at a young age).

Monique had heard of a classmate who had been cured of njarinintsy by the spirit Mampiary, and so two months later she decided to go to Ambanja on market day and see if she could find her friend, Marie, whom she knew was a medium for this tromba spirit. After two consultations, Mampiary (while possessing Marie) successfully drove out Monique's njarinintsy spirit, and Marie and Monique have remained good friends ever since. A neighbor of Marie's also directed Monique to an older woman who gave her herbal remedies to make her abort.

Monique did not go back to school that year, nor did she return to her parents' village. Instead, she moved to Ambanja with her sister, who supports herself by selling bread in the market. Marie is now Monique's closest friend, and they are together every day. In the morning Monique helps her sister make and sell bread, and by noon she returns to Marie's house. Monique is Marie's rangahy: she assists Marie at ceremonies, helps clients make appointments to consult with Marie's spirits, and she also runs errands for Marie (such as going to market and fetching water) when Marie must work elsewhere or when she is in trance. Friends and neighbors say they are lovers, but I was unable to confirm this with Marie or Monique.

As chapter 9 will illustrate, adolescence is a time of great turmoil for young girls in Ambanja, who are confronted with the expectations associated with womanhood, particularly in terms of fertility and sexuality. Marie cured Monique; Marie, in turn, has gained a much needed rangahy. Whereas the rangahy is generally a spouse, in cases where the spouse is uncooperative or nonexistent, close kin (often female) fill in. In the case of Marie, a classmate and former client is now her closest friend, her rangahy, caretaker, and perhaps her lover.[12]

MIASA NY TROMBA: MEDIUMSHIP AS WORK

Tromba spirits do not simply affect the personal lives of mediums; these spirits also play essential roles in defining a medium's place as a healer in the community. In addition, being a medium elevates a woman's status in the community; and provides a means whereby she may support herself financially. As described in chapter 6, through possession a medium can opt out of working as a wage laborer at one of the enterprises. This is facilitated by the fact that mediumship today is regarded as a legitimate and profitable profession. Mediums possess a special and particular kind of knowledge, which enables them to assist both tera-tany and vahiny.

The professionalism associated with mediumship has developed within the second half of this century. It is often said in Madagascar that spirit mediums can grow rich by working as healers, and that the most famous amass small fortunes serving important government officials. None of the mediums I interviewed made much money, although those who had a large clientele earned enough in a month to pay their rents and to cover almost all food expenses. Comparatively speaking, this is still less than they would make working six days per week at an enterprise sorting cocoa, where a female worker's monthly salary might reach a maximum of 30,000 fmg. Yet many women prefer to work as healers because this liberates them from capitalist labor relations.

TIME AND POSSESSION: THE TROMBA CALENDAR
AND CLIENT CONSULTATIONS

Working as a healer is not required but is a matter of personal choice for a tromba medium. The range and frequency of healing activities vary widely from one medium to another. Some occasionally assist kin or close friends, while others build a large clientele so that they might see half a dozen or more clients during the course of a week. Other mediums prefer to participate only in large ceremonies; at these times their spirits may be asked for advice by participants or passersby.

Although a medium has much to gain as a healer—prestige, fame, and, potentially, an income—not all mediums work as healers. This is because possession is exhausting and time consuming, and so a successful medium is one who plans ahead. After a medium leaves trance she often feels weak and stiff, especially in her arms, back, and neck, and she is usually disoriented for the rest of the day. Since spiritual consultations may take an hour, if not longer, a medium who regularly receives clients at home needs help in attending to her other duties. One medium I knew always made sure she had lunch prepared early in the morning before she would receive clients. If her children returned from school for the midday meal and found her in trance, the oldest daughter (who was fourteen years old) would cook the rice, and her father, who would be busy as the rangahy, would occasionally shout orders to her and the other children from the consultation room. The children would eat, clean up, nap, and return to school while the medium, her husband, and sometimes the client, would eat much later when the consultation was over.

There are auspicious and inauspicious times for possession, determined by the lunar calendar and the solar day. The period between the new or ascending moon (fanjava tondroeñy, "mounting moon") and full moon (fanjava bory, "round moon") is the best time to perform a tromba ceremony. This period is associated with life, vitality, growth, and well-being. The period marked by a descending moon (fanjava maty, "dead moon") and no moon (fanjava fady, "taboo moon") is a time of death and danger. This is when, for example, royal funerals are held. No spirits may be called up in a medium (and thus, out of their tombs) during these lunar phases. To do so would be dangerous, since it might bring harm or death (see figure 7.3).

Taboo phases also coincide with certain months (the word fanjava means both "moon" and "month"). As noted in chapter 5, tromba is

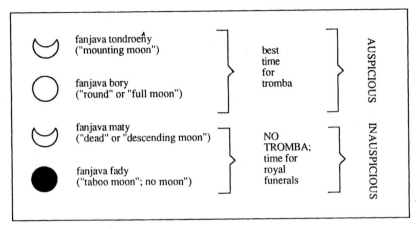

Figure 7.3.   Tromba Lunar Phases.

taboo when the royal Sakalava tombs are cleaned. These periods are mid-June to mid-July for Bemihisatra spirits, and mid-July to mid-August for the Bemazava, and they are referred to as fanjava fady ("taboo month[s]") or *sokave*. In August there is much tromba in Ambanja following the lifting of the bans. This time also corresponds with the end of the coffee harvest season, when women's and men's pockets are full of cash, enabling them to host long overdue (and very expensive) ceremonies.

To a lesser extent, similar meanings are assigned to the positions of the sun in the sky. Morning is associated with well-being, growth, and life, whereas the afternoon, when the sun is descending, is less auspicious. As illustrated by Angeline's ceremony in chapter 5, large-scale ceremonies generally begin in the morning and proceed through the night and into the next morning. It is just after dawn that a new spirit often arrives in the neophyte. All spirits also have taboo days associated with them which coincide with activities that occur on a regular basis back at the tombs: Tuesday and Thursday are among the most common for spirits active in the Sambirano. In addition, a medium may not go into trance if she is menstruating.

Determining when to hold a tromba consultation is fairly complicated, since overlapping yet distinct systems of lunar and solar time affect possession. As a result, a general rule of tromba possession is that a client must make an appointment to consult with a given spirit. This time is determined in part by when it is convenient for the medium and, more specifically, by phases of the moon and sun. Solar time is more flexible than lunar: sometimes a consultation occurs in the afternoon. In part this is because, by Sakalava notions of time, a new day does not begin at dawn, but around 2:00 P.M., when the sun is descending (for example, Friday begins on Thursday afternoon). Some mediums are willing to hold sessions with clients in the afternoon in order to allow for the constraints imposed by the workday. Thus, they might schedule consultations late in the day since people in Ambanja prefer to go to market in the morning and mediums or their clients may work at the enterprises until 3:00 or 4:00 P.M. The best time to hold a ceremony is in the morning, before 10:00 A.M., and at a time in the month when the moon is new.

MARIE AND MAMPIARY: PROBLEMS AT WORK AND SPIRITUAL INTERVENTION

As described in chapter 6, tromba possession offers mediums, who work at the enterprises, a way to opt out of wage labor, because of the cash crop fady associated with certain spirits. As a result, tromba mediumship as a profession stands in opposition to wage labor. Mediums say they do not provide services to clients for money since it is their duty or obligation to assist the living when they wish to contact the royal dead. Nevertheless, the income derived from these consultations enables a medium to survive in a world dominated by a cash economy. Again, Marie provides an appropriate example:

Marie, who lives near my house, is twenty-eight and has four spirits, the first one having arrived when she was seventeen. Her parents are both Tsimihety settlers from south of the Sambirano; she herself was born in Ambanja. She was married when she was younger, but she now lives alone. Marie has an eleven-year-old daughter who lives with Marie's mother in a village in the countryside. Two years ago Marie started to work at a local enterprise, where she sorted cocoa (since one of her spirits has coffee and cashew taboos).

One evening I woke up around 10:00 P.M. and heard someone crying and wailing. I thought it was coming from Marie's house, since I could see some people inside—maybe one or two—who appeared to be tending to someone. The crying was like that of a njarinintsy . . . later I thought I heard the person wandering about in the street at night, again crying and wailing.

A few days later one of my assistants and I went to talk to Marie to interview her about her experiences at work. She told us that she had suddenly quit her job at the enterprise. We learned that the other night I had indeed heard her crying and that that was the night she had quit her job. When we asked her why, she told us the following: "There was a young man there who was very interested in me, but I didn't like him. I tried to ignore him and brush him off whenever he made passes at me, but instead of leaving me alone, he continued to bother me even more . . . treating me like a prostitute [*makarely*]. . . . [On the last day of work] I was sitting on the ground beside a truck, sorting cocoa. He came over, sat down on the truck, and put his foot on my head!" When my assistant asked why he had done this, Marie said "Because I would not accept his advances! . . . I don't remember what happened, because I passed out [*manjary torana*] . . . I was told later that I was taken back to my house in a company car. When I got back to Ambanja and woke up I went straight to Monique's house. She then went to find my mother in her village." Marie then explained that the reason why she fainted was that her spirit Mampiary was angry. "He did not like having my head touched by something dirty [tsy tiany maloto, "he hates filth"]. . . . Mampiary also gave me a njarinintsy because he was mad . . . at the man and . . . because Mampiary did not want me to work at the enterprise any longer. . . . My mother and Monique helped me to call up the spirit [*nikaiky ny tromba*]: Mampiary said they were to have me bathe and oil my body." Then Monique added, "Before we could do this, Marie ran from the house and went wandering in the forest nearby . . . that's where you'll find the cocoa fields of [the enterprise where Marie worked]."

I then asked Marie to describe her sentiments toward Mampiary after all this happened. She said: "He was not my enemy but my friend because he helped me . . . he made the man's foot swell up for a week, and he lost his job! Ha! . . . I'd like to go back to work, but Mampiary will not let me. . . . If I want to go back to work I must first make a formal request [*hataka*] to him."

This story illustrates the role of the tromba spirit as guardian and protector of Marie, since it is the spirit who intervenes during this crisis. It also stresses the significance of problems associated with work, as well as those that may arise in interactions between men and women. These themes, of work and romance are major concerns for many mediums' clients and they will be reiterated in the discussion on mediums and their clientele in chapter 8.

During this episode, the man's actions were an affront to both Marie and her spirit. In placing his foot on her head, he violated strict rules of etiquette. In Madagascar, only individuals of higher status (elders or royalty) may raise their heads above those of other adults. If someone needs to walk through a seated crowd, they always bend over, and as they walk between others they put their hand before them and say *aza fady* ("excuse me," lit. "don't [commit a] taboo" or "pardon my taboo"). For Malagasy, the head is sacred, and so no one ever touches the head of another without first asking if they may do so. Tromba possession is among the few situations where the head may be touched by others: as illustrated in Angeline's ceremony, lesser spirits place their heads in the laps of Grandparent spirits to honor them and to acquire their blessing.[13] When sleeping in a crowded room, Malagasy generally form a circle with their feet in the middle, so that one's head does not come into contact with another person's dirty feet. When the man touched Marie's head with his foot, his action was also an affront to her spirit, since spirits reside in the heads of their mediums (cf. Feeley-Harnik 1988: 76).

Following this incident, the man was fired from his job. Marie did not return to work at the enterprise.

> In August, a month after Marie left her job, she started to work full-time as a medium. She lived in my neighborhood, and when I would pass by her house I often saw clients coming and going from there. Most often she was possessed by Mampiary who, although he is not a very powerful spirit, was well known by the people of Ambanja. At these times Mampiary would call out to me if he saw me in the street and would ask me to come watch him work. Marie held consultations with clients as often as four days a week, when the moon was in auspicious phases, and her friend Monique as always there to assist.

Within two months Marie had assembled a large clientele. During the auspicious times of the month she was able to make as much as 8,000 fmg per week. When I left the field two months later, she was still working as a healer. Her clients included equal proportions of women and men, tera-tany and vahiny, and people she knew as well as strangers. She made additional money by helping friends in her neighborhood who needed to organize large-scale possession ceremonies (romba ny tromba) to appease their own angry spirits. She was, for example, one of the mediums who appeared at Angeline's ceremony. Marie hosted some of these ceremonies for neophytes in her own house, making arrangements for musicians and inviting other mediums to participate. Marie was usually paid 1,000 to 2,000 fmg for each of her spirits that arrived at a ceremony; generally at least two of her four spirits participated.

Although Marie was able to support herself financially as a medium, describing this activity as work (asa) is problematic, since it it runs contrary to how mediums perceive their actions and, more generally, to Sakalava conceptions of work. When a tromba medium is consulting with clients, one says "miasa izy" ("she is working"), but this is not in reference to the money she might earn. Instead, it bears the same meaning as when she is washing clothes: she is busy or occupied. Tromba mediumship, according to Sakalava concepts of work, is not regarded as a form of wage labor. Furthermore, a medium does not have free access to the goods and cash that are given to her spirit(s).[14]

A medium can make use of the funds paid by clients only through prior agreement with her spirit(s), since payments are made to the tromba spirits and not directly to her. This is because a client comes to consult a spirit, and not the medium, who is simply the vehicle for communication. Payments are made to spirits in several ways. A client is expected to bring gifts of money or food to the spirit to encourage it to arrive and to ensure it will be pleased and will then cooperate. During the invocation, the client initiates the consultation with a payment of one or two silver-colored (nickel) 50- or 100-fmg pieces (vola fotsy)[15] which they place in the plate filled with water and crumbled kaolin. Once the spirit has arrived, the client offers goods for consumption which are appropriate for that spirit, such as soda pop, rum, beer, or cigarettes. These items are for the spirit, and the medium must consume all during trance. If for some reason she does not, they are put aside and used during another ceremony (this happens most often with cigarettes). Even if the actual consultation is brief, the spirit is expected to stay until it has consumed these items. Thus, none of these goods remain for use by the medium or her family after the ceremony is over.

Consultations often require one or more follow-up visits. The client may be instructed, for instance, to find or purchase certain herbs and then return to the medium's home for further instructions. I have watched spirits write up lists for this purpose which are similar to doctor's prescriptions. The final payment is made only if the cure is successful. The spirit will usually state its terms beforehand: if the cure is effective the client must pay, perhaps, 500 fmg, a piece of cloth, or a bottle of beer (charges are usually levied on a sliding scale). Again, none of the money or goods can be used by the medium or other members of her household. Only the spirit can wear the cloth, and the money should be used to buy, for example, a new hat for the spirit or to pay for a future ceremony. Mediums keep these funds separate from general household funds, often on a shelf or table in the east or northeast corner of the house, this being a sacred spot that is designated as the storage place for tromba's items (*trano ny tromba,* lit. "the tromba's house").

There is, however, a certain amount of flexibility here. Mediums do borrow from the tromba's till, but only after asking permission from the spirit. As in the case involving Angeline and her coffee fady, the spirit may be summoned and asked by the rangahy if it would make an exception. In this way, the rangahy may ask if funds from the spirit's till can be spent on something needed by the household. I am unsure how often individual mediums actually pay back these loans. Although Malagasy frequently borrow money from one another, they do not necessarily pay back the full amount. Instead, by remaining in debt, a reciprocal relationship is initiated, where the original giver is then free to make a future request of the original borrower.[16] To ask for repayment of a debt shows total disregard for this form of etiquette. This is expressed by the saying *tsy manao trosa* (lit. "[I/we] don't do [give] credit"), which implies that if one demands reimbursement it redefines the relationship between these two friends as an unequal one more akin to that between a merchant and client. As among the living, a spirit does not ask for a full repayment of the debt, but requests, instead, another favor. For example, it may ask to have a ceremony given in its honor. In this way the medium can actually sustain herself on clients' payments, although she does not consider this money to be a salary nor are her activities a form of wage labor. Tromba is work (asa) in the precolonial sense: when a medium is receiving clients, one says *asa ny tromba* ("the tromba spirit is working"). This a medium does out of duty, since she performs this work to help the living gain access to the royal ancestors.

FEEDING THE SPIRITS: MEDIUM-CLIENT RELATIONSHIPS

Within the context of tromba healing ceremonies, there are several shifting relationships between the medium and rangahy, the medium and her spirit, and the client and medium/spirit. In the context of healing sessions, the key relationship is between the client and spirit, whereas that between client and medium is secondary. A medium who works most of the month as a healer will become well known in her neighborhood. A client's choice to go to a specific medium may be based on practical or sentimental reasons: the medium lives nearby, or perhaps she is a friend or relative. Others seek her out because she is possessed by a spirit that has helped them (or someone else they know) in the past. A client may also wish to speak with a powerful spirit, and so he or she seeks out a medium who is possessed by a Grandparent. Marie's clients include friends and neighbors, although the majority are strangers (both tera-tany and vahiny) who seek the advice of a particular spirit—in her case, usually Mampiary.

The relationship between healer (medium or spirit) and client is complex. On the surface, it is based on an unbalanced form of reciprocity in which the medium provides services in exchange for money or gifts that are given to her spirit. To gain access to the spirit, the client must have the cooperation of the medium. For example, an adult with sore eyes or a child who cries too much can be treated in a single, brief consultation. The client (or, in the case of a child, another adult) explains the problem to the medium and then again to the spirit. The spirit then uses its powers to heal: perhaps it will draw circles of white kaolin around the first client's eyes, accompanying this with an incantation requesting assistance from more powerful ancestral spirits. For the child, it might prepare an herbal remedy to sooth a stomachache or sore gums. If the cures work, each client is expected to return later to make a small payment—a bottle of beer or perhaps 200 fmg. Although mediums help clients with physical ailments, more often clients suffer from complicated economic and social problems associated with work and success, or love and romance.

In a sense, the simpler the problem, the less involved the relationship between the medium-spirit and client. With serious problems, relationships may develop over time that are more symbiotic (or even, in extreme cases, parasitic). This is expressed by the proverb *"Tromban'ny teta, vola miboaka"* (lit. "It's tromba that's in the head, it's money that comes out"). This saying was popular in 1987, when it appeared on a printed lambahoany cloth that many women in Ambanja purchased. The message conveyed by this proverb is that if one wants service, one must pay for it first. Merchants in local boutiques use it to mean "don't touch the merchandise unless you plan to pay for it." For them, it is synonymous with the expression mentioned earlier: "We don't give credit" (tsy manao trosa). The proverb is also a reference to the greedy and demanding nature of tromba spirits—if you seek the advice of a tromba spirit, you may have to pay dearly for it. The extent to which this is true is determined by the nature of the client's problem, the type of cure the tromba spirit dispenses, and the personality of the medium. Although mediums do not consider their activities as healers to be a form of wage labor, the spirit-client relationship is an unequal one, since spirits are demanding and greedy.[17]

There is much folklore surrounding the centrality of tromba in the lives of the intelligentsia, with stories recounting how the most famous tromba mediums have been flown from northern Madagascar to Antananarivo to treat the urban elite. Malagasy often express great fear (SAK: *mavozobe;* HP: *mitaotrabe*) of tromba spirits because of their consuming and unpredictable nature. There are several reasons to be wary of tromba spirits. First, people who commune too often with the spirits run the risk of becoming possessed themselves. Second, tromba spirits can be reckless and they are easily angered, and so they may physically injure observers. Third, they can be very demanding of their clients, consuming an individual's wealth in exchange for spiritual advice and assistance. As Feeley-Harnik has noted, praise songs about Sakalava royalty speak of their voracious greed and how they desire to encompass and consume all that they see (1982: 30ff). Similarly, one must feed spirits if one seeks their cooperation. The tromba, as royal spirits, may, in turn, devour the fortunes of desperate clients. I have met individuals who have paid as much as 50,000 to 100,000 fmg to a series of healers as they sought treatments for what seemed to be incurable ailments.

Although I would not describe the majority of mediums I encountered as greedy, I did find it to be an appropriate description for the few who dealt in harmful or bad medicine (fanafody raty). This type of fanafody is used for self-advancement, generally at the expense of others or, more directly, to harm an adversary (this will be discussed in detail in the following chapter). Because of the nature of their work, these mediums are very cautious in forming relationships. Whereas many of Marie's clients are strangers, Marivola, who professes in private that she specializes in bad medicine, screens her clients very carefully. She and other members of her household are very careful in their daily interactions with non-kin.

MARIVOLA'S BAD MEDICINE

Marivola, who is thirty-six years old, is married and has four children. She is Arab-métisse (her father is an Arab from Yemen, and her mother, who is now dead, was Tsimihety). Marivola is a housewife, and her husband is a bookkeeper at one of the local enterprises. Marivola has four spirits; three of these she inherited from her mother.

Although Marivola possesses a number of valuable skills (she finished two years of high school and speaks French fluently) she prefers not to work. Occasionally, however, as a medium, she holds private healing sessions in her home. She does not have a steady flow of clients. She only assists individuals whom she knows well and whom she trusts. As a result, during certain months there is a flurry of tromba activity in her house, whereas other months may pass when she rarely goes into trance. The amount of activity depends upon the problems that arise in her own household and upon the demands from her limited clientele.

Marivola is very cautious about divulging any information about her work as a tromba medium, more so than most mediums I have met, because she is among the few who are willing to provide clients with bad medicine (fanafody raty). To speak of these things would mean giving away secrets. It might also bring on the wrath of her spirits, since this knowledge is sacred. She and her husband are very suspicious of non-kin, certain that out of fear or jealousy of Marivola's powers, they will try to harm them or their children with their own bad medicine. Marivola and her husband make a point of buying food and other goods from strangers or non-Malagasy. They prefer to go to the outskirts of town even for everyday items rather than going to the grocery run by their next-door neighbors and risk being harmed by them.

Marivola uses kinship to define close relations with clients; these are the only friends she trusted. When I knew her in 1987, she only received two women as clients on a regular basis, both of whom she defined as being "like sisters" (mira piravavy). The first was a woman who suffered from chronic headaches whom she helped because, as Marivola put it: "I have known her a long time, and, besides, she is Tsimihety, and so I feel I should help her, because we are like family" (mira havana). The second was a friend named Fatima.

The story of Fatima's relationship with Marivola will be covered in the following chapter. As will become clear, Fatima paid dearly for Marivola's services. In contrast to Marivola, the profile provided of Marie, above, is more typical for a medium. Marie's clients learn of her through word of mouth, and many are strangers. If Marie does not treat certain clients, it is not so much because she is suspicious of them or because she has no sentimental ties to them, but because of the limitations of the skills of her spirits. Marivola, on the other hand, is very cautious. She rarely even permits any visitors to enter her house. Instead, they must stay on the front porch or visit her in her backyard. If they appear at mealtime they are rarely greeted with "karibo, karibo sakafo," ("come in, come in and eat"), as is standard practice in Ambanja. Her cautiousness (which I often felt verged on the paranoid) is a result of the nature of her trade: since she harms others, others might try to harm her. Or, put another way, since she is preoccupied with doing ill to others, she assumes that all people are potentially her adversaries. Because trust is a major concern for Marivola and her husband, strangers are especially dangerous.

Regardless of the nature of their trades, however, for mediums such as Marie and Marivola possession transforms identity and enhances power by granting greater authority over their activities at home, at work, and in the community at large. The idioms of marriage and kinship associated with tromba facilitate the incorporation of women more readily than men. These structural principles help to create special bonds between mediums, turning friends into fictive kin. If a medium is a migrant, her ethnic identity changes, since she will be recognized by her fellow mediums as being Sakalava. As a medium for tromba spirits in the popular realm, she plays an important role in the local community, assisting vahiny and tera-tany clients in their efforts to cope with and control the events in their lives. As Part 3 will show, problems vary for tera-tany and vahiny, adults and children, and even for mediums of different statuses. It is tromba mediums and other practitioners who assist clients in making sense of the crises they encounter in their lives.

PART III

The Conflicts of Town Life

CHAPTER VIII

The Problems and Conflicts of Town Life

The Adult World

Survival in this community of strangers (cf. Robertson 1978) hinges on social and economic success. Well-being for migrants in Ambanja is not just a matter of physical health—it involves personal skills and power in relation to the local social, economic, and political orders. The problems migrants encounter also affect kin who may live elsewhere under severe conditions characterized by a scarcity of land, food, animals, or even water. As healers, tromba mediums are specialists who help others cope with the uncertainties and disorder of life. Local systems of healing reveal the nature of affliction and are indicative of local tensions. Clients come to tromba mediums when plagued by problems that fall into three general categories: physical ill health, work and success, and love and romance. The focus of this chapter is on the problems and conflicts faced by adults in Ambanja; the chapter that follows addresses the special problems that are experienced by children (especially adolescent girls).

MALAGASY CONCEPTS OF HEALING

Medical pluralism is an essential element of life in Madagascar, where a wide variety of healers and healing practices operate. In Ambanja, the domains of indigenous practices and Western biomedicine cannot be described as distinct or, as Janzen (1978) has argued for Zaire, complementary. Rather, the boundaries between these healing systems fluctuate depending heavily on the skills of the healer, the preferences of the client, and on economic constraints.

FANAFODY-GASY, FANAFODY VAZAHA

Central to Malagasy notions of healing is *fanafody,* a term that has multiple meanings. First, it is used to distinguish between different styles of healing: fanafody-gasy or "Malagasy medicine" and *fanafody vazaha* or "foreign" or "European medicine" (which I will refer to here as "clinical medicine").[1] In Ambanja, indigenous healers, or those who specialize in fanafody-gasy, include moasy (HP: ombiasy) or herbalists; mpisikidy, the diviners who specialize in the vintana, a complex zodiac system which operates in reference to time and space (see Huntington 1981); and the mediums for tromba, kalanoro, and tsiñy spirits. Here I will focus on the tromba medium as healer, who in many ways epitomizes the work of these different types of indigenous practitioners.

Ambanja also has a variety of practitioners trained in clinical medicine. Since it is a county seat, the town has a public hospital. In 1987 this was staffed primarily by female nurse-midwives and one male nurse. Usually there are also at least two medical students in residence (*stagiaires*) working at the hospital as part of their medical rotation. The primary activities carried out at the hospital are first aid, lying-in services, and the vaccination of children. Common ailments are also treated including malaria, gastrointestinal and dermatological problems, and venereal diseases. There are no operating facilities; serious emergencies must be treated in the town of Hell-ville on the nearby island of Nosy Be.

As a result of the presence of the enterprises, there is also a private workers' clinic next door to the public hospital. This is staffed by a doctor (who is also affiliated with the public hospital) and several nurses. In addition, there are satellite clinics located at each of the enterprises. Each clinic is staffed by a nurse, and the doctor tries to visit once a week (this depends largely on the condition of the roads and how well the clinic's truck is operating). In addition, the Catholic Mission runs its own small clinic, where a small charge is levied for visits (the public hospital is free). Here there are two doctors and several nurses. Both the workers' and mission's clinics have their own pharmacies, but patients at the public hospital must go to local pharmacies to fill their prescriptions. When I left the field in early 1988, the Catholic Mission was in the course of completing the construction of a new hospital with an operating room. Other services include a small leprosy hospital, maintained by the Catholic Mission in a nearby village, and there is at least one doctor who runs a private practice in town.

The term *fanafody* also means "medicine" and is used to refer to any substance that can bring about a change in an individual's state of health—be it beneficial or harmful. In this context, *fanafody* is a term applied to a wide variety of substances. These include pharmaceutical drugs dispensed by clinicians and pharmacists, as well as the rich pharmacopoeia of medicinal plants used by moasy and other indigenous practitioners. Local plants are used in several ways, such as to make infusions, so that the patient can inhale the vapors or drink the liquid as a tea; there are also preparations that can be used in bath water or applied to the body in other ways. Incantations may be said over herbs or objects to instill them with healing powers. Today the efficacy of medicinal herbs indigenous to Madagascar is being studied by biologists and botanists. Near Antananarivo is an institute for testing the medicinal properties of plants. Similarly, several foreign pharmaceutical companies have become interested in the potential curative effects of the flora of Madagascar (see Boiteau 1979; Boiteau and Potier 1976; Cordell and Farnsworth 1976; Debray et al. 1971; Pernet 1964; Plotkin et al. n.d.; Ranaivoarivao 1974). Perhaps the most famous of these is a plant called the Madagascar Periwinkle (*Catharanthus roseus*), which is used to produce drugs for childhood leukemia (Jolly 1980: 138; 1987: 173).

Although the cost of pharmaceuticals is kept to a minimum by manufacturing and packaging them in Madagascar, they can still be difficult to acquire, because they are expensive by local standards and are sold primarily through privately owned pharmacies. It is not unusual for a doctor to write a prescription for a drug that can not be found locally (or anywhere in the country, for that matter). Doctors also often write prescriptions for small quantities—sometimes less than the amount needed for treatment—to prevent patients from reselling them at a profit. The drugs available at the private clinics are limited, but they tend to be better stocked than the local pharmacies. Malarial drugs, antibiotics, and dermatological creams are prescribed most often, although they may not always be available. Many patients also prefer to buy the more expensive (yet generally unavailable) imported brands, saying they are more effective than those produced domestically. Although a black market exists, Malagasy tend to hoard pharmaceuticals rather than share or resell them, since they are so difficult to acquire. Also, pharmacists as a rule do not dispense drugs without a prescription (for a contrasting view on other regions of the Third World, see Lee et al. 1991; and Silverman, Lee, and Lydecker 1982, 1986; Silverman, Lydecker, and Lee, 1990).

Malagasy distinguish between beneficial and harmful medicine, the latter being especially important within the context of fanafody-gasy or Malagasy medicine. There is *fanafody tsara* ("good medicine") and fanafody raty (HP: ratsy; lit. "bad/evil medicine/magic"); sometimes the latter is translated into French by Malagasy speakers as *magique* or *poison*. Fanafody tsara is used to cure, while fanafody raty is used to harm one's adversaries. It is sorcerors and witches (*mpamosavy*)[2] who use fanafody raty most frequently, although moasy (herbalists) and tromba mediums (like Marivola in the previous chapter) dispense it occasionally as well. The difference here is that the mpamosavy (sorceror or witch) uses fanafody raty for his or her own sake, whereas the healer dispenses it to clients so that their well-being may improve at the expense of someone else's misfortune.

I wish to stress that each of these categories of good and bad medicine include substances with known medicinal qualities (pharmaceuticals as well as herbal substances that may be curative or poisonous), as well as other (and what are often referred to in the anthropological literature as "magical") properties that are transferred to them through actions made or words uttered by the healer. For simplicity's sake (and in order to reflect Malagasy ways of thinking) I will use the blanket term *medicine* (fanafody) when referring in general to substances that are used to bring about a change in health or well-being. *Good medicine* (fanafody tsara) refers to those substances taken willingly by a client seeking a cure, and the term *bad medicine* (fanafody raty) refers to those substances that are used to cause harm to or to influence the behavior or well-being of another person, unbeknownst to the victim. The terms *poison* and *magic* will only appear in the text where informants themselves used them. I wish to stress here that these are definitions developed for specific application within a Malagasy context, because more standard definitions, especially of magic (cf. Evans-Pritchard 1937; Frazer 1976 [1911]; Malinowski 1948; also Favret-Saada 1980) do not coincide with Malagasy conceptions of illness. (For more details on Sakalava concepts of sorcery and magic, see Gardenier 1976.)

The presence of clinical medicine in Madagascar has not led to major distinctions being drawn between substances that have a physiological as opposed to a psychological (or magical) effect. The efficacy of both fanafody-gasy (Malagasy medicine) and fanafody vazaha (foreign medicine) is recognized by Malagasy regardless of their level of education, even if they are trained as clinicians. Rather than rejecting fanafody-gasy, Malagasy intelligentsia often struggle to make sense of what they perceive to be conflicting yet coexisting systems of thought. Similarly, non-Malagasy, especially missionaries and clinicians who have lived in Madagascar for a decade or more, are often equally confused and perplexed not only by the persistence of beliefs in fanafody-gasy, but also by what they themselves perceive to be effective and powerful properties.[3]

Tromba mediums and clinicians generally respect each other's attitudes toward healing. They do not seek to discredit each other's methods or knowledge, but view them at times as complementary, at others as distinct or as providing different solutions to the same sorts of problems. The point of view involved changes with each situation. As will be shown in chapter 10, the rejection of explanations associated with fanafody-gasy is a stance taken only by extremists such as Protestant exorcists (and, as I have argued elsewhere, psychiatrists; see Sharp, in press). This is not to say that specialization does not occur. For example, it is only through clinicians that Malagasy have access to many pharmaceuticals, since strict laws prohibit their sale by nonregistered persons. On the other hand, clinicians in Ambanja never repair broken bones, because the bonesetters of the rural north are famous throughout the island for their skills in fixing even the worst compound fractures. In addition, some tromba mediums are skilled diviners who specialize in *sikidy* divination, using seeds, stones, or playing cards.

Indigenous[4] healers specialize in other problems as well. Those associated with possession are generally considered the exclusive domain of tromba mediums. For example, possession by njarinintsy spirits is a common affliction of adolescent girls, but few clinicians in Ambanja have heard of this disorder unless they grew up in the north, and even they rarely see it since it is spirit mediums and other healers who specialize in treating it. Clients may go to the clinic complaining of headaches and stiffness, but this usually occurs before they have been alerted to the possibility that a spirit might be making them ill. If there are any rules directing a hierarchy of resort (Romanucci-Ross 1977), they are very loosely defined. Roughly speaking, they are as follows: if someone feels physically ill in a way that is unfamiliar, he or she usually goes to the clinic first to receive a vaccination or a prescription, usually for antibiotics. If the treatment is unsuccessful (or prohibitively expensive) they will try other means. Sakalava are an exception to this rule. They prefer to consult moasy and tromba mediums over clinicians. Sakalava say this is because they are wary of being treated by Merina doctors.

Clearly, Ambanja's inhabitants have a wide variety of healers to consult. None, however, is so widespread and so numerous as are tromba mediums. Choices made regarding treatment and more general assistance are very personal. These depend on individuals' past experiences, their faith in (or, as noted earlier, their sentimental ties to) a given healer (or spirit), and the cost of their services, rather than simply the nature of the problem. The proliferation and professionalization of tromba mediums and other indigenous healers is, I believe, evidence of the limitations of clinical medicine in Madagascar. This includes its inability to solve problems that extend beyond physical ailments into the social realm (cf. Janzen 1978); the severe shortage of drugs and medical supplies needed to guarantee quality care; and, finally, Sakalava reluctance to consult with clinicians who are from the high plateaux.

In Ambanja, healers—be they moasy, tromba mediums, or clinicians—are thought to be skilled if they are able to cure problems that extend beyond physical ailments. Well-being is defined in broad terms and extends into the social and economic realms of human experience. Tromba mediums are especially adept at this. They serve as gatekeepers between the world of the living and the dead, and between the present and the past. When they reach the boundaries of their knowledge, they may refer to other ancestors of the spirit world for guidance and advice to assist the ailing client.[5] As ancestors it is their duty to watch over the living. They have not only a keen awareness of what comes to pass in the local community, but also the power to bring about change.

A medium's knowledge overlaps with that of clinicians: they can treat, for example, infections, malaria, sore eyes, and diarrhea. Throughout the past decade, Madagascar has become a country of scarcity, as is evident by the bare shelves in the country's pharmacies and public hospitals. In Ambanja, patients who require surgery must purchase their own gauze, bandages, and anesthesia, and then go elsewhere to have the operation performed. Often the required materials are unavailable locally, and people with serious emergencies may die before they can reach Nosy Be. The workers' and Mission's clinics are better stocked than public pharmacies. Still, sometimes as much as half of what has been ordered (and paid for) may be missing from the packages. This is what Malagasy refer to as *risoriso*, or corruption (HP, lit. "to zig-zag," "wander," or "weave in and out"), and it is very much a part of everyday life. Unlike clinicians, tromba mediums rely on local sources of ancestral power and knowledge, and they draw from an extensive and readily available pharmacopoeia of local plants.[6] Tromba mediums also rely on the power and sacred knowledge of royal ancestors.

Healers in Ambanja are problem solvers and not just curers. Because of the authority and stature that accompanies their knowledge and abilities they are often asked to assist in a variety of crisis situations. They give loans and advice, and they are frequently called upon to mediate in personal disputes among kin, between employees and employers, and between private citizens and local public authorities. They may be elected to serve on neighborhood committees, where one of their main duties is to hear local disputes. In this way, their social duties may overlap with those of enterprise directors, elected political officials, judges, and the Bemazava king. The town's judge reports that sometimes tromba spirits possess their mediums and appear in court to defend or threaten a party or order him to make a particular decision.

SICKNESS AND DEATH

Ny aretina dia toy ny akoho: mahita làlana hidirana
nefa tsy mahita làlana hivoahana: lit. "Sickness is like
a chicken: it can find the way in but it can not find
the way out," that is, sickness comes easily; it's
getting well that is difficult.

                                        —*Malagasy proverb*

Sickness and death are times when tromba mediums play crucial roles in the lives of their clients. In Ambanja, the concern for one's well-being is reflected in the greetings people use: "*Mbola tsara?*" ("[are you] still well?") and "*Salama, Salam-tsara*" ("[go] in good health"). Since many of this town's inhabitants are wage laborers, economic stability hinges on good health. Sickness may interfere with productivity or it may threaten an individual's ability to hold on to a job. Given this, it is not surprising that many of a tromba medium's clients are vahiny laborers (see plate 7).

Tromba mediums assist clients who suffer from a variety of ailments. Among the most common are sore eyes, stomachaches, bad headaches, and stiffness in the limbs, back, or neck. Mediums such as Marie, for example, possess an extensive knowledge of the local pharmacopoeia. When Marie is in trance her tromba spirit often instructs her clients to use certain medicinal plants. If these are unavailable, the spirit tells Monique, the rangahy, to go to the forest nearby to retrieve them, or the spirit might write a prescription so that the client can purchase the herbs from a moasy. Sometimes the client goes home to administer the

Plate 7.   Tromba spirit giving advice to a client. Since mediums embody ancestral power when they are possessed by tromba spirits, they are regarded as
powerful healers. A client may make an appointment for a private consultation,
or passersby may drop in unannounced at a large-scale ceremony. Occasionally
tromba spirits also give unsolicited advice: this man is being scolded for being
drunk in public in the middle of the day.

treatment or returns later to have the tromba spirit do it (or so that the
spirit can give further instructions). For most of these private consultations Marie's clients are young adults in their twenties and thirties.
Marie also participates on a regular basis at ceremonies for other mediums. When she is in trance she is often asked to treat infants and young
children who suffer from such problems as fever, chills, diarrhea, eye
infections, or crankiness.

Death is especially frightening for migrants who are away from home,
because to be far from the ancestral land means risking being separated
and lost from one's primary kin. As explained in chapter 4, some migrants have established burial societies in Ambanja. These societies ensure that the dead will be transported safely back home so that they
may rest with their ancestors. Again, tromba mediums may be important
actors in this context. They may be called upon to help the living understand the causes leading up to the death of a loved one, or they may
even fall suspect themselves.

In Ambanja, a clinical diagnosis generally is not sufficient to explain a sudden death. In a manner reminiscent of Evans-Pritchard's Azande (1937), one must determine the underlying causes: why this person at this particular time? Generally, it is one's neighbors who are suspected of being sorcerors of witches (mpamosavy) or having used bad medicine (fanafody raty) against the victim. Most often old women fall suspect because they remain at home throughout the day. If they care for their own grandchildren they also develop intimate ties with their neighbors' children, coddling and scolding them and offering them snacks while they prepare their own meals. Old women are most frequently blamed, ostracized, and shamed as witches following the death of a neighbor's child, accused of having killed the child with fanafody raty because they are jealous of another's prosperity. These older women are quite vulnerable, since they often live only with their grandchildren, without any adult kin nearby to protect them.

WITCHCRAFT ACCUSATIONS AGAINST OLD MAMA ROSE

In one neighborhood where I lived temporarily, a two-year-old child died. Although two doctors in town agreed malaria had been the cause of death, the mother, Alice, who was a nurse herself, sought out a moasy and later a tromba medium to discover the identity of the person who had brought death upon her child. For this mother, the medical prognosis was not enough—the child may have died of malaria, but she needed to know why this had happened so suddenly and at that time and place. Mama Rose, an older woman who lived next door, was identified by both healers as a witch (mpamosavy). Mama Rose's daughter, fearing for her mother's well-being and safety, took a leave of absence from her own job in a distant town to watch over her elderly mother and to make sure no harm came to her. She also called up Mama Rose's own tromba spirit to ask for advice and protection from the fanafody raty that they assumed Alice was now using to harm her. Mama Rose was an older woman in her sixties, and so this in itself was a sign of their desperation, for she had not been active as a medium for nearly ten years. After approximately six months the animosity between Mama Rose and her neighbors subsided but only after Alice had moved out of her house, leaving her husband and his child by a former marriage behind. Three months later Mama Rose's daughter finally returned to work at her job full-time. She continued to visit her mother every weekend until Alice moved away.

This story reveals the value—and the power—of tromba spirits and their mediums. As Alice seeks to make sense of a tragedy in her own life, it is a moasy and later a tromba medium who give her answers that extend beyond those that her own medical training can provide. Mama

Rose, as an old woman who lives alone, is a vulnerable target and she, in turn, relies on her own tromba spirit for comfort and support in time of crisis. As the stories that follow reveal, tromba spirits and their mediums provide a host of other services to clients who struggle with the problems of daily urban life and plantation work.

WORK AND SUCCESS

Ny asa no harena: "Work is wealth."
                                        —*Malagasy proverb*

Work or, more specifically, wage labor, is central to the lives of the majority of Ambanja's inhabitants. It is Sakalava who are most resistant to working at the enterprises, whereas vahiny, out of necessity, hold the majority of these jobs. As described earlier, most workers express the desire to be freed from the constraints of plantation labor. For many, however, these jobs are a matter of survival. Since employment activities occupy a large proportion of daily life for the majority of Ambanja's inhabitants, well-being at the job is essential. Tromba spirits answer clients' needs by providing work medicine (*ody asa*). Clients request this, for example, to encourage their bosses to grant them raises or to change the disposition of an unkind supervisor or employer.

DONÉ AND HIS TROUBLES AT WORK

Doné is a forty-one-year-old Antaisaka man from southeastern Madagascar. He came north ten years ago, having been encouraged to do so by an older brother, who had been living in Ambilobe for three years. Shortly after Doné's arrival, his brother left, and Doné decided to move to Ambanja because he had heard that it was easier to find work there. Since he knew how to drive a car, he soon found a job as a truck driver at one of the larger concessions.

After working there for four years, Doné saved up enough money to pay to have his wife come join him. She brought with her their first child, who was five years old at the time. They have since had four other children. Doné and his family live in a two-room house made of corregated tin and located on land owned by his employer. They also have access to a small field where his wife grows such subsistence crops as manioc and garden vegetables. Doné finds it harder each year to earn enough to support his family. He says that they do not starve, but now he rarely has enough cash to buy clothing for his children. (As long as parents can not afford to buy clothing for their children they are reluctant to let them attend school.)

In 1986, two of Doné's sons were caught stealing cocoa pods from his boss's fields. Although workers and passersby are permitted to take one or two pods (which one can break open, eating the seeds as a snack), these boys were found with a gunny sack filled with nearly twenty pods, which ostensibly they were preparing to sell. The foreman who found them brought them to the boss, who took them to the local jail to be fined. As Doné reported, "I did not have the cash to pay the fine, and so I went to my boss and asked him to drop the charges. Instead, he offered to help bribe the judge, but only if I promised to pay him 50,000 fmg up front" (this amount was ten times the fine). Doné felt paralyzed: "I didn't have the money to pay either the fine or the bribe. . . . I was so afraid, I thought I'd lose my job. A friend [coworker] later lent me the money . . . then I consulted a tromba spirit and asked for medicines to help me [counteract the boss's cruelty]. . . ."

"I told my story to the tromba. He told me to go collect certain types of herbs and bring these with a package of cigarettes and a small bottle of rum. I went back a second time and the spirit prepared the medicine: he blew smoke and sprinkled rum on it, and then he tied it in a small bundle. He then told me to place the bundle inside my boss's car one night, under the driver's seat."

This was not difficult for Doné to do, since he was often in the garage tending to the cars and trucks that were kept there. "A week later my boss found the bundle, and he became very frightened. He was sure that one of his workers was trying to poison him. . . . For the next month he rarely left his house and only allowed his wife or daughter to prepare his meals, even though he had several house servants! Ha ha! Later he gave all of us a small raise!" Doné felt he had triumphed. When he received his next paycheck, he used part of it to buy a bottle of beer, which he brought to the medium's house as payment for the spirit's services.

Doné's story is important because it illustrates several key issues. First, work is essential to the well-being of migrants, and their survival may depend on the actions of their employers. Second, in times of crisis a tromba medium, drawing upon local Sakalava ancestral power, may solve their clients' problems. Doné's case is not one involving impotent medicines, because Malagasy believe in the harmful effects of fanafody and the power of tromba spirits. The bundle under the car seat was an apt warning for the boss, and it proved to be very effective. Third, tromba mediums are not marginal members of this community, but essential and powerful figures who cure personal and social ills. In Doné's case the tromba medium aided the powerless and vulnerable laborer who was caught in a very sticky web of power relations with his boss.

STATUS, SUCCESS, AND POWER

In Ambanja, one can gain wealth by "working hard" (*miasa mafy*) and through various forms of medicines (fanafody). For the powerful, money can influence the outcome of decisions in the local court, and it brings influence in government. For the powerless, it is fanafody that can bring about change or relief from the hardships of everyday life. A brief example illustrates this point. In one neighborhood a very wealthy merchant was in the process of constructing a large building (he had acquired the land by bulldozing other people's houses one afternoon while the police stood by and watched). He was forced to bring this construction to a halt after a local, self-acclaimed sorceror (moasy) declared in public that he had mustered all his powers to harm the merchant and his family, and he would continue to do so as long as the construction continued. The merchant met in private with the sorceror and paid him a generous sum of money to stop his actions and to keep quiet. The construction then resumed.

An important aspect of fanafody is that the client may use it to increase his or her status, success, or power relative to that of others. As in the case involving Fatima, below, acquiring this type of assistance may require a series of intense negotiations. Her relationship with Marivola was a complex one, where a long-term, reciprocal association cemented their friendship. Marivola is a master of this sort of negotiation. Since she dispenses harmful medicines, her relationship with a client must not only be one based on trust, but also one where the client remains in debt both to her spirit(s) and to her (see, again, the discussion of Marivola in chapter 7). Fictive kinship provides a means for redefining these relationships so that such negotiations are possible (and more binding).

THE CASE OF FATIMA

Fatima and Marivola were not always friends. Mme Fatima's neighbors were amazed to see the two women visiting with each other during my stay in Ambanja, for only the year before the two had had a serious quarrel following the death of Medar, Fatima's husband. Fatima, however, decided to make amends with Marivola, because she knew that she was a powerful medium who could help her to achieve certain goals.

Medar had been a talented and respected school principal in Ambanja. He also had a fair amount of money, which he had inherited from his father. He had died suddenly at the age of forty-two, and doctors in town were unable to identify the cause of his death. Fatima was grief stricken and was certain that her friend Marivola was responsible. She assumed that Marivola was jealous of their prestige and wealth (and she was right—Marivola was jealous). Fatima's family lived in great comfort in a well-furnished, five-room cement house. They had such expensive luxury items as a color television, a VCR, an Italian-made sewing machine, and a gas stove. Furthermore, Marivola had the skills to enable her to cause such harm, for she was a powerful tromba medium who specialized in fanafody raty. During Medar's funeral and for months after Fatima made it clear to her neighbors that she believed Marivola was responsible, and all contact broke off between the two women.

But Fatima is an ambitious woman: she has six children, all of whom are enrolled in the private Catholic Mission school. In 1987 she sent her oldest son to complete his last two years of schooling at the private and very prestigious French school in the provincial capital, hoping that there he would have a better chance of passing the baccalauréat exam, thus enabling him to continue on to university and thereafter get a good job. Meanwhile, she was having trouble controlling her fifteen-year-old daughter, who, being very beautiful and coquettish, had had a string of lovers, including some of the most powerful men in town. Fatima felt it necessary to take action to protect her children. For her son she wanted fanafody to help him with his studies; for her daughter she wanted, first, to prevent other women from harming her out of anger or jealousy and, second, she wanted to control her actions and felt that a good scolding from a powerful tromba spirit might accomplish this. Because Fatima was aware of Marivola's power as a medium, she reopened communications with Marivola, visiting her on a regular basis over the course of two months. Marivola herself had much to gain from her friend. Since Fatima worked as a nurse at one of the enterprises, she could write prescriptions for drugs, and since she was well-off financially, Marivola could request loans from her friend when she was in need. Marivola eventually consented to provide the fanafody, and over the course of two months, the women met regularly to call up Marivola's most powerful spirits. Fatima paid dearly for these services, giving a total sum of 20,000 fmg to Marivola's spirits. I also watched her help Marivola acquire drugs and injections on four separate occasions.

In Madagascar, a country of economic extremes, an individual's success and power draw attention and suspicion from others (cf. Favret-Saada 1980). This is illustrated by a body of folklore that was popular a decade or two ago surrounding French ex-patriots. These stories are rich in imagery that describe Europeans who live off the bodies of the less fortunate. Europeans were suspected of being "blood thieves" (mpaka-raha) and heart snatchers (mpakafo). More recently, Indian merchants have become scapegoats in times of greatest national scarcity. Occasionally, violent outbursts occur throughout the island, directed against Indians. This violence is precipitated by the spreading of an apocryphal story in which an Indian merchant kills the child of a Malagasy beggar (katramy), striking it after it has touched a morsel of food in his shop. Such a story circulated in Madagascar in 1987, and angry Malagasy destroyed Indian-owned shops throughout the island.[7]

LOVE AND MONEY, WIVES AND MISTRESSES[8]

Tsarabe ny manambady: "Marriage is wonderful."
— words spoken by a young girl
shopping in a boutique

As outlined in chapter 4, marriage ceremonies are infrequent and relationships more generally are extremely fragile in Ambanja. By the time most adults have reached their forties, they have been involved in a series of unions, each of which has lasted only a few years. The tenuousness of relationships today is reflected in the fact that many tromba mediums and other spiritual practitioners do a lucrative traffic in love medicines (*ody fitia*) for both men and women, who hope either to hold onto a wandering partner, to cause harm to a rival, or to charm a potential mate.

Any man with money in his pocket—be he married or single—is a target for seduction. In precolonial times, polygyny was a sign of success and power for Sakalava men (particularly if they were royalty). More recently this has changed in response to the effects of colonialism. The French colonial period was marked by the transition from a subsistence economy to one characterized by wage labor, with status being measured by possessions and monetary wealth. The co-wife has slowly been replaced by the mistress, who today is ironically referred to as the *deuxième bureau* (lit. "second office"). This name conjures up images of excessive work, referring to the fact that a man has to work harder if he has a mistress. From a wife's point of view, it is also a reference to sabotage,[9] since the mistress is viewed as an enemy to the stability of the man's marriage and household. This new term has become popular within the last decade. Previously the term used was *bodofotsy* ("bedcover" or "blanket"), since a man's mistress (like his blanket) is someone he takes with him when he goes traveling (*en tourné*).[10]

Women who have children and who are involved in tenuous unions are particularly vulnerable economically. A woman who relies on a man for income to support her and her children may suffer greatly if she does not have another way in which to generate an income—a job, a small business, or the ownership of land. Although neighbors often help one another with short-term child care or cooperate in economic ventures, a premium is still placed on kinship. Thus, if a woman is a migrant without extended kin living in the area, her problems become even more severe. Fostering is still a common pattern throughout Madagascar (see, for example, Kottak 1980: 185 on the Betsileo, and Bloch 1971: 9 on the Merina). A common pattern in other parts of Sakalava territory is that children of divorced parents typically go to live with their fathers (Feeley-Harnik 1991b: 218).[11] In Ambanja, however, an additional pattern has emerged: the female-headed household. Children are often left under the care of the maternal grandmother (as in the case of Mama Rose, above), while the mother lives elsewhere, working to support not only herself and her children, but her aging mother as well.

Love and money are very important themes in Ambanja society and are subjects that appear with great frequency in the form of popular sayings. These are often printed on the colorful lambahoany cloths that local women wear as body and head wraps and include such phrases as:

"I [may] love you [a man addressing his mistress] but I'm not exchanging the-one-in-the house," that is, the legitimate wife (*Tiako anao fa tsy atakaloko ny an-trano*);

"I love my spouse" (*Tiako vady*);

"The big spouse [real wife as opposed to mistress] is the best" (*Vadibe tsara*);

"I'm so happy to see you, my Darling!'" (*Falyfaly mahita anao Cheri ê!*); and

"Can't buy me love" [lit. "You don't need money to have my love"] (*Tsy mila vola ny fitiavako anao*).

I know of only two crimes that inspire public outrage and mob violence against the perpetrator in Ambanja society: taking property from someone, or sleeping with another person's partner. With the cry of either *mpangalatra!* ("thief!") or *vamba!* ("adulterer!"), neighbors within earshot will drop what they are doing and come running. If they should catch the guilty party or parties, the mob will beat them with their fists or with broomsticks or other hard objects.[12]

Tromba mediums and their rangahy report that a majority of their clients come seeking love medicines (ody fitia), of which there are two kinds: that used by men to charm women (*ody manañgy*) and that used by women to charm men (*ody lehilahy*). The first tromba consultation I witnessed early in my fieldwork involved a male client who sought to charm his wife, who had become the deuxième bureau of a richer man. This ceremony was the client's second consultation. He had chosen to speak with Djao Kondry since this spirit is a young playboy who is knowledgeable about women, love, and romance. After recounting his problem to Djao Kondry, the client unrolled a cloth in which he had a packet of cigarettes, which he gave to the spirit as a gift. Then he withdrew a bottle of honey, some cologne, a packet of medicinal powder, and three bundles of dried leaves. The tromba poured honey and cologne on the powder and herbs, and, after saying a series of prayers, he instructed the man to put a bit in his wife's food, her bath water, and in their bed. Then she would not be able to resist him, and she would stop going to see her lover.

Migrants who are far from home are especially vulnerable when involved in tenuous unions, as the following case illustrates.

THE STORY OF LALAO

Lalao is a thirty-five-year-old Merina woman who came to Ambanja with her husband, Christôphe (who is Betsileo), approximately eight months ago. Previously they had been living in Nosy Be, where they met. Lalao did not work. Christôphe was an engineer at one of the enterprises and was transferred to Ambanja from the headquarters at Nosy Be. Christôphe has three children(ages five, ten and fifteen) by a former marriage. His first wife was Sakalava; about four years ago she died. Lalao, who had previously been his mistress, then moved into Christôphe's house and assumed the role as the youngest child's mother (she is addressed by her neighbor's by the teknonym "Maman'i'Hervé" or "Mother of Hervé"), having claimed this role during the recent circumcision of this child. Until the night of this story many women in the neighborhood had no idea Lalao was not the biological mother of all three children.

One night when I was visiting with a Betsileo neighbor named Vero, Lalao appeared at the door, sobbing uncontrollably. She told us that her husband had beaten her and that she was afraid to go back to her house. She wanted to go home to her mother in Antananarivo, but she did not have any money of her own, since her husband was in charge of household finances. Vero was at a loss what to do—she did not know this woman well and, like Lalao, she did not have free access to household funds. She decided to go across the road to Isabelle's house and ask for assistance, since Isabelle worked with Christôphe and thus knew the family better than she.

We assembled at Isabelle's house and listened to Lalao tell her story in more detail. She had learned that Christôphe now had a mistress here in Ambanja. This new mistress was an older Sakalava woman(ten years his senior). Lalao said that she had consulted a tromba medium last week, asking the spirit to give her two kinds of love medicine: one she put in her bath water (*fankamamy oditra*, lit. "makes the skin sweet") so that her husband would want her again. The spirit also gave her her some herbs to sprinkle in their bed, but they did not seem to have had any effect. Since her husband's mistress was well known in the neighborhood as a tromba medium, Lalao was certain that the mistress had used more powerful medicine to make Christôphe come home and beat her instead.

When Lalao spoke of her economic dependence on her husband and his violent behavior, the other two women(and, ultimately, I, too) began to cry. We looked over her possessions and decided that she should keep her sewing machine, so that she would have a means of support. Isabelle and I then gave her some money in exchange for some of her kitchenware. Vero did the same, taking money from her husband's till, thus giving Lalao a large proportion of their household savings (close to half a month's worth of her husband's wages). Isabelle then went to find Lalao's uncle (FaBr) to ask for assistance, but he threw her out of his house. Isabelle then appealed to Christôphe, who gave her enough money for Lalao's transportation back to Antananarivo. Lalao cried late into the night and at one point tried to poison herself by attempting to drink kerosene. Later, when she had calmed down, she fell asleep for a few hours at Vero's house. This was done against Vero's husband's wishes, for he was already furious that his wife had given her so much money. Lalao left the next morning in a transport bound for the capital.

The seriousness of Lalao's situation was evident in the other women's reponses. Among Malagasy, in times of crisis—such as sickness or death—self-composure is essential. Except for very close female kin, one never cries at these times. I myself was scolded severely on two occasions for crying, once during an interaction with an angry spirit and the other while attending a child's funeral. This episode involving Lalao was the first (and only) time I ever saw anyone cry, aside from a mother grieving over a child's death. The women present not only felt great sorrow for Lalao, but they were also graphically reminded of problems they themselves had suffered. As Vero put it, "I am so sad [mampalahelo] because she is a woman and I am a woman." Isabelle herself had suffered greatly several years ago when she learned that her husband had a mistress. This she deduced one day when she discovered that their cassette player was missing. At first she assumed that a thief had taken it, but later she realized that her husband had sold it to buy gifts for another woman. Her husband is Sakalava royalty (ampanjaka) from Ambanja, while she is Antakarana (and a commoner) from the north, and so she feels powerless to control his actions.

The following day Vero explained that she, too, had left her husband temporarily following the birth of their youngest child. An important institution associated with marriage in the high plateaux, among Merina and Betsileo, is misintaka: when a woman is unhappy with her husband she may leave him and go home to her parents. There she stays and is watched over by them. When this happens it is regarded as a separation but not a divorce (*misao-bady*). If the husband wants his wife to return he must approach her parents, bearing expensive gifts. The comparable institution among Sakalava is called *miombiky*, in which payments are made in cattle (*omby*). Whereas marriage ceremonies (and misintaka) occur frequently in the high plateaux, as one Sakalava informant put it, "only savage Sakalava living in the bush practice miombiky anymore."

Although Lalao and her husband are from the highlands, both were migrants who lived far from parents and other kin. In addition, their behavior reflects an adaptation of Sakalava customs, rather than any strict adherence to Merina or Betsileo ones. Where there is no marriage ceremony, as is true for the majority of unions in Ambanja today, there is no reparation for temporary separation. According to Merina and Betsileo custom, if a couple lives far from home, the husband, who usually controls the household finances, is obligated to give his wife money to return to her parents, if she so desires. Thus, the other women viewed Christôphe's reluctance to help Lalao as a serious breach of custom. When they pressured him, he relented and gave Isabelle some money for Lalao's carfare home. Lalao, like many women who are unemployed (typically they are married to professional men), relied on her husband for economic support. Since, as a migrant, she was unable to find kin nearby who would help her, she turned to her female neighbors, all of whom were migrants.

Neighbor's attitudes toward Lalao changed after she had left town:

> At first, these women, and others living around her house, refused to associate with Christôphe, and they stopped buying yogurt from his brother (dairy products are hard to come by and are greatly coveted in Ambanja). Two days after Lalao left, her husband's mistress moved into the house, enabling Christôphe to return to work, since she stayed at home to care for his youngest child. Soon neighborhood opinion changed in favor of Christôphe. A week later Vero's husband returned from a trip to Antananarivo and told how Lalao had appeared at his parents' house after her own parents had thrown her out on the street. He went to speak to Christôphe to learn his side of the story and was told that although Lalao appeared very upset, in fact she was the one to blame. She had squandered all of his money, insisting that it be used to buy her beautiful dresses instead of food for the children. Two months later Lalao returned to Ambanja, and tried to form a reconciliation with her husband, but he threw her out under the watchful (and approving) eye of his neighbors. She left town that afternoon.

In all of these stories, involving Mama Rose, Doné, Fatima, and Lalao, tromba mediums provide clients with a means for confronting and articulating problems they encounter in the everyday world.

Through this indigenous Sakalava institution, troubled individuals appeal to the power and knowledge of local ancestors in order to make sense of and control their lives in times of chaos. It is through tromba that the living are able to cure life's ills and uncertainties. These include sickness and death, work and success, and love and romance. Although clients usually specify these particular categories as they define their needs, the case studies provided here illustrate that these categories often overlap. As the following chapter illustrates, children, too, must cope with these and related problems.

CHAPTER IX

The Social World of Children

Children are often invisible in migration and urban studies. Much of the literature assumes that children do not live on their own, but under the care and watchful eye of adults, who may be kin, foster kin, or neighbors. As a result, their experiences are shadowed by those of their caretakers. When children appear as a discrete category in studies of African societies, most often the themes that frame their activities are economics and health. Schildkrout (1981), for example, describes the manner in which urban Hausa children assist their mothers who are confined, through purdah, to their homes. Others focus on the more insidious qualities of the institutionalization of child labor cross-culturally (Mendelievich, ed. 1979; Minge 1986). Studies in maternal and child health demonstrates that the young are the most vulnerable in times of scarcity (UNICEF-UK 1988; see also Scheper-Hughes 1987, 1992, and other essays in Scheper-Hughes, ed. 1987). Throughout the Third World, children are portrayed as passive victims of poverty whose parents (or other kin) struggle to care for them against a myriad of obstacles. Among the most vivid portraits of the effects of urban squalor on children in Africa are those found in fictional accounts drawn from authors' firsthand experiences (see, for example, Emecheta 1979). Other studies by Mead (1939, 1961 [1928]) and, more recently, those falling under the direction and editorship of J. and B. Whiting, explore the meaning of adolescence cross-culturally, or, more generally, the experiences associated with growing up in different societies (Burbank 1988; Condon 1987; Davis and Davis 1989; Hollos and Leis 1989; see also the annotated bibliographies of Gottlieb et al. 1966). Only a few studies have explored situations where urban children live alone and care for themselves, but these focus on the extreme margins of life, where children are the victims of abandonment, famine, warfare, or the untimely deaths of kin (see, for example, Ennew and Milne 1990; Reynolds and Burman, eds. 1986; UNICEF 1987).

Northern Madagascar provides a striking contrast. Village children who have successfully completed their studies in rural primary schools and who show promise for more advanced learning sometimes come to Ambanja voluntarily (and with their parents' encouragement) to continue their schooling (for a similar case from Melanesia see Pomponio 1992). They are, essentially, young migrants: since there are no dormitory facilities available, they live in town without adult supervision. Many children, as young as thirteen, live alone or share a very simple one- or two-room house with a group of other students. These children must cope, on their own, with the complexities of two realms of experience. First, they must be able to make the shift from rural to town life. Second, they must face the problems that characterize the transition from youth to adulthood. Typically, they are the children of Sakalava tera-tany or non-Sakalava settlers who live in rural areas of the Sambirano. Such children experience problems characteristic of migrants in general, yet they are more vulnerable because they are children.

Outbreaks of njarinintsy possession have accompanied this recent trend. Within the last two decades outbreaks of mass possession have occurred in local schools, and the most common victims of these reckless and dangerous spirits are adolescent girls. Throughout the late 1970s and early 1980s, as many as thirty students became possessed at one time. In several instances, school officials closed down the schools until the spirits could be appeased. Although the frequency of njarinintsy possession in Ambanja has decreased in recent years, several cases are reported annually in at least one of the three local junior and senior high schools. Unlike tromba possession, which is established and ordered, njarinintsy possession is erratic and disordered, and its victims exhibit behavior that expresses the chaos inherent to their daily lives.

Reports of similar outbreaks of group or mass possession appear elsewhere in the anthropological literature and, typically, these occur within such institutional settings as schools (Harris 1957) and, more recently, factories (Grossman 1979; Ong 1987, 1988). An assumption underlying these studies is that issues of power and powerlessness are central to mass possession movements. As with earlier discussions of tromba in this study, the significance of power for njarinintsy possession must be investigated in reference to two axes, one defined by a historical development from past to present and the other including different levels of social experience: the community, the family and the schoolyard, and the individual. Elsewhere I have argued that conflicting moral orders in this community give rise to an anomic state (Durkheim 1968) in these children, which may have severe psychological consequences (Sharp 1990).[1] This chapter will illustrate, first, that children and adults have very different possession experiences, and thus njarinintsy provides additional information on the structural significance of tromba in this community. Second, the dangers associated with njarinintsy possession uncover other dimensions of disorder in this community which, in turn, have implications for the future. These children's experiences reveal the hidden underbelly of town life, deepening the understanding of problems associated with gender, polyculturalism, and colonialism which have thus far been explored only through adults' eyes. In order to resolve these children's problems, adults of diverse origins and backgrounds pulled together, drawing upon Sakalava authority to surmount chaos and reestablish social order.

THE POSSESSED YOUTH OF AMBANJA

Although tromba possession was the main focus of this research, my attention was often drawn to the njarinintsy, volatile and unpredictable spirits whose most frequent victims are adolescent girls. No mass outbreaks occurred during 1987; thus, this discussion of njarinintsy possession in the schools is based on interviews with more than one hundred informants, including spirit mediums, schoolchildren, their parents, other family members, teachers, and other school officials. The data collected focused on three areas: informants' accounts of mass possession occurring one to six times a year between 1975 and 1980, involving anywhere from three to thirty students; interviews with five established mediums who, in the past, had experienced possession sickness and four women who had recently been struck by possession sickness (see Appendix A); and my personal observation of five cases of njarinintsy in 1987.[2] Although tromba possession is an experience shared by many adult women, the following generalizations can be made about njarinintsy: the majority of its victims are between thirteen and seventeen years of age; they are school migrants who have come from Ambanja from neighboring rural villages; and they are female and, usually, pregnant and unmarried at the time of possession. The stories of Angeline (chapter 5) and Monique (chapter 7) are typical of njarinintsy victims. Sosotra's story, which follows, provides yet another portrait.

SOSOTRA AND THE NJARININTSY

One afternoon, while my assistant and I were interviewing a medium in her home, we suddenly heard the sound of wailing coming from a small house made of palm fiber which was located directly across the yard. Two women who were sitting with us exclaimed simultaneously that there was a njarinintsy ("*misy njarinintsy é!*") and so we all quickly stood up and went outside to see what was happening. It was Sosotra, a young Sakalava woman of nineteen who lived next door. She had joined us on previous occasions while we discussed tromba and other forms of possession. At these times she was generally quiet and sullen and often complained of nightmares(*nofy raty*), headaches, and dizziness. Although my informant had counseled her to consult either a moasy or a tromba medium for these problems, Sosotra did not pay much attention, often rising abruptly (and rudely) in the middle of conversation and walking home without saying goodbye. Neighbors often commented that she was odd (adaladala), but they pitied her because she was clearly troubled by possession sickness. During the last month or so it had also become clear to all of us that she was pregnant. No one had any idea who the father was.

On this afternoon Sosotra behaved in a manner that was very different from what I had witnessed previously. She suddenly burst from her house and fell on the ground, thrashing about, wailing and then shouting fragmented words that were impossible for any of us to understand. When we tried to get near her to calm her down she only became more violent. Finally, a friend of hers, along with two older women in their fifties, lept upon her and held her down until she became quiet. Eventually her aunt (MoSi), with whom she lived, came home, and she immediately arranged to take Sosotra in a taxi to a nearby village in order to consult with a tromba medium who specialized in possession sickness. She also sent for Sosotra's mother, who arrived the next day, accompanied by two young children. Two days later I saw Sosotra and she appeared quiet, but still sullen, unwilling to talk to me or my friend, who was her neighbor, about what had happened.

Sosotra's aunt then gave the following account, while Sosotra's mother was at the market buying food for the evening meal: "These last few months have been very difficult, very hard [*sarotra be, mafy be*]. Sosotra lived here in town by herself for two years, sharing a room with two schoolmates. She started to get in trouble, staying out all night and skipping classes. When I moved here last year she came to live with me. . . . Her parents had hoped that she could finish her schooling this year but she soon became very agitated and unhappy in school. Her teachers and neighbors said sometimes she would refuse to go to classes at all; on other days she would come home by late morning. . . . She wouldn't eat all day and then she'd go to the disco with her friends and stay all night. Three months ago the njarinintsy started, and she had to drop out of school a month before the term ended. I haven't known what to do. . . . Njarinintsy is very difficult and it is dangerous. . . . We took her to a tromba [medium] and the njarinintsy came out [miboaka] and spoke to [the tromba spirit]. The tromba said, 'My grandchild [zafiko], why are you bothering this girl? Leave her alone, leave her in peace! What do you want from her?' I was frightened [mavozobe] for her, but now it all seems pretty funny . . . the njarinintsy said he wanted Sosotra for his girl-friend [sipa]! but when he saw how unhappy we were, he promised to leave if we gave him some presents. We promised to leave some honey and soda pop near a sacred madiro tree for him, and then he departed. Then Sosotra fell on the ground, delirious but calm, and in the past few days she has slept soundly, without any signs of possession."

Sosotra's story parallels that of many other njarinintsy victims: she is under twenty, a school migrant from a village, and pregnant. Her story also parallels those of other girls who were involved in outbreaks of mass possession.

SCHOOLYARD POSSSESSION

Today njarinintsy possession is most common at home; it assumes its most dramatic form in the schoolyard, however, where it also has wide-spread impact on the community. This is a relatively new phenomenon in Ambanja. The earliest report that I have recorded from northern Madagascar occurred in 1962 in a school in Diégo. Most informants say that they first heard of njarinintsy in the 1970s and that it was brought by Tsimihety migrants. Of the seventeen teachers and school officials interviewed who had either grown up in the area or who had come to Ambanja within the last ten years, all but two reported that they had never heard of this type of possession elsewhere. Of the two who had, they both said that njarinintsy behavior has changed consider-ably: fifteen to twenty years ago njarinintsy were, for the most part, clowning spirits. As one teacher, who grew up in the north, said, "When I was much younger I would occasionally see [students possessed by] njarinintsy sitting outside a school and playing guitars, calling to pas-sersby to come and sing and dance with them."[3] In more recent years, however, they have become increasingly violent. Within the last decade, possession in Ambanja's junior and senior high schools has become so commonplace that two of the three school principals have formulated policies for handling it.[4]

A typical scenario[5] reads as follows: a teacher asks a student to perform a task, perhaps an assignment at the board. The student, instead of responding, will suddenly start to wail. Eventually the sound will grow louder, and she will sob, scream, or yell obscenities. She also might stand up or run about the room. As one teacher who witnessed a case in class explained: "I had asked this girl to read a passage from a French book. Instead she started to cry and then scream! I didn't understand what was going on—I come from Antananarivo and I had never seen such a thing. When she stood up I became scared. . . . Two students ran out of the room and a third told me to come, too, so I left and went to look for help." Often four or five boys will struggle with the njarinintsy victim in an attempt to hold her down. Word travels fast when such an outbreak occurs, so that usually a school official will arrive to help. A school principal explained: "If the girl fails to answer any questions and it is clear that she is possessed, sometimes the only thing to do is to slap her across the face. . . . I remember I had to hit one student three times! Then she was suddenly quiet and confused, calmly asking me where she was and why she had just been struck."[6] After the incident is over, or at least once the girl is under control, a group of friends will escort her to the home of her parents or other close kin (who most often live in the neighboring countryside), so that these family members may take over. Even though the girl may appear calm, the spirit will stay with her, shifting from dormant to active states until a healer coaxes it to leave.

Njarinintsy is thought to be very contagious, and from 1975 to 1980, mass outbreaks of njarinintsy possession were common. When a njarinintsy victim starts to wail, other students will run from the classroom or be ordered to do so by a well-informed teacher or school official. On several occasions fifteen to twenty students became possessed at one time. Sometimes up to four boys were affected, but in all cases the outbreak was initiated by a girl, and girls always formed the majority. Angeline (see chapter 5), for example, became possessed four times in one month, and during two of these episodes as many as ten other students also became possessed, including one boy. At the height of these outbreaks in Ambanja, njarinintsy spread from the junior high school and moved across the street to the primary school.

After attempts to treat njarinintsy possession on an individual basis failed to eliminate this problem in the schools, a group of concerned parents responded by requesting that school officials also become involved. This group of adults decided to call in a powerful moasy to visit the school and determine the causes of mass possession. He said that local ancestors (tromba, razaña, and other spirits) were angry, for when the school was built by the French no regard was paid to the sacredness of ancestral ground. During construction several tombs had been moved, and a few were destroyed. This specialist insisted on the necessity of performing a joro ceremony to honor these ancestors. This decision was an unusual one, for school grounds were hardly considered an appropriate setting for this ceremony. Nevertheless, school officials consented. An ox was sacrificed and members of the community gathered to sing to and praise the ancestral spirits, asking forgiveness and permission to continue to work at the school. A photographer was also hired to take a series of pictures to commemorate the event. Following these actions, the frequency of njarinintsy possession dropped considerably that year, with only a few students still experiencing possession fits. Eventually school officials, the possessed students, and their parents met once more with a kalanoro medium, this time in secrecy at night in one of the classrooms, to appease the njarinintsy one last time.[7] This collective response came from adults of diverse origins, including Sakalava and vahiny parents and schoolteachers and officials, several of whom were from the high plateaux. Their chosen course of action reinstated social order and cohesiveness in the schools. It also led to the reassertion of local Sakalava ritual authority over domains previously usurped by a foreign colonial power.

NJARININTSY POSSESSION AND SOCIAL STATUS

As discussed earlier in chapter 5, the causes for, behavior of, and responses to tromba and njarinintsy spirits are quite distinct. Njarinintsy is a form of possession sickness that requires immediate action. Kin must step in to care for the victim before serious harm befalls her. They may need to take her to a series of healers in order to have the spirit (or spirits, since njarinintsy may occur in groups of seven) driven from her. She must be watched closely, and great care must be exercised to ensure that the spirit has departed permanently. If not, she may go mad or die. Most often njarinintsy posssession is caused by fanafody raty or bad medicine. As a result, it is necessary to determine whether possession was brought on by an adversary or if the victim accidentally came into contact with fanafody that was intended for someone else. Another cause may be that the njarinintsy has been sent by a tromba spirit because the victim has been resisting possession (as was true of Angeline).

If this is the case, additional steps must be taken to instate her as a tromba medium.

A comparison of the qualities of tromba mediums and njarinintsy victims reveals that gender, age, and other aspects of social status vary for these two forms of possession. Adult female status in Ambanja is defined by crossing thresholds marked by marriage (common law or otherwise) and childbirth. Women who have attained this status form the majority of female tromba mediums. Marriage also provides the idiom for describing tromba possession, since a spirit is said to be the medium's spouse. Furthermore, through tromba possession a woman's social ties are enhanced, so that she joins a wide network of other mediums of diverse ages and backgrounds. Also, if she chooses to become a healer, her status in the community is elevated.

The majority of njarinintsy victims, however, have never been married and have had no previous possession experience. Instead, many of these girls are single and pregnant at the time of possession (as was true with Angeline, Monique, and Sosotra). In addition, unlike tromba, njarinintsy possession is a temporary, incomplete form of possession. It is a type of possession sickness in which the possessed is a victim who requires assistance from others at a time of personal crisis. Njarinintsy spirits are not accepted companions of their victims, nor do they assist them in times of need, as do tromba spirits. They are malicious and destructive.

The data recorded in figure 7.1 (chapter 7) and Appendix A reveal several trends regarding njarinintsy. Common themes emerge in the histories of women who have experienced both possession sickness and tromba mediumship and those who have experienced only the former. These two groups can be compared in terms of age of onset of possession, schooling, tera-tany or vahiny status, and history of fertility-related traumas.

First, five of the eighteen female tromba mediums (Angeline, Leah, Marie, Beatrice, and Mariamo) have been afflicted with possession sickness (two of them have experienced it twice). In the case of all five women, possession sickness precipitated mediumship status, which followed shortly afterward: all five have Grandchildren spirits, and the fifth and oldest (Mariamo) has a more prestigious Child spirit. Leah and Marie have each been struck a second time since instating tromba spirits. Year of birth is another determinant for this group: possession sickness has not been experienced by mediums who were over the age

of thirty-four in 1987, reflecting that this is a relatively recent phenomenon in Ambanja, that it affects younger women, and that recently it has
begun to precede tromba possession.

Age, school experiences, and problems involving romance and fertility also affect the timing of episodes of possession sickness among these
(now) established mediums. Angeline, Leah, and Marie were first struck
with possession sickness between the ages of seventeen and twenty;
Beatrice and Mariamo at thirteen and twenty-six (or thereabouts), respectively. Marie experienced possession sickness three months after the
difficult birth of her first child. Angeline was struck after falling in love
with her teacher, who left to continue his studies elsewhere while she
was expected to stay behind and finish school. Finally, social status is
a factor. The women in this first group are either tera-tany or the children of settlers: Angeline, Leah, and Beatrice are Sakalava from a village
near Ambanja, Ambanja, and Nosy Be, respectively. Marie is the child
of Tsimihety settlers, whereas Mariamo was born of a Comorean father
and Sakalava mother in Ambilobe. Four of these five women have completed at least some level of junior high school and the fifth completed
primary school.

The second group (Vivienne, Sylvie, Victoria, and Sosotra), composed
of women who have been struck by possession sickness only, are predominantly Sakalava: Sylvie was born in Ambanja and Victoria and
Sosotra are from nearby villages. Vivienne is the child of a Sakalava
mother and Tsimihety father and originally came from Ambanja.[8] The
ages at which njarinintsy episodes occurred for this second group of
four women range from fourteen to early thirties; two out of four (Vivienne and Sosotra) were in junior high school. In reference to fertility,
Sylvia was struck by njarinintsy one week after a miscarriage, Victoria
following an abortion, and Sosostra following her first pregnancy by a
secret lover when she was still single.

Several themes emerge if these two categories of women are compared. First, three out of five mediums (Angeline, Leah, Marie) were
first struck by possession sickness while they were adolescents enrolled
in junior high school. Among those affected to date only by possession
sickness, two out of four (Vivienne and Sosotra) were also in junior
high school. For all five women questions surrounding female adult
status or fertility were important issues at the time. If the specific school
experiences are compared between these two groups, three of the five
students were what I refer to here as "child" or "school migrants":
Angeline, Vivienne, and Sosotra each came on their own from villages

to continue their education in Ambanja. As will become clear below, the relationships between school migration, adult status and fertility, and possession sickness are part of a larger picture framed by historically based national and community forces. Likewise, the responses to these possession episodes are linked to the internal logic of local culture, in which Sakalava customs provided an appropriate response to problems that arise from powerlessness.

THE DISORDER OF A FRAGMENTED WORLD

The members of this community, be they tera-tany or vahiny, young or old, must struggle at some level to cope with forces that challenge notions of cultural and, ultimately, personal identity. The combined forces of colonialism, polyculturalism, and subsequent métisization have led both to the erosion of Sakalava cultural values and to a blurring of ethnic boundaries. Newly arrived migrants must become enmeshed in local networks, seeking out friends and relatives who come from the same region of the country. Others attempt to become Sakalava through changes in behavior, dress, and dialect and by participating in such Sakalava institutions as tromba ceremonies. The dilemmas associated with economic survival and social integration frustrate many vahiny. As earlier descriptions of settlers' stories show, even those who feel content (tamana) in Ambanja continue to be regarded as outsiders by local tera-tany. The most vulnerable group in this context consists of children living alone, since they have neither adult guidance nor the skills to solve the problems associated with town life. The young girls who become possessed by njarinintsy are the most visible victims of this process because they suffer the consequences of unexpected (and unwanted) pregnancies.[9] They are faced with a complicated and tangled set of desires and expectations; in their possessed states they mirror the problems inherent to schooling on the coast.

COLONIAL POLICIES AND NATIONAL TRENDS: EDUCATIONAL DILEMMAS

Problems associated with education characterize the lives of children. In Ambanja, they run beyond those associated merely with high performance in school. In recent times, severe constraints levied by political and economic forces have imposed new frustrations on students. These problems are rooted in changes that occurred during the colonial period.

A comparison between today's schoolchildren and those of past generations illustrates this.

Under the French, schools were built to serve Malagasy students. Primary (FR: *primaire*) education was mandatory, and the first school for Malagasy in Ambanja was built in 1908, only a few years after the town was founded. An extensive network of primary schools was established throughout the island, with schools located even in the smallest villages. A few students were able to continue on to junior high (*collège*), high school (*lycée*), and, ultimately, to professional schools. These children joined a privileged group of students who were groomed to form a future elite class of civil servants. In the Sambirano, special preference was shown for the children of local royalty and others whose parents already worked for the colonial administration (see Crowder 1964, and Gifford and Weiskel 1974, for discussions of French colonial education policies elsewhere in Africa; see also Fallers 1965, especially chaps. 5 and 7ff).

Junior high and high schools were few in number and were generally located in urban centers so as to serve the region. As Malagasy children moved beyond primary school they left home to live in the provincial or national capitals. They were housed in dormitories, where they were placed under the strict supervision of members of a French ruling class. The school was regarded as the primary arena for the application of colonial *assimilation* policies, whereby French values were promoted and local culture was undermined (cf. Crowder 1964). The education of girls, for example, was comparable to that of French finishing schools, for they were taught homemaking skills and became well versed in the manners that were thought to be essential for women living in a cosmopolitan French society. As Alima, a member of the Bemazava royal lineage explained:

> When I was a young girl I was sent to Antananarivo to complete my studies there. . . . My father was an important man in Ambanja because he was in the direct line of succession. . . . They were very strict with us at school: we had to learn to sit and act like ladies, dressing and behaving like proper Parisian women. . . . Our studies were very rigorous, too. In addition to learning how to sew and cook French cuisine, we were instructed in math, geography, French, [and other subjects]. . . . We were both raised and schooled by French matrons. . . . I hated it there, though. We Sakalava did not like living in dormitories with borzany [derogatory term for Merina]; they are not like us: Sakalava like to bathe three to five times a day, but the Merina girls were very modest, and so they only bathed on the weekends. It was so cold there, too—we had to wash with ice cold water in the winter.

Alima and her peers are now the better educated parents and grandparents of many of the children who live in town today, filling local and provincial adminstrative posts. In spite of the difficulties she faced as a student, Alima's education served her well in the early days following Independence: under President Tsiranana she was appointed to a ministerial position and was highly regarded in the province of Antsiranana as someone who kept a watchful eye on the needs of people in the north.

In some ways, the policies established under the French have continued since Madagascar's Independence in 1960 and throughout the period leading up to the Socialist Revolution of the early to mid-1970s. Primary education has remained mandatory, and additional schools have been built in an attempt to accomodate the increasing numbers of children in both urban and rural areas. A characteristic of this French-based educational system is a series of standardized examinations that students must pass if they are to proceed to the next level. Failure and subsequent repetition of school years is not uncommon, and the numbers of enrolled students decrease dramatically as one moves up in the grades into junior high, high school, and the university.

Funds earmarked for education are limited. Schools are unable to accomodate an ever-increasing population of youth, since they lack the funds to cover costs for teachers' salaries and the maintenance and construction of buildings. As a result, schools remain overcrowded and many students are turned away. The rate of construction of new junior high and high schools continues to be slow. When they are built, they are centrally located in the larger towns. Village children are still forced to leave home if they are to continue their schooling beyond the primary level. In Ambanja, the first public junior high school was built in 1960, the year of Independence, and since 1981 there has been a high school (a new building was completed in 1987; see chapter 6). There is also a private school run by the Catholic Mission, which now extends through high school, with a small men's seminary attached. Under the French system, there was dormitory housing, but this is no longer provided except for seminary students. When teachers are asked about the problems faced by Ambanja's youth, the lack of housing is the most commonly cited factor.

The problems that confront Ambanja's youth are complicated by the contradictions between their aspirations and the political and economic realities inherent to Madagascar today. Because of the difficulty of progressing through the system, success in school is regarded with great pride by adult kin, and so students may stay enrolled in school to please their parents. Nevertheless, employment opportunities are extremely limited in Madagascar. Positions for the better educated, when they are available, often go to those who live in the capital or who have strong connections there. Well aware of these circumstances, students in Ambanja often mock their teachers publicly, asking why they should work hard when there are no jobs to be had. They often state that their parents, the peasants of the Sambirano, are rich because they own land, while the teachers, who hold university degrees, do not make enough to care adequately for their families. Should they wish to attend university, coastal students have a much lower chance of passing the national exams. In addition, it is difficult for coastal students to acquire decent scholarships because of the favoritism that characterizes the educational system. Attending university often is a painful experience because of the hostility between highland and coastal groups.

CHILDREN AND POLYCULTURALISM

As Gifford and Weiskel state in their review of French colonial educational policies in Africa, "Both in imagination and in fact, the colonial period brought into being a *civilisation m[é]tisse:* a jostling, a juxtaposition of values. The indelible education, imbedded in the mind and felt through the senses, was a blend of contrasts" (1974: 710). The emphasis on French values continued during the first administration of the government of Madagascar, from Independence until the Socialist Revolution. After the Revolution it was no longer appropriate to strive to be French. Schoolchildren experienced—and suffered the consequences of—the transition during the early years of new malagasization educational policies. These were implemented in Ambanja by 1975 (they will be described in more detail below). It was during this year that the first outbreaks of mass njarinintsy possession occurred.

I have discussed elsewhere (Sharp 1990) the manner in which mandatory education in Madagascar gave rise to adolescence as a new category of experience (cf. Ariès 1965; Lasch 1977: 12ff; Minge 1986), and how this is relevant to the moral education (Durkheim 1961) and subsequent experiences of Ambanja's schoolchildren. In essence, their preparation for adulthood, which occurs in the village, is cut short as they move to town to continue their schooling. As students under the present state system, they lack the socialization that their predecessors, such as Alima, had, for they are socialized neither by kin nor French school authorities. Instead, they fall between the cracks. Amiability between teachers and students is often blocked by interethnic hostility and prejudice: the majority of their teachers are Merina, whom many Sakalava tera-tany regard as their enemies. This prevents school teachers from being guardians, caretakers, or agents of socialization for their students.

As noted in chapter 6, malagasization has become a cornerstone of government policy following the Socialist Revolution of the 1970s, advocating the supremacy of Malagasy customs (fomba-gasy) over those of foreign origin (fomba vazaha). The effects of malagasization on education, however, have only exacerbated local tensions in schools. Whereas in the past all subjects were taught in French, today this is only true of the last year of high school and at the university. Students enrolled in public schools learn all subjects in official Malagasy, which is based on the Merina dialect, and study French only as one of many subjects. The sudden switch to an all-French curriculum is overwhelming for most students and has led to strikes throughout the country at high schools and the university. Teachers are handicapped as well. As members of the last generation that was schooled in French, they often do not know the technical terms in official Malagasy relevant to the very subjects they are trained to teach. The problems that arise through the use of different dialects can also be severe. Many teachers in Ambanja are not Sakalava (see Mme Razafy in chapter 4, for example), so that not only do teachers and students experience severe communication problems, but coastal students are at a disadvantage when compared to their counterparts in the high plateaux who are familiar with this dialect. Sakalava students also resent having to learn what they perceive as being the Merina dialect. In turn, their own values and experiences often conflict with those they are expected to advocate to the younger generation of students.

Beyond the borders of the schoolyard, these children from the villages face additional problems associated with urbanization and polyculturalism. Like adult migrants, who have come to Ambanja temporarily or permanently in search of work, students from rural areas are responsible for such basic needs as their food and shelter. Some children manage to live with extended kin (this most often involves staying under the care of maternal classificatory mothers and grandmothers). Those without relatives in town must rent a room or a small house made of palm fiber that is paid for by their absent parents, since townspeople are very reluctant to take non-kin into their homes. For example, a friend of mine had such a dwelling in her backyard which she had rented to students for three consecutive years. She explained that the boy who lived there in 1987 was quiet and studious, but he rarely had much to eat. Losing a pad of paper or set of pens could be a severe hardship. When I asked if she fed him or helped him sometimes in other ways she said flatly, "Oh no, he's not my child, he's not kin [*tsy tsaikiko, tsy havañana izy*] . . . why should I feed him? I have five children of my own to care for." Thus, these children often live without direct adult supervision, unlike those of a previous era, who were supervised by the teachers of a foreign regime.

Today, many of Ambanja's children are, in essence, child migrants faced with adult problems. In addition to keeping up with their studies, they are responsible for housekeeping, cooking their own meals, and carefully maintaining monthly budgets. They often face severe economic pressures, since the present constraints of the Malagasy economy on individual households make it difficult for many parents to give more than the bare essentials to children living away from home. If parents own land, it is easier for them to supply their children with rice and other staples. Nevertheless, these students may need to have a supplementary income to pay for extra food and school supplies, and so some turn to stealing to support themselves. In addition, since they have been freed from the constraints that would normally be set by older kin, many of these children fail to resist the attractions available in town. These include going to the cinema, drinking, dancing, and early sexual experiences. In practical terms, not only does their schoolwork suffer, but it is also a severe drain on their pocket money. Girls face the additional problem of pregnancy. Through their involvement in adult town life, Ambanja's children are often faced with dilemmas that can seriously affect their chances for higher education.

SELF-ADVANCEMENT AND FANAFODY

Just as Ambanja's adults are in competition with each other for scarce resources—work, money, and lovers—students, too, compete with each other in the schoolyard and in the classroom. For them, as with adults, fanafody is a major source of control. As mentioned above, the most frequently cited cause for njarinintsy possession is that the victim has come into contact with fanafody raty. Fanafody is acquired by consulting tromba mediums or other specialists and is usually prepared for use with a specific individual in mind. It is placed either where the intended victim will touch or walk over it—on a doorknob, on a personal item, or in a doorway—or it may be put in food or bathwater.

Fanafody may affect anyone who comes into contact with it. When attacks of njarinintsy occur in school, those concerned must determine where the fanafody was placed and whether it was prepared by an adversary of the child or child's kin, or if, perhaps, the afflicted inadvertently came into contact with something that was intended for someone else. Another explanation was illustrated by the 1980 outbreaks of mass possession cited above. When possession continued even after repeated individual consultations with healers, eventually human forces were ruled out and angry ancestors were identified as the direct cause.

As described in previous chapters, fanafody is used by adults to control their own lives; they also use it to assist their children. On numerous occasions I watched worried parents consult tromba mediums for problems related specifically to their children's performance in school (see, for example, the case of Fatima in chapter 8). Examination time in particular is one of great worry for many parents. This is not very surprising, since the performance and success rates for Ambanja's students fall well below the national average. Class rank is an important indicator of a child's success, so that parents may use fanafody not only so that their children will succeed, but so that others will fail. Following patterns set by adults, children also use fanafody against one another, but in a setting particular to their own experience: the schoolyard. For children, the use of fanafody raty is very closely tied to jealousy and fear of one another. As one young informant said when asked about tensions between students and their patterns of association, "I have no friends, I only study. The students in Ambanja are not nice people—if you do well they accuse you of using magic [magique] to succeed and then they use magic against you to make you fail."

In addition to scholastic success, social competition is also a major preoccupation of young students. Village children who have come to town for their schooling and live alone, unhampered by adult supervision, are likely to be more socially active than their town-based counterparts. Such children, in general, form the majority of those seen out at night in the streets on *promenade* (mitsangantsangana) or in bars and discos. Ambanja's youth are also sexually active at an early age—for girls this may mean as early as thirteen, whereas boys lag behind by a few years. Young students and teachers both report that competition among girls for male attention can be fierce. Teachers agree that when fights occur in the schoolyard they often center on disputes of this nature between two girls. The frequent use of fanafody raty on school grounds accounts for the common occurrence of njarinintsy attacks in school.

As proof of this, informants point out that it is the "prettiest girls" (*tsara tarehy*) who most often become possessed. One of two reasons is generally given to support this observation: other students are more likely to be jealous of them and wish to cause them harm, and njarinintsy prefer them because they are so attractive (thus Sosotra's spirit wanted her to be his girlfriend or sipa). School officials are also quick to point out that, in almost all cases, it is later learned that these girls, like Sosotra, were in the early stages of pregnancy when they became possessed.

COPING WITH PREGNANCY

Pregnancy among these girls throws the nature of these children's dilemmas into high relief, since it is an obvious sign of participation in the adult world. Cross-cultural comparison reveals that Ambanja's students share experiences with children in many other countries, where changing social patterns affect the rates of premarital pregnancy among adolescent girls (cf. Lancaster and Hamburg, eds., 1986; Worthman and Whiting 1987). In recent years, this topic has also become a concern for such international agencies as UNICEF, the World Health Organization, and Planned Parenthood International (Kulin 1988).

In Ambanja, girls tend to become sexually active before boys their own age do, sleeping with older boys or men. In addition, these village girls who live alone and unsupervised in town are more likely to become involved in the town's nightlife than town-based girls, whose relatives monitor which boys they see. Although students interviewed insist that it is unlikely that a girl who is sexually active is working as a prostitute (makarely), it is likely that she is someone's mistress (deuxième bureau). A sign that a man treats his mistress well is that he buys her expensive gifts, such as perfume, imported fabrics, and gold jewelry. He will also be expected to take her places, such as the cinema or discos, or to the more cosmopolitan centers of Nosy Be or Diégo. A schoolgirl who receives such attention is thus easy to recognize. She may become an object of envy, either for other girls who wish to have a similar relationship or who are fond of the same man, or for boys whose attentions go unrequited.

Responses by kin to adolescent pregnancy are often marked by severe sanctions. As one girl explained, "My parents were very angry and refused to speak to me for weeks." For Malagasy, a refusal to speak to the injuring party is an extreme response in moments of great anger or sadness. This can, literally, go on for weeks. It is a form of social death for the transgressor, since a refusal to communicate serves as a denial of the other's existence. In most cases, the parents will eventually accept the pregnancy, for Malagasy value children very highly. Also, this response from parents is not that unusual when viewed more broadly and historically. It parallels patterns set by adults in Ambanja, among whom short-term marriages are common.

For children in school, however, pregnancy adds special hardships for girls and it is regarded as a very serious matter. Village parents are often reluctant to send their daughters away to school, because they worry that if they live unsupervised in town they might become pregnant. A decision by parents to allow a daughter to attend school away from home is proof of their confidence in her. If she does indeed become pregnant, it is a breach of this confidence as well as a disappointment. Furthermore, school policies and economic constraints will force her to end her schooling prematurely, since it is the policy of all schools to expel the girl if officials discover that she is pregnant. Youth of Ambanja say that school officials rarely look for the boy who is responsible. (I understand, however, that at the new high school these girls may finish the term, but it is generally assumed they will leave school after the baby is born.)[10] A pregnant girl undergoes extreme hardship if the father of the child refuses to support her and the child. In response, close kin—especially the girl's mother—will usually step in and help raise and care for the child. The girl, in turn, may choose to remain in town where it will be easier for her to make a living.

As the data shows, njarinintsy spirits attack their victims in times of personal conflict. Most often they are associated with an incomplete transition to womanhood and, more specifically, with problems of fertility. Possession provides the idiom and the human body the vehicle for expressing such conflicts. From a Sakalava point of view, tromba mediumship marks a sanctioned transition to adult female status: typically it occurs among women who are in their twenties or older and who have already borne at least one child. In contrast, njarinintsy occurs at thresholds where this transition is incomplete. These experiences parallel Boddy's descriptions of northern Sudanese women who are possessed by zar spirits (1988, 1989). Njarinintsy occurs at junctures where fertility is sudden and problematic: njarinintsy victims are adolescent girls who are confronted with unwanted pregnancy and motherhood. They have not been issued into this status by supportive kin. Rather they are alone in town, and this event carries serious consequences for them.

Thus they stand on the brink of adult female status without having achieved it in culturally sanctioned ways. Were they in the village, a mate would be expected to declare paternity and support the child. They, however, are schoolgirls, sent to town to complete their studies, and they are expected to postpone motherhood. Contrary to their parents' expectations, they have become involved in the town's nightlife, sleeping with men who treat them as mistresses but not as wives.

CHILDREN AND SOCIAL CHANGE

The victims of njarinintsy possession comprise an unusual group, whose status is defined as marginal from a multiplicity of angles. They are caught in limbo between childhood and adulthood, forced prematurely to become adults before they have been fully socialized. This has the most severe consequences for schoolgirls. Should they choose to participate in the sexual realm of town life, they risk becoming targets for scorn, jealousy, and fanafody raty. If they suddenly find themselves pregnant, they must face the anger of their parents, often, abandonment by their lovers, banishment from school, and, finally, the economic necessity of finding work so that they may support their children. These dilemmas—which result from recent political, ideological, and economic changes—may be overwhelming, since these girls are young, inexperienced, and alone.

DISPLACED SAKALAVA AND INVADING SPIRITS

Themes of displacement and disorder are reiterated in concrete and symbolic ways in the context of njarinintsy school possession. As Feeley-Harnik explains (1991b, chaps. 4 and 5), the movement or displacement from village (antsabo, "at the crops") to town (ampositra, "at the post") is a disturbing aspect of recent history for the Bemihisatra-Sakalava of the Analalava region. Among the tera-tany of Ambanja, however, those who move frequently are not so much adults in search of work, wealth, or spouses (Feeley-Harnik 1991b: 279), but children who are sent on their own to further their educations and hope to draw on their training to assist their kin financially in the future. Thus, these children define an unusual category of migrants. Most often they are tera-tany or the children of settlers; but while their parents may feel established and content (tamana) in rural villages, these children must cope with problems similar to those of other newly arrived migrants in town, including the shortage of housing and the high cost of living. Their problems are compounded by those that exist at school, most notably involving the consequences of malagasization.

Marginality is a central aspect of njarinintsy possession. By contrast, to become a tromba medium, one must be well integrated into the community. Young women like Basely (chapter 7) can not become mediums unless they can afford to host the appropriate ceremonies and situate themselves within a locus of supportive kin and close friends already familiar with tromba possession. Such a status shift is not possible for adolescent schoolgirls, first, because they have not yet achieved adult status in a socially sanctioned way and, second, because they live isolated in town, far from kin. The responses to individual cases of njarinintsy possession—as with any form of sickness—reflect the necessity of collective action, in which family and friends congregate to care for and socialize with the afflicted. The responses to repeated cases of group possession were a bit different in that they involved participation that went beyond kin and friendship networks. The cooperative actions of parents and school officials eventually stabilized these girls' social positions and reintegrated them into a community of caring adults.

Disorder and fragmentation are concepts that are communicated symbolically through njarinintsy possession (cf. Lambek 1981; Ackerman and Lee 1981). Again, a comparison between tromba and njarinintsy clarifies this. First, although dialogue is a very important aspect of tromba, direct communication is not characteristic of njarinintsy. During fits of njarinintsy possession, a message of chaos and dysfunction is conveyed through the actions of the victim's body. Njarinintsy spirits express rage, taking the form of insults and physical violence directed at people and objects. The spirits' actions are sporadic and unpredictable and the words they utter consist of incomplete phrases and swearing, so that their messages are vague, fragmented, and garbled. There is a dynamic at work here between communication and power. Tromba mediums may wield much control through their words, both in a household and in the community at large, but the power of njarinintsy possession is short-lived, leading only to the temporary closing down of schools while parents and authorities seek explanations for the causes for these events. In addition, njarinintsy is an incomplete form of possession: the lifetime training and self-exploration so characteristic of tromba is not part of the njarinintsy experience. Instead, njarinintsy is a temporary state that is frightening and confusing for both victims and witnesses. This type of dangerous spirit must be driven from its victim;

only then perhaps may she anticipate becoming a tromba medium some-time in the future.

In addition, njarinintsy spirits, like the displaced children they possess, are in some sense migrants themselves. They are viewed as being a problematic and marginal category of spirits in Ambanja (and, more generally, in northwest Madagascar). Most mediums state that njarinintsy are either like tromba, referring to them as "little tromba" (tromba hely) or "bad tromba" (tromba raty). Others (such as the medium who assisted Sosotra) view them as the "children" or "grandchildren of tromba."[11] Local concern over the effects of polyculturalism and métisization are reflected in njarinintsy as well. As described earlier, Bemazava royalty are emphatic in their statements that njarininintsy are of foreign origin, brought by Tsimihety migrants from the south. From a purist stance, these are invading and troublesome spirits that belong neither in Sakalava territory nor in Sakalava royal lineages. In essence, they are perceived to be a threat to the continuation of Sakalava power and succession.

Displacement and confusion also characterize the geography of the schoolyard, the locus of outbreaks of njarinintsy possession. Here the "jostling" and "juxtaposition of values" to which Gifford and Weiskel (1974: 710) refer take on a more disturbing tone. Eventually the cause of mass outbreaks was identified as angry ancestors whose tombs had been displaced by French colonial officials. The subsequent use of the schoolyard by the community continued this disregard for Sakalava sacred space. This breach of local custom was in turn exacerbated by the presence of non-Sakalava students, Merina schoolteachers, and the programmatic curricular changes that occurred through malagasization. Thus, as indigenous and proper ancestral spirits were displaced, these njarinintsy of foreign origin began to dominate the schoolyard, sent by the ancestors to harm the living.

Additional actions by schoolchildren themselves complete this image of displacement in the schoolyard. In this setting, children compete with each other for success in school; they also compete for romantic partners. Whereas the use of fanafody is a factor of everyday adult life in the town at large, the frequency of use is especially high in the schoolyard. This is compounded by the fact that the space is small and its borders clearly demarcated. Thus, potentially everyone runs the risk of being affected. Victims of njarinintsy are often those who accidentally come into contact with substances left to harm someone else, and so, like these children and their spirits, the dangerous effects of fanafody raty may be displaced onto an unintended victim. Anger and frustration underlie this world of children, who must cope with interethnic hostilities and the problems brought on by national educational policies. Their powerlessness is aptly expressed by their frequent use of fanafody raty and through the volatile actions of the njarinintsy spirits.

In this setting, njarinintsy possession has not assumed a static form. Instead, it has changed in response to localized social and political forces. Whereas in the 1960s these were mild-mannered and clowning spirits, by the mid-1970s they had become violent and uncontrollable. Njarinintsy possession communicates marginality, as young, displaced migrants are seized by foreign entities whose erratic behavior operates as an expression of their fragmented world. Ironically, it is the actions of these marginalized children that led to the reassertion of Sakalava power. Such an outcome, however, was possible only through the active participation of adults.

RESPONSES TO SCHOOLYARD POSSESSION:
SAKALAVA REVIVALISM

There is no question that njarinintsy disrupts the social order in school and even in the community at large. The solutions chosen were varied. At first, kin were responsible for ensuring that individual children were treated by a local healer. By 1980, however, mass possession occurred with alarming frequency in the junior high school, involving at least one outbreak each week for over a month. The more intensive solutions that followed were embedded in a local, dominant cultural logic, prompted by the actions of a culturally and socially alienated group of youth. In essence, Sakalava traditionalism provided the appropriate responses at a time of acute personal and community crisis. Prior to these mass possession events, schools and other buildings constructed by the French or the state were not viewed as appropriate settings for joro ceremonies for honoring ancestors. Thus, the boundaries of sacred space were broadened as a result of these events.[12]

Malagasization played an important role in the incidence of and responses to outbreaks of njarinintsy in ways that at first appear contradictory, since, in part, malagasization may be viewed as the root or cause of the problem—but it also provided appropriate responses and solutions. Mass outbreaks of group possession coincided with the institutionalization of malagasization in Ambanja. This policy was formulated at a national level to foster a sense of *national identity and culture* among all Malagasy speakers. Those students who were affected by njarinintsy were members of the first classes that took their exams in Malagasy, and their possession can be viewed in part as a form of symbolic protest against this new educational policy. Yet another aspect of malagasization, however, is an emphasis on the need to respect *local customs,* and so the hosting of a joro ceremony on school grounds was a logical application of this policy. By 1980 this aspect of local Sakalava culture provided the appropriate answers for children struggling with the problems of urbanization and state education. Since it involved the participation of adults and school officials, tera-tany and vahiny (among whom there were Merina) came together to honor and recognize the authority of local Sakalava ancestors.

The effects of this decision were eventually felt beyond the confines of the town's schoolyards, since it set in motion a chain of events that led to the institutionalization of Sakalava authority and power over the local tanindrazaña. When the decision was made to build a new high school in Ambanja, living and dead royalty held sway over all major decisions. Similarly, the approval of the royal tromba spirits was—and continues to be—required if state-owned boats wish to fish in the sacred waters off Nosy Faly (see chapter 6; for an interesting contrast see Ong 1988).[13] Thus, it was a fragmented, incomplete form of possession, involving non-Sakalava spirits, which led to the reintegration of alienated youth and the reassertion of local Sakalava power.

The question that remains is what form njarinintsy possession will assume in the future. Njarinintsy has begun to become an integral part of tromba, often preceding mediumship among the younger women of Ambanja. It already appears to be taking a dominant role in ushering girls into womanhood in cases where their female social status is problematic. In addition, the playboy Grandchildren—whom some say were at one time njarinintsy—now frequently possess Ambanja's children. Perhaps they will replace the royal spirits of Nosy Faly in dictating the direction of local culture through this future generation of mediums, who must make sense of new tensions shaped by this ever-changing world of urbanization and polyculturalism.

CHAPTER X

Exorcising the Spirits

*The Alternative Therapeutics of
Protestantism*[1]

I wish to end this study with a discussion of an alternative form of healing offered by an unusual group of vahiny in northwest Madagascar. Protestant exorcists serve as a final option in a locally conceived hierarchy of resort (Romanucci-Ross 1977), especially for problems associated with spirit possession and madness. A wide array of indigenous practitioners (including tromba, kalanoro, moasy, mpisikidy) play key roles in diagnosing and treating the symptoms associated with these categories of experience.[2] However, if their repeated efforts fail to improve the health status of a patient she (usually with her kin) may seek treatment from other healers whose training is derived from nonindigenous (Western and Christian) sources.

Two factors account for this reluctance on the part of Sakalava patients and their kin to consult with Protestant exorcists. First, ethnic factionalism is key. Although exorcists working in northern Madagascar are all Malagasy, they are rarely Sakalava, and many come from the high plateaux. The fact that they are strangers creates an interesting dynamic in the context of therapy. Second, Protestants embrace a competing view of reality and, more specifically, of possession. Since they consider tromba spirits to be evil, few Sakalava are willing to seek out their treatments. In some cases, however, the exorcists' healing approaches and philosophy offer a welcome escape from the otherwise unavoidable problems that accompany possession.

The therapy offered by Protestants also carries important implications for the study of the ongoing dynamics of identity and power. As shown throughout this work, tromba is a mainstay of social life in Ambanja, yet a minority of women eventually choose to opt out of mediumship. One's social status is raised by virtue of being a medium and healer, but the possession experience has its problems. As all mediums say, their spirits make them "suffer" (*mijaly*). From a Sakalava perspective, once a spirit is instated, possession is permanent, and a medium must accept the suffering that accompanies this status as part of her fate. A few, however, find the associated hardships to be intolerable. Exorcists offer these mediums a way to be freed of their spirits. In order to do so, however, a medium must reject Sakalava respect for and beliefs about royal ancestors. Exorcists also expect their clients to convert to Protestantism, thus permanently embracing a worldview contrary to that of their own culture.

SAKALAVA PERCEPTIONS OF POSSESSION AND MADNESS

In Ambanja, when mediums and other informants describe possession they sometimes compare it to madness (adala, adalaña; also, *marary saina, very saina/jery*, "sick" or "lost mind"). Even though possession and madness are regarded as distinct categories of experience, they overlap somewhat in their causation, symptomatology, and treatment. According to Sakalava informants, possession and madness define a spectrum of symptoms where severity is an important distinction. In this model, tromba possession and madness occupy opposite poles, and possession sickness falls somewhere in between (see figure 10.1). This spectrum of experiences ranges from a good, powerful, and inescapable state to a destructive, dangerous, and frightening illness.

Tromba possession is distinct in that it is an accepted form of behavior and experience, involving periodic changes in personality, dress, and other characteristics as the medium moves in and out of trance. Although tromba spirits periodically may cause harm to a medium—making her sick if they are angry, for example—they are generally regarded as sacred, powerful, and beneficial entities that look after the medium, her kin, and her clients.

Njarinintsy, masoantoko, shay-tuan and bilo are evil, reckless, and uncontrollable spirits. Since they simultaneously are forms of spirit possession and sickness (*marary*), they occupy a position somewhere between tromba and madness. As described in chapter 9, a njarinintsy, for example, is a generic spirit that has no personal name. Although it

TROMBA	POSSESSION SICKNESS	MADNESS
controlled: medium enters/exits trance at will	uncontrolled: fits of possession	uncontrolled: victim does not have fits but experiences madness as a constant state of being characterized by socially unacceptable behavior
caused by a spirit that is identifiable (it has a name, distinct personality, dress, etc.)	unidentified, generic spirit that has no name	may be caused by a spirit, but the spirit does not possess the victim
communication is possible: one can have a dialogue with the spirit as if it were a living human being	communication is possible, but difficult: spirit is usually angry and uncooperative; the victim's speech is fragmented	communication is very difficult, if not impossible: victims often make no sense when they speak
permanent: medium has her spirit(s) for life	temporary and dangerous sickness; she must be cured or will risk further harm	possibly permanent, dangerous form of sickness: it is very difficult, if not impossible, to cure
powerful, good	dangerous, bad	dangerous, bad

Figure 10.1.   Characteristics of Possession and Madness (Sakalava interpretations).

possesses and controls the body of its victim, this (as well as other forms of possession sickness) is temporary, and it is regarded as a special form of illness that ceases when the spirit is driven from its victim. During fits of possession a victim may be described as being temporarily mad, suffering from a "sick mind" or "sick spirit" (marary saina) because she periodically and uncontrollably shouts obscenities, attacks people, or wanders aimlessly through the streets. If the harmful spirit(s) is not driven from the victim it may have long-lasting effects, ultimately driving her permanently insane or even killing her.

Madness is a general illness category defined very broadly by more serious forms of deviant behavior which are fairly constant and long-term. Madness is a frightening problem, for, as an extreme illness category, it is very difficult to cure. It is defined in reference to possession, but it is not the same. Madness may be caused by an angry spirit, brought upon its victim by a tromba because she is resisting possession, or by a malicious spirit, such as a njarinintsy, which has been allowed to stay too long within her. One of the primary problems with madness, however, is it does not necessarily result from a foreign entity that actually *resides in* the victim. The intangibility of the problem is part of what makes it extremely difficult to treat.

Possession offers other clues for understanding Sakalava conceptions of madness. Whereas tromba is good (tsara) and sacred (masina), madness, like possession sickness, is bad (raty). Communication is also an important factor in distinguishing these categories from one anther. Tromba spirits have full-fledged personalities that enable them to converse and interact with the living. The speech of njarinintsy and similar spirits, on the other hand, is angry and garbled. The mad occupy the other polar extreme: they speak nonsense and this is a constant state for them, unlike the fits that characterize possession sickness.

Although madness may sometimes be confused with possession sickness (especially at onset), it is a distinct category because it is viewed as an extreme and potentially permanent state of being. In Ambanja there were two individuals who were often seen in public places and who were labeled as mad (adala, adalaña). One was an Antandroy man who wore women's clothing and who carried a stick, which he would swing at passersby. The second was a Comorean woman who, even though she had kin in town, preferred to sleep outside and eat out of garbage heaps. In contrast, the behavior of a victim of possession sickness may be very odd or frightening, but after a fit has ended she appears normal and does not remember what happened. The significance of the breaking of social norms in labeling the mad is evident in the manner in which the diminuitive term *adaladala* is applied. It is used, in a teasing way, to describe anyone who acts odd or silly. As the following story illustrates, a person must be seriously ill to be called *adala* or *adalaña*.

THE CASE OF VICTORIA

One of the more spectacular public displays of njarinintsy violence that I witnessed occurred one afternoon on the main street of Ambanja. As this case illustrates, the application of the label of possession sickness became increasingly problematic, eventually leading those who knew Victoria to relabel her as mad (adalaña).

One afternoon I was standing in line in the Peasant's Bank. Suddenly all three bank tellers ducked behind the counter just as a rush of water flew through the air and hit a crowd of people to my right. I spun around and saw a woman in her thirties standing on the veranda. It was my neighbor Victoria, who often suffered from attacks of njarinintsy. She was soaking wet, holding a bucket in the hand of her limp right arm, and she had a faraway stare. I also noticed that she had one black eye. An older woman started to yell at Victoria, telling her to get away from the bank and leave her alone. Instead, Victoria suddenly made another rush for the interior of the bank, threatening the woman with her empty bucket, waving it in her direction as if to pitch more water on her. Two young men escorted the older woman out, and Victoria, after wandering around the bank for a minute or two longer, departed, walking aimlessly, as if drunk, down the main street and past the post office. The three bank employees, giggling nervously, peered out from under the counter and, then, cautiously, stood up and continued their work. When the older woman was out of sight two customers explained to the rest of us in line that the woman whom Victoria was aiming for was her nasty (*masiaka*) mother-in-law.

Victoria had been plagued by njarinintsy for over a year; as she told me once, "I suffer too much" (*Izaho mijaly loatra*). She could often be seen wandering through the streets of Ambanja, wailing and crying, and she argued on a daily basis with her spouse and his kin. Within the last three months her fits of possession happened so frequently that some of my neighbors joked that you could tell the time of day by when Victoria would wander by. Others were disturbed by her behavior: as an old schoolteacher of hers sadly explained, these days it was more common to see Victoria in a possessed state than out of one. He and others stated that njarinintsy should not be like that—generally the victim has fits and then she is fine, but Victoria always seemed to be possessed. One of her friends speculated that perhaps Victoria had been sick for so long from njarinintsy possession that it had started to drive her insane (adalaña), that she had started to lose her mind (very jery).

All who knew Victoria agreed that her story was very sad (mampalahelo). Victoria was Sakalava from a nearby village. After completing two years of high school she had met her (common law) husband, who was a truck driver for a northern transport company, and she dropped out of school to accompany him to Diégo where he lived. She had been a gifted student and soon found work at a local business as a bookkeeper. Victoria had always hoped to finish her studies at the private French School there, something that her husband had promised he would help her do if she came to live with him. But ten years later and after having had three children, she was still working long hours. She still dreamed of learning more French and studying Italian. Two years ago her husband had lost his job and he had insisted that they return to Ambanja, a town she hated. There had been much tension (and violence) in her marriage during the last four years. This had increased within the past eighteen months, after her husband had learned that she had secretly had an abortion. As a neighbor explained: "Her husband became very angry with her, and he beat her on and off for several days. The noise was terrible! . . . Two neighbors had to go to the house to stop him. . . . Now her mother-in-law is angry at her, because she won't do anything she is told."

At this point the attacks of njarinintsy began. Her in-laws took her to two healers, but neither succeeded in driving the spirit(s) from her. They then summoned Victoria's mother and sister, who lived in a village thirty kilometers from Ambanja. As Victoria's sister later explained, they took her to a series of expensive healers, but all were unable to encourage a spirit of any kind to speak. Even when a kalanoro made all sorts of promises to leave very expensive items at a sacred spot for the spirit to consume, the only signs that Victoria was troubled by spirits were that she would sob uncontrollably and thrash about on the floor during the healing sessions. Her kin had become increasingly worried, because now they were not sure how to cure (*mitaha*) Victoria. Her mother and sister went home, leaving her in her husband's care.

Two nights after the episode in the bank Victoria struck again. She had wandered aimlessly into a bar where her husband was drinking with his brother, some friends, and two women reputed to be prostitutes. As the proprietor later explained in disbelief, Victoria had suddenly rushed behind the bar, grabbing bottles of expensive imported whiskey and rum and smashing them on the floor. Her husband jumped up and grabbed her, dragged her out into the street, and then he began to pound her with his fists. His brother and two other men finally stopped him, and Victoria was escorted home. The next day her in-laws again summoned Victoria's mother and sister, and told them to take her home to their village. By this time everyone who knew Victoria was certain that she was not sick with possession sickness but was insane. Within the week her sister and mother came from their village and, after spending the night, they took her to the provincial hospital in Diégo. I later learned from her sister that Victoria had spent one month in the asylum and that she was now "quite content [tamana] living by herself in Diégo. . . . She has not suffered from an attack since we brought her there."

Victoria's story reveals how kin, as well as members of the community at large, were actively involved in assessing Victoria's problem and, ultimately, relabeling it as madness rather than possession sickness. Several factors led to this reassessment of her condition. First, her fits were not short-lived, but instead had begun to dominate her life—to see her out of a possessed state had become an unusual event. The level of violent behavior was typical of njarinintsy, but the frequency of her unusual social misconduct led others to believe that it was more than this. Even the most gifted healers of the region could not drive any spirit from her. Furthermore, if she had a spirit, it was odd that it would never talk, even in fragmented speech. The decision to take Victoria to the asylum was one of last resort, only after the efforts of a series of indigenous healers had failed.

THE LIMITATIONS OF CLINICAL MEDICINE

As Victoria's story illustrates, clinical medicine (and, more specifically, psychiatry) provides one option of last resort for extreme cases of possession and madness. The choice to go to the psychiatrist or the exorcist is a personal matter and the actions of patients and their kin reveal no particular trend of favoring one over the other. More often, however, patients leave the asylum for the exorcists, rather than the other way around.

As I have argued elsewhere (Sharp, in press), the efficacy of psychiatric medicine in northern Madagascar is hampered by a multitude of factors. Problems in part result from a reliance on drug therapy in a country where prescribed medications are often unavailable in local pharmacies (cf. Sachs and Tomson 1992; Vogel and Stephens 1989; for contrast see Lee et al. 1991; Silverman, Lee, and Lydecker, 1986; and Silverman, Lydecker, and Lee, 1990). The practice of isolating patients from kin while they are in the asylum also runs contrary to indigenous therapeutic practices.[3] In turn, as others have argued (Zola 1978; see also Dunk 1989; Lock 1984; Ong 1988; Pappas 1990), the medicalization of disorder often empowers the doctor while silencing the patient. To quote Taussig (1980b: 8), this leads to "the alienation of the patient's self-understanding and capacity" to articulate the causes of her suffering. In Madagascar, a reliance on Western-derived clinical approaches means that the psychiatrist and patient have radically different perceptions of illness. In essence, they suffer from what I have referred to as "conflicting epistemological realities" that block treatment.[4] Clinical medicine denies the legitimacy of the subjective experience of possession.

Ethnic differences between patients and clinicians are also significant. Malagasy doctors working in the north are generally strangers to the region and rarely see possession (or know that a patient is possessed). Several factors account for this: some informants stated that it is taboo (fady) for njarinintsy victims, for example, to receive injections, and mediums are generally reluctant to mention their spirits to doctors for fear of being ostracized. Also, Sakalava—regardless of whether or not they have spirits—generally avoid clinics because they do not want to come into contact with Merina doctors.

As this chapter will show, exorcism is likewise an extreme choice of therapy, yet a few Sakalava opt for it because it offers powerful alternatives for those who have endured great suffering. Even though exorcisms are painful and frustrating for patients, exorcists are successful healers because they first accept and then transform the patient's explanations for and experiences of possession and madness. During Protestant healing rituals possession is viewed as an appropriate idiom for describing illness, and madness is redefined as normative, not deviant, behavior. Ultimately this approach carries significant implications for the empowerment of both the patient and the healer and it may lead to a permanent transformation of the patient's identity.

CATHOLIC AND MUSLIM PERSPECTIVES ON POSSESSION

Ambanja, a large town, is a religious center for Catholics, Muslims, and Protestants. To a large extent the membership of these faiths is defined by the ethnic and geographic divisions that exist in Madagascar. The majority of Sakalava belong to no church (tsy mivavaka; "don't pray"). Those who do are either Catholic or Muslim (the latter is true especially if they are royalty). Rarely are they Protestant—Sakalava generally define themselves in opposition to those other ethnic groups whose members are. Since it is the Protestants who specialize in exorcism in Madagascar, they will be the primary focus of this chapter. Before discussing their activities, however, I will first provide a brief overview of Catholic and Muslim ideas about possession, many of which overlap. In addition, Catholic and Muslim points of view throw into high relief the relative severity or strictness of the Protestant stance.[5]

CATHOLIC ENCULTURATION AND ATTITUDES TOWARD POSSESSION

As a response to enculturation policies, the Catholic church in Ambanja takes a laissez-faire attitude toward possession. Although it does not openly condone tromba possession, it does not prohibit it either, as do the Protestants. Among Ambanja's Catholics, Sakalava religion is a subject of intellectual interest. During interviews that I conducted with priests and nuns (who were European as well as Sakalava) their collective approach to possession was generally philosophical or theological in nature. They would return my questions by asking: "What is it—is the spirit real, or is it a delusion that people believe in? How do we explain it? Is it psychological? What is its social and cultural signifi- cance?" (cf. Estrade 1979). Several Sakalava clergy have written their theses in France on Sakalava religion, with a special emphasis on tromba (see, for example, Jaovelo-Dzao 1983, 1987). Clergy who show an inter- est in local culture may be invited periodically by Sakalava parishioners to observe tromba ceremonies. Given these attitudes, it is not surprising that the majority of mediums I interviewed over the course of a year were Catholic, and many sent their children to the local mission school. Just after Easter I visited several mediums in their homes where I found palm frond crosses that they had acquired at mass. In several instances Grandchildren spirits identified themselves as Catholic, as were their mediums (although this news of Catholic spirits shocked church offi- cials). As mentioned earlier, mediums sometimes call on the Christian God, Andriamanitra ("The King of Heaven"), rather than using *Zana- hary,* the collective name for ancestors, when they invoke their tromba spirits.

All priests are trained exorcists, but the Catholic church in Ambanja does not offer this service to its parishioners. Instead, the diocese has an official exorcist who lives in a remote town on the east coast of the island. Whereas Protestants view tromba and other spirits as demons and possession as the work of Satan, the Catholic point of view is more compatible with the Sakalava one. As one Italian priest stated, "It is a matter of faith . . . if a woman comes to me and says that she is troubled by spirits, I encourage her to pray with me, because this seems to help." In those cases where a parishioner seeks greater assistance from a priest, she may be told to go to the Protestants to be exorcised and then to return to her own church to pray. This is what happened in the case of a woman named Vivienne (see below).

ISLAM

Muslims in Ambanja are fairly tolerant in their attitudes towards posses- sion. Islamic tolerance is also due, in part, to the fact that in Ambanja men are most active in Islam. Possession is common cross-culturally within the context of Sunni Islam, which recognizes the possibility of possession by jinn (see, for example, Crapanzano 1973, 1977b, 1983; Eikelman 1968; I.M. Lewis 1986, especially chap. 6; I.M. Lewis et al., eds. 1991; Nimtz 1980). Among the Muslims of Ambanja, tromba and other Sakalava spirits are relabeled as such, and are called jiny or devoly (devils, demons).[6] Although all mosques in town have an area or separate building set aside where women may pray, ordinarily no more than ten women attend on a regular basis, and so few members would be mediums. It is not unusual for Muslim men, who are active at the mosque, to have spouses who are not Muslim or who are observant only during Ramadan (Ramzan). Some Muslim men have wives who are tromba mediums, and many Muslims consult mediums, moasy, and other indigenous healers when they are ill. Muslims in Ambanja also have their own specialists called *badry* (so named after the text they use and the ritual they perform), whose healing powers are derived from books written in Arabic.[7] In Ambanja, exorcisms are occasionally held at mosques to drive out spirits from the possessed, but more often adherents see no conflict between possession activities and Islam. The few who seek to have jiny exorcised tend to be men and not women. In such cases it is the priest or *fondy* (also referred to sometimes as the *mwalimo*, from the kiSwahili word *mwalimu*) who performs the exorcism. This generally involves the burning of incense and group prayer at the mosque.

The one exception is a reformist group that I will refer to as Modern Islam. Modern Islam was formed in 1979 by members drawn from an assortment of mosques who found the attitudes of Muslims in town to be too lenient—and syncretic—for their tastes. Members of this group view themselves as more literary and "pure" in their approach to Islam. They stress the necessity of learning how to read and write Arabic (most members of other mosques learn prayer strictly through memorization). Also, more recently, Modern Islam has sought to impose greater restrictions on women by introducing the veil and purdah. So far this has been met with great resistance from local women, so that the female membership of this group lags far behind that of men (there are approximately ten women to sixty or seventy men). Modern Islam also stresses the need to be "scientific." Its leaders are vehemently opposed to the work of moasy, tromba mediums, and other indigenous healers. If njarinintsy possession is suspected, for example, the afflicted is instructed to go to the hospital first to make sure that her shaking is not caused, perhaps, by malaria. As one member put it, "If it is truly possession, we believe that it is the work of the devil; we are like Christians in this respect."

Leaders of Modern Islam are able to perform exorcisms, but as of 1987 only one possession case had ever been treated. This involved a tromba medium named Berthine (see Appendix A) who chose to convert because her new husband was a Muslim; it was necessary to rid her of her spirit before she could join. The exorcism involved the following steps. First, she had to break the tromba's taboos (fady). Second, all of the spirit's paraphernalia were burned in the mosque. Third, she was asked to pray with others in the mosque. When the tromba spirit cried out, the Koran was placed on her head and the spirit was driven out of her through prayer, as if it were a jiny. Afterward, she was instructed to pray for five days, five times a day. As will be clear from the discussion below, these rituals parallel those that occur during Protestant exorcisms.

THE *FIFOHAZANA* OR PROTESTANT EXORCISTS

Nearly all Protestant sects in Madagascar conduct exorcisms. Some have special curing retreats where exorcists work full-time; two of the most active groups are the Lutherans and the FJKM.[8] The exorcist movement and its associated specialists are referred to as *fifohazana* (HP: "awakening," "revival"; from the verb *mifoha*, "to wake," "to arise"); they are also called mpiandry (HP: "shepherds"). Since I am specifically interested in those activities that are related to spirit possession, I will refer to them here as *exorcists*. Satan (*Satany*) and devils (*devoly*) are thought to cause misfortune, and so the exorcist's goal is to drive spirits out of the bodies of their victims. In general terms, individuals usually fall ill because they have no faith in Jesus (*Jesosy*).

Exorcists have received special training as healers and they form a special branch of their respectives churches. The majority are Malagasy, and they include pastors, evangelists, and parishioners. They are male and female, and they come from a wide variety of backgrounds, including peasants and educated professionals. Ethnic affiliation reflects the geographical distribution of Protestant missionary activities throughout the island: typically they are Merina and Betsileo from the highlands. There are also Antandroy, Antaisaka, and Antaimoro from the south and southeast and Tsimihety from the west and north. Rarely are they Sakalava or Antakarana. In Ambanja, several churches hold exorcism ceremonies on a regular basis. The FJKM church, which is by far the largest Protestant church in town, is most actively involved in this, and has more than a dozen trained specialists. Others include the Lutheran church and a small Pentecostal group that calls itself the Fifohazana Church, which broke off from the FJKM over a decade ago.

Exorcists gain inspiration and guidance from prophets, and each

church has its own. According to FJKM records, the fifohazana movement was started in the 1880s by a Betsileo man from the high plateaux
named Rainisoalambo. He was a diviner (mpisikidy) who suffered from
severe and incurable skin problems. He had a dream in which he was
told to go to the church, and so the next day he threw away his medicines
(fanafody-gasy) and went there with his children. Eventually he built
his own church in Soatanana, near Fianarantsoa, where he began to
heal others. Soatanana is now a major center for fifohazana training and
healing activities for numerous churches (Anonymous 1962; Rasamoela
1975; Trexler 1989). Although each church has its own prophets, the
Lutherans pride themselves on having the only living prophet, who is
named Nenilava ("Tall Mother"). Nenilava is Antaimoro and is the
daughter of an herbalist (HP: ombiasy) who converted to Lutheranism
when she was young. Her visions and wisdom concerning the teachings
of Christ make her a central figure in her church (cf. Trexler 1989).

The style of dress and methods of healing are fairly standard among
different Protestant groups. The clothes they wear during exorcism sessions reflect a blending of Calvinist dress of more than a hundred years
ago, combined with high plateaux styles (see plate 8 and the last two
photos in Estrade 1977). Exorcists always dress in white and keep their
bodies well covered. Men generally wear long-sleeved shirts and long
pants, and women wear long-sleeved blouses and ankle-length skirts.
Both men and women sometimes wear long white robes that have puffy
sleeves and dog-eared collars that are tied close to the throat. Some also
wear bulky white shawls, reminiscent of the lamba worn by Merina.
Many wear a wimple, wrapping a white cloth around their foreheads
and then tying it at the back of the head. These clothes may be worn
every day like a uniform or only during healing sessions. The quality
and elaborateness of clothing often reflect the amount of church treasury
funds available for exorcism activities.

The role of an exorcist can be a part- or full-time occupation. Some
exorcists assist only during healing sessions that occur on Sundays after
regular services, while for others it is a way of life, such as those who
live in healing retreats (see below). The majority became exorcists after
they or someone close to them was healed. Exorcists treat all forms of
illness, including physical ailments such as blindness, headaches, lame-
ness, troubled thoughts, restlessness, madness, and possession. Satan
and devils cause illness and suffering, and the exorcist heals by driving
them out of their victims through the laying on of hands (HP: fametra-
han-tànana) and through prayer (vavaka). The exorcist's strength and

Plate 8.   *Fifohazana* exorcist driving spirits out of a patient while others watch and wait their turns. Note that the exorcist has placed her hand on the patient's head.

power are derived from the Holy Ghost (*ny Fanahy Masina*) and for this reason Lutherans refer to exorcisms as *asa sy fampaheresana* ("work and empowerment"). Exorcists prefer to work in groups of three, reflecting the power of the trinity. Groups of other sizes are acceptable, but exorcists avoid working alone. As one put it, "When you work alone you may think that the power is in you, forgetting that it is derived from the Holy Spirit . . . if you are too proud you might fail in your work." Exorcisms occur frequently in Ambanja: throughout 1987 I witnessed approximately a dozen, and I heard of more than twenty others. Five of the sessions I witnessed took place at the Lutheran church where I lived, where one of the pastors was trained as an exorcist.

The purpose of these healing sessions is to cure specific ills as well as to ensure general well-being in the congregation. Some churches schedule sessions on a regular basis, such as on the first Sunday of each month. Private, intensive sessions can be arranged for those who suffer from serious problems. Exorcists may apply their powers at home as well, treating themselves and members of their households, or they may be called into a patient's home to work. Some patients come on their own, but most often they are accompanied by kin. The majority of patients are adolescent girls who are plagued by njarinintsy and other forms of possession sickness; older women (thirty or older) who wish to rid themselves of tromba spirits; and those whom kin label as mentally ill (adala). Serious problems can not be cured in one session but require a number of visits to ensure that the spirit(s) has left permanently. If the patient is not a Protestant she or he is also expected to convert and become a regular member of the church.

EXORCISM AS THERAPY

Exorcism sessions are electrifying events that are exhausting for both exorcist and patient, and they can be frightening for young children and for the uninitiated. During these sessions a patient's kin may also be present, as may parishioners, who have been encouraged to attend so that they may assist by praying and singing. Parishioner participation is necessary for several reasons. First, prayers and hymns are imbued with the power of the Word of God. Second, spirits enjoy music and so hymns help to draw them out of their victims. Third, by participating in these sessions parishioners are witnesses of God's work.

Exorcisms have several stages. If the exorcists are not in their robes, they will don the proper attire before they begin (often this is done with great ceremony at the front of the church). All church services open with the singing of hymns, and this is also true for exorcisms. The session then proceeds with readings from the Bible and most often these include the following passages:[9]

> Then he said to them: 'Go forth to every part of the world, and proclaim the Good News to the whole creation. Those who believe it and receive baptism will find salvation; those who do not believe will be condemned. Faith will bring with it these miracles: believers will cast out devils in my name and speak in strange tongues; if they handle snakes or drink any deadly poison, they will come to no harm; and the sick on whom they lay their hands will recover.'
>
> (Mark 16: 15–18)[10]

> [Ary hoy Izy taminy: Mandehana any amin'izao tontolo izao hianareo, ka mitoria ny filazantsara amin'ny olombelona rehetra. Izay mino sy atao batisa no hovonjena; fa izay tsy mety mino no hohelohina. Ary izao famantarana izao no hanaraka izay mino: hamoaka demonia amin'ny anarako izy; hiteny amin'ny fiteny izay tsy mbola hainy izy; handray menarana izy; ary na dia misotro zava-mahafaty aza izy, dia tsy hampaninona azy izany; hametra-tànana amin'ny marary izy, dia ho sitrana ireny.]

> Jesus repeated, 'Peace be with you!', and said, 'As the Father sent me, so I send you.' Then he breathed on them, saying, 'Receive the Holy Spirit! If

you forgive any man's sins, they stand forgiven; if you pronounce them unforgiven, unforgiven they remain'

(John 20: 21–23)

[Ary hoy indray Jesosy taminy: Fiadanana ho anareo; tahaka ny nanira-han'ny Ray Ahy no anirahako anareo kosa. Ary rehefa nilaza izany Izy, dia nanisy fofonaina, ka hoy Izy taminy: Raiso ny Fanahy Masina; na helok'iza na helok'iza no avelanareo, dia voavela izany; ary na an'iza na an'iza kosa no tsy avelanareo, dia tsy voavela izany.]

In addition to these passages, which speak of the laying on of hands and the healing powers of God, exorcists may read others that refer specifically to the problems of those who have come to be cured. These people are asked to form small groups at the front of the church and sit on the ground on a mat. Amid the singing, the exorcists lay their hands upon the heads of these people and pray quietly for their health and well-being. Patients with more serious problems are then called before the congregation and are healed separately.

The tenor of sessions directed at helping more serious cases is very different, especially when possession is the cause of the problem. During sessions for tromba possession, for example, the spirit is first reidentified as a demon or as Satan. The spirit must be encouraged to come forth so that it may then be driven from the body of its victim. These actions echo and draw from those of a tromba ceremony, where the spirit arrives by possessing the medium, announces its name, and converses with the audience. An exorcism, however, it not a joyful event but a frightening and volatile one because the spirit is quickly angered when confronted by the exorcists. If there are several exorcists present, they divide into groups (preferably into threes) and they work together with each patient; periodically they change places, rotating from one patient to another. In this way the intensity of the healing power directed at each person is great and is varied. As parishioners sing, the exorcists shout at the spirits in the imperative voice, a form that in most cases is used in Malagasy only to address naughty children, animals,[11] and demons: "Voka!" ("Get out!"), "Mivoka amin'ny ianarana Jesosy!" ("Get out in the name of Jesus!").

As the exorcism progresses, the language becomes more powerful and the volume increases as exorcists shout their orders and parishioners sing louder and more intensely. This is usually when the spirit arrives. If it is a tromba, curses may suddenly issue forth from the mouth of the patient; if it is a njarinintsy, the victim will start to wail loudly, scream, and sob. Possessed patients usually collapse periodically on the ground, at which point the exorcist orders them to "get up!"(*mifoha!*). The exorcist speaks directly to the spirit, encouraging it to engage in a dialogue. He asks, "Who are you!? Why have you possessed this person!? What do you want?" and, in hearing the answers, he shouts back again, "Get out! get out you devil!" (Voka! *Voka devoly!*) or "Go back to the desert from whence you came!" (*Handeha amin'ny tany karakaina!*). These sessions can be violent, not only because the patient may fall or thrash about but because the exorcist, in wrestling with the spirit, may push at or tug on the patient's body. Sometimes an exorcist repeatedly pushes a patient to the ground and then orders the patient to "get up! Rise up in the name of Jesus!"[12]

Eventually, the wailing will stop and the patient will regain consciousness, feeling exhausted. The hymns become quieter, and the session will end with a prayer to bless all who are present. This session will be followed by at least one more session, generally later that week, to ensure that the spirit has departed permanently. One unusual case that I witnessed involved three members of an Antandroy family (mother, father, and thirteen-year-old son). It was the mother who originally requested to have a tromba exorcised, but soon it was clear that the father, too, had a bilo spirit. Each time the father's spirit was driven from him it would then move into the body of his wife or son, so that each person in turn had to have this spirit exorcised. This required several weeks of intensive work, involving six exorcists who worked with the patients two or three times each week.

Following these healing sessions, the exorcists, pastor, or congregation members visit patients in their homes to make sure they are well. If a patient had a tromba spirit, she will be instructed to bring all of the spirit's paraphernalia to the church, so that it can be burned or otherwise destroyed. Patients are also expected to return to the church for Bible study and prayer and they are encouraged to join the church as permanent members.

Being an exorcist is difficult and involves great dedication. As one confided:

One of the problems in being an [exorcist] is that people here [in Ambanja] think I'm like a moasy [herbalist]—they want to be able to come just once, be cured, and leave. Maybe they think I am more powerful than most moasy but, still, I am the same to them. If they ask me to come to their house to help them, I always ask them if they use fanafody . . . that is our [the fifohazana's] way. They may say no, but sometimes I think they are hiding that they do use it, because they are afraid to say yes. For us, we are not like the moasy, because we expect the person to become a member of the church, to choose to be Christian. It is no good if I come and exorcise them and then I don't see them again. . . . I think some people think, "he is an exorcist, so why don't we have him come and see what happens?" . . . One time a well-known woman here in town . . . had me come to her house. . . . I think her husband had a tromba [spirit], or maybe he is a little crazy [adala]?—but I am not sure. His wife had me come exorcise him—and I gave him a book to study, but they didn't come to the church. . . . Being an exorcist is difficult—people will come to you at any time—sometimes in the middle of the night—because they are afraid and they ask if they can sleep here in our house. We take them in, we share their problems. . . . I am not as strong as they think I am, I have my faults, I sin, too, sometimes. But this is why I have chosen to be an [exorcist].

THE PROTESTANT TOBY (CAMPS) OR CURING RETREATS

Several Protestant churches have centers for faith healing which are called *toby* (HP, lit. "camp") and which I will refer to as "curing retreats." The Lutherans are most famous for this, having established a large retreat in the high plateaux near Fianarantsoa. The mother church, which is located in a suburb of Antananarivo, also hosts regular healing sessions. In 1987 a new retreat was being built in the outskirts of this city so that there would be a second hospital that was more centrally located on the island. Many patients come to the Lutherans seeking the guidance of the Prophet Nenilava, who moves back and forth between the two centers. Smaller, usually rural retreats, can be found throughout the island.

Exorcists and their patients live full-time at these curing retreats. Primary curing activities involve the laying on of hands and intensive prayer sessions. Sometimes the kin of seriously ill patients will come and request that the exorcists accompany them home. A group of them (preferably three) will join the household temporarily to watch over and heal the sick person, and room and board is provided as payment for their services. Because the bonds that develop between the exorcists and the patient's kin can be strong, sometimes an exorcist later marries someone from the patient's household.

In northwest Madagascar, near Ambanja, there are three FJKM curing retreats. The closest was established in 1986 and lies eight kilometers from the town (and one kilometer off the main road). The work of these Protestant exorcists tends to be ecumenical in nature, reflected by the fact that although all those living at the retreat are members of the

FJKM church, the deacon (HP: *iraka*), who moves between the three retreats, is Anglican, as is the Antaimoro planter who donated the land. The FJKM church also has sought to combine efforts with other churches in order to establish an additional center in Ambanja.

The retreat near Ambanja occupies one-third of a small village, which has a total population of approximately two hundred people. It consists of a large open area about the size of a soccer field, surrounded by numerous structures, including an outdoor kitchen and shaded eating space; an unfinished (roofless) church; a long rectangular building that has four apartments in which the exorcists live; and three small, two-room houses that are for patients and their kin. The church is constructed of concrete. All other buildings are modest structures made from traveler's palm.

Eight adult exorcists (four men and four women, including two married couples), and about a dozen children are the retreat's full-time residents. At any given time there are three to five patients living there who are usually accompanied by one or two of their kin (such as parents, spouses, or siblings). The exorcists are Tsimehety, Betsileo, and Antaimoro, whereas the majority of the villagers are Sakalava as well as Antaimoro settlers. Patients are of diverse backgrounds and include fairly equal proportions of tera-tany and vahiny: when I visited in April 1987, they were Sakalava, Antakarana, and Tsimehety from the north; Comorean; and Antaimoro migrants from the south. Flanking the settlement on one side are fields, where the exorcists grow manioc, rice, maize, and greens. On the other are the villagers' dwellings, a Catholic church, a schoolhouse, and a playing field.

Like the majority of their patients, exorcists are poor, yet therapy itself is free and thus practical, since they rely on the power of the Holy Spirit to heal. Exorcists live solely off donations and the bit of food they can eke out of the land. As is true for hospital care throughout Madagascar (and elsewhere in the Third World) patients are expected to cover all of their own expenses, so kin accompany them to make sure they have clean clothing and food to eat. The cost of a long-term stay at the retreat can create serious hardships. Such was the case for an elderly Antakarana couple who had been living at the retreat for six months so that their son could be treated for madness. As the father explained:

> Here it is very hard for us, we have five other children . . . two, who live nearby, come to visit and bring us rice when they can. Here rice is very expensive, half again as much as it is in the market in Ambanja. I must work in other people's coffee and cocoa fields for money, and my wife helps others

in their houses. We always need money to buy rice and other food, nivaquine [for malaria] and aspirin. Since there is no car that goes to Ambanja, it is very hard for us to travel to and from this village. We are not sure how much longer we can stay.

Most patients who come to this retreat are adults. They suffer from an assortment of problems. The majority (male and female) are mentally ill. The second largest group consists of single women who are suffering from tromba and other forms of possession. There are also those who are crippled (*kalemy*) and, finally, those with more general ailments, the most common being skin problems. When I visited the retreat outside Ambanja in April 1987, there were five patients there: two Sakalava women who suffered from tromba possession; a young Antaimoro boy, about age ten, who appeared to be mentally handicapped (as one exorcist said, "When he first came here he didn't even know how to use silverware"); a Comorean man in his late thirties who was diagnosed as mentally ill (*marary saina*), who sat and talked to himself; and the young Antakarana man whose father is quoted above and who was also said to be mad. The majority of patients who come here have previously sought help from indigenous healers but found no cure. Some patients may stay for months, while others have remained for years.

Each exorcist is responsible for several patients, who in turn have three exorcists assigned to them. The treatments they administer take several forms. First, everyone is expected to pray (mivavaka) three times a day, since prayer weakens Satan. Second, laying on of hands (fame-trahan-tànana) occurs twice a week. The notion of community is constantly stressed, and thus fictive kinship is a key defining principle for social relations among exorcists and patients. The pastor and deacon are referred to as "father" (papa or baba), and exorcists refer to each other as siblings, expecting patients and their kin to address them in this manner as well.[13] There is also a strong emphasis placed on the importance of work, and so patients labor in the kitchen, fields, and elsewhere according to their individual abilities and strengths. When one Sakalava villager was asked to describe the exorcists, she said "they work very, very hard" (*miasa mafibe izy*).

Three times a year the FJKM fifohazana exorcists hold reunions, and the location rotates between the three curing retreats in the northwest. One of my assistants went to observe a reunion during Pentecost, which lasted for two days. Much time was spent praying and singing hymns or working in the compound, and a communal feast was held where meat was served. This meal was a great luxury that the exorcists at this retreat could ill afford: since they receive little if any money from the mother church, their daily diet generally consists of a meager dish of boiled manioc and bananas, often with no rice. In all, 695 people attended. This official head count included the ten patients and their kin. The patients consisted of the five currently in residence at this retreat, plus five others who came from the two other retreats. These patients included three women who were suffering from tromba possession (see accounts of Vivienne, below, and Mona, who appears later in this chapter; also Appendix A); two men who were mentally ill (marary saina); and a woman with a child who had a severe case of diarrhea. The other participants consisted of seventy exorcists, other novices training to be exorcists, and congregation members, including those who had come for first communion.

Throughout the night the exorcists healed through the laying on of hands. Participants were split into two groups, so that the majority stayed outside while the ten patients were taken to be healed separately inside one of the houses. As one exorcist explained to my assistant, this was done because healing sessions can be upsetting to watch, since sometimes Satan can make patients act violently.

SEEKING CURES FOR POSSESSION: THREE CASE STUDIES

The stories that appear below all concern extreme cases. The first involves a woman who, like Victoria, suffered from problems that shifted between possession sickness and madness. The other two are women who refused to accept tromba mediumship as a permanent manifestation of their lives. Although all three of these patients are Sakalava, they each took a radical step in the therapeutic process, seeking assistance from non-Sakalava Protestants for their problems. Two of these women have chosen to convert, thus abandoning Sakalava culture for a new religious system.

VIVIENNE

Vivienne is from a family where many of the women are tromba mediums. Her older classificatory sister is an established medium who receives many clients in her home and who was one of my key informants (see Alice in Appendix A). Another classificatory sister is Berthine(see above) who had her spirit exorcised by members of Modern Islam.

Vivienne is the daughter of a Sakalava mother and Tsimihety father. She is fifteen years old and she attends junior high school to the north in Ambilobe. She was raised by her mother, who was Catholic and who died when

Vivienne was twelve. Her father lives in Diégo. Following her mother's death
he arranged for Vivienne to live with his brother and his brother's wife, who
are both members of the FJKM church. Throughout the summer Vivienne
has been living with her aunt (MoSi) in Ambanja. Although her aunt is not
Christian, she decided to bring Vivienne to the Pentecostal retreat that my
assistant attended.

For one year Vivienne has been very sick, troubled by a njarinintsy spirit.
As her aunt explained: "Sometime she is crazy [adala izy é]! . . . If I ask her
to set the table, she puts spoons under the tablecloth; at other times she
cooks with hair! . . . She swears [vetaveta] and she has tried to hit her uncle!
Now she lives with me. . . . Sometimes she cries and laughs suddenly—this
even happened when she was at school! I took her to the Catholic priest and
he told me to take her to the Lutherans [around the corner]. We went there
one Sunday, but nothing happened. So then I took her to the FJKM church.
Her father's relatives want her to come and stay here [at the retreat], but
Vivienne refuses, saying that she is Catholic and that she has no intention
of changing her religion."

Vivienne and her aunt later returned to the retreat, where they lived for
four weeks. Here Vivienne took part in healing and prayer sessions several
times each day. After two weeks she felt stronger (hery) (and, as her aunt
and the exorcists noted, she had also become more cooperative) and she
started to work in the fields. Three months later she returned to school.
Vivienne occasionally attends Sunday services at the FJKM church. When
her Sakalava friends tease her about this, she states flatly that she goes for
her health and she insists that she has not converted.

I later asked one of the Lutheran exorcists about Vivienne, who
stressed that, in his opinion, she was not possessed, but was mad (marary
saina):

She doesn't look at you when you talk, but she gazes around and talks to
herself. That is not like someone with njarinintsy. I remember I asked her
if there was anything troubling her and she said yes, that there was a boy
who had tried to harm her with fanafody—he pretended that he loved her
and sweet talked her, but she later realized he didn't care about her at all.
This is so common! . . . With these young girls it is always a problem with
a boy. I told her to forget about it, that there were better ones out there. I
tried to heal her and to help her, stressing that she must come back with
her family—I am not a doctor, I can not cure someone in just one session!
But she never came back. I think that she must have gone to the FJKM
church because she has relatives who pray there. This is better, because her
kin will be there with her and, besides, their work is the same as mine. They
know how to heal the same way as I do.

ELISABETH

Elisabeth is forty-two years old and the daughter of Sakalava parents. She
was raised in a small village northwest of Ambanja. When she was very

young (five years old) she had already begun to show signs of tromba possession, and by the age of seven her parents had held a ceremony to instate
a fairly powerful Child spirit within her. Neighbors were skeptical of this
development, finding it difficult to believe that a girl so young could have
a tromba spirit; nevertheless, she soon had clients who came from other
villages and towns seeking her spirit's advice. By the age of fifteen she had
two other spirits, a Child and a Zafin'i'fotsy Grandparent.[14] As Elisabeth
put it, mediumship was a very difficult (*sarotra be*) experience. For much of
her childhood she fell sick periodically, suffering from chronic weakness,
dizziness and fainting spells, terrible headaches, and frequent nightmares.

At age seventeen Elisabeth convinced her parents to let her go live with her
sister in Ambanja. She had previously visited the town on many occasions,
preferring it to the sleepy village in which she grew up. In Ambanja she took
her first lover who eventually became a common-law spouse. This relationship lasted for three years. She later met her husband, Claude, with whom
she lived on and off for twelve years. Eventually she grew tired of this relationship. As she put it, all Claude wanted was the money she earned as a
medium. As in her childhood, she frequently fell ill and sometimes was unable
to get out of bed for weeks at a time. This made it extremely difficult for
her to carry water, go to market, or care for her two children, especially
when her husband was not with her. Twice spirit mediums had diagnosed
her tromba spirits as the cause, and by the age of thirty-five she had held
the appropriate ceremonies to have two additional spirits instated. Each time
her health only improved temporarily. She also spent much time and money
seeking help from other local healers and doctors, all to no avail. Repeatedly
she was told by friends and kin that her spirits were responsible for her bouts
of illness, and she had become frustrated nearly to the point of panic. Unable
to earn enough money to host additional ceremonies to appease her spirits,
her health only worsened.

In 1984, Elisabeth's sister took her on the ferry to the nearby island of
Nosy Be, where they sought out the Protestant exorcists at the FJKM church
there. After several weeks of intense healing sessions (three times a week for
four weeks), Elisabeth was finally freed from her spirits. Like the majority
of mediums, she did not recall what took place during these interactions
between her spirits and the exorcists, but she described the process as frightening and exhausting (*mavozo aho, kajobe aho*), followed by a sense of
elation after each session. She has since converted to this church, and is now
among their most highly respected exorcists. She lives in Nosy Be, two blocks
from the pastor's house. She has not, however, visited with her kin since
this time. Only her sister comes to see her, since others, especially her parents,
are ashamed that Elisabeth keeps the company of Merina Protestants.

ZALOKY

Zaloky is approximately fifty years old (although, as described in chapter
2, she is easily mistaken for a woman who is much older). Zaloky's life as
a medium is fairly typical for older Sakalava tera-tany women. She was

married at age sixteen and, at age thirty-two, after the births of three of her four children, she became possessed by the transitional Child spirit Zaman'i'Bao(see chapter 5). Within two years she had become a respected healer in the area and she had a steady flow of clients. At age thirty-five her husband died. She describes the next five years as difficult and bitter ones because of struggles with her children over land rights (again, see her story in chapter 2). She eventually married (by common law) her second husband Marcel, a Tsimihety migrant laborer who had been a regular client of hers when seeking guidance from Zaman'i'Bao for problems related to work or physical ailments.

Zaloky describes her past activities as a medium as very difficult: "Zaman'i'Bao is a very powerful spirit, and his mediums must be strong [mahery]. It was a difficult life: I had many [clients]! too many! [*bemaro! beloatra!*] . . . they would come whenever they wanted, it didn't matter how I was feeling. . . . You know, Zaman'i'Bao, he is hard on his mediums, he spits up blood. . . . Some days I would not be able to get up after a session [with a client] . . . my back and neck would be so sore; one day I saw black spots for three days! It was terrible . . . when a tromba spirit gets angry, he makes you sick. . . . I didn't have the money to host a ceremony to make him happy, and this really frightened me. I wondered, is he going to kill me? . . . Marcel, who had gone to the FJKM church as a child, told me to go there to have the spirit driven out, but I didn't want to. I was so afraid! [*mavozo é!*]. We live near the newly built Lutheran church, and my spirit didn't like that either. They would start to sing and I could hear them in my house. I'd get scared, because sometimes Zaman'i'Bao would arrive suddenly and be very angry, especially when they sang the hymn "Jesosy Tomponay" ["Jesus our Master"]. . . . Then one day I just wandered into the church, [possessed by] the tromba [spirit]! Can you imagine! I don't remember what happened, but Marcel and the pastor say they stopped the service right there and drove out the spirit. . . . that was ten years ago. . . . Now Marcel and I pray there every week. . . . They take care of me; they are my family [HP: *fianakaviana*]." Zaloky is now a respected elder in the church. She and Marcel have fallen into economic hardship within the last few years and they continue to be troubled by land disputes with her children. The Lutherans give them food and she in turn has decided to will her land to this church (unless a disco next door overruns her homestead first).

Vivienne, Elisabeth, and Zaloky have each suffered from a form of possession which is fairly typical for Sakalava women their respective ages. Vivienne is an adolescent troubled by problems of love and romance, and she suffers from njarinintsy possession. Elisabeth and Zaloky were established mediums for Child and Grandparent spirits that commonly appear among women of their backgrounds and ages. All three are also unusual, however, and even marginal, in other ways. Vivienne's problems with possession are extreme, now bordering on madness. Elisabeth's career as a medium began at an exceptionally early age. Rather than accepting her fate, she has suffered terribly throughout her life, unable to cope with her status as a spirit medium. Regardless of her actions, she continued to be plagued by illnesses caused by her tromba spirits. For Zaloky, an older woman, the more mundane forms of suffering associated with mediumship eventually were intolerable. Although she had many clients, trance exhausted her and she found demands of visitors to her house to be too great. This was compounded by the terrible conflicts with her children over land rights.

These three women present extreme cases for yet another reason: although they are tera-tany, they eventually sought solutions through a nonindigenous institution dominated by peoples from the high plateaux. In the case of Vivienne, the Protestant exorcists may be able to help her through a serious illness—whether it is possession sickness or madness—coaxing it to leave and then giving her continued support. Elisabeth and Zaloky, on the other hand, are women who have rejected the role of tromba medium, choosing instead to be freed permanently from possession. They have come to the exorcists hoping to have their spirits driven from them because they find the suffering they experience as mediums unbearable. This is a pattern that has emerged in the Lutheran church, where, in addition to Zaloky, two other Sakalava have joined for reasons associated with tromba. The first is an old man (in his sixties) who, like Zaloky, had a tromba spirit exorcised and who later joined the congregation. He and Zaloky felt their ties to the local community were fragmented: Zaloky was embroiled in a bitter quarrel with her children over land inheritance, and this older man was unmarried and had no children. Another Sakalava convert was a twenty-year-old man who joined because he was deeply distressed by the suffering that he saw his mother and ex-wife endure as tromba mediums.

Seeking the assistance of the exorcists reflects a deliberate choice to opt out of and thus be free from the institution of spirit possession, which in many ways epitomizes what it means to be Sakalava. This involves embracing, at least in part, Protestantism as a new faith, either by drawing on the power of the exorcists for convenience's sake to drive out unwanted tromba spirits, or through the more permanent act of conversion. In choosing this route, however, one becomes, in a sense, less Sakalava, not only because one rejects tromba, but also because Sakalava look disfavorably upon Protestant vahiny. As the stories of these three women show, this choice may also mark a shift away from kin and Sakalava identity: two of these former mediums have chosen

to become members of new Christian communities that in many ways
are like newly found kin.

THE POWER OF PROTESTANT HEALING

Exorcists' clients are drawn from a variety of backgrounds; one thing
that they all share in common is that they are desperate. Other healers—indigenous and clinical—have failed to relieve their suffering.
Their distress may be compounded by their marginality within the local
Sakalava community. Pertinent factors here include understanding the
following: the manner in which practitioners of this alternative healing
system cope with a competing epistemological reality derived from Sakalava culture, the significance of power in the therapeutic context, the
relevance of structural shifts in identity, and the meaning of community.

REDEFINING THE SYMBOLIC ORDER THROUGH AN
ALTERNATIVE EPISTEMOLOGICAL SYSTEM

As I have argued elsewhere (Sharp, in press), understanding the therapeutic efficacy of Malagasy exorcists is a difficult task. Csordas, in his
work with charismatic Christians in the United States, stresses that efficacy and outcome hinges on an assessment of procedures (such as rituals) used by therapists as well as the process (or experiences) undergone
by patients. Anthropologists need to have a clearer understanding of
patients' subjective experiences of "encounters with the sacred, episodes
of insight, or changes in thought, emotion, attitude, meaning, behavior"
(1988: 121). An analysis of exorcists in Madagascar reveals the relevance of their approaches and epistemological model to therapeutics.
A key aspect here is that exorcists use invasive conversionary tactics
that require the active participation of the patient and, if possible, her
kin. Through this process the meaning of suffering is transformed and
often, in turn, the patient's definition of self is also altered.

Patient and healer may have radically different perceptions of illness
and personal disorder. As Taussig (1980b) has argued, medical care
may serve as a method to silence the patient rather than one through
which to communicate with and comprehend her perceptions of her
illness. In northwest Madagascar, ultimately therapeutic success or failure hinges on the healer's ability to comprehend the patient's epistemological reality. To rely on the knowledge of indigenous healers to solve

problems associated with possession and madness means to embrace the logic of the cultural system from which they originate. For example, established mediums typically specialize in tromba possession because they grasp the deep-rooted internal cultural logic that shapes the significance of royal ancestors and the nature of their needs and whims (cf. Lévi-Strauss 1963a). For the exorcist, on the other hand, an oppositional stance to this internal logic is central, since conversion is the ultimate goal. Paradoxically, to achieve this goal, the sharing of ideas must be part of the process. The exorcist helps the patient by redefining her conception of reality (and, ultimately, her identity). The patient, in turn, must embrace the Protestant belief system to be fully healed.

This is a dialogic process, one that is clearly evident in cases involving possession. Ironically, exorcists do not deny the existence of spirits; rather, they refuse to distinguish between different categories, *relabeling all spirits* (tromba, kalanoro, njarinintsy, and so forth) as demons (devoly). As Greenfield (1992) illustrates, the strength of a group of Spiritist healers in southern Brazil lies in the syncretic nature of their healing practices. They rely on an assortment of models of illness causation, including the teachings of the spiritist Allan Kardec, modern physics, and Candomblé, Umbanda, and other Afro-Brazilian religions. Their work attracts clients because their ideas make sense to people of diverse origins who populate the polycultural, urban world of Brazil. Protestant exorcists in Madagascar are not nearly so liberal (or eclectic) in their approaches. Nevertheless, within the therapeutic context there is still a sharing and overlapping of information between Sakalava and Christian systems. Exorcists would never, for example, draw on the power of a tromba spirit to heal, yet they do rely on a form of possession involving the Holy Spirit to achieve a similar end. In addition, the exorcist's approach is participatory, designed to engage the patient in a continuous dialogue about her life and the meaning of spirits for her. Prayers, hymns, and sermons serve as didactic tools to transform the patient's way of perceiving her illness as well as the world more generally.

In contrast to the tolerance of Catholic enculturation policies, Protestant churches in Madagascar have always made conscious and deliberate attempts to define their doctrines in reference—and opposition—to indigenous beliefs (fomba-gasy) (Gow 1979; Mutibwa 1974; Trexler 1989; see also entries authored by Sibree, Pearse, Dahle, Haile, Davidson, and others in the journal of the London Missionary Society [LMS] 1881–1900). As zealous evangelists, the ultimate goal of these exorcists is to undermine a patient's beliefs by simultaneously acknowledging their legitimacy. In reference specifically to tromba possession, they accept the pervasiveness of these spirits' taboos (fady), and then, in turn, they declare that "tromba [itself] is taboo" (fady tromba), an expression that operates like other fady in Madagascar to mark difference, distinguishing ethnic groups from one another.

The power of communication is central to the act of exorcism, especially when exorcists engage the spirits themselves. Just as an accordionist or valiha player entices tromba spirits to arrive in their mediums, Protestant healers use their own music to encourage the spirits to possess patients. Their style of interaction with these spirits parallels that of tromba mediums, or other indigenous healers, who seek to placate or cajole a spirit into staying (in the case of a tromba) or departing peacefully (as with a njarinintsy). Exorcists, however, take this one step further: they taunt, scold, and lecture spirits and then they drive them, with force, from their victims. Exorcists fully comprehend the meaning of possession in the lives of their patients, and they seek to alter their ways of perceiving their experiences. Thus, on the one hand, exorcists successfully integrate two seemingly divergent or conflicting epistemologies. On the other, through conversionary tactics, they undermine indigenous cultural logic.

WORK, INDEPENDENCE, AND EMPOWERMENT

Protestants draw on the indigenous symbolic order in other ways to heal as well as transform the patient's sense of the world. For example, they supply new meanings for the concept of work (asa). As described in previous chapters, ideas surrounding work are highly charged for the Sakalava, whose lives are shaped by the plantation economy of the Sambirano. Preferably, work should be framed by economic independence involving such activities as caring for one's own fields. If one works to serve another, this should only be done for Sakalava royalty, and not in the sense that characterizes the enterprises, where work means alienated wage labor.

In the healing retreats of the northwest, a new Protestant work ethic has emerged (cf. Weber 1991 [1930]; see also Comaroff and Comaroff 1991: 140ff). When patients have the strength, they are expected to assist with daily chores, cooking in the kitchen, cleaning the church and other structures, and assisting in the fields. Such participation serves to integrate them into daily community life. It also stresses the duty that one has to serve God, the master of us all, a concept aptly expressed in the hymn mentioned by Zaloky, "Jesosy Tomponay," or "Jesus our Master." Women who have abandoned mediumship continue to perform sacred work, but for a Christian deity rather than for royal ancestors.

The significance of work carries over into other exorcist activities, where themes of power and dominance are important. For example, healing sessions are referred to as "work and empowerment" (asa sy fampaheresana). The exorcist's conversionary tactics are invasive, requiring the patient to submit to God's power. Exorcism also may be empowering for the patient, however, since she is required to become actively involved in the therapeutic process (cf. Taussig 1980b). Elisabeth, in choosing to be trained as an exorcist, has taken the final step. Her "work" is what will shape her new identity as a Sakalava convert and as an active Protestant.

STRUCTURAL SHIFTS AND REDEFINING IDENTITY

As noted above, those who opted for exorcism were already marginalized for a variety of reasons, including madness, alienation from kin, or cultural dislocation resulting from migration. A final factor contributing to their marginality is especially notable. Even though all mediums I interviewed considered tromba possession to be a difficult experience, the majority accepted it as their lifelong fate. During the course of this research, however, I met five women who had opted for exorcism. Vivienne, Elisabeth, and Zaloky sought respite from tromba mediumship, possession sickness, or madness. A fourth woman was Mona, who attended the Pentecostal retreat. She was thirty-four and had three tromba spirits. Mona had suffered immensely during the previous six years from a host of problems for which no indigenous healer could find a cure, and she hoped that if her spirits were driven from her, her health would return. Finally, Berthine chose another route: she had a tromba spirit exorcised as part of her conversion to Islam. The afflicted may already be marginal even before becoming a Christian. Vivienne shared many of the problems of school migrants (chapter 9); in addition, she suffered from the complex problems associated with madness. Others already felt somewhat alienated from Sakalava kin or friends, as was true for Elisabeth and Zaloky (and the two men who converted to Lutheranism; see above). Thus, in at least three of these cases, *it is not spirit possession that marks a Sakalava woman's marginal status* (I.M. Lewis 1966, 1971,

1991, and essays in I.M. Lewis et al., eds., 1991) *but her inability to cope with it.*

The exoricist's power plays a pivotal role in the process of redefining such a woman's identity. This is evident in the style of social interaction that occurs during healing sessions, where the exorcist and patient assume dominant and submissive positions. While an exorcist stands, the patient kneels before him or her. Exorcists will often touch the head of the patient, either with their hands or the Bible (see plate 8). This is a highly charged, symbolic gesture, that violates Malagasy rules of status etiquette. As noted in the story of Marie (chapter 8), the head is sacred and should not be touched. This is especially important if the patient is a tromba medium (and, even more so, if she is in the process of entering trance), since these royal spirits are said to sit (mipetraka) in her head. Only elders and royalty can raise their heads about others. Thus, the patient, in accepting the exorcist's mode of treatment, submits to Protestant authority. Only once the patient embraces Christianity through conversion is the relationship between patient and exorcist defined as an equal one.

Thus, the power of the exorcist to transform a patient's identity is rooted in the manipulation of the indigenous symbolic order. Structural shifts in identity may be partial or complete. Nevertheless, they define a central aspect of this therapeutic process, since a Sakalava patient must embrace beliefs that run contrary to her own culture if the therapy is to work. A medium must deny the existence of royal ancestors and be willing to relabel them as demons. She also must accept that the Holy Ghost is more powerful than tromba and that a Christian God is her savior and guardian. Finally, she must submit to the power and authority of a community peopled by non-Sakalava vahiny. Should she convert, her identity no longer hinges on her ethnicity; rather, she is relabeled as a *Christian*. If she is trained to be an exorcist, like Elisabeth, her new work (asa) as a shepherd (mpiandry) (rather than a tromba medium) defines who she is.

JOINING A COMMUNITY OF STRANGERS

The concept of community is generally assumed to be central to religious experience (Durkheim 1965 [1915], especially Bk. 1; V. Turner 1969: chaps. 3 and 4), and, more specifically, in charismatic Christian communities, where the collective provides a supportive environment for those

who otherwise feel socially, culturally, politically, or economically dis-
enfranchised (see, for example, Comaroff 1985; Finkler 1985; Jules-
Rosette 1975; Kehoe 1989; La Barre 1992 [1962]; Lawless 1988;
McGuire 1982; for a fictional account from Africa see also Achebe
1959). An important dimension of the healing methods used by Malagasy exorcists is that, in severe cases, the patient must live apart from
her original community and within the confines of the curing retreat.
Thus, the concept of the Protestant community itself is viewed as therapeutic. Here patients are accompanied by kin and they are under the
constant, watchful eye of exorcists. This practice is rooted in Malagasy
culture, regardless of ethnic origin: throughout Madagascar, the room
where a sick person convalesces can quickly become overrun by a constant stream of kin and other visitors. Similarly, patients at Protestant
curing retreats are never left alone.

On a grander scale, the retreat is also simultaneously a model Sakalava village and an alternative Christian community. The retreat near
Ambanja, for example, has been built in the middle of an already existing village, and the dwellings of other inhabitants are indistinguishable
from those of the exorcists. Only the Protestant church and an outdoor
communal kitchen stand out. Patients are expected to become active
members of this community, taking part in the prayer sessions that occur
several times a day and, as mentioned above, assisting in the work that
keeps the retreat operating.

In the retreat, the notion of "cure" is relative and is subjectively
defined, the concept of community playing a key role. Although
(ex-)patients may continue to be troubled by their illnesses, they find
that their eccentricities are usually better tolerated by others if they join
a Protestant congregation or if they continue to live at the curing retreat.
For example, the symptoms of madness that originally were viewed as
extreme forms of social deviancy are redefined as the normative behavior
of individuals who have been blessed. The assessment of therapeutic
success also hinges on the healer's subjective point of view, for in this
context the cure is conditional, based on conversion to a new faith. It
is, however, highly unusual for Sakalava to convert to Protestantism.
Although such a choice is viewed as a major triumph for the exorcists,
among Sakalava, converts such as Elisabeth are anomalies and even
pariahs. Since they risk being abandoned by kin, mediums who choose
to convert will stay close to the Protestant community. In so doing, they
gain, as Zaloky said, new "family."

Just as fictive kinship was pivotal in the context of tromba, it is also operational in these new Christian communities. Those who embrace Christianity are defined as "brothers" and "sisters" of one another, and all are children before God, the Father. Through exorcism rituals, patients break from Sakalava structural relationships and adopt new, Christian ones. In addition, a subtle shift in ethnic affiliation occurs: since the majority of Protestants are from the high plateaux, the kin terms used are not those of Sakalava village or town networks, but others derived from highland dialects. This shift is reflected in Zaloky's choice of language, since she uses a high plateaux term (fianakaviana) when she says that the Lutheran church is her new "family."

Even though the final step of conversion may relieve the suffering of these Sakalava women, it nevertheless raises other questions about the future of tera-tany identity in the Sambirano. Karp, for example, reports that within a year's absence from Tesoland in Kenya, all of the mediums he knew had converted to Christianity and no longer practiced possession (personal communication; see also Karp 1987, 1989). In Ambanja, however, I do not anticipate that Protestantism will make major inroads into the community of Sakalava tera-tany, because for them this faith is too strongly associated with French colonial and Merina enemies. At present, conversion is rare and is a last resort, for the price one pays is very high. Elisabeth and Zaloky are extreme cases that involve women who desperately sought relief and found it only by joining this isolated community of strangers.

Conclusion

*Toward a Reassessment of the Possessed
and the Dispossesed*

This has been a study in the politics of culture. Against this backdrop of a polycultural community, I have sought to show that identity is not static or "one-dimensional." Rather, as Cohen (1976) has argued, there exists an interdependence between power relationships and symbolic action. Furthermore, the dynamic nature of identity in Ambanja is part of a historical process shaped by such forces as colonialism and voluntary migration. Tromba possession provides a rich terrain for exploring how identity is experienced in private, social, economic, and political realms, since it mediates between the competing categories of tera-tany and vahiny, or insider and outsider. In order to understand the complexities of this problem, this investigation has required, as Apter (1992) advocates in his study of Yoruba religion, an exploration of the "deep meanings" (cf. Geertz 1973) embedded in ritual form. Such meanings reveal the links between knowledge and power: through the realm of tromba possession one may gain access to the most potent forms of local knowledge, which are sacred and linked to the royal ancestors. Ultimately, such knowledge affects personal and collective well-being.

In concluding, I would like to reevaluate a number of assumptions (or questions) that have been critical throughout this work. First, this study has sought to explore the manner in which symbolic power may extend beyond the temporary realm of ritual. Thus, how might religious experience be politically charged (again, see Cohen 1976; also Apter 1992 and Lan 1985) and have long-term effects on everyday life? Second, who exactly are the "dispossessed" members of what some might label a "peripheral" society of the world?

These two questions are especially pertinent to studies of possession and, more specifically, the relevance of social status for determining participation patterns. If we assume the perspective of Ambanja's inhabitants, tromba possession is not a peripheral experience, but a significant force within indigenous culture. Similar to Giles' study from the East African coast (1987), the data presented here contradict the assumed impotence of the possessed. This case from Ambanja reveals the manner in which ritual form may be used to manipulate oppressive forces that affect the personal lives of migrant laborers or the collective experiences of Sakalava. In this context, the human body provides a powerful medium for the articulation of problems that characterize urban life.

In this vein, the significance of tromba can only fully be understood if it is explored in relation to indigenous notions of identity, which operate on personal, social, and cultural levels. As this study has shown, tromba mediumship alters identity and may be permanently empowering for tera-tany and vahiny. Today saha for royal spirits maintain considerable control over the production of local knowledge and the manipulation of power structures. More recently, they have been able to direct economic development that threatens to alienate them of their tanindrazaña. So long as the sacredness of ancestors is honored in the Sambirano—and by the state—Sakalava may be able to maintain their control over the use of local territory. Such was the case that Lan (1985) described for Zimbabwe in the 1970s; the questions to be addressed in Madagascar are what roles will new generations of mediums play in this arena, and what will be the future of the Sambirano?

In the popular realm, tromba possession is pivotal for understanding concepts of alienation and well-being. Tromba offers the potential for first-generation female migrants to strengthen their personal networks and become recognized as tera-tany in their own lifetimes. Through this process, mediums gain access to an extensive and locally embedded network of relationships based on equality and reciprocity. These they may exploit to find work, gain access to local resources, and acquire assistance in times of need. As healers, they may also extend their networks to include clients, freeing themselves from the requirements of wage labor. Thus, mediumship offers migrant women a means to overcome the greatest difficulty or social affliction they face. Tromba enables them to become tamana, or content, in Ambanja.

Spirit mediums, in turn, mediate the migration experiences of others in several ways. First, even though tromba mediumship is primarily a female experience, men may also extend or strengthen their personal networks through sisters, wives, and lovers who are mediums. Second, tromba possession ceremonies and, more specifically, healing rituals, have been a central focus of this investigation since they reveal the nature of local power and the problems of the vulnerable. Tromba simultaneously provides a setting for expressing individual and social ills and a means to alleviate them. Polyculturalism and a plantation economy shape the most common forms of affliction—physical, romantic, and economic problems.

Throughout this work I have sought to place women as well as children in more visible positions vis-à-vis migration studies. Migration as a process may involve the active participation of women: not all remain in homesteads for the primary purpose of reproducing labor (Meillassoux 1982; Richards 1951). Many, like their male counterparts, branch out on their own in search of work and economic independence. This is a worldwide trend (Little 1973; Ong 1987; Nash and Fernandez-Kelly, eds. 1983; Schuster 1979) and warrants continued scrutiny. As I have shown, children define an unusual category of migrants who must cope with the challenges of this social process. In Ambanja, njarinintsy may be a pervasive force in their lives, operating as a culturally sanctioned form for expressing the chaos that characterizes contemporary urban life (cf. Taussig 1987). Thus, the experiences of children as well are in need of more careful cross-cultural study.

More generally, I have advocated that analyses of the migration process will remain shallow if symbolic realms are overlooked. Material considerations are certainly an essential aspect of the problems associated with relocation, since survival hinges on one's ability to find housing, work, and so forth. In addition, kin who remain behind rely on a migrant's economic success. As this study from Ambanja shows, however, other factors come into play and may be just as significant as purely material matters. The first involves the manner in which identity is defined, since different social categories enjoy different levels of access to local power structures. Second, there are subgroups of migrants, each defined by the manner in which indigenous Sakalava perceive them as well as by their personal, sentimental ties to a particular region. There also are several other key concepts involved here. Land and work, for example, are symbolically charged and are significant concerns for teratany and vahiny alike. Put another way, it is not simply access to land or labor that assures well-being or success for the migrant—in Madagascar or elsewhere—but also the sentimental and symbolic values assigned to these and other realms of experience.

In returning to the questions asked above, what I have sought to prove is that ritual form, and, more particularly, healing rituals, supply a rich and varied ground upon which to explore problems inherent to everyday life. Historical analysis reveals the dynamic nature of tromba: as local perceptions of what it means to be Sakalava have changed, tromba has altered in form yet remains a central defining principle for local identity. Thus, in northwest Madagascar, participation in tromba is not evidence of powerlessness or marginal status. Rather, as the work of Protestant exorcists show, it is those who are unable to cope with Sakalava identity and mediumship status who are truly dispossessed.

Appendices

Glossary of Malagasy Terms

ADALA; ADALAÑA   "Madness," "to be insane"; the diminutive form is *adala-dala*, which means "to be odd" or "silly."

ANDRIAMANITRA   "Ruler of Heaven"; the Christian God; compare Zanahary, below.

ANDRIAN-/NDRAM-   Prefixes used to designate royal descent. When Sakalava royalty die they receive a new praise name (*fitaha*) which generally begins with this prefix. This new name will also be the one used if a person becomes a tromba spirit.

ANDRIANTOMPOENIARIVO   The founding ancestor of the Bemazava-Sakalava dynasty.

ANTANDROY[1]   Malagasy peoples from southern Madagascar; they are, for the most part, pastoralists. Sometimes this term is used generally to encompass other peoples such as the Bara and Mahafaly.

ANTAISAKA, ANTAIFASY, ANTAIMORO   Malagasy peoples of the southeast coast.

ANTAKARANA   Northern neighbors of the Sakalava. They share common origins with and, culturally, they are very similar to the northern Sakalava.

AMPANJAKA; AMPANJAKABE   "Royalty" or member of a royal lineage, "ruler."

ASA, MIASA   "Work," "to work," as in *miasa ny tromba*, "the tromba [spirit or medium] is working" (compare to *fanompoaña*, below).

BAKA ANDRANO   "Coming from the water," referring to the spirits of Sakalava royalty who chose to drown themselves rather than serve under the Merina. These are *Zafin'i'fotsy* spirits (see below).

BAKA ATSIMO   "Coming from the south," that is, tromba spirits that are entombed near Mahajanga. These are *Zafin'i'mena* spirits (see below).

---

[1] I have not listed the names of all Malagasy ethnic groups, but only those that appear repeatedly throughout the text of this study. See chapter 3 for a more complete list.

BEMAZAVA-SAKALAVA   The northernmost dynastic branch of the Sakalava kingdoms; the people who are indigenous to the Sambirano Valley.

BEMIHISATRA-SAKALAVA   Neighbors of the Bemazava who occupy the territory to the south of Ambanja as well as the the small island of Nosy Be, where one of their rulers is located.

BETSILEO   Malagasy peoples of the southern high plateaux.

BETSIMISARAKA   Malagasy of the east coast.

BORZANY   A derogatory term used by Sakalava to refer to the Merina.

CÔTIERS   "People of the coast," a term applied to virtually all Malagasy except the Merina and Betsileo of the high plateaux.

DADY, DADILAHY, DADIBE   "Grandparent, "grandfather," "great-grandparent." These kinship terms are used to refer to the oldest (and greatest) of the tromba spirits. Sometimes they are also used to refer to the medium (*saha*) as well; see also *zanaka* and *zafy*.

DEUXIÈME BUREAU   Lit. "the second office" or mistress. An older term for this is *bodofotsy*, lit. "bedcover" or "blanket."

DOANY   "Royal residence"; also a form of possession brought to the south by Antandroy migrants who have worked in the north.

DRAKÔ, ZALAHY, KAMARADY   Terms of endearment used between women (*drakô*) and between men (*zalahy*); *kamarady* (from the French *camarade*) is a general term used for either gender.

ENCULTURATION   A policy of the Catholic church which encourages the tolerance of local beliefs and customs, emphasizing syncretism over orthodoxy.

ENTERPRISES (FR: ENTREPRISES)   Large-scale state-owned plantations.

ÉTRANGER   French for "foreigner," "stranger." Malagasy also used *vazaha* (see below) when referring to North Americans and Europeans, especially if they are Anglo.

FADY   "Taboo"; *faly* (which can also mean "happy") is an older form of this word (as with *Nosy Faly* or "Island of Taboos").

FANAFODY   "Medicine." There are several categories of fanafody: *fanafodygasy* or "Malagasy medicine" and *fanafody vazaha* or "foreign/European medicine" (that is, clinical medicine). There is also *fanafody tsara* or "good medicine" and *fanafody raty/ratsy* or "bad medicine" (sometimes translated in French as *magique* or *poison*).

FANOMPOAÑA, ASAMPANJAKAÑA   "Royal service" or "royal work" that is performed by Sakalava out of obligation to their rulers. This is distinct from other forms of work (*asa*).

FATIDRA   "Blood brotherhood" or "sisterhood."

FIFOHAZANA; MPIANDRY   "[Those who] rise up"; "shepherds": Protestant exorcists.

FJKM   Abbreviation for Fiongonana Jesosy Kristiany Malagasy (Malagasy Church of Jesus Christ). Formed in 1970, it is actively involved in exorcist activities.

FOMBA-GASY, FOMBANDRAZANA/-RAZAÑA   "Malagasy customs" or "customs of the ancestors." These terms refer to aspects of Malagasy culture which predate the colonial period. They are often contrasted to *fomba vazaha*.

FOMBA VAZAHA   "European [usually specifically French] customs."
In the context of religion, *fomba-gasy* refers to indigenous religion, as opposed to religions of foreign origin, such as Islam and Christianity.

HITADY HARENA/VOLA/ASA   "to search for fortune/money/work." These are expressions that are used frequently by migrants when they give their reasons for coming to Ambanja.

JORO   Ceremonies that honor ancestors and where *omby* (cattle) are sacrificed.

KALANORO   A nature spirit that lives in the forest and eats raw food. It is described as being short with long hair, red eyes, and feet that point backward. Mediums for kalanoro must capture them and this enables them to become powerful healers. While a kalanoro medium is working he or she can not be seen by clients, but must sit behind a drapery.

KITAMBY, KISALY, SALOVA; LAMBAHOANY   Forms of Sakalava dress: The *kitamy* is a waist wrap worn by men; the *kisaly* and *salova* (also called *salovaña*) together form the clothes worn by Sakalava women. The kisaly is draped over the head or shoulders and is generally accompanied by a matching salova, which women wrap around their bodies and tie at the waist or chest. A *lambahoany* is a factory-made cloth that can be used as any of these three pieces of clothing (*lamba* is the general term used for cloth throughout Madagascar).

LOLO   Spirits of lost souls, ghosts.

MAHABO, ZOMBA   The royal tomb(s) of the northern Sakalava and the Antakarana. Zomba is also the name for the royal residence.

MAFANA, MIFANA   "Hot" postpartum practices followed by the majority of Malagasy; see also *ranginalo*.

MALAGASIZATION (MALGACHISATION)   National policy of Madagascar that emphasizes Malagasy language, customs, and so forth over those of foreign origin.

MAKARELY   "Prostitute."

MAPINGO   Wooden staff held by tromba spirits. That of more powerful spirits is usually tipped with embossed silver.

MAROVAVY, AMBIMANAÑY   Female tomb guardian; see also *ngahy*.

MERINA   The dominant ethnic group of Madagascar, both in terms of numbers and political influence.

MÉTIS, MÉTISSE   Offspring of unions of mixed origins (male and female forms); for example: Arab-métis: male child of Malagasy (usually Sakalava) and Arab parents.

MOASY (HP: OMBIASY)   A type of healer, usually one who specializes in herbal remedies.

MORENGY   Public boxing matches.

MPAMOSAVY   A "witch" or "sorceror."

MPISIKIDY   "Diviner."

NGAHY   Male tomb guardian; see also *marovavy* (compare to *rangahy*).

NGAOMA   "Homesick," "malcontent"; the opposite of *tamana*. One might also say *te ho mody*, which expresses the desire to return home.

NJARININTSY, MASOANTOKO, SHAY-TUAN, BILO   Types of evil spirits that cause possession sickness.

RANGAHY   Interpreter for a tromba spirit (compare to *ngahy*).

RANGINALO   "Cold" postpartum practices followed exclusively by Sakalava; see also *mafana, mifana*.

RAZAÑA, RAZANA   "Ancestors" (generic term).

REBIKY   Dance held to honor royalty.

ROMBA NY TROMBA   Tromba ceremony, distinct from a private consultation with a medium.

SAHA   Mediums for the greatest of the royal tromba spirits. In general, this term is only applied to mediums who have been tested to make sure their spirits are authentic; they live in the village near the royal tomb of their spirit(s).

TAMANA   To be "content" (for example, where one lives); the opposite of *ngaoma*.

TANY FOTSY/MALANDY   "White earth" or kaolin, which has cool healing properties.

TANINDRAZAÑA, TANINDRAZANA   The "ancestral land."

TERA-TANY (HP: TOMPONTANY)   "Children of the soil" (HP: "masters" or "possessors of the soil"); the indigenous people of a region. In the Sambirano, these are the Bemazava-Sakalava.

TSIÑY   A nature spirit that is generally associated with a sacred tree. Tsiñy mediums are powerful healers.

TROMBA   Sakalava royal ancestral spirits. This term is also used to refer to the institution, the possession experience, and mediums for such spirits.

TSIMIHETY   Migratory pastoralists of Madagascar. They form one of the most established and best documented of the migrant groups that have moved into northern Madagascar.

VADY   "Spouse."

VAHINY   "Guests"; Malagasy migrants.

VAMBA   "Adultery," "adulterer."

VAZAHA   "Strangers" or foreigners, especially those of European origin.

VINTANA   Malagasy cosmological zodiac system.

ZANAKA   "Children;" the second of the three generational categories of tromba spirits; see also *dadilahy* and *zafy*.

ZAFY   "Grandchildren"; the most recent and least powerful of the three generations of tromba spirits; see also *dadilahy* and *zanaka*.

ZAFIN'I'MENA, ZAFIN'I'FOTSY   these are abbreviated forms of *Zafinibolamena* and *Zafinibolafotsy*, or "Grandchildren of Red metal/Gold" and "Grandchildren of White metal/Silver." These labels correspond to two major descent groups of Sakalava (including both living royalty and tromba spirits); Antakarana are also members of the Zafin'i'fotsy dynasty. See also *baka atsimo* and *baka andrano,* above.

ZANAHARY   Collective term for all ancestors, also used to refer to the more distant original ancestors. Compare to Andriamanitra, above.

APPENDIX B: LIST OF THE POSSESSED

Medium Name/Age	Ethnicity	Residence Status	Marriage/Children	Possession History	Economic Activities	Schooling
			Tromba Mediums: Female			
BASELY (7) age: 19	Tsimihety FA/MO: Tsimihety from Maromandia MO died when Basely was 12	child of settlers considers self t-t born in Ambanja	single no children	17: diagnosed with tromba, but not instated, said to be crazy (adala)	works as Marivola's housekeeper	finished primary school
ANGELINE (5) age: 20	Sakalava FA/MO: Sakalava	t-t born in village near Ambanja	18–present: 1st husband (T/CW) 1 pregnancy, miscarried	17: njarinintsy 20: Mampiary and Djao Kondry (GC)	does not work, husband works as supervisor at enterprise	completed junior high school
BERTHINE* (10) age: 20	Betsileo FA: Betsileo MO: Sakalava (sister of Alice)	child of settler (gp); considers self t-t born in village near Ambanja 18–20: Ambanja	19–present (IW): 1st husband no children	16?: name unknown 19: exorcised in mosque as requirement for conversion (husband is a Muslim)	does not work, supported by husband	2–3 yrs. of junior high school
LEAH age: 20	Sakalava FA: unknown MO: Sakalava (MO's MO Betsileo, sister of Gertrude)	t-t born in Ambanja	19–20: married (CL) now separated; 20: abortion	18: njarinintsy 19: Be Ondry and Mampiary (GP) 20: masoantoko	prostitute? occasionally receives clients as a medium	2–3 yrs. of junior high school
ALICE* (10) age: 28	Betsileo FA: Betsileo MO: Sakalava (sister of Berthine)	child of settler (gp); considers self t-t; born in village near Ambanja 17–20: Nosy Be (1 yr. at school) 20–present: Ambanja	18–?: 1st husband (CL), 1 child 6 yrs. (2 dead); 25–present: 2nd husband (CL) no additional children	6: claims 3 tromba arrived, but not instated until later. 17: Djao Kondry and Mampiary (GC) 26: Kotofanjava, Tontoño and Raovoay (C)	husband works at restaurant; she is a full-time medium, attends ceremonies regularly; she owns their house, each has a rice field	most of high school
MARIE (8) age: 28	Tsimihety FA/MO: Tsimihety from Maromandia	child of settlers, considers self t-t; born in Ambanja	17–27: married (CL), now separated, child age 11 (lives with Marie's mother)	17: njarinintsy (child 3 mos. old) 18: Mampiary (GC) and Andriantahiry (C) 20: Kotolavazaha (C) 25: Mampiamihy (GC) 28: njarinintsy at work	husband worked, she had some clients as a medium 27–28: worked at enterprise; 28–present: full-time medium; attends ceremonies regularly	finished junior high school

(continued)

Medium Name/Age	Ethnicity	Residence Status	Marriage/Children	Possession History	Economic Activities	Schooling
		Tromba Mediums: Female (Continued)				
BEATRICE age: 30	Sakalava FA/MO: Sakalava	t-t (Nosy Be) born on Nosy Be; 26–28: Diégo; 29–present: Nosy Be	20–27: 1st husband (CL), separated; 4 children 28–30: 2nd husband (CL), separated	26–28: masoantoko 28: tromba ceremony, spirit did not arrive 30: spirit exorcised by FJKM Protestants	supported by husbands and mother in Nosy Be	1–2 years junior high school
FLUERETTE age: 32	Antaimoro FA: Antaimoro MO: Sakalava	child of settler and t-t (GP); considers self to be t-t; born in Ambanja 18–23: in school at Nosy Be	24–present: 1st husband (CL) (met in Nosy Be), 2 children, 12 and 2 yrs.	14: Kely Sanga (C) 18: Djao Kondry (GC)	husband is schoolteacher, she is secretary at same school; they own their house; no clients but she attends some ceremonies	finished high school at private school in Nosy Be
PERLINE age: 33	Sakalava FA/MO: Sakalava	t-t, born in Ambanja	18–22: 1st husband (CL); 24–present: 2nd husband (CL), 0 children, (infertile); 2nd husband's 2 children by former marriage live with them; until recently, so did Perline's sister	22: Mampiary (GC) 26: "armchair" tromba (will not disclose name) (C?) receives many clients as a medium	runs small grocery with aid from husband; she owns the house and store	1 year of high school (private Catholic school)
MONA (10) age: 34	Sakalava FA/MO: Sakalava	t-t (Nosy Be) born in Nosy Be	22–present: 1st husband (CL)	26: 1st tromba (GC?) 27: 2 other tromba (will not disclose spirits' names) (GC?) 28–34: very sick 34: attempted to have spirits exorcised by FJKM Protestants at Pentecostal retreat	works part-time in bars in Nosy Be	1 year junior high school

MARIAMO (7) age: 34	Comorean-métisse FA: Comorean; MO: Sakalava (mo died when A was 12)	settler? born in village near Ambilobe; 16–17: Diégo; 17–33: Mahajanga and environs; 33: moved to Ambanja with 2nd husband	16 + 2 weeks: 1st husband (CL), 0 children (infertile); 33–present: 2nd husband (CL), cares for 8-yr-old son of husband's sister	13: tromba hely (?) followed by Mbotimahasaky (C?) 22: went to ceremony at royal tombs near Mahajanga, possessed by Djaomorengy, Djaomarangimbato, and Rakotoraimboly (GC/ C?)	worked as prostitute in Diégo, Mahajanga; present husband owns land, helps him farm; receives clients regularly, and attends many ceremonies	finished primary school
MARIVOLA (7 and 8) age: 36	Arab-métisse FA: Arab MO: Tsimihety (died when Marivola was 22)	settler, born in Befandriana 22: moved to Ambanja with her husband	17–present (CW): 4 children, ages 15, 13, 12, 5	23: Mena Moasy (C) 25: Kotofanjava (C) 28: Raleva (C) 32: Ndramandenta (GP) (all but Kotofanjava were inherited from her mother)	husband works as a bookkeeper at local enterprise; she runs small grocery, occasionally receives clients as a medium	completed 2 years of high school (private Catholic school)
GERTRUDE (6) age: 37	Betsileo FA/MO: Betsileo	child of settlers; born in Fianarantsoa, age 5 moved to Ambanja with parents	17–30: 1st husband (CL), now separated; 3 children, ages 20, 14, 12; 1 child, age 7, by a lover	29: Mampiary and Djao Kondry (GC)	supported by husband, 29: worked briefly at enterprise until realized she was possessed by tromba with coffee and cashew taboos; occasionally receives clients; lame, so rarely attends ceremonies; sells rum; oldest son is laborer at an enterprise	1 year junior high school
ELODIE age: 39	Sakalava FA: unknown (Merina?, left before she was born) MO: Sakalava	t-t born in Ambanja	15–20: 1st husband (CL); 21–present: 2nd husband (CL), separated 1 year, has had 6 children, 2 dead	15: Lava Sanga (C) 35: Mampiary (GC)	17–25: worked at tapioca factory; 25–34: worked off and on at other plantations or enterprises; 35–present: works in bar; owns her house and 2 others in neighborhood; no clients but attends ceremonies	part of junior high school

(continued)

Medium Name/Age	Ethnicity	Residence Status	Marriage/Children	Possession History	Economic Activities	Schooling
			Tromba Mediums: Female			
ELISABETH (10) age: 42	Sakalava FA/MO: Sakalava	t-t, born in small village near Ambanja	17–20: first husband (CL); 21(?): 2nd husband (CL) live together off and on for 12 years, 2 children	5: signs of tromba; 7: Child spirit instated (name unknown); by age 15 two other spirits, one a Child (Kotofanzava?), the other a Grandparent; by age 35: two other tromba (1C, 1 GP) instated. All spirits exorcised in 1984 by FJKM church	earned money as a medium; supported by husband; sells produce in the market and from her home. Owns some farmland in the countryside	finished primary school
ZALOKY (2, 10) age: 50	Sakalava FA/MO: Sakalava	t-t, born in Ambanja	16–35: 1st husband (CL), widowed, 4 children 30 +; 40–50: 2nd husband (CL, later PW), no other children	32: Zaman'i'Bao (C) 40: exorcised by Lutheran Protestants	she owns her house and small rice field; present husband works part-time at enterprise, he is also a night watchman; they sell scrap material, beg for food; in the past she received clients as a medium, attended ceremonies	finished primary school
			Saha at Nosy Faly			
DADIBE or AÑEVA, ("Beauty") age: 39	Antakarana FA/MO: Antakarana	t-t, born on Nosy Faly 25?–31: Toamasina 31–present: Nosy Faly, now lives in tomb village, saha for founding ancestor of the Bemazava	21?–31: 1st husband (CL), separated, has 2 children, ages 20 and ?	25: Tontoño, Kotomavila and Raleva (C) 33: Andriantoemponiarivo (royal tromba) (GP) (following death of previous saha)	previous work? present: in addition to being saha, sells matches and sugar	some primary school
MBOTISOA age: 50	Sakalava FA/MO: Sakalava	t-t, born in village near Ambanja 44: moved to Nosy Faly, as saha, lives in tomb village	married 25 + years (T), 44: widowed, 3(?) children over 30 years	first after age 20, 2nd before age 40; 40: royal tromba (Andriamandefitriarivo?) (GP)	works as saha, supported by villagers and royalty who visit	some primary school

Male Mediums

ROMAIN age: 30	Betsileo FA: Betsileo MO: Sakalava	settler?; born in Analalava, has lived in Mahajanga, Fianarantsoa, Nosy Be, Ambilobe; arrived in Ambanja 2 yrs. ago	22–25: 1st wife, (CL), separated, 1 child, lives with ex-wife in Ambilobe	24: Boxer (GC) (would not disclose name; very violent)	28–present: runs small grocery (sells matches, kerosene, and rum); works as sikidy (diviner), occasionally attends ceremonies	1 year junior high school
GABY age: 38	Sakalava FA/MO: Sakalava	t-t, born in village near Ambanja 18: moved to Ambanja	29–36: 1st wife, (CL), separated, no children	16: Raleva (C) 37: Raovoay (C)	18–present: carpenter; receives clients, attends ceremonies	finished primary school

Possession Sickness Only #

VIVIENNE* (10) age: 15	Tsimihety FA: Tsimihety MO: Sakalava (MO died when Vivienne was 12)	child of settler, considers self t-t, born in village near Ambanja; 12–13: Ambanja; 14–present: at school in Ambilobe	single, no children	14–present: njarinintsy? insane (adala)? attempts at exorcism by Lutheran and FJKM churches and FJKM Pentecostal retreat	under the care of FA's brother and his wife (Ambilobe) and MO's sister (Ambanja)	presently enrolled in junior high school in Ambilobe
SOSOTRA (9) age: 19	Sakalava FA/MO: Sakalava	born in village near Ambanja	single, pregnant	19: njarinintsy dropped out of school, pregnant	unemployed	1 year high school
SYLVIE age: 21	Sakalava FA/MO: Sakalava	t-t, born in Ambanja 18–20: Nosy be; 21–present: Ambanja	19–present: 1st husband (CL); 20: 1 pregnancy, miscarried, treated at hospital	20–present: njarinintsy, 1st attack 1 week after miscarriage	18–20: worked for sugarcane enterprise, Nosy Be	1 year junior high school
VICTORIA (10) age: 32	Sakalava FA/MO: Sakalava	t-t, born in village near Ambanja; 19–30: Diégo; 30–present: Ambanja	22–present: 1st husband (CL), 3 children, ages 8, 6, 3; abortion age 30	30–32: njarinintsy soon after husband learned of abortion; kin brought her to wide assortment of healers; fits stopped when brought to asylum in Diégo (and when separated from abusive husband)	secretary in local government office	finished university

(continued)

KEY

Names and circumstances from personal histories have been altered slightly to conceal the identity of these informants.
Mediums are listed chronologically by age.

Personal details:

Alima (10): name of medium, followed by chapter in which she is mentioned.

19–20: age in 1987.

Resident status:

t-t tera-tany.

settler: informant plans to settle permanently in Ambanja.

child of migrant: unless stated otherwise, "child of migrant" means that at least one parent was born elsewhere and moved to Ambanja.

(gp): next to "child of migrant" means that it was a grandparent who moved to Ambanja. Thus the parents of the possessed person are children of migrants. In these cases, the medium considers herself to be be tera-tany and not vahiny.

Marriage status/children: †

		Possession history: #	
(CL):	common law	(GC):	Grandchild spirit	tromba
(T):	traditional (Sakalava)	(C):	Child tromba spirit	
(CW):	Catholic wedding	(GP):	Grandparent spirit	tromba
(IW):	Islamic wedding			
(PW):	Protestant wedding			

* Alice & Berthine are sisters; Vivienne is their classificatory sister (their mothers are sisters).

† Many informants have had (or do have) temporary lovers; an assumption of the label "marriage" is that the couple lives in the same household and they consider one another to be "spouses" (vady). Also, the number of children refers to live births unless stated otherwise.

For other cases of possession sickness preceding tromba mediumship, see: Angeline, Leah, Marie, Beatrice, and Miriamo, above. *Economic activities: Work* refers to *wage labor.* Mediums who are unemployed are housewives. Activities as spirit mediums are listed under this column since personal consultations with clients and participation in ceremonies bring income into the medium's house, albeit indirectly through her spirits.

Notes

NOTES TO CHAPTER ONE

1. The Bemazava are the northernmost branch of Sakalava, who today comprise the fifth largest ethnic group in Madagascar (see chapter 3). Although *Bemazava-Sakalava* is the most precise term used to refer to the inhabitants of the Sambirano Valley, it is also very cumbersome. As a result, throughout this study I will refer to them simply as the *Sakalava*, except when discussing them in reference to historical developments or when comparing them to their neighbors, the *Bemihisatra-Sakalava* who live to the south on the main island and on the smaller offshore island of Nosy Be.

2. The term *tromba* can be confusing for non-Malagasy speakers, since this label is used to describe the possession experience, possession as a religious institution (both specifically among the Sakalava and as a more general, blanket term throughout Madagascar), a particular category of spirits, and a medium who is possessed by this type of spirit. In addition, as explained in the textual notes, there is no difference between singular and plural forms in dialects of Malagasy: one determines number by context or by other signifiers ("one tromba" compared with "three tromba," for example). In this study I have sought to clarify the meaning of the word *tromba* by using the following phrases throughout the text: "tromba spirit," "tromba possession," and "tromba medium." Where the term *tromba* appears alone, it refers to tromba as a religious institution.

3. This population figure is based on data from the 1986 census (Madagascar 1986).

4. Morgan has described the latter stance as follows: "Not all critical anthropologists adhere to orthodox Marxism. Some prefer a phenomenological and humanistic, yet politically informed, approach to sickness and healing" (1990: 945).

5. The original French spelling of this word was *malgachization*. Throughout this study I will use *malagasization*, which reflects the post-Revolution pronunciation.

6. I do not seek to provide a detailed history of Madagascar; for discussions on precolonial and colonial periods see especially M. Brown (1978); Ellis (1985); Heseltine (1971); Stratton (1964); and Thompson and Adloff (1965).

7. For a discussion of the problems encountered by African nations in the transition to socialism see Munslow (1986; as well as other authors in Munslow, ed. 1986); and Fagen et al. (1986).

8. A functional analysis is, to some extent, inevitable, however, since it will underlie any study in which the author seeks to answer the question *why* spirit possession occurs in a particular cultural setting or point in time. My point here is that functionalism is not the primary theoretical approach found in the writings of the authors listed here (who would, no doubt, argue against the suggestion that it is there at all).

9. There are numerous examples of the application of the marginality or deprivation argument, including those that predate I.M. Lewis's seminal article (1966); for a sampling, see Beattie (1961); Gomm (1975); Harris (1957); and Shack (1971).

10. It is not my purpose here to provide an exhaustive overview of different interpretations of possession, but rather, through a sampling, to give the reader a sense of the nature of this complex debate. A common pattern in studies of possession is to provide such an overview, and so I defer to my predecessors rather than duplicate their efforts. For two informative and succinct discussions see Lambek (1981, especially chaps. 4 and 5) and Morsy (1991).

11. These conceptions of *self* and *person* are derived from Mauss (1987) and will be discussed in detail in chapter 7.

12. *The New York Times, Le Monde,* and other newspapers ran stories on the attempted coup that occurred in the summer of 1991. As a result, some reporters at that time sought to give their readers a glimpse of Malagasy culture.

13. Feeley-Harnik's careful study, *A Green Estate,* provides a new and detailed analysis of the Bemihisatra-Sakalava of Analalava. In the context of the discussion here, it represents an important shift away from high plateaux studies. In addition, within the past two years there has been increased activity in the south and on the coasts, especially involving ecological studies.

14. Many towns and cities in Madagascar have more than one name: a foreign name (usually given by the French) and a Malagasy one. Throughout this study I will follow current practice in Madagascar and use Malagasy names. The one exception is Diégo-Suarez (a name given to this northern port by Portuguese explorers). *Antsiranana* is the Malagasy name for this provincial capital (as well as the corresponding province), yet people living in the north prefer to refer to it affectionately as *Diégo.* I have decided, likewise, to refer to it as *Diégo,* since this prevents readers from confusing *Antsiranana* with *Antananarivo* (both cities are referred to frequently in the text).

15. Out of respect for the privacy of my informants and assistants, I have sought for the most part to conceal their identities. Thus, all names that appear here are pseudonyms unless the party requested otherwise or where it would

be impossible to conceal who they are (such as current rulers). In addition, case studies are usually composites of several informants, and the majority of place names have been altered.

NOTES TO CHAPTER TWO

1. Two species of shade trees predominate here. The Malagasy names for them are *montany* and *bonara*. I have been unable to identify their scientific names.

2. See Gade (1984) for an interesting discussion of ylang-ylang fields creating a "smell-defined space" in Nosy Be.

3. This was still under construction in January 1988.

4. Because of a paucity of literature on the history of the northern Saka-lava—and coastal peoples in general—much of the data acquired for this chapter have been drawn from the oral historical accounts of informants. The most valuable written sources for general background information on this region are: Baré (1980, 1982); Boucabeille (1897); Dalmond (1840); De Foort (1907); Dury (1897); and Mellis (1936); see also Feeley-Harnik (1978, 1982, 1991b), Lombard (1988), and Raison-Jourde, ed. (1983).

5. As I noted in chapter 1, throughout this study I will use the general term *Sakalava* to refer to the indigenous inhabitants of the Sambirano. Since this present chapter addresses their historical origins, I have taken care to refer to them by their exact name, the Bemazava (branch of the) Sakalava. I also use this term here so as to distinguish the Bemazava from the Bemihisatra-Sakalava, their neighbors who live to the south and on Nosy Be.

6. For more detailed accounts of Sakalava royal history, see, for example, Baré (1973), Feeley-Harnik (1978, 1982, 1988, 1991b), Guillain (1845), Lombard (1988), Noël (1843), Raison-Jourde (1983, especially the map on p. 44), Schlemmer (1983), and Valette (1958).

7. All Sakalava royalty will eventually have at least two names: the first is the name they use when they are alive, the second is a posthumous praise name (*fitahina* [Lombard: 1988]) which commemorates their great deeds. Thus, *An-driantompoeniarivo* means "the king who was worshiped by the multitudes" (*andrian-*, royal prefix; *tompoeny* "to honor, worship"; *arivo*, "thousand" or "many"). Since many royalty also become tromba spirits after they die, this second name is often referred to as the "tromba name" (*ny ianarana ny tromba*). Although today very few people honor the rule, in the past it was *fady* or taboo to utter a royal person's living name after he or she had died. In general, I will respect this rule, except where it becomes necessary to distinguish the living person from the spirit. The significance of this rule will become clear in Part 2.

8. For analyses of the ritual and other symbolic applications of the Sakalava expression "each/both," see Feeley-Harnik's (1991b) ethnography of the Analalava region.

9. In the case of Millot, 80 percent of his lands were acquired through the French government, the other 20 percent from sales by private farmers.

10. The reasons for this are complex and I will not detail them here. Simply put, Millot has remained private as a result of the shrewd understanding on the part of the company's managers of the laws and restrictions that affect private ownership and international trade in Madagascar.

11. De la Motte St. Pierre's property has changed names and ownership several times throughout the century. By the 1920s it was referred to as the Société Agricole du Sambirano. In 1929 some lands were sold to the Compagnie Nosybéenne d'Industries Agricoles (CNIA). By the 1930s it went by the name of Compagnie de Cultures Coloniales (CCC) and then in the 1950s became the Compagnie de Cultures Cacayères (CCC). It appears to have eventually merged with CNIA, and then in 1964 all CCC holdings were divided into two farms: CNIA, based in the village of Ambohimena, and SOMIA (Société Malgache d'Industrie et d'Agriculture) in Bejofo. Regardless of these transactions, the present holdings of CNIA and SOMIA are roughly equivalent to what de la Motte St. Pierre had laid claim to at the turn of the century.

12. A hectare is equivalent to ten thousand square meters or approximately 2.47 acres.

13. Similarly, the prison in Analalava provided labor for that region as well (Feeley-Harnik 1991b: 7).

14. As Feeley-Harnik describes in her account of the Analalava region, movement and relocation are very much a part of Sakalava *royal* history, as each ruler seeks to establish a new residence following the death of his or her predecessor: royal death pollutes the earth, making it too "hot" (*mafana*) and "filthy" (*maloto*) for future habitation. In reference to the period of French occupation, however, she reports: "By the early twentieth century, Sakalava . . . were not known for moving about like Tsimihety, Merina, or Betsileo. On the contrary, French ethnographers since the turn of the century described the Sakalava as dying out in the face of more vigorous competitors for their land" (1991b: 2).

15. This remark also serves as an illustration of Malagasy attitudes toward other African peoples. The word *Senegal* is Malagasy slang for non-Malagasy peoples of African descent. Also, cannibalism is a theme that is reiterated by Malagasy when they seek to distinguish themselves from other African peoples of the mainland.

The ambivalence felt by the Bemazava toward the French is reflected in a story told by an informant in reference to this event. His father, a man who was appointed as a local official by the French, spoke harshly to Verdure of the incident and reminded him that his forces had been invited to the Sambirano so that they could help the Bemazava, not so that they could murder them.

16. For a vivid example of the introduction of clocks in southern Africa see Comaroff and Comaroff (1991: xi).

NOTES TO CHAPTER THREE

1. The "official" number of ethnic groups fluctuates over time, as is reflected by earlier national censuses. Thus, for 1950 there were eleven ethnic categories;

in 1959, nineteen; in 1968 and 1971, twenty. These changes have occurred as a result, for example, of the decision of whether or not to include the peoples of the island of St. Marie as a separate ethnic group (St. Marians hold dual Malagasy and French citizenship). In addition, at one time a group may be delegated to a separate category, and at other times it is subsumed under a larger one. Several groups, who were conquered or dominated by Sakalava, are often included under the Sakalava label. These are the Makoa, who are the descendants of African slaves; the Vezo, a fishing people of the southwest; and their neighbors, the Masikoro, who are herders and cultivators (Astuti 1991; Kottak 1986: 3; Lombard 1986). Little is known about the Mikea, who are forest-dwelling hunter-gatherers, and so they may not appear on maps or in census materials (Fanony 1986). Dez (1964) provides a brief discussion of the number of recognized ethnic groups after Independence.

2. Following a system established under the French colonial government, today the national political system of Madagascar is arranged hierarchically in national, provincial, county, (in the past, district), and city governments. The lowest level in the hierarchy consists of households; these are grouped into neighborhood administrative units. Each neighborhood elects a president. His (or her) main duties include hearing disputes among local residents and serving as their local representative in the city government. All newly arrived residents are expected to register with the neighborhood president, providing their name, age, the number of members of their household, and information on their point of origin and sometimes their ethnicity. One of the purposes of these logbooks is to collect census data for the national government.

3. Another interpretation of the term *Sakalava,* given to me by an informant, is that it refers to the "long tresses" or braids that Sakalava men used to wear (see Feeley-Harnik 1988: 77).

4. A number of Malagasy informants expressed great anxiety over the scene in the film *2001: A Space Odyssey* when the astronaut's lifeline is cut by the computer, Hal, and his body sails out into space. Since it would be impossible to retrieve his body, it can never lie in the tomb with his ancestors.

5. As any traveler in the south knows, animals are prestige items among Malagasy pastoralists. Nowhere is this more obvious than in the territory of the Mahafaly, where the horns of zebu, sacrificed at funerals, are mounted on tombs. These may number more than one hundred on large tombs.

6. The exact origin of this term is unclear. Many informants thought it was a combination of the French and Sakalava words for "land" or "soil" (*terre* and *tany*), but more likely it is a compound word formed from the Sakalava terms *teraka* ("child/children") and *tany* ("land," "soil"), so that literally it means "children of the soil." The equivalent term used elsewhere in Madagascar is *tompo-tany* or *tompontany*, which means " masters" or "owners of the soil/ land" (cf. Bloch 1971; Feeley-Harnik 1991b). Lambek (1981: 17–19) reports that in Mayotte, the concept of *tompin* is also central. The most significant role associated with this status is that tompin elders have the final say in village affairs. As Feeley-Harnik has also remarked, the term *zanatany* ("children of the soil/land") is used in the Analalava region to refer to those who were born

locally, and it includes decendants of vahiny and tompontany. Thus, in Analalava, *zanatany* may be used to obscure differences between, essentially, insiders
and outsiders (personal communication). I have not heard the term *zanatany*
used in this manner in Ambanja however, and the use of the term *tompontany*
appears to mark differences in dialect in this community, since it is non-Sakalava
who employ it.

7. The population for the entire county (Fivondronana) was 93,791, of
which 493 were foreigners. The ratio of male to female was close to 1:1, with
46,508 men to 46,790 women. In the town of Ambanja the ratio for adults of
eighteen to fifty-nine years of age is 4,122 males: 4,185 females. The ratio drops
sharply at sixty years of age to 497: 277 for reasons I have yet to determine.

8. Throughout this study I will use Antandroy as a representative group for
southern peoples (such as Mahafaly and Bara), and Antaimoro for peoples of
the southeast (such as Antaisaka).

9. As Feeley-Harnik reveals in her study *A Green Estate*, which focuses on
the Bemihisatra-Sakalava in Analalava, movement is very much a part of Sakalava history and it takes several forms. First, following the death of each ruler,
his or her successor must move the *doany* or royal residence to a new location
because the earth is "filthy" and "hot" (*maloto sy mafana*). Disputes over
succession may also lead to migration (usually northward) as new dynasties are
established. Second, virilocal residence is the most common pattern of movement among commoners following marriage. Third, she describes how Sakalava
migrate as wage earners *within their own territory,* moving from rural villages
to the urban center (the "post") of Analalava in search of work or fortunes
(*hitady asa, hitady harena*). For a discussion of the tensions underlying local
labor migration see especially chapters 4 and 5 in her book.

10. See Astuti (1991: 234ff) on the importance of distance (either symbolic
or actual) between village and tomb.

11. Again, very little has been written on the history of religion among the
Bemazava; in this section I will rely heavily on the works of Fr. Jaovelo-Dzao
(1983, 1987). Jaovelo is a priest who is Bemazava-Sakalava. He is trained as
an anthropologist and has written extensively on religion (including both traditional or indigenous Sakalava religion as well as those of foreign origin).

12. In contrast to the rigidness of Bemazava-Sakalava constructions of identity, Astuti (1991) has argued that the Vezo of southwest Madagascar perceive
their identity as being fairly flexible: "Vezoness" hinges not so much on place
of birth or kin ties but rather on skills that are associated with coastal life.
These include, for example, fishing, boat building, and being able to walk on
sand. If a person fails to perform in such ways, then he or she is not Vezo.

13. Kottak (1980: 170) has noticed a similar pattern in his comparative
study of two villages of highland Betsileo: "As descendants of the first settlers,
all Tranovondro claim superior status (as *tompotany* [SAK: *tera-tany*], owners
or caretakers of the land) to more recent immigrants, who have obtained their
estates through purchase, grants, and Merina policy. Yet only the senior Tranovondro of Ivato—the ceremonial, judicial political and economic center of a
major rice plain region—invoke this claim." Again, compare Lambek (1981:
17–19) for the case of Mayotte.

NOTES TO CHAPTER FOUR

1. Malagasy often have several names. The first is the name given at birth, which may or may not be accompanied by a family name. If the family is Christian, a child will acquire a Christian name when he or she is baptized, and this will be the name used on official documents. Family members may continue to address them by their original name or by their Christian name. Many people also have nicknames, such as Boba (after a cartoon character) and Mme Tsarazanaka, or "the Lady [with the] beautiful children." Adults change their names following the birth of the first child, adopting a teknonym (thus Papan'i'Vero and Maman'i'Vero are "Father/Mother of Vero"). Although the teknonym is the most commonly used name when addressing adults, I have decided to use the birth or Christian name instead, since most readers will find the teknonyms confusing.

2. The drought in the south has been so severe in recent years that some villages rely on government trucks to bring water.

3. The salary that Roland paid his workers was high by Malagasy standards: a well-paid male laborer at one of the better enterprises might make 35,000 fmg, which is slightly higher than the salary paid to a junior high school teacher with a high school degree. In terms of the cost of living in Madagascar, 30,000 fmg would buy enough rice to feed a family of two adults and two small children; 1,500 fmg per month would cover the rent for a small house (with one or two rooms) made from traveler's palm.

4. The full ramifications of this will be discussed in detail in chapter 9.

5. When I began this study in Ambanja, I had assumed that blood-brotherhood and blood-sisterhood (fatidra) would be used by migrants to establish ties in the community (see Tegnaeus 1952; also Feeley-Harnik 1991b: 271ff). Throughout the course of my fieldwork, however, I found no evidence of this happening. As Part 2 will show, other forms of fictive kinship are operative, especially within the context of tromba possession.

6. Because this study focuses primarily on the everyday lives of commoners in Ambanja, what appears here is an oversimplification of Sakalava royal social structure. For a more detailed discussion, especially in regard to the complexities and dilemmas associated with male as opposed to female royal descent, see Feeley-Harnik (1991b, especially chap. 2).

7. Today in the Sambirano few informants can recall how Bemazava kinship operated prior to French contact or in the early colonial period. As a result, I am relying heavily here on Feeley-Harnik (1982, 1984, 1991b) and Baré (1980, especially chap. 4, pp. 179–235). Also note that Feeley-Harnik (1991b) prefers to translate firazaña as "ancestries."

8. Here Baré is drawing from Goody's (1958) discussion of optative kinship, as well as Goodenough (1956) on unrestricted systems (see also Baré 1980: 185).

9. Highlanders especially delight in the Sakalava tendency to adopt French terms, often applying them in creative—and, as the following examples reflect, bawdy—ways. In 1987, two popular terms for women's panties were *garde-*

manger ("pantry") and *je t'aime* ("I love you," which is a reference to imported undergarments that had phrases like this embroidered on them).

10. From a Sakalava point of view, unions cemented by a ceremony and common-law unions are both considered to be forms of marriage (*manambady*). I will therefore use the term *marriage* as my informants did, referring to any relationship where both members of a couple referred to each other as *vady* ("spouse") and where they inhabited the same domicile.

11. I wish to thank Michael Lambek for drawing my attention to the fact that these differences existed during a visit to my field site. For comparative data see his brief discussion of "rangginalu" in Mayotte (1992: 242).

12. Ranginalo appears to be unique to the northern Sakalava. Although Baré makes no mention of ranginalo among the Bemihisatra-Sakalava of Nosy Be, Feeley-Harnik reports that the Bemihisatra of Analalava identify ranginala as Sakalava, saying it is "stronger" (see discussion below) than mafana (for which highlanders are the archetypal example) (personal communication). According to my informants in Ambanja, the southern Sakalava of the Morondava region (Menabe) are mifana (mafana). Antakarana who live to the north of the Sambirano are mifana or "hot" like other Malagasy.

13. Bloch, in his treatments of Merina burial (1982) and circumcision (1986) rituals, also speaks of this opposition between hot and cold. Hot is associated with women, who are polluting and disruptive to the harmony of the collective or deme; cold is associated with harmony, collectivity, and the tomb. Bloch acknowledges that heat is associated with childbirth for the Merina, but he overlooks the healing powers of heat that characterize postpartum practices.

14. Tensions between maternal and paternal ties appear to be historically rooted, at least in the context of royal succession. Feeley-Harnik (1991b) writes of the dilemmas that arise with the shift that occurred through the selection of heirs who were "children of women" (zanaka[n] vavy) rather than "children of men" (zanaka[n] lahy). In a discussion of this theme Noël has also stated that "paternity [has] always been considered dubious among the Sakalava, because of the extreme laxity of morals" (1843, vol. 19: 292, as quoted in Feeley-Harnik 1991b: 82).

NOTES TO CHAPTER FIVE

1. Authors generally refer to tromba as being the spirits of Sakalava *princes.* This is, however, misleading, since both male and female members of royal lineages may become tromba. Throughout the province of Diégo (Antsiranana) there are a number of well-known female tromba: for example, the royal Bemazava lineage has several female spirits. The term *prince* is misleading as well, because it implies not only the absence of princesses, but also of kings and queens. For these reasons I prefer to use the term *royalty* when referring to rulers and other members of their lineages.

2. Tsiaraso III, who is the present Bemazava king, does on occasion visit Nosy Faly.

3. *Atsimo* is the name of the tomb in Mahajanga province in which these

royalty are entombed (Ramamonjisoa, personal communication). Some informants also say that the name is derived from *tsimo,* which means "wind." The term refers to the idea that tromba are out in the air when they are neither in the tomb nor in a medium.

4. In Ambanja, early June is often a time of much tromba. Following this, however, are "taboo months" *(fanjava fady)* for certain categories of spirits: mid-June to mid-July is fady for Bemihisatra spirits, and the period from mid-July to mid-August is fady for the Bemazava. These taboo months are associated with times when royal work (fanampoaña) is being performed at their respective tombs. Since this period is associated with death and danger, it is said that the tomb "door is closed" *(mifody ny varavaraña)* so that the royal spirits may not leave and possess the living. Similarly, tromba possession is also forbidden during any month when a member of the royal family has died. The month when the door is once again open *(mibiaña)* is August *(Volambita).* Finally, if there is an eclipse, no tromba possession may occur during that month.

5. In this study, I wish to distinguish between *spirit possession* and *trance,* the former referring to the experience as it is socially defined and constructed, the latter describing the physiological changes felt by the medium. In other words, *possession* refers to Sakalava perceptions of the spirit, as it takes control of the medium's body, and *trance* refers to the medium's altered state of consciousness. I am not certain if all of the mediums I observed actually entered trance (Sakalava stress that there is "fake" tromba: *tromba mavandy* or "tromba who lie"), but since trance is assumed by Sakalava to be part of the medium's experience I, too, will assume that the majority experienced this altered state of consciousness.

6. A valiha is a type of zither made from a large piece of bamboo. It is held vertically in the lap and the strings are plucked with the fingers and thumbs. It is unusual to find a valiha player at a ceremony in Ambanja, since today there are very few musicians in the area who know how to play this instrument.

7. Students in Ambanja and other coastal areas lag behind highland children in their schooling; it is not unusual for junior high school students to be in their late teens and for high school students to graduate when they are in their early twenties. In addition, Angeline's experience with njarinintsy possession typifies that of many adolescent schoolgirls. These topics will be discussed in chapter 9.

8. According to compass direction, the closest royal tombs are at Nosy Faly and lie north of Ambanja. The spirits who appear at Angeline's ceremony all come from tombs in the south (boka atsimo), near Mahajanga.

9. As Feeley-Harnik explains, this is a form of mead used at royal celebrations and to cleanse filth associated with death or wrongdoing (1991b: 594).

10. Spirits' names appear in capital letters to designate when they arrive.

11. Tromba, of course, as royal ancestors, are also razaña. To avoid confusion, I will use the term *razaña* only when referring to the ancestors of commoners.

12. Lambek (1981: 70ff) refers to this as the "communication triad" of possession, which involves the sender (host or medium), the receiver (spirit), and the intermediary (others with whom the spirit converses).

13. One informant stated that in the past individuals with leprosy could not be placed in the family tomb. I am not sure if this was true, since the disease does not appear to be stigmatized today.

14. Non-Sakalava Protestants, too, honor their dead at this time but, as I heard a Lutheran pastor stress during a sermon, they were not to leave goods such as honey or rum at the gravesites to *feed* the dead, since this is a pagan Malagasy custom (fomba-gasy). They could, however, leave flowers or candles to *honor* them.

15. Feeley-Harnik describes lolo as spirits who have not achieved ancestor status (1991b: 405); see also Lombard's discussion (1988: 117ff). Astuti (1991) reports that among the Vezo *lolo* means "tomb" and it is thus equated with known ancestors.

16. For the Highland Merina, *vazimba* are the spirits of the little people who are said to be the island's original inhabitants. See also Lombard (1988: 17) on the southern Sakalava of Menabe.

17. The term *njarinintsy* is often capitalized; since there is not one but a multitude of njarinintsy spirits I have decided not to capitalize this term in the text (compare, however, Sharp 1990). Feeley-Harnik translates Njarinintsy as "Mother Cold" while my informants in Ambanja defined it as "The Fellow/ The One who is Cold."

18. Among my informants, however, a few were skeptical about this structural affinity to tromba; these tended to be members of the Bemazava royal lineage. They stated that more recent tromba spirits, such as Mampiary, Be Ondry, and Djao Kondry are not tromba spirits but simply njarinintsy who have taken names and who are trying to achieve royal status. According to Feeley-Harnik (1991a: 88), "be hondry," like njarinintsy and "masantoko," is an evil spirit (lolo) who possesses in order to kill.

19. Heurtebize (1977) has described this form of possession among the Antandroy. He reports that a decade ago Antandroy sometimes returned from the north with a new form of possession, called *doany,* which means "tomb," but by 1987 doany possession was rare (Heurtebize, personal communication). See also Lombard's description of bilo among the southern Sakalava of Menabe (1988: 17). Finally, for an intriguing discussion of bilo and economic change among the Masikoro see Fieloux and Lombard (1989).

NOTES TO CHAPTER SIX

1. For an example from the Betsileo see Kus (1984).

2. The oldest category (Grandparents) reveals the greatest amount of "collapsing" of generations. In other words, the names of some spirits have been forgotten. Still, I wish to stress here that the genealogy in figure 6.1 spans two centuries of Sakalava history (this should be clearer through a comparison with figure 2.3). Others are much deeper than this one.

3. In other regions of Madagascar (especially the highlands) *lambamena* is the term used for a burial shroud. Other names for cloths that are worn by tromba mediums during possession are *kokoy* (these are generally white cotton cloths with striped borders; they are similar to the *kikoi* of coastal Kenya) and

the purple striped, cotton *soboya* (from Arabic, *sobaiha*[?]). Originally the latter were made of handwoven silk and were imported by Comorean and Arab merchants from Arabia. Kokoy were also handwoven, although I am not sure if they were imported or made locally. Now they are produced by factories in Madagascar. For a more detailed discussion of Sakalava textiles see Feeley-Harnik (1991a).

4. I was never able to learn why these tromba spirits have towels. Terrycloth is a coveted imported item and I assume that it is associated with European customs of bathing because these tromba wash their hands fairly frequently and they use the towel for drying. One informant, with whom I traveled, gave me a long lecture on how Europeans are unclean, because they do not bathe as often as Sakalava, and told me that when a person bathes the upper body alone this is called a *douche vazaha* ("European shower").

5. *Andrian/m-* and *Ndran/m-* are variants of the same prefix, which signifies royal descent.

6. Spirits that dress like Mampiaminy appear to be more common to the south in, for example, the Analalava region (see Feeley-Harnik's description, 1991a: 110, n. 16) and Mahajanga (as she in turn reports the account in Estrade 1977: 59).

7. According to the 1986 census, the total population of Ambanja was 26,288 (25,945 nationals, who are almost exclusively Malagasy, and 343 foreigners or *étrangers*). The population by age group (male and female) was as follows:

> 0–5 years: 5,182
> 6–17 years: 11,682
> 18–59 years: 8,307
> 60 and up: 774

8. Sugar plantations were established in Nosy Be in the eighteenth century; sugar was also one of the first cash crops planted in the Sambirano (see chapter 2). Rum would have been available to the Sakalava earlier than this, since it was already being distilled on other islands of the Indian Ocean. Rum may also have been produced locally from other vegetable sources.

9. The third crop of importance here is cocoa. Interestingly, it is not recognized as a taboo for any tromba. I often joked with informants that it was only a matter of time before it, like coffee and cashews, became an important *fady*, a suggestion that most mediums found to be ridiculous.

10. For other discussions of the symbolic meanings associated with money cross-culturally, see, for example, Shipton (1989) and Taussig (1980a, especially chap. 7).

11. For example, in the town of Ambanja, tromba ceremonies are generally held inside people's houses. Passersby become aware of tromba because they can hear the music, but they cannot see the mediums. This is quite different from the countryside, where open-air, shaded platforms are built in the center of villages to serve as the sites for tromba cermonies. Perhaps this practice occurred because villagers rarely fell under the scrutiny of colonial officials whereas townsfolk had to be wary of their watchful eye. (The mediums who

appear in plate 6 are sitting on such a platform.) See also the platform ("meeting house" or *fatsina*) that appears in Feeley-Harnik (1991b: plate 29, p. 336).

12. This action on his part is highly unusual (and fady) for a Sakalava king. Rulers should only "visit" royal tombs after they have died. Tsiaraso I's actions may perhaps be attributed to the fact that he is Catholic and is also somewhat uncomfortable in general about being an ambanjakabe.

NOTES TO CHAPTER SEVEN

1. *Self* and *person* are generally overlapping or may even be indistinguishable since the concept of an individually, psychologically conceived self is not universal cross-culturally. In the context of tromba possession, however, they are in some ways distinguished by private and public realms. For a medium, selfhood is a private or personal experience, and it is in this sense that I use the term, as Mauss did.

2. A detailed discussion of this process extends beyond the scope of this present study. Suffice it to say here that the level of self-reflection that occurs, for example, in the context of Western schools of psychiatry and psychology is not something that characterizes Malagasy culture (see Sharp, in press). If we assume that language shapes in part the way we perceive the world, the Malagasy language is structured in such a way so that the speaker will avoid drawing attention to himself or herself. For example, a common Malagasy sentence structure is the passive voice, where the first-person pronoun often drops out completely. Thus, individuals who speak at too great a length about their problems are perceived as egotistical and rude (for a discussion of this among Vakinankaratra see Keenan 1974).

3. Ideally, these should be zanakan' vavy and zanakan' lahy, or "children of women" and "children of men" (for a detailed discussions of the significance of these categories in royal rituals see Feeley-Harnik 1991b). This complementarity of male and female in ritual contexts is something Malagasy share with Melanesian peoples (Betsy Traube, personal communication).

4. Two of the nineteen women surveyed were infertile. I am also unsure if three others had been pregnant prior to becoming a medium. One of the two men interviewed was married prior to possession. Figure 7.1, which provides information on total number of marriages, also reveals that mediums, throughout the course of their possession histories are similar to a significant number of adults in the general population, since they have been engaged in more than one union in their lifetimes.

5. Although a few mediums I encountered had acquired their spirits in adolescence, I know of only three cases of children possessed by tromba. Elisabeth first showed signs of possession around age six, and by age seven her parents had hosted a ceremony to have a Child spirit instated in her. I also saw a young girl (about age eight) become possessed by Mampiary during the course of a royal Antakarana ceremony. Finally, Alice claimed that that she first showed signs of possession by three tromba spirits around age six, although no spirits were instated until much later (again, see Appendix A). These three cases are

unusual, and the authenticity of such stories are questioned by Sakalava: when one of my assistants heard that Alice claimed to have become a medium at such an early age, she said: *"ma! mavandy izy é!"* ("what! oh—she's lying!").

6. To compare a human being to a dog is probably the most derogatory statement that one can make about another person in Madagascar. In this context, Perline uses it to stress how dire Basely's situation is.

7. Most often, the reasons given for not performing fatidra in Ambanja were either that the ceremony was too expensive or that the informant did not know how to do it. It is still common practice, however, elsewhere in Madagascar. Huntington, for example, has a Bara blood-brother (1973 and personal communication). Descriptions from Sakalava territory can be found in Lombard (1988: 84), who describes in detail the materials needed for the ceremony, and Feeley-Harnik (1991: 271ff).

8. *Miralahy* ("brothers") and *miravavy* ("sisters") are terms of reference. Terms of address used by siblings are *zoky* (for an older sibling) and *zandry* (for a younger sibling) (see chapter 4).

9. In Haitian vodou, mediums (female or male) may choose to marry a spirit. In doing so, she or he must save one day out of the week for the spirit spouse: on such days the medium may not date or have sexual intercourse. In return, the spirit is a benevolent guide and caretaker in ways that parallel those of a loving spouse (Brown 1991: 248, 306ff). In the Sudan, a medium may be a bride of zar, where medium and spirit have sexual relations (I.M. Lewis 1991: 3). Crapanzano also describes the Moroccan Tuhami's relationship with the she-demon 'A'isha Qandisha as a sexual one (1983). Tromba possession in Ambanja is not described as a sexual relationship, however.

10. I encountered no married men with spirits. I assume that a man's wife would address her husband's spirit as "brother-in-law" (rañao), since a man's spirit is his brother.

11. Lambek (1988b) also provides an account of this, describing its psychological significance for the children of mediums in Mayotte. In Alice's household the process is very much the same.

12. If they are lovers, potentially this relationship would set up interesting structural parallels with male rangahy, since Marie might be conceived of as Monique's spouse in the context of tromba. I do not have enough data on this at this time, and to date I have not seen references to other similar relationships in the literature on tromba.

13. As will become clear in chapter 10, Protestant exorcists, seeking to undermine the authority of tromba spirits, will place their hands or the Bible on medium's heads.

14. Similarly, Lambek (1981: 9) reports for Malagasy speakers in Mayotte that "*asa* conveys a sense of seriousness and responsibility, an activity carried out in the context of long-range goals and of a moral system." It is used to refer to a large class of activities and performances, of which possession is one.

15. This is not a lot of money. In 1987, 50 fmg would buy five small bananas, and 100 fmg would buy a papaya or one cup of rice.

16. In Haitian vodou spirits also make loans. A client may prefer this, even at usurous rates that exceed credit card interest charges, because of the value

of the reciprocal bond (see the example in Brown 1991: 63ff). Kenyon (1991: chap. 6) also reports that zar leaders in the Sudan have begun to provide economic support to those in need.

17. There are different interpretations of this from elsewhere in Madagascar. Estrade has also recorded this proverb, translating it as "Teta's royal spirit, money appears." He states the expression is used to describe government officials who accept bribes; those who give such bribes are like the spirit Teta's victims who have been fooled by a fake tromba (Estrade 1977: 307; also reported in Feeley-Harnik 1991a: 111–112, n. 23). Raison-Jourde (1983: 58) and Chazan-Gillic (1983: 472) report that among the southern Sakalava *tromba antety* and tromba andrano are two opposing categories of spirits, the latter being "tromba of the earth" as opposed to those of the water.

NOTES TO CHAPTER EIGHT

1. There has been much debate in medical anthropology over the construction of an appropriate label for what is generally referred to as "Western biomedicine" (or some variant of this). Part of the problem is the propensity among many anthropologists to want to oppose things Western to all other systems. I find the label "bio-medicine" to be inadequate, since it emphasizes a *biological* model. It also implies that indigenous medicine cannot fit into this paradigm, although the biomedical properties of many local medicinal plants are now well known in such countries as Madagascar and the People's Republic of China, for example. Although I prefer the term "cosmopolitan" (see Dunn 1976), it, too, is problematic, since some assume that *cosmopolitan* implies *urban* (Dunn, however, does not intend it to be used in this way). Even though Malagasy use the terms "Malagasy" and "foreign" to distinguish the two, "foreign" is misleading, since it does not include practices that show influence from Arabs, Indians, Comoreans, and so forth. "Clinical" is a more appropriate label in Madagascar since it is the setting—the clinic—which provides the most distinguishing characteristic between "Western" and "traditional" or what I prefer to call "indigenous" Malagasy forms of healing.

2. One person's healer might be said to be another's sorceror, but as the story of the merchant's construction project shows (see below), there are self-professed sorcerors living in Ambanja.

3. My purpose here is to emphasize the pervasiveness of beliefs, not to prove or disprove the efficacy of treatments. Much has already been written on the power of belief in the context of magic and healing more generally. For different perspectives on this subject see Cannon (1942); Favret-Saada (1980); Lévi-Strauss (1963a, 1963b); Hahn and Kleinman (1983); and Moerman (1983).

4. In this discussion of medicine and healing practices I have chosen to use the term *indigenous* rather than *traditional* since the latter implies a static form from the past that never changes. *Indigenous* is also a problematic term, yet here it provides a satisfactory shorthand manner in which to distinguish Malagasy-derived healing practices from those that at least originally were of Western origin. In other words, I am relying on this term as a way to distinguish the

differences between fomba/fanafody-gasy (tromba, moasy, mpiskidy) and fomba/fanafody-vazaha (clinical medicine).

5. Although I have never attended a kalanoro ceremony, my understanding is that they, too, consult other spirits, including tromba. Informants report that these consultations are suspenseful—and even comical—since the kalanoro sometimes departs suddenly, asking its audience to wait while it goes to find out the details of the problem. Its return is sudden and surprising, the spirit's squeeky voice breaking the silence to inform the audience what it has just learned or seen elsewhere by speaking with ancestors or other spiritual parties.

6. The local pharmacopoeia has caught the attention of at least one local clinician, see Raherisoanjato (1985).

7. I heard versions of this story in Antananarivo, Nosy Be, Ambilobe, Diégo, and Ambanja. Interestingly, no violence occurred in Ambanja, although there were outbursts in neighboring towns. The same series of events have occurred at least twice in the last fifteen years in Madagascar.

8. Portions of this section have appeared elsewhere in a different context; see Sharp (1990).

9. The term *deuxième bureau* was coined by the French during World War II to refer to that branch of the military which was responsible for espionage activities.

10. Feeley-Harnik also notes that Bodofotsy is a common woman's name in the high plateaux (personal communication).

11. For a discussion of how Vezo fathers ritually claim their children, see Astuti (1991, especially chaps. 5 and 6).

12. This account, as well as the discussion of njarinintsy that follows in chapter 9, may lead the reader to believe that violence occurs frequently in this community. On the contrary, Malagasy are quite reserved, and violence—particularly in public—is very unusual. As a result, such behavior is thrown into high relief because it is such an extreme divergence from the norm.

NOTES TO CHAPTER NINE

1. This chapter draws in part from the descriptions and arguments presented in an earlier article: for more detailed discussions on the moral dilemmas faced by Ambanja's schoolchildren and the subsequent anomic and psychological consequences associated with town life and adolescence see Sharp (1990).

2. For simplicity's sake, in this chapter *njarinintsy* will serve as a blanket term for all forms of possession sickness described in chapter 5.

3. Njarinintsy, like tromba spirits, love music.

4. Feeley-Harnik reports that njarinintsy possession has existed in the Analalava region since at least the 1970s, and it continues to be deadly and chaotic in form.

5. This scenario is a composite drawn from the descriptions given by school officials, teachers, and other observers.

6. During the 1970s corporal punishment in schools was made illegal. This is the only circumstance I know of in Ambanja where striking a student is still permitted.

7. The responses to njarinintsy which are detailed here are those of public school administrators, the majority of whom grew up in this area of Madagascar. Although the Catholic church in Ambanja is far more accepting of Sakalava cultural practices than are Protestants and Muslims, Catholic school officials have refused to hold a joro. As a schoolteacher said, "This is, after all, a *Catholic* school." In 1987, however, I learned that the Catholic church did perform joro for newly constructed village churches. This conflict in policy may be a result of the fact that the head of the Catholic school is from the highlands and there are many Europeans teaching there. The monsignor of Ambanja, who supervises the building of the churches, is himself Sakalava and therefore is more respectful of local traditions. His actions also reflect the *enculturation* policies of the Church following Vatican II.

8. More detailed descriptions of Victoria's and Vivienne's stories appear in chapter 10. Vivienne, although she was only fifteen when I met her in 1987, had moved around considerably in the last few years. That summer she was living in Ambanja and was enrolled in school in Ambilobe, a town to the north.

9. Abortion is illegal in Madagascar, and for this reason it was very difficult to collect data on it in Ambanja. There are indigenous abortifacients available. In addition, there are a number of skilled M.D.s in the northern province who do a lucrative trade in performing abortions, and many of their clients are adolescent girls.

10. In 1987 I heard that an important school official in Ambanja gave an address at a national teachers' meeting where he argued that boys are equally responsible for pregnancy; members of the audience, however, did not show much interest in this idea.

11. Feeley-Harnik (personal communication) notes that in the 1970s in the Analalava region the spirit "Be Hondry" (Be Ondry) was considered a deadly and chaotic njarinintsy, but as of 1987 he has been elevated to the status of tromba and is recognized as having healing powers. A similar process may have occurred in Ambanja, where a few informants described Be Hondry and other Grandchildren spirits as njarinintsy.

12. As noted earlier in chapter 8, the concept of the traditional or traditionalism is highly problematic. I have chosen to use this terminology here since it underscores that this response among local Sakalava was unusual and marked a break from contemporary custom.

13. Today, throughout Madagascar, it is common practice to host a joro ceremony (or its equivalent) prior to the opening of a new state-owned building. Evidence of a past joro frequently can be seen in Antananarivo, for example, where the horns of sacrificed zebu cattle may rest atop fences and walls surrounding a factory.

NOTES TO CHAPTER TEN

1. Portions of this chapter appear in a discussion of therapeutic efficacy in another article (see Sharp, in press): these include the overview of fifohazana healing, the case studies of Elisabeth and Vivienne, and figure 10.1.

2. There is an extensive literature in anthropology which addresses the efficacy of indigenous healers in treating mental illness, as well as other forms of affliction (see Fabrega 1970; Janzen 1978; Kiev, ed. 1964; Kiev 1972; Lebra 1982; Lévi-Strauss 1963a, 1963b; Prince 1964; Sow 1980; Taussig 1987, 1989; Torrey 1986; V. Turner 1964).

3. Bloch (1971: 59–60) for example, gives a brief description of a visit to an asylum in the high plateaux. He reports that patients lived in great fear of witchcraft from "heart thieves" (*mpaka-fo*) because they were surrounded by strangers. In essence, the asylum is oftentimes little more than a prison (see also Sharp, in press).

4. A discussion of the applicability of psychiatric diagnoses cross-culturally is beyond the scope of this chapter. Several authors identify psychiatry as being most effective when applied to Western, middle-class whites (see, for example, Marsella and White, eds. 1982; Meltzer 1978; Pande 1968; Pederson 1982). Kleinman (1978, 1980) suggests that psychiatry can be applied effectively cross-culturally if the psychiatrist comprehends the patient's "explanatory model" of illness. Kleinman's stance has its limitations, however, since it overlooks the depth of the patient's subjective experience. He assumes that mainstream psychiatric practices can be effective as long as the psychiatrist has a grasp of the patient's cultural background. Also, as Pappas (1990) argues, Kleinman's model does not include an assessment of power within the therapeutic context. Thus I prefer to speak of competing epistemologies (Sharp, in press) since this emphasizes the complexity of the cross-cultural therapeutic encounter.

5. Spirit possession has long been a focus of interest for theologians; for other perspectives see, for example, Eikelman, Pazder, Peaston, and Salman in Prince, ed. (1968).

6. My informants did not describe spirits as occupying a second world apart from that of the living, as explained elsewhere in the literature (see Boddy 1989: 3ff, 269ff; Lambek 1981: 26; P. Stoller 1989, especially 48–49).

7. For an account of similar practitioners elsewhere in Madagascar see Mack (1986: 65) on the *katibo,* specialists who use sacred books called *sorabe.*

8. Until recently the Anglican church had no exorcists. This changed in 1987 when the Anglican bishop, who was a missionary from the United Kingdom, was trained as an exorcist by the Lutherans. He chose to do so not so much because he felt the need to drive out demons, but so that he could learn how to converse with and thus more effectively assist parishioners who believed that they were possessed.

9. These passages are central to defining the work of Pentecostal groups worldwide. For additional references see Goodman (1988); Jules-Rosette (1975); La Barre (1992 [1962]); and Sundkler (1961).

10. English text is taken from *The New English Bible* (Oxford and Cambridge University Presses, 1970); the Malagasy is taken from the Protestant Bible produced by Fikambanana Mampiely Baiboly Malagasy (1986).

11. For an analysis of the use of the active voice with animals see Bloch (1972).

12. Trexler (1989: 12) reports that a decade ago Lutheran exorcists would hit their patients with such force that in three cases they died; recently they

have become more restrained in their actions. I never saw an exorcist strike anyone.

13. As was explained earlier, Malalgasy kin terms and terms of address are determined by the sex of the speaker and the person to whom they are referring. Since the majority of exorcists come from the high plateaux and the south, they tend to use Merina and related terms, thus: *pirahadahy* "brothers," *pirahavavy* "sisters"; *rahavavy* "sister" for male speaker, *anabavy* "sister" for female speaker, and so forth. As with Sakalava, alternative terms of address are determined by relative age: *zoky* for "older sibling" and *zandry* for "younger sibling."

14. Elisabeth was reluctant to give the names of her exorcised spirits.

References

Achebe, Chinua
  1959   *Things Fall Apart*. New York: Ballantine Books.
Ackerman, S. E., and Raymond L. M. Lee
  1981   Communication and Cognitive Pluralism in a Spirit Possession
            Event in Malaysia. *American Ethnologist* (8) 4: 789–799.
Althabe, Gérard
  1969   *Oppression et Liberation dans l'Imaginaire: Les Com-
            munautés Villageoises de la Côte Orientale de Madagascar.*
            Paris: François Maspero.
  1980   Les Luttes Sociales à Tananarive en 1972. *Cahiers d'Etudes
            Africaines* 20: 407–447.
Andriamihamina, R., N. Trevet, T. de Commarmond, J-L. Rabenandrasana,
and R. Perier
  1987   *Ambanja, Etat Actuel.* Projet Urbain dans les Faritany, Service
            de l'Urbanisme et de l'Aménagement, Direction de l'Archi-
            tecture de l'Urbanisme et de l'Habitat, Direction Générale
            de l'Equipement, Ministère des Travaux Publics. Antana-
            narivo.
Anonymous
  1962   *Fanazavana momba ny Fifohazana.* Ambatoreny-Soatanana,
            Madagascar: publisher unknown [FJKM?].
Apter, Andrew
  1992   *Black Critics and Kings: The Hermeneutics of Power in
            Yoruba Society.* Chicago: University of Chicago Press.
Arens, W., and Ivan Karp
  1989   Introduction. In *Creativity of Power: Cosmology and Action
            in African Societies.* W. Arens and I. Karp, eds., xi–xxix.
            Washington, D. C.: Smithsonian Institution Press.

311

Ariès, Philippe
1965   *Centuries of Childhood: A Social History of Family Life.*
            Robert Baldick, trans. New York: Vintage Books.
Astuti, Rita
1991   *Learning to Be Vezo: The Construction of the Person among
            Fishing People of Western Madagascar.* Ph.D. diss., London
            School of Economics and Political Science.
Aubert, Jean-Marie
1987   L'Inculturation de l'Eglise Catholique dans le Nord de Mada-
            gascar. Paper presented at the Colloque d'Histoire, Antsira-
            nana, July 27–August 1, 1987.
Baer, Hans A.
1982   On the Political Economy of Health. *Medical Anthropology
            Newsletter* (14) 1: 1–2, 13–14.
1986   Sociological Contributions to the Political Economy of Health:
            Lessons for Medical Anthropologists. *Medical Anthropology
            Quarterly* (17) 5: 129–131.
Baer, Hans A., Merrill Singer, and John H. Johnsen
1986   Introduction: Toward a Critical Medical Anthropology. *Social
            Science and Medicine* (23) 2: 95–98.
Baré, Jean-François
1973   Successions Politiques et Légitimité: l'Exemple Sakalava du
            Nord (1700–1800). ASEMI, 4: 4.
1980   *Sable Rouge: Une Monarchie du Nord-ouest Malgache dans
            l'Histoire.* Paris: Editions L'Harmattan.
1982   Histoire et Présent dans les Monarchies Sakalava du Nord-
            Ouest. *Omaly sy Anio* 16: 173–176/180[?].
1983   Remarques sur le Vocabulaire Monarchique Sakalava du
            Nord. In *Les Souverains de Madagascar.* F. Raison-Jourde,
            ed., 153–172. Paris: Karthala.
Bartholomew, Robert E.
1990   Ethnocentricity and the Social Construction of "Mass Hys-
            teria." *Culture, Medicine and Psychiatry* 14: 455–494.
Bastide, Roger
1978   *The African Religions of Brazil.* Baltimore: Johns Hopkins
            University Press.
Beattie, John
1961   Group Aspects of the Nyoro Spirit Mediumship Cult. *Rhodes-
            Livingstone Institute Journal* 30: 11–38.
Belrose-Huyghues, Vincent
1979   At the Origin of British Evangelism: The Dream of Madagas-
            car. In *Madagascar in History: Essays from the 1970s.* R. Kent,
            trans. and ed., 252–268. Albany, Calif.: The Foundation for
            Malagasy Studies.
Birkeli, Fridtjov
1957   The Church in Madagascar. *International Review of Missions*
            (46) 182: 155–163.

Blacking, John, ed.
    1977   *The Anthropology of the Body*. A.S.A. Monograph, no. 15. New York: Academic Press.

Bloch, Maurice
    1968   Tombs and Conservatism among the Merina of Madagascar. *Man* (3) 1: 94–104.
    1971   *Placing the Dead: Tombs, Ancestral Villages, and Kinship Organization in Madagascar*. New York: Seminar Press.
    1972   Why Do Malagasy Cows Speak French? *!Kung* (London School of Economics Anthropological Society). 28–30.
    1982   Death, Women, and Power. In *Death and the Regeneration of Life*. M. Bloch and J. Perry, eds., 211–230. Cambridge: Cambridge University Press.
    1986   *From Blessing to Violence: History and Ideology in the Circumcision Ritual of the Merina of Madagascar*. Cambridge: Cambridge University Press.
    1989   *Ritual, History and Power: Selected Papers in Anthropology*. London School of Economics Monographs on Social Anthropology, no. 58. London: The Athlone Press.

Boddy, Janice
    1988   Spirits and Selves in Northern Sudan: The Cultural Therapeutics of Possession and Trance. *American Ethnologist* (1) 1: 4–27.
    1989   *Wombs and Alien Spirits: Women, Men, and the Zar Cult in Northern Sudan*. Madison: The University of Wisconsin Press.

Boiteau, P.
    1979   *Précis de Matière Médicale Malgache avec Fomulaire*. Antananarivo: La Librairie de Madagascar.

Boiteau, P., and P. Potier
    1976   The Urgent Search for Medicinal Plants. *CNRS Research* 3: 33–39.

Boucabeille, (Lt.)
    1897   De Tananarive à Diégo-Suarez. *Notes, Reconnaissances et Explorations*, vol 2., semestre 2 (August), 93–112.

Bourguinon, Erika
    1973   *Religion, Altered States of Consciousness, and Social Change*. Columbus: Ohio State University Press.

Brown, Karen McCarthy
    1991   *Mama Lola: A Vodou Priestess in Brooklyn*. Berkeley, Los Angeles, Oxford: University of California Press.

Brown, Mervyn
    1978   *Madagascar Rediscovered: A History from Early Times to Independence*. London: Damien Tunnacliffe.

Bunge, Frederica M., ed.
    1983   *Indian Ocean: Five Island Countries*. Second edition. Department of the Army Area Handbook Series, Publication no. DA

Pam 550–154. Washington, D.C.: American University for the Secretary of the Army.

Burbank, Victoria K.
1988   *Aboriginal Adolescence: Maidenhood in an Australian Community.* New Brunswick: Rutgers University Press.

Cannon, Walter B.
1942   Voodoo Death. *American Anthropologist* (44) 2: 169–181.

Chandon-Moët, Bernard
1957   Christianisme et Différenciation Ethnique: Les Catholiques de la Basse-Betsiboka (Madagascar). *Archives de Science Sociales des Religions* 1: 103–113.

Chazan-Gillic, Suzanne
1983   Le Fitampoha de 1968 ou l'Efficacité Symbolique du Myth de la Royauté Sakalava dans l'Actualité Politique et Economique Malgache. In *Les Souverains de Madagascar.* F. Raison-Jourde, ed., 451–476. Paris: Karthala.

Cohen, Abner
1969   *Custom and Politics in Urban Africa: A Study of Hausa Migrants in Yoruba Towns.* Berkeley and Los Angeles: University of California Press.
1976   *Two-Dimensional Man: An Essay on the Anthropology of Power and Symbolism in Complex Society.* Berkeley, Los Angeles, London: University of California Press.

Colson, Elizabeth
1969   Spirit Possession among the Tonga of Zambia. In *Spirit Mediumship and Society in Africa.* J. Beattie and J. Middleton, eds., 69–103. London: Routledge and Kegan Paul.
1970   Coverts and Tradition: The Impact of Christianity on Valley Tonga Religion. *Southwestern Journal of Anthropology* (26) 2: 143–156.
1971   *The Social Consequences of Resettlement: The Impact of the Kariba Resettlement upon the Gwembe Tonga.* Manchester: Manchester University Press.
1977   A Continuing Dialogue: Prophets and Local Shrines among the Tonga of Zambia. In *Regional Cults.* R. P. Werbner, ed., 119–139. ASA Monograph 16. New York: Academic Press.

Comaroff, Jean
1985   *Body of Power, Spirit of Resistance: The Culture and History of a South African People.* Chicago: University of Chicago Press.

Comaroff, Jean, and John Comaroff
1991   *Of Revelation and Revolution: Christianity, Colonialism, and Consciousness in South Africa.* Chicago: University of Chicago Press.

Condon, Richard G.
1987   *Inuit Youth.* New Brunswick: Rutgers University Press.

Cordell, G., and N. Farnsworth
    1976   A Review of Selected Potential Anti-Cancer Plant Principles.
                Heterocycles (4) 2: 393–427.
Covell, Maureen
    1987   *Madagascar: Politics, Economics, and Society.* London:
                Frances Pinter Publishers.
Crapanzano, Vincent
    1973   *The Hamadsha: A Study in Moroccan Ethnopsychiatry.*
                Berkeley, Los Angeles, London: University of California
                Press.
    1977a   Introduction. In *Case Studies in Spirit Possession.* V. Crapan-
                zano and V. Garrison, eds., 1–39. New York: John Wiley.
    1977b   Mohammed and Dawia: Possession in Morocco. In *Case Stud-
                ies in Spirit Possession.* V. Crapanzano and V. Garrison, eds.,
                141–176. New York: John Wiley.
    1983   *Tuhami: Portrait of a Moroccan.* Chicago: The University of
                Chicago Press.
Crapanzano, Vincent, and Vivian Garrison, eds.
    1977   *Case Studies in Spirit Possession.* New York: John Wiley.
Crowder, Michael
    1964   Indirect Rule—French and British Style. *Africa* (34) 3:
                197–205.
Csordas, Thomas
    1988   Elements of Charismatic Persuasion and Healing. *Medical An-
                thropology Quarterly* (2) 2: 121–142.
Dalmond, Pierre
    1840   *Mission Saclave 1840.* Manuscript in the Archives of the Insti-
                tut Supérieur de Theologie et de Philosophie de Madagascar,
                Antsiranana.
    n.d.   *Exercises en Langue Sakalava et Betsimisaraka 1841–1844.*
                Recherches et Documents no. 3. Antsiranana: Institut
                Supérieur de Theologie et de Philosophie de Madagascar.
David-Bernard, Eugène
    1943   *La Conquête de Madagascar.* Paris: Fernand Sorlot.
Davidson, Andrew
    1889   The Ramanenjana or Dancing Mania of Madagascar. *Antana-
                narivo Annual and Madagascar Review* (4) 8: 19–27.
Davis, Susan Schaefer, and Douglas A. Davis
    1989   *Adolescence in a Moroccan Town.* New Brunswick: Rutgers
                University Press.
Debray, M., H. Jacquemin, and R. Razafindrambao
    1971   *Contribution à l'Inventaire des Plantes Médicinales de Mad-
                agascar.* Paris: ORSTOM (Office de la Recherche Scientifique
                et Technique d'Outre-Mer).
Decary, Raymond
    1933   *L'Androy (Extrême Sud de Madagascar): Essai de Mono-
                graphie Régionale.* 2 vols. Paris: Société d'Editions.

1956   La Notion du Travail chez les Malgaches. *Encyclopédie Men-
            suelle d'Outre-More.* July–August: 71–72.
1966   La Première Mission Catholique à la Baie de Saint-Augustin
            en 1845. *Bulletin de Madagascar* 243: 779–788.

De Foort, (Captain) E.
1907   *Etude Historique et Ethnologique sur le Secteur d'Ambato-
            Boéni.* Tananarive: Imprimerie Officiel, Colonie de Madagas-
            car et Dépendances.

Delval, Raymond
1967   Les Musulmans à Madagascar—Problèmes Contemporains
            (résumé et situation). In *Arabes et Islamisés à Madagascar et
            dans L'Océan Indien,* 57–58. Antananarivo: Le Centre d'Ar-
            chéologie de la Faculté des Lettres et des Sciences Humaines
            de l'Université de Madagascar.
1987   L'Islam dans le Nord de Madagascar. Paper presented at the
            Colloque d'Histoire, Antsiranana, July 27–August 1, 1987.

Deschamps, Hubert
1959   *Les Migrations Intérieures à Madagascar.* Paris: Berger-
            Levrault.

Dez, Jacques
1967   De l'Influence Arabe à Madagascar à l'Aide de Faites de Lingu-
            istique. In *Arabes et Islamisés à Madagascar et dans L'Océan
            Indien,* 1–20. Antananarivo: Le Centre d'Archéologie de la
            Faculté des Lettres et des Sciences Humaines de l'Université de
            Madagascar.

Dez, M.
1964   Les Groupes Ethniques de Madagascar. *Bulletin de L'Acade-
            mie Malgache* (42) 1: 23–24 [actual publication date: 1966].

Downs, R. E., and S. P. Reyna, eds.
1988   *Land and Society in Contemporary Africa.* Hanover, N.H.:
            University Press of New England for the University of New
            Hampshire.

Doyal, Lesley
1979   *The Political Economy of Health.* Boston: South End Press.

Dunk, Pamela
1989   *Greek Women and Broken Nerves in Montreal.* Medical An-
            thropology 2: 29–45.

Dunn, Fred
1976   Traditional Asian Medicine and Cosmopolitan Medicine as
            Adaptive Systems. In *Asian Medical Systems: A Comparative
            Study.* C. Leslie, ed., 133–158. Berkeley, Los Angeles, London:
            University of California Press.

Durkheim, Emile
1961   *Moral Education: A Study in the Theory and Application of
            the Sociology of Education.* E. K. Wilson and H. Schnurer,
            trans. New York: The Free Press.
1965   *The Elementary Forms of the Religious Life.* Joseph Ward

Swain, trans. New York: The Free Press. (Originally published in 1915.)

1968   *Suicide: A Study in Sociology*. J. A. Spaulding and G. Simpson, trans. New York: The Free Press.

Dury, S. V.

1897   De Tsaratanana à Nossi-Be. *Notes, Reconnaissances et Explorations*, vol 2., semestre 2 (November), 413–445.

The Economist

1989   *A Debt to Nature*. The Economist (London), August 31.

Eikelman, Dale

1968   The Islamic Attitude towards Possession States. In *Trance and Possession States*. Raymond Prince, ed., 189–192. Montreal: Proceedings of the Second Annual Conference, R. M. Bucke Memorial Society 4–6 March 1966.

Elling, R. H.

1981   The Capitalist World System and International Health. *International Journal of Health Services* 11: 21–51.

Ellis, Stephen

1985   *The Rising of the Red Shawls: A Revolt in Madagascar 1895–1899*. Cambridge: Cambridge University Press.

Emecheta, Buchi

1979   *The Joys of Motherhood*. London: Heineman International.

Ennew, Judith, and Brian Milne

1990   *The Next Generation: Lives of Third World Children*. Philadelphia: New Society Publishers.

Epstein, A. L.

1958   *Politics in an Urban Community*. Manchester: Manchester University Press.

Estrade, Jean-Marie

1977   *Un Culte de Possession à Madagascar: Le Tromba*. Paris: Editions Anthropos.

1979   Une Autre Lecture du Tromba. *Taloha* 8: 95–110.

Evans-Pritchard, E. E.

1937   *Witchcraft, Oracles and Magic among the Azande*. Oxford: Clarendon Press.

Fabrega, Horacio, Jr.

1970   On the Specificity of Folk Illnesses. *Southwestern Journal of Anthropology* 26: 304–314.

Fagen, Richard R., Carmen Diana Deere, and José Luis Coraggio, eds.

1986   *Transition and Development: Problems of Third World Socialism*. New York: Monthly Review Press.

Fallers, Lloyde A.

1965   *Bantu Bureaucracy: A Century of Political Evolution among the Basoga of Uganda*. Chicago and London: University of Chicago Press.

Fanony, Fulgence

1986   A Propos des Mikea. In *Madagascar, Society, and History*.

C. Kottak et al., eds., 133–142. Durham: Carolina Academic Press.

Faublée, Jacques
1954   *La Cohésion des Sociétés Bara*. Paris: Presses Universitaires de France.

Favret-Saada, Jeanne
1980   *Deadly Words: Witchcraft in the Bocage*. C. Cullen, trans. New York: Cambridge University Press.

Feeley-Harnik, Gillian
1978   Divine Kingship and the Meaning of History among the Sakalava (Madagascar). *Man* n.s. 13: 402–417.
1982   The King's Men in Madagascar: Slavery, Citizenship and Sakalava Monarchy. *Africa* (52) 2: 31–50.
1984   The Political Economy of Death: Communication and Change in Malagasy Colonial History. *American Ethnologist* (11) 1: 1–19.
1986   Ritual and Work in Madagascar. In *Madagascar, Society and History*. C. Kottak, J-A. Rakotoarisoa, A. Southall, and P. Vérin, eds., 157–174. Durham: Carolina Academic Press.
1988   Sakalava Dancing Battles: Representations of Conflict in Sakalava Royal Service. *Anthropos* 83: 65–85.
1991a   Cloth and the Creation of Ancestors in Madagascar. In *Cloth and Human Experience*. Annette B. Weiner and Jane Schneider, eds., 73–116. Washington, D.C.: Smithsonian Institution Press.
1991b   *A Green Estate: Restoring Independence in Madagascar*. Washington, D.C.: Smithsonian Institution Press.

Fieloux, Michèle, and Jacques Lombard
1989   La Fête de l'Argent ou le "Bilo" du Coton. *Cahiers des Sciences Humaines* (25) 4: 499–509.

Fikambanana Mampiely Baiboly Malagasy [Malagasy Bible Distribution Society]
1986   *Ny Soratra Masina dia ny Testamenta Taloha sy ny Testamenta Vaovoa* [Old and New Testament (Protestant version)]. Antananarivo: Fikambanana Mampiely Baiboly Malagasy.

Finkler, Kaja
1985   *Spiritualist Healers in Mexico*. South Hadley, Mass.: Bergin and Garvey.

Firth, Raymond
1967   Ritual and Drama in Malay Spirit Mediumship. *Comparative Studies in Society and History* (9) 2: 190–207.

Frankenberg, Ronald
1988   Gramsci, Culture, and Medical Anthropology: Kundry and Parsifal? or Rat's Tail to Sea Serpent? *Medical Anthropology Quarterly* (2) 4: 324–337.

Frankenberg, Ronald, ed.
  1988   Essay for the Development of Critical Medical Anthropology.
            Medical Anthropology Quarterly 2: 4.
Frazer, (Sir) James G.
  1976   "Sympathetic Magic" and "Magic and Religion." *The Golden
            Bough: A Study in Magic and Religion,* 52–219, 220–243.
            Third edition. New York: St. Martin's Press (Third edition,
            originally published in 1911.)
Frère, Suzanne
  1958   *Madagascar: Panorama de l'Androy.* Paris: Editions
            AFRAMPE, M. Pailhé et ses Frères.

Fry, Peter
  1976   *Spirits of Protest: Spirit Mediums and the Articulation of Con-
            sensus among the Zezuru of Southern Rhodesia (Zimbabwe).*
            Cambridge: Cambridge University Press.
Gade, Daniel W.
  1984   Redolence and Land Use on Nosy Be, Madagascar. *Journal of
            Cultural Geography* (4) 2: 29–40.
Galliéni, (General) J. S.
  1900   *La Pacification de Madagascar (Operations d'Octobre
            1896 à Mars 1899).* Paris: Librairie Militaire R. Chapelot
            et Ce.
  1908   *Neuf Ans à Madagascar.* Paris: Librairie Hachette et Cie.
Gardenier, W.
  1976   *Witchcraft and Sorcery in a Pastoral Society: The Central
            Sakalava of West Madagascar.* Ph.D. diss., Rice University,
            Houston.
Geertz, Clifford
  1973   *The Interpretation of Cultures.* New York: Basic Books.
Gifford, Prosser, and Timothy C. Weiskel
  1974   African Education in a Colonial Context: French and British
            Styles. In *France and Britain in Africa: Imperial Rivalry and
            Colonial Rule.* P. Gifford and W. R. Lewis, eds., 663–711.
            New Haven: Yale University Press.

Giles, Linda L.
  1987   Possession Cults on the Swahili Coast: A Re-examination of
            Theories of Marginality. *Africa* (57) 2: 234–258.

Gluckman, Max
  1954   Rituals of Rebellion in Southeast Africa. In *Order and
            Rebellion in Tribal Africa,* 110–137. New York: The Free
            Press.

Gomm, Roger
  1975   Bargaining from Weakness: Spirit Possession in the South
            Kenya Coast. *Man* 10: 530–543.

Gontard, M.
  1971   La Situation Religieuse à la Madagascar en 1897. *Bulletin de
            Madagascar* 300: 405–417.

Goodenough, W. H.
  1956   Residence Rules. *Southwestern Journal of Anthropology* 12: 22–37.
Goodman, Felicitas D.
  1988   *How About Demons? Possession and Exorcism in the Modern World.* Bloomington: Indiana University Press.
Goody, Jack, ed.
  1958   *The Development Cycle in Domestic Groups.* Cambridge Papers in Social Anthropology, no. 1. Cambridge: Cambridge University Press.
Gottlieb, David, Jon Reeves, and Warren D. TenHorton
  1966   *The Emergence of Youth Societies: A Cross-Cultural Approach.* New York: The Free Press.
Gow, B. A.
  1979   *Madagascar and the Protestant Impact.* New York: Africana Publishing Company.
Grandidier, A. and G. Grandidier, eds.
  1903–   *Collection des Ouvrages Anciens Concernant Madagascar.* 9
  1920   vols. Paris: Comité de Madagascar.
Gray, Robert
  1969   The *Sheitani* Cult among the Segeju of Tanzania. In *Spirit Mediumship and Society in Africa.* J. Beattie and J. Middleton, eds., 171–187. New York: Africana Publishing Company.
Greenfield, Sidney M.
  1992   Spirits and Spiritist Therapy in Southern Brazil: A Case Study of an Innovative, Syncretic Healing Group. *Culture, Medicine and Psychiatry* 16: 23–51.
Grossman, Rachel
  1979   Women's Place in the Integrated Circuit. *Southeast Asia Chronicle* 66: 2–17.
Gueunier, Noel-Jacques, and Fulgence Fanony
  1980   Le Mouvement de Conversion à l'Islam et le Rôle des Confréries Musulmanes dans le Nord de Madagascar. *Asie du Sudest et Monde Insulindien* (11) 1–4: 151–168.
Guillain, Charles
  1845   *Documents sur l'Histoire, la Géographie, et le Commerce de la Partie Occidentale de Madagascar.* Paris: Imprimerie Royale.
Hahn, Robert A.
  1985   Culture Bound Syndromes Unbound. *Social Science and Medicine* 21: 165–171.
Hahn, Robert A., and Arthur Kleinman
  1983   Belief as Pathogen, Belief as Medicine: "Voodoo Death" and the "Placebo Phenomenon" in Anthropological Perspective. (Perspectives on the Placebo Phenonmenon.) *Medical Anthropology Newsletter* (14) 4: 3, 16–19.

Harris, Grace
1957   Possession "Hysteria" in a Kenya Tribe. *American Anthropologist* (59) 6: 1046–1066.
Hart, Donn V., Phya Anuman Rajadhon, and Richard J. Coghlin
1965   *Southeast Asian Birth Customs: Three Studies in Human Reproduction.* New Haven: Human Relations Area Files Press.
Hellmann, Ellen
1948   *Rooiyard: A Sociological Survey of an Urban Native Slum.* Rhodes-Livingston Papers no. 13. Capetown: Oxford University Press.
Heseltine, Nigel
1971   *Madagascar.* New York: Praeger Publishers.
Heurtebize, George
1977   Le Traitement du "Doany" dans l'Androy. *Omaly sy Anio* 5–6: 373–385.
Hobsbaum, Eric
1983   Introduction: Inventing Traditions. In *The Invention of Tradition.* Eric Hobsbawm and Terence Ranger, eds., 1–14. Cambridge: Cambridge University Press.
Hollos, Marida, and Philip E. Leis
1989   *Becoming Nigerian in Ijo Society.* New Brunswich: Rutgers University Press.
Hopkins, Nicholas S.
1972   *Popular Government in an African Town; Kita, Mali.* Chicago: Chicago University Press.
Hübsch, Bruno
1987   Les Débuts de la Communauté Catholique à Antsiranana. Paper presented at the Colloque d'Histoire, Antsiranana, July 27–August 1, 1987.
Huntington, Richard
1973   *Religion and Social Organization of the Bara People of Madagascar.* Ph.D. diss., Duke University, Durham, N.C.
1981   Time and Space in Madagascar: Spatial Indicators of Social Process. *Symbols* Winter: 2–12.
Huntington, Richard, and Peter Metcalf
1979   *Celebrations of Death: The Anthropology of Mortuary Ritual.* New York: Cambridge University Press.
Janzen, John
1978   *The Quest for Therapy: Medical Pluralism in Lower Zaire.* Berkeley, Los Angeles, London: University of California Press.
Jaovelo-Dzao, Robert
1983   *Anthropologie Religieuse Sakalava: Essai sur l'Inculturation du Christianisme à Madagascar.* Thèse de Troisième Cycle en Ethno-Théologie. Faculté de Theologie Catholique, Université des Science Humaines de Strassbourg.
1987   *Anthropologie Religieuse Sakalava: Essai sur l'Inculturation*

du Christianisme à Madagascar. Recherches et Documents no. 2. Antsiranana: Institut Supérieur de Théologie et de Philosophie de Madagascar.

Jolly, Alison
1980   *A World Like Our Own: Man and Nature in Madagascar.* New Haven: Yale University Press.
1987   Madagascar, a World Apart. *National Geographic* (171) 2: 148–183.
1988   Madagascar's Lemurs on the Edge of Survival. *National Geographic* (174) 2: 131–161.

Judic, Bruno
1987   Les Jésuites à Madagascar au XIXe Siècle: Formation Spirituelle et Réalités. Paper presented at the Colloque d'Histoire à Antsiranana, July 27–August 1, 1987.

Jules-Rosette, B.
1975   *African Apostles: Ritual and Conversion in the Church of John Maranke.* Ithaca, N.Y.: Cornell University Press.

Kane, Stephanie
1988   Sùrreal Taboo and the Embera-Gringa. Paper presented in the session on "Magical Realism and Capitalist Critique in Latin America" at the Annual Meetings of the American Anthropological Association, Phoenix, November.

Karp, Ivan
1985   Deconstructing Culture-Bound Syndromes. *Social Science and Medicine* (21) 2: 221–228.
1987   Power and Capacity in Rituals of Possession. Paper presented at the Symposium on African Folk Models and Their Application, Uppsala, August 23–30.
1989   Power and Capacity in Rituals of Possession. In *Creativity of Power. Cosmology and Action in African Societies.* W. Arens and I. Karp, eds., 91–109. Washington, D.C.: Smithsonian University Press.

Karp, Ivan, and Patricia Karp
1979   Living with Spirits of the Dead. In *African Therapeutic Systems,* Z. A. Ademuwagun et al., eds., 22–25. Waltham, Mass.: Crossroads Press.

Keenan, Elinor Ochs
1974   *Conversation and Oratory in Vakinankaratra, Madagascar.* Ph.D. diss., University of Pennsylvania, Philadelphia.

Kehoe, Alice B.
1989   *The Ghost Dance: Ethnohistory and Revitalization.* Fort Worth: Holt, Rinehart and Winston.

Kehoe, Alice B., and Dody H. Giletti
1981   Women's Preponderance in Possession Cults: The Calcium-Deficiency Hypothesis Extended. *American Anthropologist* (83) 3: 549–561.

Kendall, Laurel
1985   *Shamans, Housewives, and Other Restless Spirits: Women*

in Korean Ritual Life. Honolulu: University of Hawaii Press.

1988   *The Life and Hard Times of a Korean Shaman: Of Tales and the Telling of Tales*. Honolulu: University of Hawaii Press.

Kent, Raymond K.
1968   Madagascar and Africa: Part II. The Sakalava, Moroserana, Dady and Tromba before 1700. *Journal of African History* (9) 4: 517–576.

Kent, Raymond K., ed.
1979   *Madagascar in History: Essays from the 1970s*. Albany, Calif.: The Foundation for Malagasy Studies.

Kenyon, Susan M.
1991   *The Five Women of Sennar: Culture and Change in Central Sudan*. Oxford: Oxford University Press.

Keyes, Charles F.
1981   The Dialectics of Ethnic Change. In *Ethnic Change*. C. F. Keyes, ed., 4–30. Seattle: University of Washington Press.

Kiev, Ari
1972   *Transcultural Psychiatry*. New York: The Free Press.

Kiev, Ari, ed.
1964   *Magic, Faith, and Healing*. New York: The Free Press.

Kleinman, Arthur
1978   Concepts and a Model for the Comparison of Medical Systems as Cultural Systems. *Social Science and Medicine* 12: 85–93.

1980   *Patients and Healers in the Context of Culture*. Berkeley, Los Angeles, London: University of California Press.

Koritschoner, H.
1936   Ngoma ya Sheitani. *Journal of the Royal Anthropological Institute*. 66: 209–219.

Kottak, Conrad P.
1980   *The Past in the Present: History, Ecology, and Cultural Variation in Highland Madagascar*. Ann Arbor: The University of Michigan Press.

1986   Introduction. In *Madagascar: Society and History*. C. Kottak et al., eds., 1–7. Durham: Carolina Academic Press.

Kottak, C. P., J-A. Rakotoarisoa, A. Southall, and P. Vérin, eds.
1986   *Madagascar: Society and History*. Durham: Carolina Academic Press.

Krippner, Stanley
1987   Cross-Cultural Approaches to Multiple Personality Disorder: Practices in Brazilian Spiritism. *Ethos* (15) 3: 273–295.

Kulin, Howard E.
1988   Adolescent Pregnancy in Africa: A Programmatic Focus. *Social Science and Medicine* (26) 7: 727–735.

Kus, Susan
1984   Time as Space and Space as Time in Nineteenth Century Imerina, Madagascar. Paper presented in the session on "The Mate-

rial Correlates of Social Structural Models" at the Annual Meetings of the American Anthropological Association, Boulder, November.

La Barre, Weston

1970   *The Ghost Dance.* Garden City, N.Y.: Doubleday and Company.

1992   *They Shall Take Up Serpents: Psychology of the Southern Snake-Handling Cult.* Prospect Heights, Ill.: Waveland Press. (Originally published in 1962.)

Lambek, Michael

1980   Spirits and Spouses: Possession as a System of Communication among the Malagasy Speakers of Mayotte (Comoro Islands). *American Ethnologist* (7) 2: 318–331.

1981   *Human Spirits: A Cultural Account of Trance in Mayotte.* New York: Cambridge University Press.

1988a   Graceful Exits: Spirit Possession as Personal Performance in Mayotte. *Culture* (Canada) (8) 1: 59–69.

1988b   Spirit Possession/Spirit Succession: Aspects of Social Continuity among Malagasy Speakers in Mayotte. *American Ethnologist* (15) 4: 710–731.

1992   Taboo as Cultural Practice Among Malagasy Speakers. *Man* 27: 2: 245–266.

Lan, David

1985   *Guns and Rain: Guerrillas and Spirit Mediums in Zimbabwe.* Berkeley, Los Angeles, London: University of California Press.

Lancaster, Jane B., and Beatrix A. Hamburg, eds.

1986   *School-age Pregnancy and Parenthood: Biosocial Dimensions* New York: Aldine De Gruyter.

LaPierre, Jean William

1966   Problèmes Socio-culturels de la Nation Malgache. *Cahiers Internationaux de Sociologie (Paris)* 40: 57–73.

Lasch, Christopher

1977   *Haven in a Heartless World: The Family Beseiged.* New York: Basic Books.

Lawless, Elaine

1988   *Handmaidens of the Lord: Pentecostal Women Preachers and Traditional Religion.* Philadephia: University of Pennsylvania Press.

Leacock, Seth, and Ruth Leacock

1972   *Spirits of the Deep: A Study of an Afro-Brazilian Cult.* Garden City, N.Y.: Doubleday Natural History Press.

Le Bourdiec, Françoise, Paul Le Bourdiec, and René Battistini, directors

1969   *Atlas de Madagascar.* Prepared by L'Association des Geographes de Madagascar, Bureau pour le Développement de la Production Agricole. Antananarivo.

Lebra, William P.

1982   Shaman-Client Interchange in Okinawa: Performative Stages in Shamanic Therapy. In *Cultural Conceptions of Mental*

Health and Therapy. A. Marsella and G. White, eds., 303–315. Dordrecht: D. Reidel Publishing Company

Lee, Philip R., Peter Lurie, Milton M. Silverman, and Mia Lydecker
   1991   Drug Promotion and Labeling in Developing Countries: An Update. *Journal of Clinical Epidemiology* 44: Suppl. 2: 49S–55S.

Leiris, Michel
   1958   *La Possession et ses Aspects Thèâtraux chez les Ethiopiens de Gondar.* Paris: Plon.

Lévi-Strauss, Claude
   1963a   The Effectiveness of Symbols. In *Structural Anthropology.* C. Jacobson and B. G. Schoepf, trans., 186–205. New York: Basic Books.

   1963b   The Sorceror and His Magic. In *Structural Anthropology.* C. Jacobson and B. G. Schoepf, trans., 167–185. New York: Basic Books.

Lewis, Gilbert
   1980   *Day of Shining Red: An Essay on Understanding Ritual.* Cambridge: Cambridge University Press.

Lewis, I. M.
   1966   Spirit Possession and Deprivation Cults. *Man* (1) 3: 307–329.

   1971   *Ecstatic Religion: An Anthropological Study of Spirit Possession and Shamanism.* Baltimore: Penguin Books.

   1986   *Religion in Context: Cults and Charisma.* Cambridge: Cambridge University Press.

   1991   Introduction: *Zar* in Context—The Past, the Present and the Future of an African Healing Cult. In *Women's Medicine: The Zar-Bori Cult in Africa and Beyond.* I.M. Lewis et al., eds., 1–16. Edinburgh: Edinburgh University Press for the International African Institute.

Lewis, I. M., Ahmed Al-Safi, and Sayyid Hurreiz, eds.
   1991   *Women's Medicine: The Zar-Bori Cult in Africa and Beyond.* Edinburgh: Edinburgh University Press for the International African Institute.

L'Hermite, R.
   1968   Les Spiritains et l'Implantation Catholique à Madagascar au Milieu du XIXème Siècle. *Bulletin de Madagascar* (18) 266–277: 699–713.

Lim, Linda Y. H.
   1983   Capitalism, Imperialism, and Patriarchy: The Dilemma of Third-World Women Workers in Multinational Factories. In *Women, Men and the International Division of Labor.* J. Nash and M. P. Fernandez-Kelly, eds., 70–91. Albany: State University of New York Press.

Linton, Ralph
   1927   Rice, a Malagasy Tradition. *American Anthropologist* 29: 654–660.

1933   *The Tanala: A Hill Tribe of Madagascar.* Anthropological Se-
           ries, vol 22. Chicago: Field Museum of Natural History.
1943   Nativistic Movements. *American Anthropologist.* 45:
           230–240.
Little, Kenneth
1957   The Role of Voluntary Associations in West African Urbaniza-
           tion. *American Anthropologist* 59: 579–596.
1962   Some Traditionally Based Forms of Mutual Aid in West Afri-
           can Urbanization. *Ethnology* (1) 2: 197–211.
1973   *African Women in Towns: An Aspect of Africa's Social Revo-
           lution.* Cambridge: Cambridge University Press.
Lock, Margaret
1984   Licorice in Leviathan: The Medicalization of Care for the
           Japanese Elderly. *Culture, Medicine and Psychiatry* 8:
           121–139.
Lombard, Jacques
1973   *La Royauté Sakalava: Essai d'Analyse d'un Système Politique.*
           Antananarivo: ORSTOM.
1986   Le Temps et l'Espace dans l'Idéologie Politique de la Royauté
           Sakalava-Menabe. In *Madagascar: Society and History.* C.
           Kottak et al., eds., 143–156. Durham: Carolina Academic
           Press.
1988   Le Royaume Sakalava du Menabe: Essai d'Analyse d'un Sys-
           tème Politique à Madagascar. Collection Travaux et Docu-
           ments no. 214. Paris: Editions de l'ORSTOM.
London Missionary Society (LMS)
1881–   *Antananarivo Annual and Madagascar Review.* Vols 1–6. An-
1900   tananarivo.
Mack, John
1986   *Madagascar: Island of the Ancestors.* Exhibition catalogue.
           London: British Museum Publications Ltd.
Mack, John, narrator
1989   *Tromba Possession by Spirits.* Film made for the American
           Museum of Natural History by Jeremy Marre, director and
           producer. From "The Nature of Music Series." A Harcourt
           Films Production with R. M. Arts and Channel 4.
Madagascar (Government of)
1950–   *Monographies.* Census data, Province de Diégo-Suarez, Prefec-
1971   ture de Diégo-Suarez, Sous-Prefecture d'Ambanja. Antanana-
           rivo: Ministère de l'Intérieur, Service des Affaires Générales et
           Territoriales; and Archives Nationales, Tsaralalana.
1986   [Census for the town and county (Fivondronana) of Ambanja.]
           Ambanja: Service du Planification.
Madagascar-FTM
1986   Sarintanin-Dàlana/Carte Routiere, Madagascar. Road map for
           Madagascar. Antananarivo.
Malinowski, Bronislaw
1948   *Magic, Science, and Religion.* Garden City, N.Y.: Doubleday.

Marsella, Anthony J., and Geoffrey M. White, eds.
  1982   *Cultural Conceptions of Mental Health and Therapy.* Dordrecht: D. Reidel Publishing Company.

Martin, Emily
  1987   *The Woman in the Body: A Cultural Analysis of Reproduction.* Boston: Beacon Press.

Marx, Karl
  1964   Contribution to the Critique of Hegel's Philosophy of Right. In *Early Writings.* T. B. Bottomore, ed. and trans., 43–59. New York: McGraw-Hill Book Company.

Mauss, Marcel
  1979   *Sociology and Psychology: Essays.* London: Routledge and Kegan Paul.
  1987   A Category of the Human Mind: The Notion of Person; the Notion of Self. In *The Category of the Person: Anthropology, Philosophy, and History.* Michael Carrithers, Steven Collins and Steven Lukes, eds., 1–25. Cambridge: Cambridge University Press.

Mayer, Philip, with Iona Mayer
  1971   *Townsmen or Tribesmen: Conservatism and the Process of Urbanization in a South African City.* Capetown: Oxford University Press.

McGuire, Meredith
  1982   *Pentecostal Catholics: Power, Charisma, and Order in a Religious Movement.* Philadelphia: Temple University Press.

Mead, Margaret
  1939   —*From the South Seas: Studies of Adolescence and Sex in Primitive Societies.* New York: William Morrow and Company.
  1961   *Coming of Age in Samoa: A Psychological Study of Primitive Youth for Western Civilization.* New York: Dell Publishing Company. (Originally published in 1928.)

Meillassoux, Claude
  1968   *Urbanization of an African Community: Voluntary Associations in Bamako.* American Ethnological Society Monograph no. 45. Seattle: University of Washington Press.
  1982   *Maidens, Meal and Money.* Cambridge: Cambridge University Press.

Mellis, J. V.
  1936   *Volamena et Volafotsy: Nord et Nord-Ouest de Madagascar.* Tananarive [Antananarivo]: Imprimerie Moderne de l'Emyrne, Pitot de la Beaujardière.

Meltzer, J. D.
  1978   A Semiotic Approach to Suitability for Psychiatry. *Psychiatry* 41: 435–458.

Mendelievich, E., ed.
  1979   *Children at Work.* Geneva: International Labour Office.

Minge, Wanda
  1986   The Industrial Revolution and the European Family: "Child-
              hood" as a Market for Family Labor. In *Women's Work: De-
              velopment and the Division of Labor by Gender*. E. Leacock
              and H. Safa, eds., 13–24. New York: Bergen and Garvey.
Mitchell, J. Clive
  1956   *The Kalela Dance: Aspects of Social Relationships among
              Urban Africans in Northern Rhodesia*. Rhodes-Livingston In-
              stitute Paper no. 27. Manchester: Manchester University Press.
Moerman, Daniel E.
  1983   Physiology and Symbols: The Anthropological Implications of
              the Placebo Effect. In *The Anthropology of Medicine*. L.
              Romanucci-Ross, L. Tancredi, and D. Moerman, eds.,
              156–167. New York: Bergin Publishers.
Molet, L.
  1959   *L'Expansion Tsimehety: Modalités et Motivations des Migra-
              tions Intérieures d'un Groupe Ethnique du Nord de Madagas-
              car*. Mémoires de l'Institut Scientifique de Madagascar (Paris),
              IRSM Series C, 5: 1–196.
Morgan, Lynn M.
  1987   Dependency Theory in the Political Economy of Health: An
              Anthropological Critique. *Medical Anthropology Quarterly*
              (1) 2: 131–154.
  1990   The Medicalization of Anthropology: A Critical Perspective
              on the Critical-Clinical Debate. *Social Science and Medicine*
              (30) 9: 945–950.
Morsy, Soheir
  1978   Sex Roles, Power and Illness in an Egyptian Village. *American
              Ethnologist* 5: 137–150.
  1979   The Missing Link in Medical Anthropology: The Political
              Economy of Health. *Reviews in Anthropology* (6) 34: 9–363.
  1991   Spirit Possession in Egyptian Ethnomedicine: Origins, Com-
              parison and Historical Specificity. In *Women's Medicine: The
              Zar-Bori Cult in Africa and Beyond*. I.M. Lewis et al., eds.,
              189–208. Edinburgh: Edinburgh University Press for the Inter-
              national African Institute.
Munslow, Barry
  1986   Introduction. In *Africa: Problems in the Transition to Social-
              ism*. B. Munslow, ed., 1–39. London: Zed Books, Ltd.
Munslow, Barry, ed.
  1986   *Africa: Problems in the Transition to Socialism*. London: Zed
              Books, Ltd.
Murray, Colin
  1981   *Families Divided: The Impact of Migrant Labour in Lesotho*.
              Johannesburg: Raven Press Ltd.
Mutibwa, P. M.
  1974   *The Malagasy and the Europeans: Madagascar's Foreign*

Relations 1861–1895. Atlantic Highlands, N.J.: Humanities Press.

Nash, June
1979   *We Eat the Mines and the Mines Eat Us: Dependence and Exploitation in Bolivian Tin Mines.* New York: Columbia University Press.

Nash, June, and Maria-Patricia Fernandez-Kelly, eds.
1983   *Women, Men and the International Division of Labor.* Albany: State University of New York Press.

Navarro, Vicente
1976   *Medicine Under Capitalism.* New York: Prodist.

Nelson, H.D. et al.
1973   *Area Handbook for the Malagasy Republic.* Washington, D.C.: The American University.

Nimtz, August H., Jr.
1980   *Islam and Politics in East Africa: The Sufi Order in Tanzania.* Minneapolis: University of Minnesota Press.

Noël, Vincent
1843   Recherches sur les Sakalava. *Bulletin de la Société Géographique,* Série 2, 19: 275–295.

Obeyesekere, Gananath
1977   Psychocultural Exegesis of a Case of Spirit Possession in Sri Lanka. In *Case Studies in Spirit Possession.* V. Crapanzano and V. Garrison, eds., 235–294. New York: John Wiley and Sons.
1981   *Medusa's Hair: An Essay on Personal Symbols and Religious Experience.* Chicago: University of Chicago Press.

Ong, Aihwa
1987   *Spirits of Resistance and Capitalist Discipline: Factory Women in Malaysia.* Albany: State University of New York Press.
1988   The Production of Possession: Spirits and the Multinational Corporation in Malaysia. *American Ethnologist* (15) 1: 28–42.

Ortner, Sherry
1974   Is Female to Male as Nature Is to Culture? In *Women, Culture, and Society.* Michelle Z. Rosaldo and Louise Lamphere, eds., 67–87. Stanford: Stanford University Press.

Ottino, Paul
1965   Le Tromba (Madagascar). *L'Homme* (5) 1: 84–94.

Pande, S. K.
1968   The Mystique of Western Psychotherapy: An Eastern Interpretation. *Journal of Nervous and Mental Disease* 146: 425–432.

Pappas, G.
1990   Some Implications for the Study of the Doctor-Patient Interaction: Power, Structure, and Agency in the Works of Howard Waitzkin and Arthur Kleinman. *Social Science and Medicine* (30) 2: 199–204.

Parkin, David
1982   Introduction. In *Semantic Anthropology*. D. Parkin, ed., xi–li.
            New York: Academic Press.
Parry, John, and Maurice Bloch, eds.
1989   *Money and the Morality of Exchange*. Cambridge: Cambridge
            University Press.
Payer, Lynn
1989   The Land of the Lemurs. *The New York Times*, October 29.
Pazder, L. H.
1968   The Attitudes of Catholic Missionaries in Eastern Nigeria.
            In *Trance and Possession States*. Raymond Prince, ed.,
            86–188. Montreal: Proceedings of the Second Annual
            Conference, R. M. Bucke Memorial Society 4–6 March,
            1966.
Peaston, Monroe
1968   Possession and Trance States: A Protestant View. In *Trance
            and Possession States*. Raymond Prince, ed., 193–195. Mon-
            treal: Proceedings of the Second Annual Conference, R. M.
            Bucke Memorial Society 4–6 March, 1966.
Pederson, Paul
1982   The Intercultural Context of Counseling and Therapy. In *Cul-
            tural Conceptions of Mental Health and Therapy*. A. Marsella
            and G. White, eds., 333–358. Dordrecht: D. Reidel Publishing
            Company.
Pernet, M. R.
1964   Ethno-Botanique et Plantes Médicinales de Madagascar: Bilain
            d'un Siècle d'Etudes. *Bulletin de l'Academie Malgache* (42) 1:
            31–33.
Plotkin, M., V. Randrianasolo, L. Sussman, and N. Marshall
n.d.   *Ethnobotany in Madagascar: Overview, Action Plan, Data-
            base*. A Report to IUCN/World Wildlife Fund.
Pomponio, Alice
1992   *Seagulls Don't Fly into the Bush: Cultural Identity and Devel-
            opment in Melanesia*. Belmont, Calif.: Wadsworth Publishing
            Co.
Powdermaker, Hortense
1962   *Coppertown: Changing Africa. The Human Situation on the
            Rhodesian Copperbelt*. New York: Harper and Row Pub-
            lishers.
Prince, Raymond
1964   Indigenous Yoruba Psychiatry. In *Magic, Faith, and Healing*.
            Ari Kiev, ed., 84–120. New York: The Free Press.
Prince, Raymond, ed.
1968   *Trance and Possession States*. Montreal: Proceedings of the
            Second Annual Conference, R. M. Bucke Memorial Society,
            4–6 March, 1966.
Pryor, Frederic L.
1988   *Income Distribution and Economic Development in Madagas-*

car: Some Historical Statistics. World Bank Discussion Paper No. 37. Washington, D.C.: The World Bank.

Rabenoro, Césaire
1986   *Les Relations Extérieures de Madagascar de 1960–1972.* Paris: Editions L'Harmattan.

Raherisoanjato, Annie G.
1985   *Essai sur la Géographie Médicale du Faritany d'Antsiranana.* Thesis in Medicine (Diplome d'Etat, Doctorat en Médicine), Université de Madagascar, Faculté de Médicine.

Raison, F.
1970   Le Catholicisme Malgache: Passé et Présent. *RFEPA,* May: 78–99.

Raison-Jourde, Françoise
1983   Introduction. In *Les Souverains de Madagascar: L'Histoire Royale et ses Résurgences Contemporaines.* F. Raison-Jourde, ed., 7–68. Paris: Karthala.

Raison-Jourde, Françoise, ed.
1983   *Les Souverains de Madagascar: L'Histoire Royale et ses Résurgences Contemporaines.* Paris: Karthala.

Rajoelina, Patrick
1988   *Quarante Années de la Vie Politique de Madagascar 1947–1987.* Paris: Editions L'Harmattan.

Ramamonjisoa, Janine
1984   Blancs et Noirs: Les Dimensions de l'Inégalité Sociale. *Cahiers des Sciences Sociales, Université de Madagascar* 1: 39–76.

Ramamonjisoa, Suzy Andrée
1984   Symbolique des Rapports entre les Femmes et les Hommes dans les Cultes de Possession de Type Tromba à Madagascar. *Bulletin Academie Malgache* (63) 1–2: 99–110.

Ranaivoarivao, E.
1974   Vers la Démocratisation des Plantes Médicinales à Madagascar. *Bulletin de Madagascar* (330) 580–591.

Raolison, Régis Rajemisa
1966   *Dictionnaire Historique et Géographique de Madagascar.* Fianarantsoa: Librairie Ambozontany.

Rasamoela, Joela
1975   *Ny Fampianarana: Napetra-dRangahy Rainisoalambo ao Soatanana.* Antananarivo (?): Publisher unknown (FJKM?).

Rason, R.
1968   Le Tromba chez les Sakalava. *Civilisation Malgache* 2: 207–214.

Raybeck, D., J. Shoobe, and J. Grauberg
1989   Women, Stress, and Participation in Possession Cults: A Reexamination of the Calcium Deficiency Hypothesis. *Medical Anthropology Quarterly* (3) 2: 139–161.

Reiter, Rayna, ed.
1975   *Toward an Anthropology of Women.* New York: Monthly Press.

Reynolds, P., and S. Burman, eds.
    1986   *Growing Up in a Divided Society.* Johannesburg: Ravan Press, in Association with the Centre for Cross-Cultural Research on Women, Queen Elizabeth House, Oxford.

Richards, Audrey
    1951   *Land, Labour and Diet in Northern Rhodesia; An Economic Study of the Bemba Tribe.* London: Oxford University Press for the International African Institute.

Robertson, A. F.
    1978   *Community of Strangers: A Journal of Discovery in Uganda.* London: Scolar Press.

Romanucci-Ross, Lola
    1977   The Hierarchy of Resort in Curative Practices: The Admiralty Islands, Melanesia. In *Culture, Disease, and Healing: Studies in Medical Anthropology.* D. Landy, ed., 481–487. New York: Macmillan Publishing Company.

Rosaldo, Michelle Z., and Louise Lamphere, eds.
    1974   *Woman, Culture, and Society.* Stanford: Stanford University Press.

Rosaldo, Renato
    1980   *Ilongot Headhunting 1883–1974: A Study in Society and History.* Stanford: Stanford University Press.

Rouget, Gilbert
    1980   *La Musique et la Trance.* Paris: Gallimard.

Russillon, H.
    1908   *Un Culte Dynastique avec Evocation des Morts chez les Sakalava: Le Tromba.* Paris: Picard.

Ruud, Jorgen
    1960   *Taboo: A Study of Malagasy Customs and Beliefs.* Oslo: Oslo University Press.

Sachs, L., and G. Tomson
    1992   Medicines and Culture—A Double Perspective on Drug Utilization in a Developing Country. *Social Science and Medicine* (34) 3: 307–315.

Sahlins, Marshall
    1985   *Islands of History.* Chicago: University of Chicago Press.

Salman, D. H.
    1968   The Attitude of Catholicism towards Possession States. In *Trance and Possession States.* Raymond Prince, ed., 183–185. Montreal: Proceedings of the Second Annual Conference, R. M. Bucke Memorial Society 4–6 March, 1966.

Scheper-Hughes, Nancy
    1987   Introduction: The Cultural Politics of Child Survival. In *Child Survival: Anthropological Perspectives on the Treatment and Maltreatment of Children,* 1–29. Boston: D. Reidel Publishing Company.

1990   Three Propositions for a Critically Applied Medical Anthro-
            pology. *Social Science and Medicine* (30) 2: 189–197.
1992   *Death without Weeping: Everyday Violence in Northeast Bra-
            zil.* Berkeley, Los Angeles, London: University of California
            Press.

Scheper-Hughes, Nancy, ed.
1987   *Child Survival: Anthropological Perspectives on the Treatment
            and Maltreatment of Children.* Boston: D. Reidel Publishing
            Company.

Scheper-Hughes, Nancy, and Margaret Lock
1987   The Mindful Body: A Prolegomenon to Future Work in Medi-
            cal Anthropology. *Medical Anthropology Quarterly* (1) 1:
            1–36.

Schildkrout, Enid
1981   Young Traders of Northern Nigeria. *Natural History* (90) 6:
            44–53.

Schlemmer, Bernard
1983   La Domination Royale au Menabe: Détournement Colonial,
            Survivance et Décomposition. In *Les Sourverains de Madagas-
            car.* F. Raison-Jourde, ed., 391–408. Paris: Karthala.

Schuster, Ilsa M. Glazer
1979   *New Women of Lusaka.* Palo Alto, Calif.: Mayfield Publishing
            Company.

Scott, James
1985   *Weapons of the Weak.* New Haven: Yale University Press.

Scudder, Thayer
1966   Social Anthropology, Man-Made Lakes and Population Relo-
            cation in Africa. *Anthropological Quarterly* (41) 3: 168–176.

Service Topographique and Bureau des Domaines, Nosy Be
n.d.   [Miscellaneous land deed records for Nosy Be and the Sambi-
            rano Valley since 1897.]

Shack, William A.
1971   Hunger, Anxiety, and Ritual: Deprivation and Spirit Posses-
            sion among the Gurage of Ethiopia. *Man* (6) 1: 30–43.

Sharp, Lesley A.
1985   Social Change, Social Protest: The "Dancing Mania" in Nine-
            teenth Century Madagascar. Paper presented in the session on
            "Charisma" at the Annual Meetings of the American Anthro-
            pological Association, Washington, D.C., December.
1990   Possessed and Dispossessed Youth: Spirit Possession of School
            Children in Northwest Madagascar. *Culture, Medicine and
            Psychiatry* 14: 339–364.
In press   Exorcists, Psychiatrists, and the Problems of Possession in
            Northwest Madagascar. *Social Science and Medicine.*

Shipton, Parker
1989   *Bitter Money: Cultural Economy and Some African Meanings
            of Forbidden Commodities.* Monograph Series, no. 1. Wash-
            ington, D.C.: American Ethnological Society.

Shoumatoff, Alex
    1988a   Our Far-Flung Correspondents: Look at That. *The New Yorker,* March: 62–83.
    1988b   P.S. A Leap to the Lost Continent. *Condé Nast Traveler,* November: 118–125, 158–162.
Silverman, Milton, Philip R. Lee, and Mia Lydecker
    1982   The Drugging of the Third World. *International Journal of Health Services* (12) 4: 585–595.
Silverman, Milton, Philip R. Lee, and Mia Lydecker
    1986   Drug Promotion: The Third World Revisited. *International Journal of Health Services* (16); 4: 659–667.
Silverman, Milton, Mia Lydecker, and Philip R. Lee
    1990   The Drug Swndlers. *International Journal of Health Services* (20); 4: 561–572.
Singer, Merrill
    1986   Developing a Critical Perspective in Medical Anthropology. *Medical Anthropology Quarterly* (17) 5: 128–129.
Slawecki, Leon M. S.
    1971   *French Policy towards the Chinese in Madagascar.* Hamden, Conn.: The Shoe String Press.
Smith, Alison
    1963   The Southern Section of the Interior, 1840–84. In *History of East Africa.* Roland Oliver and Gervase Mathew, eds., 253–296. Oxford: Clarendon Press.
Société Malgache
    1973   *A Glance at Madagascar.* Antananarivo: Librarie Tout pour l'Ecole.
Southall, Aidan
    1979   White Strangers and their Religion in East Africa and Madagascar. In *Strangers in African Societies.* W. A. Shack and E. P. Skinner, eds., 211–227. Berkeley, Los Angeles, London: University of California Press.
    1986   Common Themes in Malagasy Culture. In *Madagascar, Society and History.* C. Kottak et al., eds., 411–426. Durham: Carolina Academic Press.
Sow, I.
    1980   *Anthropological Structures of Madness in Black Africa.* J. Diamanti, trans. New York: International Universities Press.
Stoler, Ann Laura
    1985   *Capitalism and Confrontation in Sumatra's Plantation Belt, 1870–1979.* New Haven: Yale University Press.
Stoller, Paul
    1989   *Fusion of the Worlds: An Ethnography of Possession among the Songhay of Niger.* Chicago: University of Chicago Press.
Strathern, Andrew J.
    1984   . *A Line of Power.* London: Tavistock Publications.

Stratton, Arthur
    1964   *The Great Red Island*. New York: Charles Scribner's Sons.
Sundkler, Bengt
    1961   *Bantu Prophets in South Africa*. London: Oxford University Press.
Taussig, Michael T.
    1980a   *The Devil and Commodity Fetishism in South America*. Chapel Hill: University of North Carolina Press.
    1980b   Reification and the Consciousness of the Patient. *Social Science and Medicine* 14B: 3–13.
    1987   *Shamanism, Colonialism, and the Wild Man: A Study in Terror and Healing*. Chicago: University of Chicago Press.
    1989   The Nervous System Part I: Homesickness and Dada. *Kroeber Anthropological Society Papers* 69–70: 32–61.
Tche-Hao, Tsien
    1967   The Social Life of the Chinese in Madagascar. In *Immigrants and Associations*. L. A. Fallers, ed., 87–102. The Hague: Mouton.
Tegnaeus, Harry
    1952   *Blood-brothers: An Ethno-Sociological Study of the Institutions of Blood-Brotherhood with Special Reference to Africa*. New Series, Publication no. 10. Stockholm: The Ethnographic Museum of Sweden.
Thompson, E. P.
    1967   Time, Work-Discipline, and Industrial Capitalism. *Past and Present* 38: 56–97.
Thompson, Virginia
    1987   Madagascar. In *Africa South of the Sahara*, 614–636. London: Europa Publications.
Thompson, Virginia, and Richard Adloff
    1965   *The Malagasy Republic: Madagascar Today*. Stanford: Stanford University Press.
Torrey, E. Fuller
    1986   *Witchdoctors and Psychiatrists: The Common Roots of Psychotherapy and Its Future*. Revised edition of *The Mind Game*. Northvale, N.J.: Jason Aronson.
Trexler, Edgar R.
    1989   The Prophetess of Madagascar. *The Lutheran, September* 27: 10–13.
Tronchon, Jacques
    1974   *L'Insurrection Malgache de 1947: Essai d'Interprétation Historique*. Paris: François Maspero.
    1975   L'Antagonisme Hovas-Côtiers: Un Cliché Ambigu. *Le Monde*, May 29.
Turner, Bryan
    1984   *The Body and Society: Explorations in Social Theory*. Oxford: Basil Blackwell.

1987   *Medical Power and Social Knowledge*. Beverly Hills: Sage Publications.
Turner, Victor
1964   An Ndembu Doctor in Practice. In *Magic, Faith, and Healing*. A. Kiev, ed., 230–263. New York: The Free Press.
1969   *The Ritual Process: Structure and Anti-Structure*. Ithaca: Cornell University Press.
1987   *The Anthropology of Performance*. New York: PAJ Publications.
UNICEF (United Nations International Children's Emergency Fund)
1987   *Children on the Front Line: The Impact of Apartheid, Destabilisation and Warfare on Children in Southern Africa*. New York: UNICEF.
UNICEF-U.K.
1988   *The State of the World's Children*. Oxford: Oxford University Press.
Valette, J.
1958   1700–1840—Histoire du Boina. *Bulletin de Madagascar*. 149: 851–858.
Van Gennep, Arnold
1904   *Tabou et Totémisme à Madagascar: Etude Descriptive et Théorique*. Paris: Bibliothèque de l'Ecole des Hautes Etudes.
Vérin, Pierre
1967   Introduction: Les Arabes dans l'Océan Indien et à Madagascar. In *Arabes et Islamisés à Madagascar et dans L'Océan Indien*. pp. a–c. Antananarivo: Le Centre d'Archéologie de la Faculté des Lettres et des Sciences Humaines de l'Université de Madagascar.
Vérin, Pierre, and Georgette Versinger
1970   Les Débuts de la Mission Quaker et l'Exploration du Moyet-Ouest par Joseph Sewell en 1875. *Bulletin de Madagascar* 290–291: 567–594.
Vincent, Joan
1974   The Structuring of Ethnicity. *Human Organization* (33) 4: 375–378.
Vogel, R. J., and B. Stephens
1989   Availability of Pharmaceuticals in Sub-Sahran Africa: Roles of the Public, Private and Church Mission Sectors. *Social Science and Medicine* (29) 4: 479–486.
Wafer, Jim
1991   *The Taste of Blood: Spirit Possession in Brazilian Canclomblé*. Philadelphia: University of Pennsylvania Press.
Wallace, Anthony
1956   Revitalization Movements. *American Anthropologist* 58: 264–281.
Weber, Max
1964   *The Theory of Social and Economic Organization*. A. M. Henderson and T. Parsons, trans. New York: The Free Press.

1991   *The Protestant Ethic and the Spirit of Capitalism.* Talcott Par-
            sons, trans. London: Harper Collins Academic. (Originally
            published in 1930.)

Wilson, Peter J.
1971   Sentimental Structure: Tsimihety Migration and Descent.
            American Anthropologist 73: 193–208.

The World Bank
1980   *Madagascar: Recent Economic Developments and Future
            Prospects.* Washington D.C.: The World Bank.

Worsley, Peter
1968   *The Trumpet Shall Sound: A Study of Cargo Cults in Melane-
            sia.* New York: Schocken Books.

Worthman, Carol M., and John M. Whiting
1987   Social Change in Adolescent Sexual Behavior, Mate Selection,
            and Premarital Pregnancy Rates in a Kikuyu Community.
            Ethos (15) 2: 145–165.

Zola, Irving
1978   Medicine as an Institution of Social Control. In *The Cultural
            Crisis of Modern Medicine.* J. Ehrenreich, ed. 80–100. New
            York: Monthly Review Press.

Index

Printed in the United Kingdom
by Lightning Source UK Ltd.
118911UK00001

60 4119931 6

9 780520 207080